ENABLING THE BUSINESS OF AGRICULTURE 2016

COMPARING REGULATORY GOOD PRACTICES

WORLD BANK GROUP

ISBN (paper): 978-1-4648-0772-5
ISBN (electronic): 10.1596/978-1-4648-0781-7
DOI: 10.1596/978-1-4648-0772-5

Cover image: "Farmers Market #1" © Julie Ford Oliver, www.juliefordoliver.com. Used with the permission of Julie Ford Oliver. Further permission required for reuse.

Cover design: Communications Development Incorporated.

CONTENTS

Boxes

Figures

Map

Tables

FOREWORD

Augusto Lopez-Claros
Director
Global Indicators Group
World Bank Group

Juergen Voegele
Senior Director
Agriculture Global Practice
World Bank Group

The challenge of feeding a world population of 9 billion people by 2050 can be met only through vibrant, productive, profitable and sustainable food and agriculture sectors, particularly in developing countries, where the bulk of food is grown and consumed. Similarly, well-functioning agricultural markets and agribusinesses that are inclusive and efficient—and that optimize the sustainable production and distribution of food—are essential for a food-secure future for all.

The numbers relating to the agriculture and food sectors are stark and the challenges multifaceted. Currently, more than 800 million people go to bed hungry every day. Food demand is projected to rise globally by at least 20% over the next 15 years, with the largest increases in Sub-Saharan Africa, South Asia and East Asia. At the same time, agriculture is both a contributor to climate change, accounting for 25% of greenhouse gas emissions, and is adversely affected by it. Agricultural value chains need to be dynamic, productive and efficient if the sector is both to thrive in the face of climate change and to be part of the solution.

The World Bank Group's *Enabling the Business of Agriculture (EBA)* project measures and monitors regulations that affect the functioning of agriculture and agribusiness. The ultimate aim is to promote smart regulations that ensure efficient processes that support thriving agribusinesses as well as safety and quality control.

Building on the findings of a pilot phase last year, the World Bank Group is pleased to present this first full edition of *Enabling the Business of Agriculture: Comparing Regulatory Good Practices*. It provides analysis and results from 40 countries, covering all world regions and all income groups.

Eighteen indicators, covering six topics, have been developed to address various aspects relating to production inputs and market enablers that facilitate farmers, firms and producers to sell their goods and services. The indicators measured in this year's report cover seed, fertilizer, machinery, finance, transport and markets. Four additional topics—land, water, livestock, and information and communication technology—are under development and will be included in next year's report. Two overarching themes—environmental sustainability and gender—have also been explored so that the indicators being developed encourage inclusive and sustainable practices.

Given the significant public interest in the *EBA* project, and as part of its commitment to openness and transparency, the *EBA* team continues to seek input from relevant stakeholders and experts to further strengthen the research methodology and analytics as well as expand country coverage. We invite you to provide comments on the *EBA* website at http://eba.worldbank.org/.

As the international development community accelerates efforts to achieve the new Sustainable Development Goals, particularly SDGs 1 and 2, which call for ending extreme poverty and hunger by 2030, sustainable development of the food sectors and agriculture must be at the front and center of the global community's response. This publication and its findings contribute to that overall effort.

Augusto Lopez-Claros

Juergen Voegele

ACKNOWLEDGMENTS

Enabling the Business of Agriculture 2016 was prepared jointly by the World Bank's Agriculture Global Practice, under the general direction of Juergen Voegele, Ethel Sennhauser, Preeti Ahuja and Mark Cackler and the Development Economics Vice Presidency's Global Indicators Group, under the general direction of Augusto Lopez-Claros. Federica Saliola and Farbod Youssefi managed the project, with the support from Tea Trumbic, Cesar Chaparro-Yedro and Raian Divanbeigi. The team would like to acknowledge the support of Indermit Gill and Melissa Johns. Current and former team members included Dinah Bengur, Liwam Berhane, Gerawork Bizuneh, Martha Branigan-Sutton, Rong Chen, Dariga Chukmaitova, Davida Louise Connon, Côme Dechery, Robert de l'Escaille, Nuria de Oca, Nealon Devore, Sarah Diouri, Margarita Diubanova, Soha Eshraghi, Julia Isabel Navarro Espinal, Leopoldo Fabra, Felix Frewer, Taras Gagalyuk, Arnau Gallard-Agusti, Bill Garthwaite, Gabriel Simoes Gaspar, Slavena Georgieva, Jean Philippe Lodugnon Harding, Pilar Jano, Marketa Jonasova, Edna Kallon, Marina Kayumova, Milan Kondic, Maksat Korooluev, Alva Kretschmer, Valerie Marechal, Jason McMann, Thibault Meilland, Arturo Francisco Bonilla Merino, Charlotte Merten, Nina Paustian, Aditi Poddar, Anis Ragland, Kateryna Schroeder, Justin Lee Schwegel, Samjhana Thapa, Yasmine Umutoni, Marielle Lily Walter, Lechi Zhang and Yucheng Zheng. Assisting with data collection were Ayuen Ajok, Ibrahim Alturki, Omar Alzayat, Yulia Amanbaeva, Sasha Boshart, Luiza Casemiro, Esperanza Pastor Núñez de Castro, Salma Ehsan Cheema, Maria-Magdalena Chiquier, Marie-Lily Delion, Timila Dhakhwa, Laura Diniz, Iana Djekic, Xiaquan Fang, Cecile Ferro, Albina Gasanbekova, David William Green, Megan Hyndman, Tatiana Ivanicichina, Parviz Jabarov, Gulnur Kerimkulova, Julian Koschorke, Yuhan Liu, Felipe Magofke, Charlotte Filiz Merten, Yedesdes Y Mudessir, Meirzhan Myrzaliyev, Trang Nguyen, Maria Antonia Quesada Gamez, Parvina Rakhimova, Byron Sacharidis, Valentina Saltane, Stephanie Samayoa, Atik Kiran Shah, Bungheng Taing, Herve Tchakoumi, Hulya Ulku, Jedadiah Douglas Winter, Xiao, Beibei Yan, Cem Berk Yolbulan, Diana Zeng, Geyi Zheng, Jingwen Zheng and Lilin Zheng. The team is grateful to local consultants who supported data collection or helped the team during the *EBA* team's country visits: Arun Saha (Bangladesh), Sidiki Soubeiga (Burkina Faso), Fitsum Aregawi (Ethiopia), Mohammad Issa Mousa (Jordan), Olayvanh Singvilay (Lao PDR), Tidiane Diarisso (Mali), Mohammed Bajeddi (Morocco), Dalfino Hoster Guila (Mozambique), Khin Sw Swe Aye (Myanmar) and Mohamed Osman Hussein (Sudan). The team is grateful for administrative assistance to Maisha Hyman, Rose Gachina, Monique Pelloux and Ramon Yndriago.

Andrew Goodland, Chris Jackson, Aart Kraay and Patrick Verissimo reviewed the full draft report and provided feedback. The team is also grateful for valuable comments and reviews provided by external experts as well as colleagues across the World Bank Group, in particular those in the 40 World Bank Group country offices and those working on several key areas investigated by the report. The team would especially like to acknowledge the hard work of the following individuals in the country offices who helped distribute questionnaires and validate the data: Faten Abdulfattah, Nada Abou-Rizk, Ruvejda Aliefendic, Moustafa Alver, Luis A. Aviles, Amadou Ba, Purna Bahadur Chhetri, Tran Bao Thi Nguyen, Julia Barrera, Raul Barrios, Amina Beidari Bertho, Aurelien Beko, Oliver Braedt, Olena Bychyk, Barbara Calvi, Mudita Chamroeun, Marie Genevieve Compaore, Luis Constantino, Tesfahiwot Dillnessa, Hadidia Djimba, Hosna Ferdous Sumi, Carlos Francisco Siezar, Larisa Fugol, Augusto Garcia, Patricia Gutierrez, Mistre Hailemariam Mekuria, Michael Hamaide, Amani Haque, Jairi Hernandez, Van Hoang Pham, Chris Jackson, Kutemba Kambole, Leszek Kasek, Gwladys Nadine Isabelle Kinda, Krista Kroff, Seenithamby Manoharan, Chanhsom Manythong, Joanna Mariscal, Kunduz Masylkanova, Mohamed Medouar, Tania Meyer, Manolo Morales, Mayela Murillo, Alice Museri, Aymen Musmar Ali, Belinda Mutesi, Alex Mwanakasale, Judith Mziray, Clarisse Nhanbangue, Anne Njuguna, Francisco Obreque, Alice R. Ouedraogo, Bigyan Pradhan, Maria Theresa Quinones, Nikos Schmidt, Daniel Sellen, Tara Shrestha, Vatthana Singharaj, Bintou Sogodogo, Heinz Strubenhoff, Tamara Sulukhia, Sugata Talukder, Tam Thi Do, Miss Thiri, Shewaye Yalew Shumye and Sergiy Zorya. Comments on the report were received from: Alejandro Alvarez de la Campa, Jamie Anderson, Maria Antip, Oya Pinar Ardic Alper, Joshua Ariga, Raimonds Aronietis, Sarat Babu Gidda, Derek Baker, Thomas Bauer, Keith Belk, Todd Benson, Shawki Bhargouti, Jos Bijman, Zhao Bing, Florentin Blanc, Marcel Bruins, Balu Bumb, Victor Bundi Mosoti, Stefano Burchi, Francois Burgaud, Jacob Burke, Christina Katharina Busch, Frederic Bustelo, Yi Cai, Jo Caldihon, David Casanova, Julie Caswell, Lawrence Clarke, Rick Clayton, Mark Constantine, Joe Cortes, Gily Cowan, Barney Curtis, Morgane Danielou, Roger Day, Alexandra de Athayde, Philip de Leon, Claus Deblitz, Klaus Deininger, Chistopher Delgardo, Hans Dellien, Brigitte Dias Ferreira, Eugenio Diaz-Bonilla, Grahame Dixie, Carel du Marchie Sarvass, Stefano Duilgheroff, Indira Ekanayake, Jorge Escurra, Natalia Federighi de Cuello, Erick Fernandes, Vincenzo Ferraiuolo, Francis V. Fragano, Ade Freeman, Francois G. Le Gall, Pierra Jean Gerber, John Gibson, Ian John Douglas Gillson, Tanja K. Goodwin, Naoki Goto, Lars Nikolajs Grava, David Groenfeldt, Arian Groot, Vincent Guyonnet, Thomas Hammond, Craig Hanson, Adelaida Harris, Robert John Hatton, Terhi Havimo, Tazeen Hasan, Norbert Henninger, Thea Hilhorst, Martin Hilmi, Marlynne Hopper, Jens Hügel, Ankur Huria, Sarah Iqbal, Juan Carlos Izaguirre, Devra Jarvis, Peter Jeffries, Chakib Jenane, David John, Scott Justice, Jari Kauppila, John C. Keyser, Josef Kienzle, Kaoru Kimura, Olivia Kiratu, Matthew Kirk, Justin Kosoris, Musa Kpapa, Dilip N. Kulkarni, Charles Kunaka, Andrea Kutter, Andrzej Kwiecinski, Lloyd Le Page, Zvi Lerman, Steven Lonergan, Isabel Lopez Noriega, Youlia Lozanova, Dibungi Luseba, Nathaniel Makoni, John McDermot,

Michael McGowan, Ruth Meizen-Dick, Frederic Meunier, Niels Morel, Nancy Morgan, Mohinder Mudahar, Jorge Munoz, Ajay Nair, Shankar Narayanan, Nick Nwakpa, Francois Onimus, David Orden, Theresa Osborne, Washington Otieno, Maria Claudia Pachon, Maria Pagura, Enrique Pantoja, Roy Parizat, Valentina Paskalova, François-Marie Patorni, Judith Payne, Andrew Peters, Patrick Philipp, Ugo Pica-Ciamarra, Caroline Plante, Natalia Pshenichnaya, Markus Reinisch, Alain Reocreux, Romano Righetti, Philippe Benjamin Rivoire, Loraine Ronchi, Max Rothschild, Judith Rudolph, Marieta Sakalian, Salman M. A. Salman, Aguiratou Savadogo-Tinto, Sara Savastano, Susanne Scheierling, Andres Seargent, Harris Selod, Carlos Sere, Bekzod Shamsiev, Walter Simon de Boef, Melvin Spreij, Victoria Stanley, Nancy Sundberg, Johan Swinnen, Virginia Tanase, Michael Tarazi, Felipe Targa Rodriguez, Dhanaraj Thakur, David Tipping, Muhabbat Turdieva, Joyce M. Turk, Laurian Unnevehr, Kishor Uprety, Anke van den Hurk, Kees van der Meer, Kristine Van Herck, Suzanne van der Velden, Panos Varangis, Grégoire Verdeaux, Francesco Versace, Laura Villamayor, Bert Visser, Brian Wickham, Joshua Seth Wimpey, Bruce Wise, Justin Yap, Winston Yu and Ivan Zavadsky.

The *Enabling the Business of Agriculture* program was developed in partnership with several donors, whose funding and support makes this report possible: the Bill & Melinda Gates Foundation, the Department for International Development (DFID), the Danish Ministry of Foreign Affairs, the United States Agency for International Development (USAID) and the Government of the Netherlands.

The *Enabling the Business of Agriculture 2016* outreach strategy is being executed by a communications team led by Indira Chand and Sarwat Hussain, supported by Hyun Kyong Lee and Zia Morales. The development and management of the *Enabling the Business of Agriculture* website and technical services were supported by Varun V. Doiphode, Andres Baquero Franco, Fengsheng Huang, Kunal Patel, Rajesh Sargunan, Vinod Vasudevan Thottikkatu and Hashim Zia.

The report was edited and designed by Communications Development Incorporated, led by Bruce Ross-Larson and including Joe Caponio, Mike Crumplar, Lawrence Whiteley and Elaine Wilson.

The *Enabling the Business of Agriculture 2016* report benefited from the generous input from a network of more than 2,500 local experts, including lawyers, business associations, private sector representatives, farmers' organizations, academics, government officials and other professionals actively engaged in the policy, legal and regulatory requirements in the 40 countries covered during the second year. Please note that the data published in the report and online represent a unified response based on the answers the team received from various respondents and sources and are not attributed to any particular respondent. Wherever possible, answers were corroborated by official fee schedules, laws, regulations and public notices. The names of those wishing to be acknowledged individually are listed at the end of the report and are made available on the website at: http://eba.worldbank.org.

ABOUT ENABLING THE BUSINESS OF AGRICULTURE

Agriculture and the business created by it are major sources of income and employment for a large share of the world's people. Vital for food security and poverty reduction, the business of agriculture affects rural livelihoods everywhere.

Growing food demands call for greater attention to strategies to develop the business of agriculture. Indeed, meeting the rising food demand of a global population expected to reach 9 billion people by 2050 is a major challenge—even more so in the face of increasingly adverse natural conditions.[1] The evolution of urban food demand in developing regions illustrates the need for agricultural value chains and institutional settings that are both more efficient and more effective.

An enabling environment for the business of agriculture is critical to respond to evolving market trends. It includes macroeconomic and sector-specific laws, policies, regulations, support services, information structures and labor force preparedness. It sets the stage for all business activities that have to do with producing goods on farms and transporting them to processors and consumers. Understanding this environment can help create policies that facilitate doing business in agriculture and increase the investment attractiveness and competitiveness of countries.[2]

Enabling the Business of Agriculture 2016 measures regulations that impact firms in the agribusiness value chain, providing data and analysis that allow policy makers to compare their country's laws and regulations with those of others.

Clear and accessible laws foster a business environment that benefits all market players—from farmers, including the more vulnerable such as female farmers and smallholders, to consumers and large investors. But when regulations are too complex, unpredictable or discriminatory, they raise costs and cut incentives to enter formal and competitive markets. A World Bank study in Ethiopia in 2012 showed that a weak regulatory system that fails to guarantee seed quality results in farmers paying higher prices for seed of suboptimal quality, with yields up to 50% lower than expected.[3] In Mali agricultural cereal traders ranked regulatory uncertainty among the toughest barriers to market entry.[4]

What does *Enabling the Business of Agriculture 2016* measure?

Enabling the Business of Agriculture 2016 enables policymakers to identify and analyze legal barriers for the business of agriculture and to quantify transaction costs of dealing with government regulations. Ten topics have been developed to cover different aspects of production inputs and market enablers: seed, fertilizer, machinery, finance, markets, transport, information and communication technology (ICT), land, water and livestock. Two overarching themes—gender and environmental sustainability—have been investigated to ensure that the indicators being developed encourage inclusive and sustainable practices. Although women are 43% of the global agricultural workforce, they face many constraints that limit their participation in agricultural value chains. This report includes a review of issues that are restrictive for

women in the topics covered. Because of agriculture's dependence on natural resources, the environmental sustainability topic investigates plant genetic resources and water resources management. Both will be developed further next year.

The choice of indicators was guided by a review of academic literature and case studies and by consultations with key stakeholders, including civil society organizations, partner institutions, practitioners, public and private sector representatives, researchers and technical experts.

Regulations are the bedrock of a country's enabling environment. Well-designed laws and regulations—supported by strong institutions and efficient administrative procedures—are necessary for agriculture to prosper.

The *Enabling the Business of Agriculture* methodology targets smart regulation in each of the measured areas for inputs and enablers. Smart regulation—striking the right balance in ensuring proper enforcement of essential safety and quality control while avoiding excessive regulatory burdens for value chain players—is good for the business of agriculture. It can improve services and products and lower costs. *EBA* considers more than the sheer number of regulations and does not necessarily promote deregulation. In fact, several indicators, such as fertilizer quality control and domestic plant protection, promote more regulation since the laws and regulations need to set appropriate standards in these areas to ensure health and food safety.

Enabling the Business of Agriculture 2016 presents two types of indicators. *De jure* or "legal" indicators stem directly from reading the laws and regulations to measure their quality. *De facto* or "time and motion" indicators reflect the efficiency of a country's regulatory environment—such as the number of procedures and the time and cost to register fertilizer products, register seed for sale and export agricultural goods. All indicators were designed using specific rules that are applied equally across countries to ensure that the data are comparable.

A key development presented in this year's report is the scoring methodology for legal indicators on six topics: seed, fertilizer, machinery, finance, markets and transport. This methodology assigns scores to certain legal and regulatory dimensions and serves one of the main objectives of the *Enabling the Business of Agriculture* project: to

provide governments with defined good practices that can inform policy-making and trigger reforms based on the examples of other countries. The scoring groups various data points for all six topics around three cross-cutting categories:

- **Operations** indicators measure the requirements for local companies to enter the market and conduct agribusiness activities.

- **Quality** control indicators measure the regulations governing plant protection, the safety standards for users of agricultural machinery and the quality control associated with seeds and fertilizer products.

- **Trade** indicators measure trade restrictions on exporting agricultural products, importing fertilizer and tractors and transporting goods across borders.

Comparative results on countries' laws and regulations help identify weaknesses and highlight ways to overcome them. The scores were developed at the indicator, topic and cross-cutting category levels (table 1). The rules for scoring each question are described by topic in the *Topic Data Notes* (appendix B).

Time and motion indicators, although presented and analyzed in the report, are not assigned a particular score (table 2). The reason is that some processes are clearly necessary, as with the tests for evaluating and registering new seed varieties and the technical review by a variety release committee, while others may be redundant, as with additional ministerial approval after the technical review. Since the times for taking the tests depend both on regulations and country cropping seasons, it would be unfair to penalize countries for their geographical conditions. The individual good practices have been singled out and scored under

TABLE 1 Assigning scores to legal and regulatory dimensions helps governments define good practices

	OPERATIONS	QUALITY CONTROL	TRADE	
SEED	Seed registration (0–100) Seed development and certification (0–100)			**SEED SCORE (0–100)**
FERTILIZER	Fertilizer registration (0–100)	Fertilizer quality control (0–100)	Fertilizer import requirements (0–100)	**FERTILIZER SCORE (0–100)**
MACHINERY	Tractor dealer requirements (0–100)	Tractor standards and safety (0–100)	Tractor import requirements (0–100)	**MACHINERY SCORE (0–100)**
FINANCE	Microfinance institutions (0–100) Credit unions (0–100) Agent banking (0–100) E-money (0–100) Warehouse receipts (0–100)			**FINANCE SCORE (0–100)**
MARKETS	Production and sales (0–100)	Plant protection (0–100)		**MARKETS SCORE (0–100)**
TRANSPORT	Truck licenses (0–100)		Cross-border transportation (0–100)	**TRANSPORT SCORE (0–100)**
	OPERATIONS SCORE (0–100)	**QUALITY CONTROL SCORE (0–100)**	**TRADE SCORE (0–100)**	

TABLE 2 Time and motion indicators reflect the efficiency of administrative processes related to a country's regulatory system

	OPERATIONS	QUALITY CONTROL	TRADE
SEED	Seed registration: Procedures, time and cost		
FERTILIZER	Fertilizer registration: Procedures, time and cost		Fertilizer imports: Cost of import permit and importer registration for importers of fertilizer
MACHINERY			Tractor imports: Cost of import permit and importer registration for importers of tractors
FINANCE			
MARKETS			Agricultural exports: Documents, time and cost (per shipment)
TRANSPORT	Truck licenses: Time, cost and validity of company licenses, truck permits and vehicle inspections		

the legal indicators. They were grouped in the categories on operations and trade requirements. The methodology on time and motion indicators will be further developed next year.

Building on findings presented in the 2015 progress report covering 10 countries, *Enabling the Business of Agriculture 2016* covers 40 countries in seven regions (map 1).[5] Different criteria have been used to select the countries, including ensuring adequate representation of all regions and different levels of agricultural development. Data collection will be further scaled up to 60 countries in 2016.

How are the data collected?

Enabling the Business of Agriculture indicators are based on primary data collection through standardized questionnaires completed by expert respondents in each target country. Once the data are collected and analyzed, several follow-up rounds address and clear up any discrepancies in the answers the respondents provide, including conference calls and written correspondence. The preliminary answers are then finalized and shared with governments for further validation.

The data in this report are current as of March 31, 2015, and do not reflect any changes to the laws or administrative procedures after that date. Figure 1 shows the steps in the process from data collection to public release.

Chosen from the private sector, the public sector and civil society, respondents include firms, academia, financial institutions, professional associations, farmer organizations and government ministries and agencies. These individuals and organizations know their countries' laws and regulations and how they affect people involved in agriculture. Involving various experts increases the accuracy of the data by balancing the possible biases of different stakeholders. So reaching out to both the private and public sectors helps compare the perspectives of all parties.

Enabling the Business of Agriculture data are collected in a standardized way to ensure comparability across countries and over time. Following the methodological foundations of *Doing Business*,[6] questionnaires use a standard business case with assumptions about the legal form of the business, its size, its location and the nature of its operations for each topic applied for all countries (table

3). Assumptions guiding respondents through their completion of the survey questionnaires vary by topic (see *Topic Data Notes* in appendix B). In addition, in the interest of comparability, the values in the assumptions are not fixed values but proportional to the country's gross national income (GNI) per capita.

What does *Enabling the Business of Agriculture* not measure?

Many elements that shape a country's enabling environment are not captured by *Enabling the Business of Agriculture* indicators. Broader macro-level aspects pertaining to the political, social and economic spheres of a country, for example, shape the climate of its economy, but are not now an area that *EBA* covers.

Policies, institutions, infrastructure and support services—many shaping a country's capacity to implement and enforce its regulations—are also key determinants of the enabling environment that *Enabling the Business of Agriculture 2016* has not targeted. Other variables characterizing the market—such as prices, stock market trends, government expenditures and investments—are not directly comparable and require

MAP 1 Geographical coverage of *Enabling the Business of Agriculture 2016*

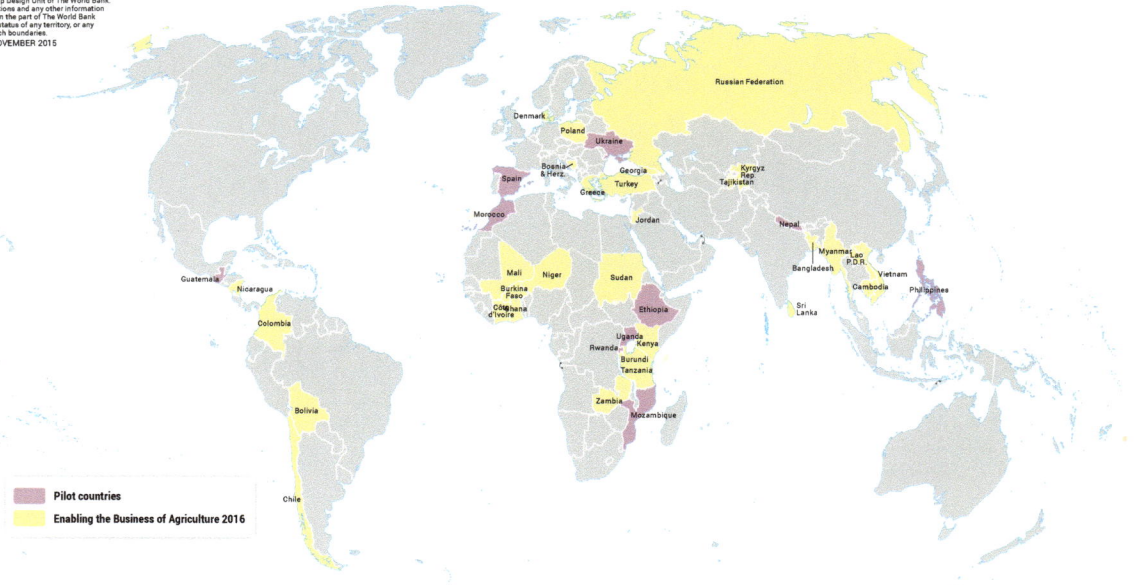

This map was produced by the Map Design Unit of The World Bank.
The boundaries, colors, denominations and any other information
shown on this map do not imply, on the part of The World Bank
Group, any judgment on the legal status of any territory, or any
endorsement or acceptance of such boundaries.
IBRD 42022 | NOVEMBER 2015

Pilot countries
Enabling the Business of Agriculture 2016

a methodology outside the scope of *EBA*'s current capacity. While *EBA* is interested in expanding into these areas, they are not covered by this report's indicators.

Much activity in rural areas, from employment to the production and sale of goods, happens through informal channels. The complexity of regulations and the time and cost they impose, could be reasons for this, as could the quality of institutions, extension services and physical infrastructure. The current focus of indicators presented in this report is on measuring official laws and regulations and not these other areas.

Benchmarking has its benefits and limitations. Quantitative data and benchmarks can be effective in stimulating debate about policy, enhancing the ability of policymakers to assess progress over time and making meaningful international comparisons. But using assumptions to ensure global coverage and comparability across countries can generalize and exclude some context-specific information. To address some of these limitations, understand what regulatory reforms are most effective and see how these issues are shaped by the context, data must be consistently collected over a number of years to combine global benchmarks with context-specific information.

What is in this year's report?

This year's report presents the main results of the team's effort over the last 12 months to collect and analyze new data and to develop indicators that can help governments make informed decisions about the enabling environment for agribusiness activity in their countries.

Feedback is welcome on the data, methodology and overall project design to make future *Enabling the Business of Agriculture* reports even more useful. Feedback can be provided on the project website: http://eba.worldbank.org.

FIGURE 1 Data collection, verification and analysis

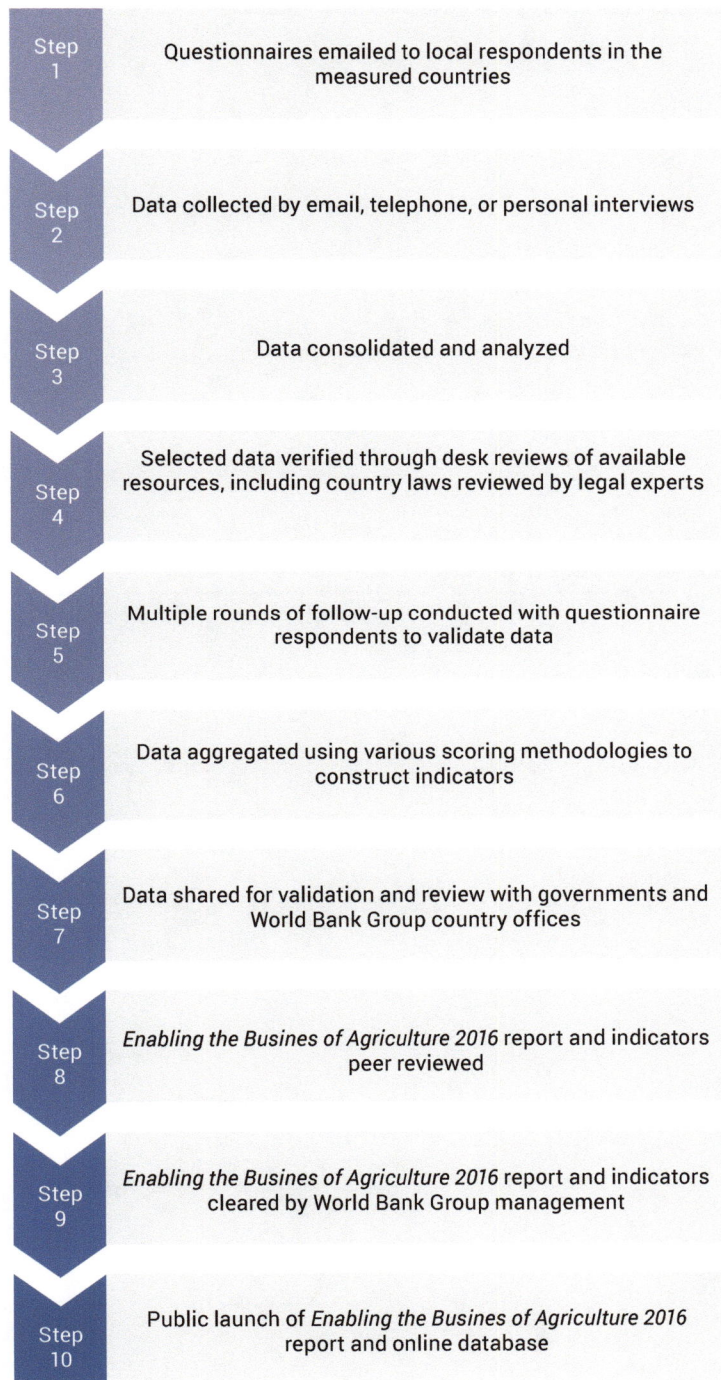

Step 1	Questionnaires emailed to local respondents in the measured countries
Step 2	Data collected by email, telephone, or personal interviews
Step 3	Data consolidated and analyzed
Step 4	Selected data verified through desk reviews of available resources, including country laws reviewed by legal experts
Step 5	Multiple rounds of follow-up conducted with questionnaire respondents to validate data
Step 6	Data aggregated using various scoring methodologies to construct indicators
Step 7	Data shared for validation and review with governments and World Bank Group country offices
Step 8	*Enabling the Busines of Agriculture 2016* report and indicators peer reviewed
Step 9	*Enabling the Busines of Agriculture 2016* report and indicators cleared by World Bank Group management
Step 10	Public launch of *Enabling the Busines of Agriculture 2016* report and online database

TABLE 3 *EBA* **questionnaires use a standard business case with assumptions**

	ASSUMPTIONS USED TO STANDARDIZE THE BUSINESS CASE
SEED	*The seed variety:* Is a maize variety that has been developed by the private sector. Is being registered for the first time in the country. Has not been registered in any other country. If maize varieties are not being developed by the private sector in the country, is an imported maize variety, which may have been previously registered elsewhere.
FERTILIZER	*The business:* Is a fertilizer importer. Imports fertilizer to sell in the country. Has registered at least one new fertilizer product in the country. Does not operate in an export processing zone or an industrial estate with special import or export privileges. *The fertilizer product:* Is a new chemical fertilizer product that has not previously been registered in the country.
MACHINERY	*The business:* Is an importer or dealer of agricultural tractors. Does not operate in an export processing zone or an industrial estate with special import or export privileges. *The tractor:* Is a new or second-hand two-axle/four-wheel drive (4WD) tractor.
FINANCE	High-income countries are not measured by the finance topic. *Microfinance institutions:* Can take deposits, lend and provide other financial services to the public. Are licensed to operate and supervised by a public authority. *Credit unions:* Are member-owned, not-for-profit financial cooperatives that provide savings, credit and other financial services to their members.

(continued)

TABLE 3 *EBA* **questionnaires use a standard business case with assumptions (continued)**

	ASSUMPTIONS USED TO STANDARDIZE THE BUSINESS CASE
MARKETS	*The business:* Performs general agricultural trading activities. Does not operate in a special export processing zone. *The contracted product:* Is the most produced non-processed non-cereal product in terms of gross production value (current million U.S. dollars).[a] *The export product and trading partner:* Is defined and grouped as cash crops, cereals, fruits and vegetables according to the Harmonized Commodity Description and Coding System 1996 version (HS 96).[b] For each country, the combination of the product and the partner country that represents the highest five-year average export value (in U.S. dollars) is selected. *The shipment:* Is transported via a 20-foot full container-load. Weighs 10 metric tons. Is assumed to comply with any fumigation requirement for the packing material (such as wood pallets), treated and marked accordingly.
TRANSPORT	*The business:* Is a limited liability company. Is 100% domestically owned. Has between 5 and 10 employees. Owns a maximum of five trucks and each truck has two axles and a loading capacity of 20 metric tons.[c] Rents a garage. Transports agricultural products within the country, including perishable goods. Does not transport fertilizers, pesticides or any hazardous products.

Note

a. All data are sourced from FAOSTAT, using the production data of 2012 (the latest available year). Cereal crops are excluded from the analysis because they are less suitable for agricultural production contracts due to certain characteristics, including the high risks of side-selling due to well-developed local or export markets, the reduced need for technical assistance in order to meet market specifications and the smaller price differentials at each point in the supply chain.

b. All data are sourced from the UN Comtrade Database, using the export data from 2009–13.

c. A truck is defined as one tractor unit, excluding the trailer.

Notes

1. FAO 2009.

2. FAO 2013.

3. World Bank 2012.

4. Diallo and others 2010; Staatz and others 1989.

5. Pilot countries were Ethiopia, Guatemala, Morocco, Mozambique, Nepal, the Philippines, Rwanda, Spain, Uganda and Ukraine. For more information on the *EBA 2015* progress report, please visit http://eba.worldbank.org.

6. *http://www.doingbusiness.org.*

References

Diallo, B., N. Dembélé and J. Staatz. 2010. "Analyse des prix de parité en Afrique de l'Ouest: Le cas du riz depuis la crise de 2007–2008. Rapport de synthèse proviso ire." Food Security Collaborative Working Paper 57243, Michigan State University, Department of Agricultural, Food and Resource Economics.

FAO (Food and Agriculture Organization). 2009. *How to Feed the World by 2050.* Rome: FAO.

———. 2013. *Enabling Environments for Agribusiness and Agro-industries Development: Regional and Country Perspectives.* Rome: FAO.

Staatz, J.M., J. Dioné and N. Dembélé. 1989. "Cereals Market Liberalization in Mali." *World Development* 17 (5): 703–18.

World Bank. 2005. *Doing Business 2006: Creating Jobs.* Washington, DC: World Bank.

———. 2012. *Agribusiness Indicators: Ethiopia.* Washington, DC: World Bank.

1. OVERVIEW

The *Enabling the Business of Agriculture 2016* report covers 40 countries in seven regions. Ten topics have been developed to measure regulations that can impact firms in the agribusiness value chain, providing data and analysis that allow policy makers to compare their country's laws and regulations with those of others. A scoring methodology that is based on good practices in relevant regulatory dimensions has been developed for 6 of the 10 topics measured: seed, fertilizer, machinery, finance, markets and transport; the remaining topics (land, water, livestock and ICT) will be further developed and scored next year.

Enabling the Business of Agriculture promotes smart regulations that ensure safety and quality control while at the same time promote efficient regulatory processes that support agribusinesses. Regulation in agriculture is justified to address market failures and protect safety, health and the environment. But some governments do not tackle these issues through appropriate regulation. Regulations may introduce burdensome procedures that shift economic activity to greater informality and corruption without even attaining the original objectives.[1] So it is important to assess the efficiency and quality of specific regulations. The *EBA* methodology highlights smart regulation in each of the measured areas. This methodology has been informed by an extensive literature review and consultations with experts.

For chemical fertilizers, for example, controls are necessary to prevent damage to the soil and adulterated fertilizer use but excessive tests that prolong fertilizer registration for years and cost thousands of dollars are difficult to defend.[2] Similarly burdensome import procedures, which require fertilizer importers to make purchases months in advance, can hinder market access. *EBA* assigns higher scores to countries with laws requiring the labeling of fertilizer and prohibiting the sale of open or

mislabeled fertilizer bags. At the same time, countries that allow the private sector (including foreigners) to import fertilizers or do not require re-registration if the product has been already registered in another country are also seen as following good practices and given high scores.

Smart regulations can improve products and services and lower costs for agribusinesses. Specific country examples in the agricultural sector show the impact of good regulatory reform on improving the supply and lowering the prices in the seed and mechanization markets in Bangladesh and Turkey,[3] in the fertilizer sector in Bangladesh,[4] Kenya[5] and Ethiopia[6] and in the maize industry in Eastern and Southern Africa,[7] among others.

But apart from these country-specific examples, there are few data that can help to better understand the link between regulations and agricultural productivity on a global scale. Extensive literature on the matter focuses on the existence or quantity of regulations, but few studies look at the quality of those regulations.[8] *EBA* attempts to fill this gap by assessing regulatory quality across a wide range of countries, thus providing a basis to understand how regulations affect economic outcomes.

Where are agribusiness regulations smarter?

A color coding system displays a synthetic measure of a country's *EBA* score in a particular topic to signal a country's adoption of good practices and areas where improvement is needed (table 1.1).

Colombia, Denmark, Greece, Poland and Spain score above average in all topics measured (dark green or green in table 1.1).[9] In general, these countries have a higher number of smart regulations in the topics covered. Although they share a substantial number of good practices, they also have room for improvement.

Colombia displays strong and efficient fertilizer registration norms, laws that support financial inclusion and adequate market regulation, but still has low safety standards for machinery. Poland has the top score for regulations related to cross-border transport, seed development and certification and fertilizer quality control, but lacks certain regulations for warehouse receipts, which would complement the existing collateral regime to obtain a loan for agriculture production.

Burkina Faso, Burundi, Ghana, Myanmar and Niger score below average on all topics (red or dark red in table 1.1), which suggests there is room for improvement in adopting the identified good practices across several topics (box 1.1). But in most countries the performance is more mixed — there are a number of good regulatory practices and at the same time areas for improvement. Bosnia and Herzegovina has solid regulations for plant protection and fertilizer but lacks regulations for credit unions and e-money. Morocco and Mozambique have weak regulations in agricultural finance but strong regulations for the registration, certification and development of new seed varieties. Vietnam has strong regulations for fertilizer quality control and plant protection, but lags in requirements for tractor dealers and safety standards for machinery.

How do regions perform?

The regulatory quality and efficiency of OECD high-income countries stand out in all topics as measured by *EBA*, followed by Latin America and the Caribbean and Europe and Central Asia (figure 1.1). South Asia and Sub-Saharan Africa show levels of regulatory strength that are lower or equal to the *EBA* global average across all measured areas. The two countries in the *EBA* sample from the Middle East and North Africa region—Jordan and Morocco—combine fairly strong regulations on seed and

TABLE 1.1 Colombia, Denmark, Greece, Poland and Spain score above average in all *EBA* topics

COUNTRY	SEED	FERTILIZER	MACHINERY	FINANCE	MARKETS	TRANSPORT
BANGLADESH	light green	orange	orange	light green	light green	orange
BOLIVIA	light green	orange	orange	light green	light green	light green
BOSNIA AND HERZEGOVINA	orange	green	orange	red	green	light green
BURKINA FASO	orange	orange	orange	orange	orange	orange
BURUNDI	orange	orange	orange	red	orange	orange
CAMBODIA	light green	orange	red	orange	orange	orange
CHILE	green	orange	orange	N/A	green	orange
COLOMBIA	light green	green	light green	green	green	light green
CÔTE D'IVOIRE	orange	light green	orange	orange	orange	orange
DENMARK	green	light green	light green	N/A	green	green
ETHIOPIA	orange	orange	red	light green	orange	orange
GEORGIA	light green	light green	orange	light green	green	light green
GHANA	orange	orange	orange	orange	orange	orange
GREECE	light green	green	light green	N/A	green	green
GUATEMALA	light green	light green	orange	light green	green	light green
JORDAN	light green	light green	orange	red	light green	light green
KENYA	green	orange	orange	light green	orange	light green
KYRGYZ REPUBLIC	light green	orange	light green	light green	light green	light green
LAO PDR	orange	orange	red	orange	orange	light green
MALI	orange	light green	red	orange	orange	light green
MOROCCO	green	orange	light green	red	light green	orange
MOZAMBIQUE	green	orange	orange	red	light green	light green
MYANMAR	orange	orange	red	red	orange	red
NEPAL	orange	orange	red	light green	light green	orange
NICARAGUA	orange	light green	orange	light green	orange	light green
NIGER	orange	orange	red	orange	orange	orange
PHILIPPINES	green	orange	light green	light green	orange	orange
POLAND	light green	green	light green	N/A	green	green
RUSSIAN FEDERATION	light green	light green	light green	N/A	light green	orange
RWANDA	red	orange	orange	light green	orange	orange
SPAIN	light green	green	light green	N/A	green	green
SRI LANKA	orange	light green	orange	orange	orange	orange
SUDAN	light green	orange	light green	red	orange	orange
TAJIKISTAN	orange	orange	light green	orange	light green	light green
TANZANIA	light green	light green	light green	light green	orange	light green
TURKEY	light green	light green	light green	light green	orange	light green
UGANDA	orange	orange	light green	light green	orange	light green
UKRAINE	light green	light green	light green	orange	green	orange
VIETNAM	orange	light green	red	light green	light green	orange
ZAMBIA	light green	orange	orange	light green	orange	light green

● Top performing countries, defined as those with topic scores above 85, indicating a high number of good practices in place as measured by *EBA*.

● Countries with a score above the sample average in a particular topic.

● Countries with a score below the sample average in a particular topic.

● Countries with topic scores below 30, indicating a low number of good practices.

High-income countries—Chile, Denmark, Greece, Poland, Russian Federation and Spain— are not measured under *EBA* finance indicators
(see *Topic Data Notes* in appendix B).

BOX 1.1 Several good regulatory practices have been identified across topic areas

Seed

✓ Variety release committee with representation of the private sector, which meets shortly after each cropping season.

✓ The availability online of an official variety catalog updated after each cropping season and specifying agro-ecological zones.

✓ Availability of initial seed classes to the private sector, which is granted access to breeder and foundation seed, and to material stored in the national gene bank.

✓ In countries where the certification is compulsory, official fee schedules for certification activities are publicly available, and nongovernmental inspectors and/or laboratories can be accredited to carry out part or all of seed certification activities.

Fertilizer

✓ Efficient and affordable fertilizer registration for companies, without the need for re-registration.

✓ Timely availability of fertilizer by the private sector through streamlined import procedures.

✓ Good quality fertilizer by requiring appropriate labeling and prohibiting open fertilizer bags.

Machinery

✓ Streamlined import procedures to facilitate timely availability and delivery of agricultural tractors.

✓ Appropriate testing of agricultural machinery to ensure imported tractors suit country conditions.

✓ Tractor registration and appropriate after-sales service to improve tractor durability.

✓ Compliance with national and international performance standards to ensure high-quality tractors.

✓ Enforcement of safety standards such as roll-over protective structures and seatbelts.

Finance

✓ Effective microfinance institutions by balancing supervision and the ability to take deposits.

✓ Reliable credit unions complying with disclosure and liquidity standards.

✓ Payments and other financial services accessible digitally and through retail agents.

✓ Electronic receipts issued by warehouse operators that farmers can pledge to secure a loan.

Markets

✓ Robust phytosanitary protection framework, including national surveillance activities, pest lists, pest risk analysis and domestic and import quarantine procedures.

✓ Efficient and affordable requirements to export major agricultural products, including membership, licensing and per-shipment documentation.

✓ Laws that do not obstruct the production or sale of agricultural goods domestically and a legal environment that facilitates the establishment and commercial operations of farmers' organizations.

Transport

✓ Promotion of fair competition and professionalism by establishing quality criteria for access to the transport sector through efficient licensing and mandatory technical inspections.

✓ Increased competition in the domestic market by reducing additional discriminatory requirements and granting transport rights to foreign trucking companies.

✓ Reduced market distortions by discouraging queueing systems and price interventions and promoting freight exchange platforms for road transport services.

✓ Facilitation of cross-border transport by harmonizing or mutually recognizing road transport standards among regional trading partners.

FIGURE 1.1 Regional performance on *EBA* indicators

Average score on *EBA* topics (0—100)

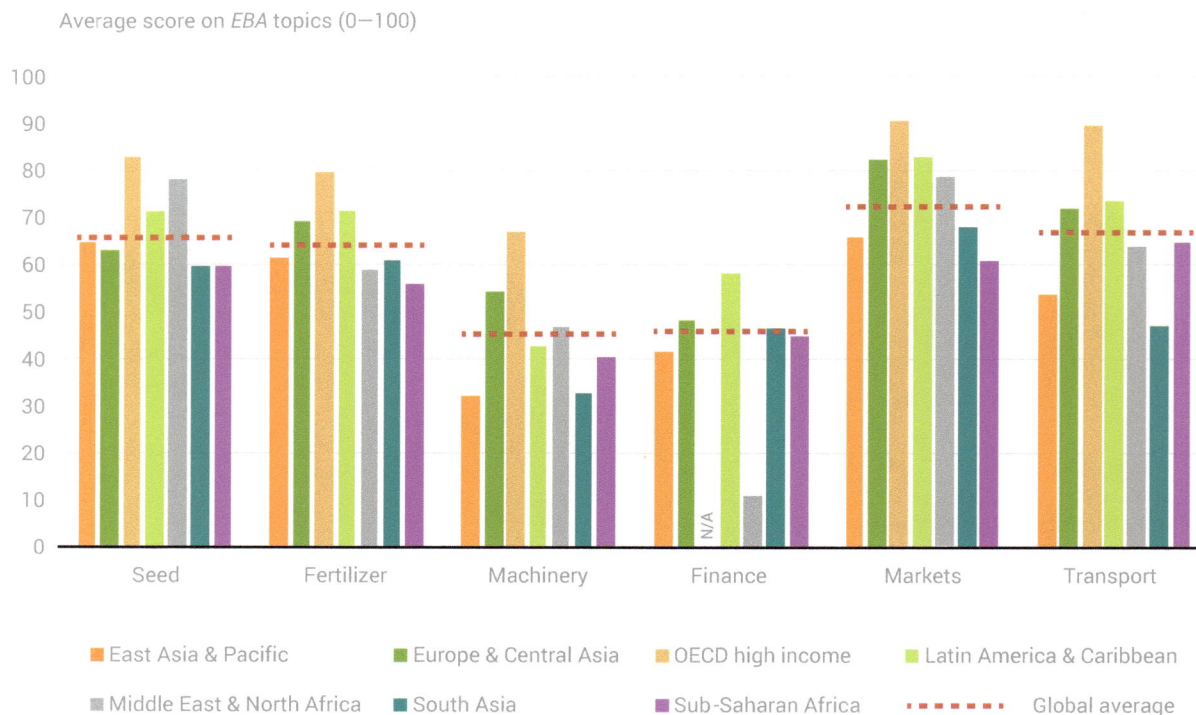

Source: *EBA* database.

Note: The *EBA* sample covers countries in East Asia and the Pacific (5), Europe and Central Asia (7), Latin America and the Caribbean (4), Middle East and North Africa (2), OECD high income (5), South Asia (3) and Sub-Saharan Africa (14). OECD high-income countries are not measured under the finance topic.

markets, with insufficient legal coverage in finance.

Variation is also observed among countries within a region. In Sub-Saharan Africa, Kenya and Tanzania perform above average, driven mainly by their good regulations in place for machinery and finance, while Niger and Burundi are among the countries with fewer good practices in agribusiness regulation overall (figure 1.2).

How do agribusiness regulations vary across levels of income and agricultural development?

A country's regulations are linked to its growth[10] and development.[11] High-income countries have better agribusiness regulations across the areas measured by *EBA*

topics than lower-income countries (figure 1.3). The correlation found between country income levels and average scores is quite strong across topics.[12]

The relevance of agriculture in an economy varies significantly across countries. *EBA* uses a classification of agricultural transformation that combines agriculture's contribution to GDP and the share of population dedicated to agriculture. The countries are divided in three groups: agriculture-based, transforming and urbanized.[13] Urbanized countries have on average smarter regulations for agribusiness than transforming and agriculture-based countries (figure 1.4). As more data are collected over time, measuring agribusiness regulations and reforms may shed light on the relationships among regulations, economic growth and agricultural transformation.

What is the relationship between efficiency and the quality of regulations?

EBA captures three key aspects of the agribusiness sector: operations, quality control and trade (see *Methodology* in appendix A). Better regulation for market access contributes to firm creation, market efficiency and competition,[14] with concrete evidence in the agricultural sector.[15] Well-designed regulations improve outcomes while enhancing agricultural productivity.[16] Efficient rules on exports and imports can improve the quantity, quality and variety of food at lower prices.[17] While the importance of these three areas has been demonstrated, it is not clear whether they come at the expense of each other—whether rules that promote easy and nondiscriminatory entry into the market

FIGURE 1.2 In Sub-Saharan Africa, countries show different levels of regulatory good practices

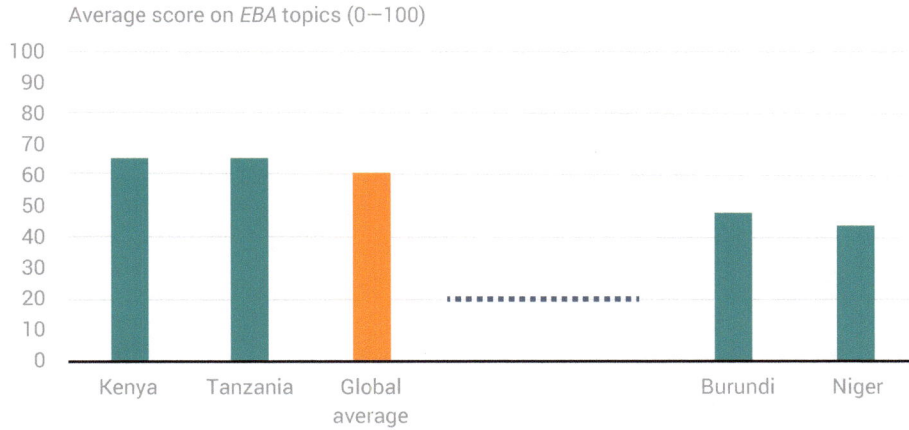

Average score on *EBA* topics (0—100)

Kenya, Tanzania, Global average, Burundi, Niger

Source: EBA database.

FIGURE 1.3 High-income countries have regulations in place that reflect a higher regulatory quality

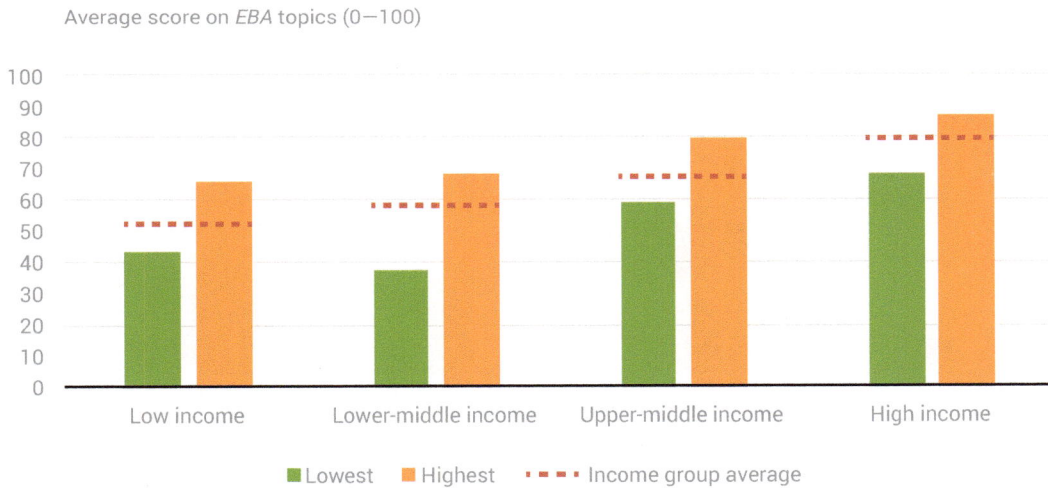

Average score on *EBA* topics (0—100)

Low income, Lower-middle income, Upper-middle income, High income

■ Lowest ■ Highest ∎ ∎ ∎ Income group average

Source: EBA database.

Note: The *EBA* sample covers high-income (6), upper-middle-income (4), lower-middle-income (19) and low-income (11) countries.

are compatible with rules that enhance safety and quality control.

EBA data clearly show that countries performing well on operations across topics also have strong laws for quality control (figure 1.5). Good regulations promote quality while helping the market work efficiently; they are complements rather than substitutes. And countries with higher scores on operations also tend to have effective and more streamlined trade requirements (figure 1.6).

EBA also measures the efficiency of administrative procedures, such as fertilizer and seed registration, with their corresponding time and cost components. Countries with stronger regulations for market operations in a particular area display different levels of efficiency in those processes. While some regions pay an efficiency cost (in actual cost or time) to put the regulations in place, others combine regulatory strength with procedural efficiency.

FIGURE 1.4 Urbanized countries have a better *EBA* performance than transforming and agriculture-based countries

Average score on *EBA* topics (0—100)

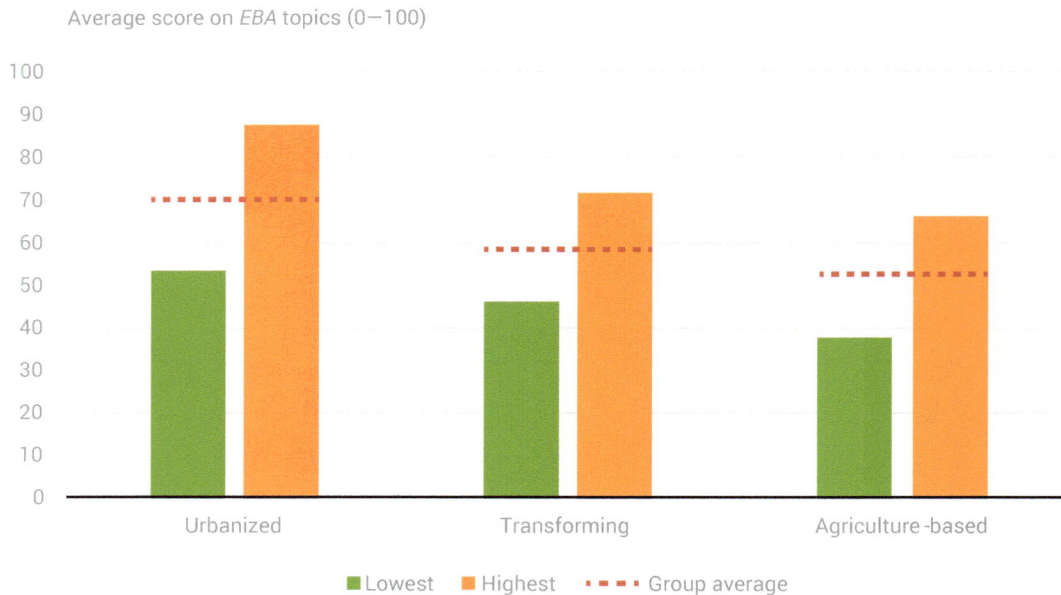

Source: EBA database.

Note: EBA countries are divided into three groups. Urbanized countries have a contribution of agriculture to GDP below 25% and a share of active population in agriculture below 25%: Bosnia and Herzegovina, Chile, Colombia, Denmark, Georgia, Greece, Jordan, Kyrgyz Republic, Morocco, Nicaragua, Poland, Russian Federation, Spain and Ukraine. Transforming countries have a contribution of agriculture to GDP below 25% and a share of active population in agriculture over 25%: Bangladesh, Bolivia, Côte d'Ivoire, Ghana, Guatemala, Lao PDR, Sri Lanka, the Philippines, Tajikistan, Turkey, Vietnam and Zambia. Agriculture-based countries have a contribution of agriculture to GDP over 25% and a share of active population in agriculture over 50%: Burkina Faso, Burundi, Cambodia, Ethiopia, Kenya, Mali, Mozambique, Myanmar, Nepal, Niger, Rwanda, Sudan, Tanzania and Uganda.

In registering new seed varieties, for example, firms in Latin America and the Caribbean pay a much higher cost than firms in the Middle East and North Africa to adhere to similar rules that guarantee an effective and safe registration process (figure 1.7). Companies in South Asia spend more time than those in East Asia and the Pacific to comply with similar requirements (in regulatory quality) to register fertilizer products (figure 1.8).

Are agribusiness regulations discriminating against the private sector, foreign or small companies?

Participation and investment in agriculture by private sector enterprises—big or small, domestic or foreign—can generate such benefits as higher productivity and access to capital and markets.[18] But these benefits depend on a wide range of factors including regulatory measures to improve both the business climate and the effective competition; for low-income and middle-income countries it is essential to avoid discriminating against different types of investors.[19]

To measure regulatory discrimination against the private sector, *EBA* data cover the eligibility of private companies to import machinery, register fertilizer, produce breeder or foundation seeds and be accredited in seed certification. The data also cover the possibility for foreign companies to import fertilizers or perform transport activities in the country. And they cover a minimum capital requirement to start a farmers' cooperative or a minimum number of trucks to establish a trucking company, which could impede small players in the market (see

Alternative ways of presenting the data in appendix C).

In general, countries perform well in terms of nondiscrimination, with an average of 14 of 18 good practices embedded in the countries' relevant laws and regulations. Greece, Denmark, Georgia, Poland, Spain and Zambia have the highest number of nondiscriminatory regulations in place while Ethiopia, the Lao People's Democratic Republic and Myanmar have the fewest (figure 1.9). More than 95% of countries allow the private sector to import tractors and fertilizers, but only a third allow them to carry out the seed certification process. While 38 countries allow foreign companies to transport goods into their country from outside, only 4 allow them to transport goods between two locations within the country.

FIGURE 1.5 Countries with smarter regulations on market operations also promote quality control

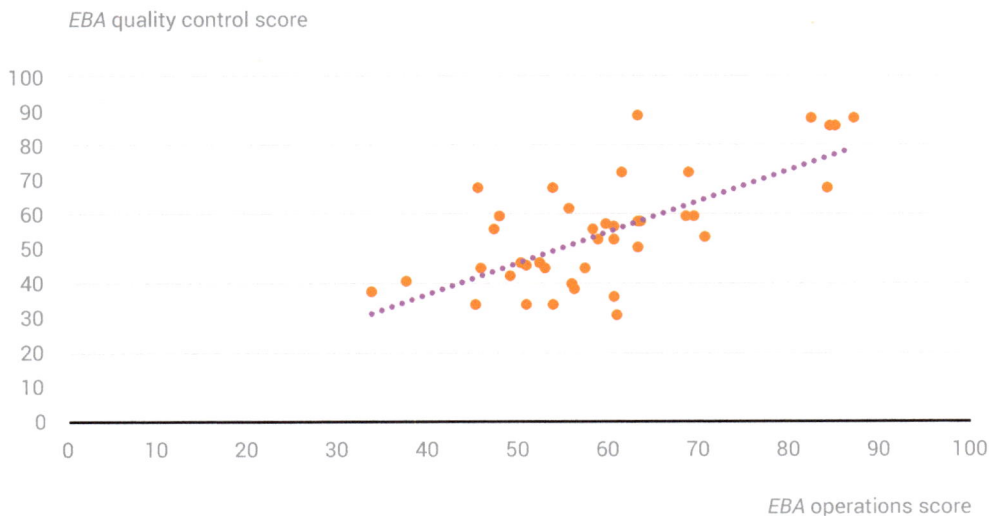

EBA quality control score

EBA operations score

Source: EBA database.

Note: The figure compares the operations score with the quality control score. The correlation between the two scores is 0.70. The correlation is significant at 1% after controlling for income per capita. The operations score is an average of the scores of indicators classified in the operations category. The quality control score is an average of the scores of indicators classified under the quality control category.

FIGURE 1.6 Better rules on market operations are associated with more efficient trade requirements

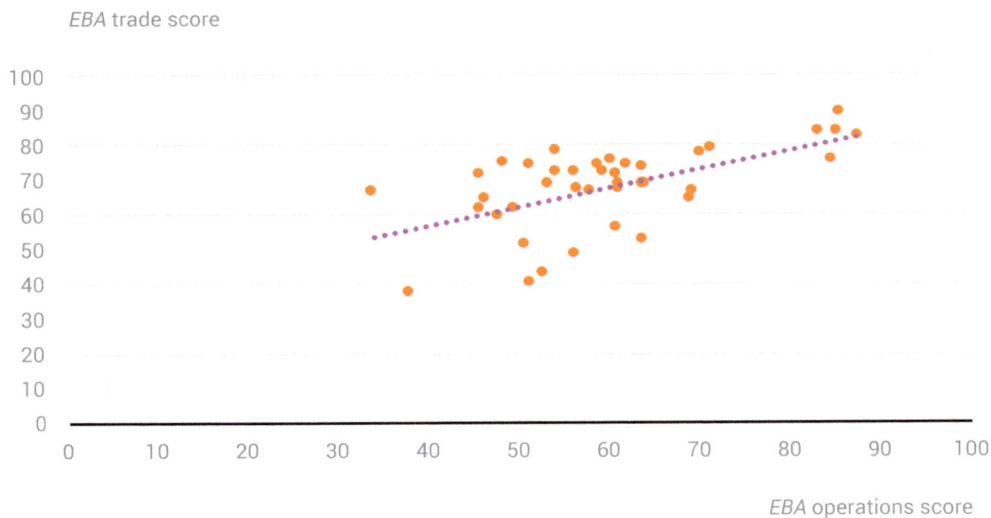

EBA trade score

EBA operations score

Source: EBA database.

Note: The figure compares the operations score with the trade score. The correlation between the two scores is 0.59. The correlation is significant at 1% after controlling for income per capita.

FIGURE 1.7 Regions with similar rules show different costs for registering a new seed variety

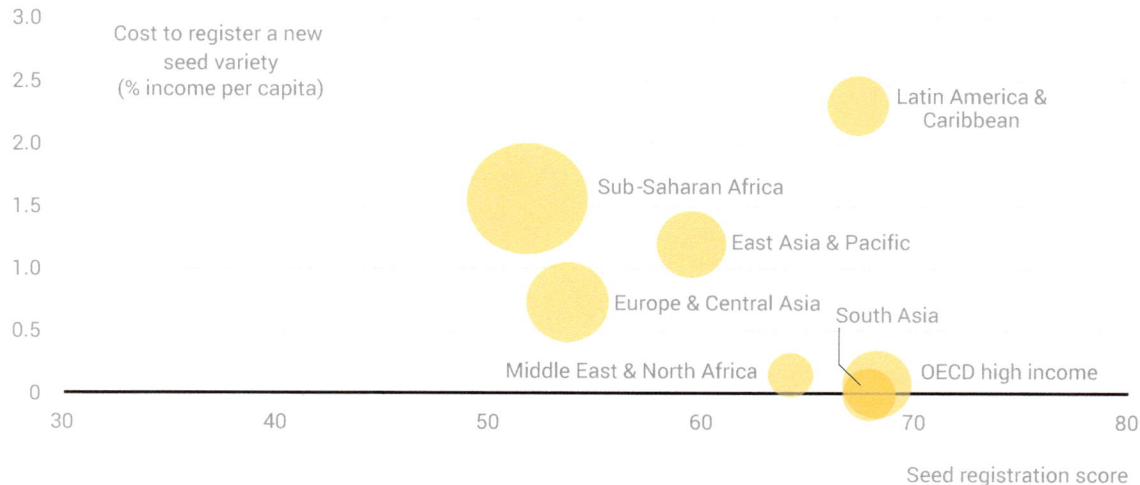

Source: *EBA* database.

FIGURE 1.8 Regions with similar rules have different time durations in fertilizer registration

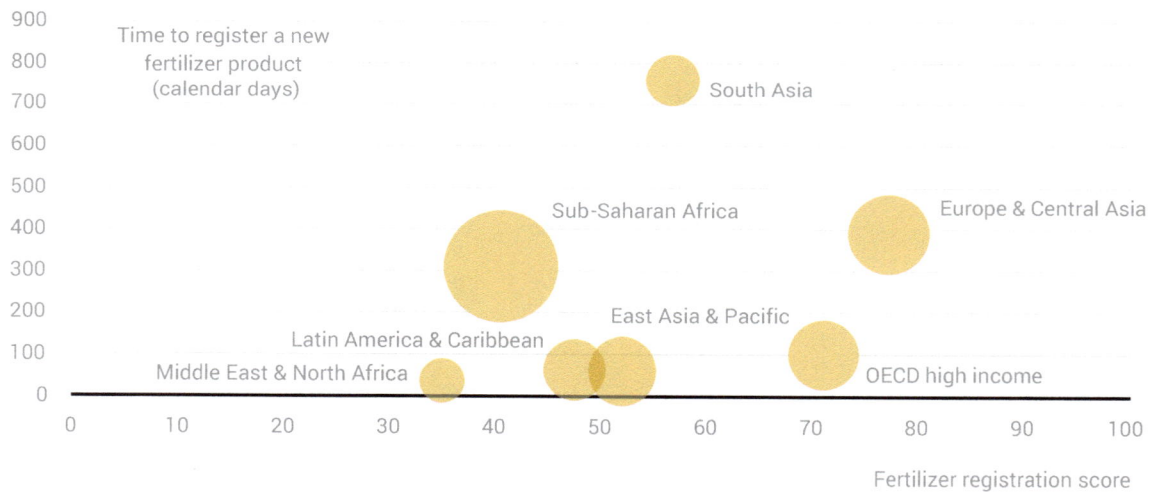

Source: *EBA* database.

FIGURE 1.9 Agribusiness rules in Greece are the least discriminatory, while Ethiopia, Lao PDR and Myanmar have potential to improve

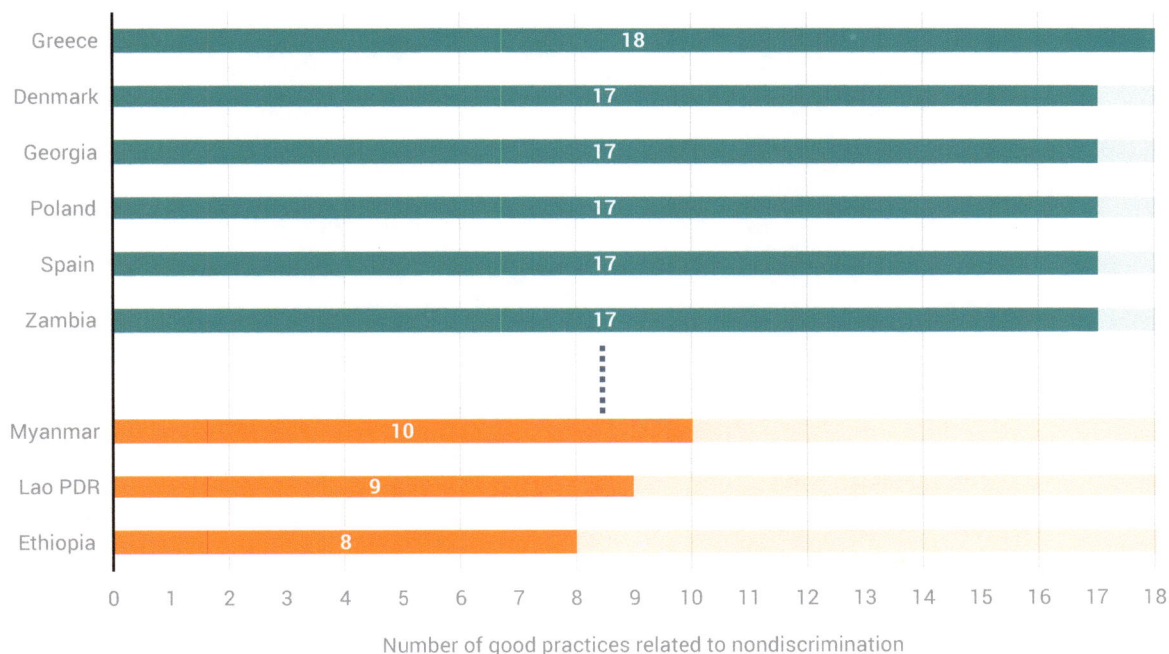

Number of good practices related to nondiscrimination

Source: EBA database.

Is regulatory information accessible for agribusiness?

Access to information about agribusiness regulations and requirements is also important. Across topics, *EBA* data measure whether governments make regulatory information available to the public, such as the specific licensing requirements, the official fee schedule of various regulatory processes and the catalogs of registered seed varieties or fertilizer products. Also taken into consideration is whether the information and services are accessible online or electronically (see *Alternative ways of presenting the data* in appendix C).

Denmark and Spain comply with 9 of the possible 10 good practices.

Rwanda (with only one) and Burundi, Côte d'Ivoire, Ethiopia and Ghana (with two) can still improve to make regulatory information more accessible for participants in the agribusiness value chain (figure 1.10). While 75% of the countries have official catalogs listing new seed varieties or fertilizer products, fewer than half make them available online.

FIGURE 1.10 Specific information on requirements for agribusiness are most accessible in Denmark and Spain and least accessible in Rwanda

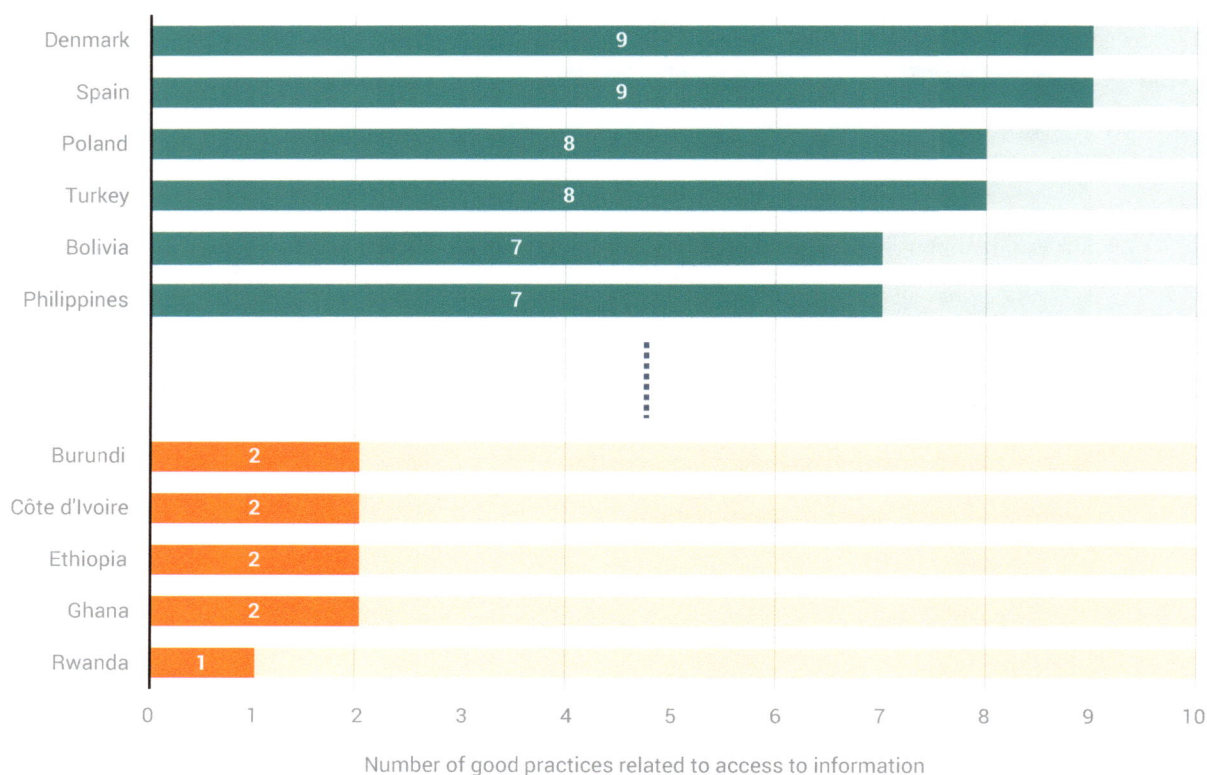

Number of good practices related to access to information

Source: EBA database.

Notes

1. Clark 2014; Van Stel and others 2007.

2. Gisselquist and Van Der Meer 2001.

3. Gisselquist and Grether 2000.

4. Lio and Liu 2008.

5. Freeman and Kaguongo 2003.

6. Spielman and others 2011.

7. Langyintuo and others 2010.

8. Literature on the association between quality of regulation and the productivity of considered agricultural inputs includes Lio and Liu (2008) and Kraay and others (2010), using governance indicators produced by Kaufmann and others (2006) in 199 countries.

9. High-income countries—Chile, Denmark, Greece, Poland, Russian Federation and Spain—are not measured under the *EBA* finance indicators.

10. Divanbeigi and Ramalho 2015; Eiffert 2009.

11. Acemoglu and others 2005; Aghion and Burlauf 2009.

12. The correlation between income per capita and the average of *EBA* scores in the 6 topics is 0.59.

13. See note in figure 1.4.

14. Ciccone and Papaioannou 2007; Klapper and others 2006; Sarria-Allende and Fisma 2004.

15. See papers cited in endnote 2–6 for examples.

16. See endnote 8.

17. Moïsé and others 2013.

18. FAO 2014.

19. Global Harvest Initiative 2011; FAO 2012.

References

Acemoglu, D., J. A. Robinson and S. Johnson. 2005. "Institutions as a Fundamental Cause of Long-Run Growth." *Handbook of Economic Growth* 1A: 386–472.

Aghion, P., and S. Burlauf. 2009. "From Growth Theory to Policy Design." Working Paper 57, Commission on Growth and Development.

Ciccone, A., and E. Papaioannou. 2007. "Red Tape and Delayed Entry." Working Paper 758, European Central Bank, Frankfurt am Main.

Clarke, G. 2014. "Does Over-Regulation Lead to Corruption? Evidence from a multi-country firm survey." *Academic and Business Research Institute* LV14025.

Divanbeigi, R., and R. Ramalho. 2015. "Business Regulations and Growth." Policy Research Working Paper 7299, World Bank, Washington, DC.

Eiffert, B. 2009. "Do Regulatory Reforms Stimulate Investment and Growth? Evidence from the Doing Business Data, 2003–07." Working Paper 159, Center for Global Development, Washington, DC.

FAO (Food and Agriculture Organization). 2012. *The State of Food and Agriculture 2012: Investing in Agriculture for a Better Future*. Rome: FAO.

Freeman, H.A., and W. Kaguongo. 2003. "Fertilizer Market Liberalization and Private Retail Trade in Kenya." *Food Policy* 28 (5–6): 505–18.

Gisselquist, D., and J. Grether. 2000. "An Argument for Deregulating the Transfer of Agricultural Technologies to Developing Countries." *The World Bank Economic Review* 14 (1): 111–27.

Gisselquist, D., and C. Van Der Meer. 2001. "Regulations for Seed and Fertilizer Markets: A Good Practice Guide for Policymakers." Rural Development Working Paper 22817, World Bank, Washington, DC.

Global Harvest Initiative. 2011. *Enhancing Private Sector Involvement in Agriculture and Rural Infrastructure Development*. Washington, DC: Global Harvest Initiative.

Kaufmann, D., A. Kraay and M. Mastruzzi. 2006. "Governance Matters IV: Governance Indicators for 1996–2004." Working Paper, Washington, DC: World Bank.

Klapper, L., L. Laeven and R. Raghuram. 2006. "Entry as a Barrier to Entrepreneurship." *Journal of Financial Economics* 82: 591–629.

Kraay, A., D. Kaufmann and M. Mastruzzi. 2010. *The Worldwide Governance Indicators: Methodology and Analytical Issues*. Washington, DC: Brookings Institute.

Langyintuo, A.S., W. Mwangi, A. Diallo, J. MacRobert, J. Dixon and M. Baziger. 2010. "Challenges of the Maize Seed Industry in Eastern and Southern Africa: A Compelling Case for Private-Public Interventions to Promote Growth." *Food Policy* 35 (4): 323–31.

Lio, M., and M.C. Liu. 2008. "Governance and Agricultural Productivity: A Cross-National Analysis." *Food Policy* 33 (6): 504–12.

Moïsé, E., C. Delpeuch, S. Sorescu, N. Bottini and A. Foch. 2013. "Estimating the Constraints to Agricultural Trade of Developing Countries." OECD Trade Policy Paper 142, OECD, Paris.

Sarria-Allende, V., and R. Fisma. 2004. "Regulation of Entry and the Distortion of Industrial Organization." Working Paper 10929, National Bureau of Economic Research, Cambridge, MA.

Spielman, D.J., D. Kelemwork and D. Alemu. 2011. "Seed, Fertilizer and Agricultural Extension in Ethiopia." Ethiopia Strategy Support Program II Working Paper 020, IFPRI, Addis Ababa.

Van Stel, A., D. J. Storey and A. Roy Thurik. 2007. "The Effect of Business Regulations on Nascent and Young Business Entrepreneurship." *Small Business Economics* 28 (2): 171–86.

2. SEED
STRENGTHENING SEED SYSTEMS

Imagine a farmer, Jelena, who sustains her family by growing corn and vegetables. A newly formed variety release committee will release improved seed varieties in her country. With this reform, Jelena will also be able to consult an online variety catalog indicating which varieties perform best in her region. All seed sold in the country will be certified to ensure quality. With improved seed varieties, subsistence farmers like Jelena can increase the yield and quality of their crops so that they can sell the surplus on the domestic market.

EBA seed indicators measure laws and regulations on the development, evaluation, release and quality control of improved seed varieties. Improved varieties are a key technology for improving agricultural productivity.[1] Smart regulation of the seed sector can ensure that laws and regulations do not obstruct the timely introduction of improved varieties to the market.

Seed registration, the first seed indicator, was selected for study because burdensome and inconsistent regulations can reduce the number of improved varieties that are released and eligible for commercialization. In countries that require registration of new seed varieties, replacing burdensome regulations with smart ones—preventing long and costly procedures while guaranteeing quality seed—can make improved varieties available to farmers in a timely manner and in sufficient quantity for planting.[2] Smarter regulations that include the private sector in the release process will provide more transparency and incentivize the private sector to release new varieties in the country.

Seed development and certification, the second seed indicator, is comprised of two components—development and certification. The first component measures regulations that support the private sector's involvement in developing new varieties. This is particularly important since public sector investments in agricultural research, including plant breeding, have declined in many countries since 1997, leaving the task to the private

sector. In some countries regulations limit the private sector's role in the development of new seed varieties, preventing companies from accessing initial classes of seeds. The *EBA 2015* progress report presented Ethiopia, where the public sector's monopoly consistently resulted in shortages of initial seed classes for smallholder farmers and agribusinesses.[3] Regulations that limit the private sector's access to initial classes of seed or genetic resources stored by national gene banks reduce the resources available to the private sector for developing new varieties.[4] In addition, protecting the property rights of seed developers spurs further innovation.[5]

The second component of this indicator captures aspects of the seed certification process. The aim of mandatory seed certification is ensuring the genetic purity and varietal identity of seed varieties. But when the process is government-run, overburdened public authorities and nontransparent bureaucracy can delay the commercialization of new varieties and give rise to corruption. One way to ensure the transparency of the certification is through the public availability of costs associated with government-run certification. Seed certification by nongovernmental inspectors and laboratories reduces the burden on the public sector and speeds the certification process.

The data cover the following areas:

- **Seed registration.** This indicator measures the efficiency of the registration, including the variety release

committee, the content, availability and frequency of the variety catalogue updates and the time and cost to register a new variety (which is not scored).

- **Seed development and certification.** This indicator measures the protection of plant breeders' rights, the access to initial classes of seed and germplasms, the licensing systems for public varieties and additional testing requirements for materials imported for research and development. In addition, this indicator addresses the availability of an official fee schedule for certification and whether third parties can perform it.

The *EBA* country scores vary from 28 to 94 points over all 40 countries (figure 2.1). This variation in scores has to do with the performance of the countries in both the seed registration and the seed development and certification indicators. Overall countries tend to score better in the latter, which focuses on the protection of plant breeder rights, the access to genetic material and initial classes of seed and quality controls. Nevertheless, some countries are exceptions, Bangladesh, Burkina Faso, Côte d'Ivoire, Ethiopia, Ghana, Kenya, Lao PDR, Nepal, Nicaragua and Turkey score higher on the seed registration indicators.

Countries can score lower or higher for different reasons. For the lowest performers, such as Bosnia and Herzegovina, Ghana, Niger, Rwanda and Uganda,

FIGURE 2.1 Countries mostly score better on seed development and certification indicators, while seed registration proves more challenging

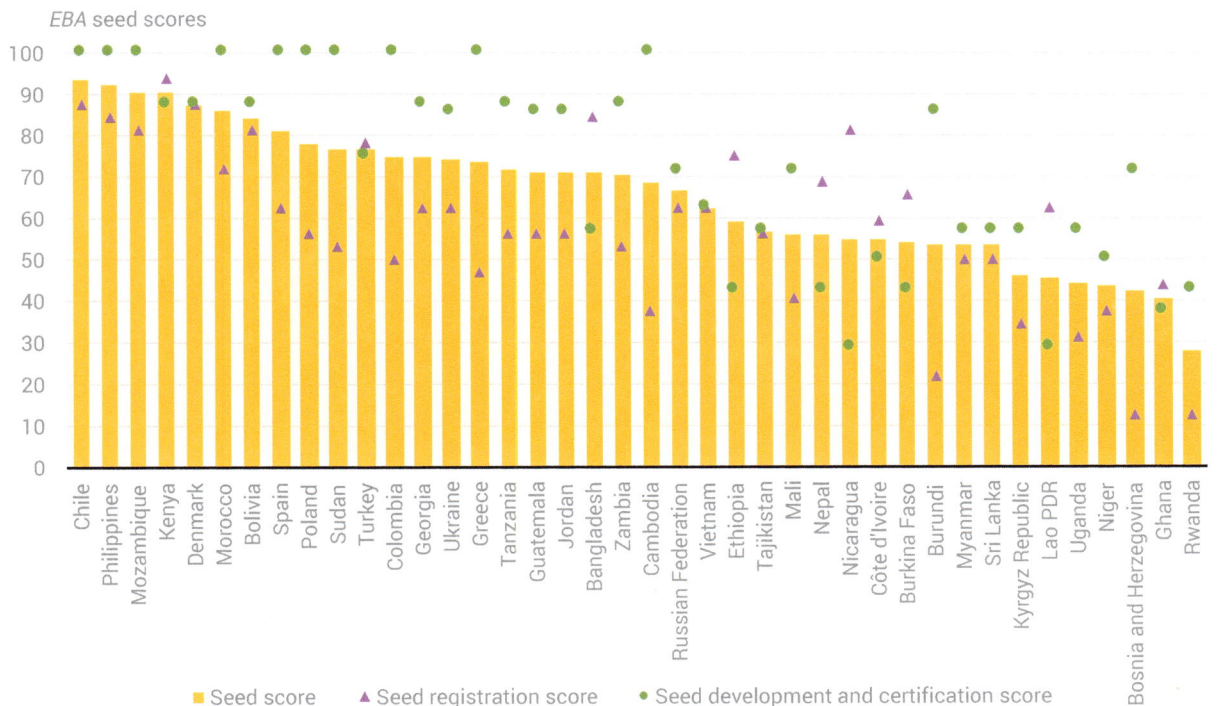

EBA seed scores

Legend: ■ Seed score ▲ Seed registration score ● Seed development and certification score

Source: EBA database.

the low scores are often from a lack of implementation of laws and regulations. Laws in Bosnia and Herzegovina, Ghana, Niger and Rwanda establish variety release authorities, but in practice the authorities are not operational. In addition, the lack of transparency in mandatory procedures also hurts a country's overall score. In four of the five lowest scoring countries (Ghana, Niger, Rwanda and Uganda), certification of cereal crops is mandatory, but there is no official fee schedule for the certification performed by the public sector.

Chile, Denmark, Kenya, Mozambique and the Philippines perform the best overall, all with scores over 80 in both the seed registration and the seed development and certification indicators. In these countries, good seed laws are in place and include provision for the flexibility of the variety release committee, the transparency and efficiency of seed registration and seed certification

activities (when required). They also support the involvement of private sector initiatives in the seed systems. But a good score does not mean those countries cannot improve in certain aspects. In Chile, Denmark and the Philippines the national catalogs listing registered seed varieties do not offer information on agro-ecological zones. Moreover, Kenya does not have an official fee schedule for the certification of seed varieties and Mozambique's national catalog listing registered seed varieties is neither available online nor updated according the country's cropping seasons.

Links between private and public sector breeding activities are greater in the OECD high-income countries surveyed

Plant breeders create new seed varieties by crossing and selecting specific beneficial traits. Increasing the number of

sources from which private plant breeders can access initial classes of seed produced by the public sector supports private plant breeders' involvement in the country's plant breeding system. But restrictive regulations can obstruct new variety development by the private sector.

In practice links between the private and public sectors take several forms—from producing breeder and foundation seed developed by public sector breeders and made available to private breeders to implementing licensing systems that allow private breeders to use local public varieties to multiply and market their seed. Allowing private breeders access to genetic materials stored in the national gene banks also supports effective collaboration between private and public actors. These practices help private breeders acquire varieties developed or conserved by the public sector and benefit from greater resources for their breeding activities (box 2.1).[6]

BOX 2.1 Good practices for involving the private sector in developing new varieties

- Should grant and protect plant breeders' rights.

- Should allow private companies to use local public varieties to produce breeder/pre-basic seed and foundation/basic seed for the domestic market.

- Should conserve germplasm in national public gene banks and make them accessible to the private sector for research and development of new seed varieties.

- Should allow local public varieties to be licensed to private sector companies for multiplication and commercialization in the domestic market.

- Should facilitate the import of nonregistered materials for research and development.

Regulations that best support private sector involvement in the breeding system are found in Cambodia, Chile, Colombia, Georgia, Greece, Jordan, Kenya, Morocco, Mozambique, the Philippines, Poland, Spain and Sudan.

By contrast, of the 40 countries surveyed, 9 do not grant the private sector access to breeder seed of local public varieties (Bangladesh, Burkina Faso, Ghana, Lao PDR, Mali, Nicaragua, Niger, Tajikistan and Turkey). Nor do Burkina Faso, Lao PDR and Nicaragua grant access to foundation seed of local public varieties. So breeders and seed companies are likely to market fewer seed varieties.[7]

Countries such as Myanmar, the Russian Federation, Tanzania, Ukraine and Zambia impose minor limitations, such as preventing private companies from importing materials for research and development of new varieties without further government field-testing. Similarly, Bolivia, Bosnia and Herzegovina and Denmark do not have systems for licensing public varieties to private seed enterprises for production and sale in the domestic market. Such practice often hampers commercialization of varieties bred by public sector institutes and universities, leaving newly developed varieties on laboratory shelves rather than in crop fields.

Registration costs vary the most among the lower-middle-income and low-income countries

In countries where registration is compulsory, a new variety of seed must pass specific tests commonly performed over one or more cropping seasons. The first tests are intended to measure the variety's distinctiveness, uniformity and stability (DUS). In most countries, a new variety of seed must also pass the value for cultivation and use (VCU) tests, which identify the advantage of the new seed over already-registered varieties. The data from these tests are reviewed by a scientific committee, which either releases the variety or advises another official body that the variety is eligible to be released.

Across income groups, relative registration costs are the lowest among high-income countries (figure 2.2). Registration costs among countries in this group show little variation—except in Russia, where registering up to five new varieties a year is free—with costs as a percent of income per capita at 6% in Chile, 7% in Poland, 8% in Denmark, 9% in Greece and 10% in Spain.

In Bangladesh, Bolivia, Guatemala, Morocco, Myanmar, Sri Lanka and Ukraine the cost is well below 40% of income per capita. But outliers such as Nicaragua, Sudan and Vietnam, where costs reach 834%, 722% and 426% of income per capita respectively, make lower-middle-income countries the income group with the most expensive registration for a new variety of seed.

There is also great variation among low-income countries. In Nepal and Uganda registering a new variety is free, whereas registration costs reach 79% and 89% of income per capita in Ethiopia and Mozambique.

Most countries have variety release committees

At the end of the registration process, the variety release committee (VRC) approves the results of several years of new variety development by plant breeders in line with VRC standards.[8] But a requirement to register a new variety of seed that is not supported by rules that ensure a flexible and effective process may discourage breeders from releasing new varieties. Of the 40 countries surveyed, 39 legally mandate the establishment of a VRC (although in Bangladesh, Guatemala and the Philippines registration of cereal varieties is not mandatory). Among them, Bosnia and Herzegovina, Cambodia and Niger have yet to establish their VRCs in practice. To reduce delays affecting the release of improved varieties into the market and the farmers, the registration and release process needs to allow seed companies to start producing the newly released variety for the next cropping season (box 2.2). In practice, this means that the release of a new variety by a VRC should be possible before each cropping season starts. Among the surveyed countries, 7 have a VRC that is fully flexible and meets on demand, and 22 have a VRC that meets after each cropping season (table 2.1). Registration applicants are thus informed about the VRC decision far enough in advance to start production.

In addition to the frequency of VRC meetings, *EBA* seed indicators measure the involvement of the private sector in the variety release decision-making.

FIGURE 2.2 The lower-middle-income and low-income countries show the greatest variation in official registration costs

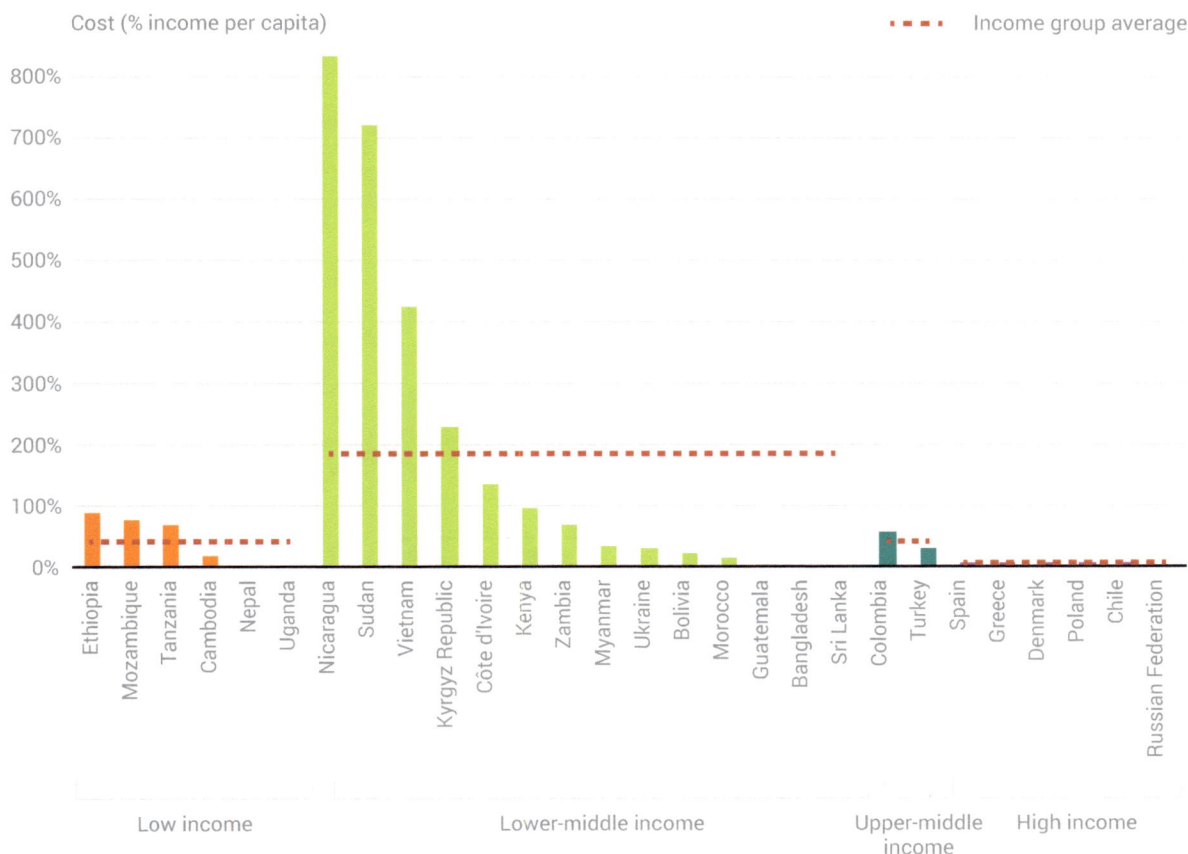

Cost (% income per capita)

- - - - Income group average

Low income   Lower-middle income   Upper-middle income   High income

Source: EBA database.

In practice, the representation of other stakeholders within the VRC may raise private sector confidence in the variety registration and release process. Of the 36 countries with an established VRC, Colombia, Ethiopia, Jordan, Lao PDR, Myanmar, Russia, Rwanda, Sri Lanka, Tajikistan, Ukraine and Vietnam do not include representatives of the private sector (figure 2.3).

In addition to the VRC review and decision, countries may require additional formalities that delay the release of the new variety without providing any additional technical verification. In 14 of the surveyed countries, the decision of the VRC does not automatically lead to the release of the variety. In practice,

additional administrative formalities must be satisfied for the variety to be released. In Kenya a registration applicant will be delayed on average 31 days in releasing a new variety.

Once released, the information relating to new varieties should be accessible, reliable and useful.[9] *EBA* seed indicators measure accessibility through the availability of an online version of the national variety catalog listing the latest varieties released in the country. Of the 40 surveyed countries, 30 have a national variety catalog, but only 19 make it available online. Bangladesh, Bolivia, Burkina Faso, Ethiopia, Georgia, Jordan, Kenya, the Kyrgyz Republic, Lao PDR, Mali, Morocco, Mozambique, Niger, Tanzania and

Zambia have variety catalogs, but they are not updated after each cropping season, so information about new varieties is not released as soon as it is available.

Bangladesh, Burkina Faso, Ethiopia, Guatemala, Kenya, Mali, Mozambique, Nepal, Niger, Russia, Tajikistan, Tanzania, Ukraine and Vietnam have national variety catalogues that specify agro-ecological zones—areas indicated by the national seed registration authority as regions in which growers can expect optimal results for specific seed varieties. Specifying agro-ecological zones enables agricultural producers to use new seed varieties properly according to the soil, landform and climatic characteristics of their farms, increasing crop yields.

BOX 2.2 Good practices for evaluating and registering new varieties

- Should include both private and public sector representatives in the VRC.

- VRC should meet after each round of DUS/VCU tests.

- Should allow new seed varieties to be released immediately after a favorable decision of the VRC.

- Should maintain an up to date national variety catalog listing, with agro-ecological zones and available online.

TABLE 2.1 Variety release committees meet after each cropping season in most countries

VARIETY RELEASE COMMITTEE	NUMBER OF COUNTRIES	COUNTRIES
Meets on demand	7	Bangladesh, Bolivia, Colombia, Côte d'Ivoire, Kenya, Lao PDR, Nepal
Meets after each cropping season	22	Chile, Denmark, Ethiopia, Greece, Jordan, Kyrgyz Republic, Mozambique, Myanmar, Nicaragua, Philippines, Poland, Russian Federation, Spain, Sri Lanka, Sudan, Tajikistan, Tanzania, Turkey, Uganda, Ukraine, Vietnam, Zambia
Does not meet after each cropping season	1	Morocco
Established but does not meet	6	Burkina Faso, Burundi, Georgia, Ghana, Mali, Rwanda
Not established	4	Bosnia and Herzegovina, Cambodia, Guatemala, Niger

Source: EBA database.

Seed quality certification in surveyed countries is mainly government-run

Seed certification subjects registered seed to controls and inspections, before it reaches farmers and other agricultural producers.[10] Certification processes commonly include field inspections, laboratory analysis, packaging and labeling. Most countries surveyed (31 of 40) establish a mandatory government-run seed certification system for cereal seed (figure 2.4). While quality control offered by government-run systems can ensure the quality of seed sold in the country, efforts may also be hindered by the limited resources available to regulatory bodies in charge of inspections, testing and labeling. While this may slow the certification process, it can also improve the quality of new seed varieties.

Regulations that allow accreditation of nongovernmental inspectors or laboratories to carry out certain certification activities can reduce potential delays caused by an overburdened public authority (box 2.3). This option allows accredited private companies to support the public sector in the certification process, increasing the speed and efficiency of quality control and ensuring that quality seed is delivered to market on time.[11] Seed companies and other private institutions can be accredited to carry out part or all of the maize seed certification process in Bolivia, Côte d'Ivoire, Denmark, Georgia, Ghana, Greece, Kenya, Niger, Spain, Tanzania, Vietnam and Zambia.

Conclusion

Strengthening seed systems through smart regulations is an essential component to the creation of an enabling environment for the business of agriculture. This year's findings show that laws and institutions are mostly in place, but with some differences in the developed indicators and challenges in implementation of the laws. There is room for improvement in all countries surveyed, such as:

- **Transparent variety release procedures allowing new varieties to be available in time for farmers and other stakeholders.** In Bolivia the variety release committee includes an equal number of public and private sector representatives, and meets on demand to prevent delays in the release of the new variety.

- **Laws that protect plant varieties developed by plant breeders to ensure sustained breeding efforts in the country.** Tanzania, which already had a law granting and protecting the rights of plant breeders over their new varieties, became bound by the 1991 UPOV Act in November 2015.

- **A legal environment that facilitates the private sector's access to**

FIGURE 2.3 In the majority of countries studied with a variety release committee, the private sector is involved in the variety release process

Number of countries

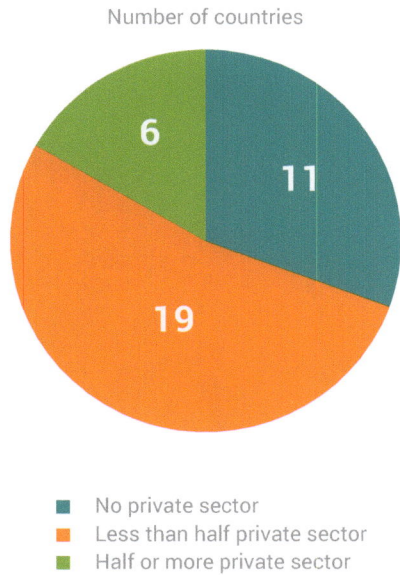

- No private sector
- Less than half private sector
- Half or more private sector

Source: EBA database.

BOX 2.3 Good practices for countries requiring mandatory certification

- Should provide for an option for companies (self-accreditation) and private institutions (third-party accreditation) to be accredited for the performance of part or all of the certification process.

- Should provide seed producers with official fee schedules that detail the costs associated with the certification performed by the public authority.

FIGURE 2.4 *EBA* countries with mandatory maize certification predominantly restrict its implementation to public sector actors

Number of countries

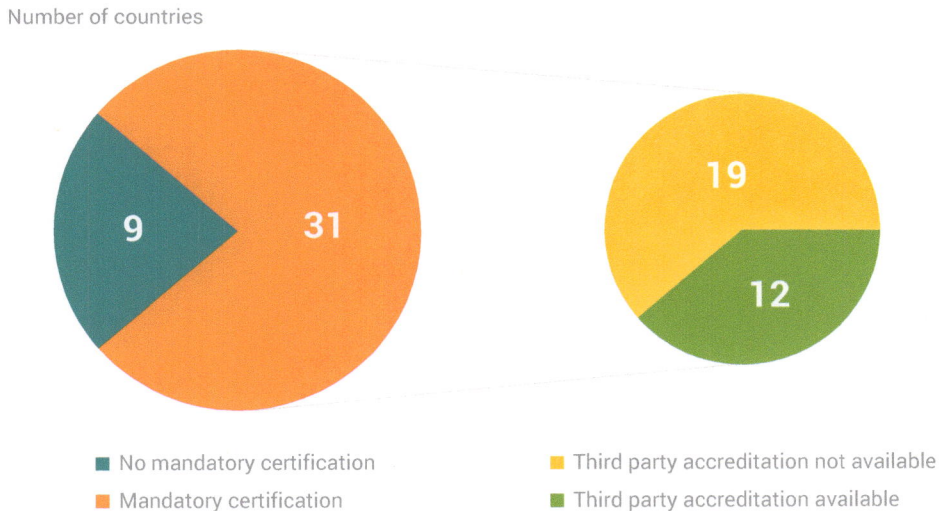

- No mandatory certification
- Mandatory certification
- Third party accreditation not available
- Third party accreditation available

Source: EBA database.

initial classes of seed and materials for research and development and involves private sector companies in the multiplication and commercialization of public varieties. In Côte d'Ivoire the seed law allows nongovernmental entities to be accredited by ministerial decree for the multiplication of plant materials.

- **A quality control system that provides transparent costs and options for the accreditation of third party inspectors or laboratories.** In Burkina Faso the fee payable for seed quality control is provided by law and proportional to production area.

Improving laws and regulations that affect the development, evaluation, release and quality control of improved varieties is an important step. Research shows that improved seeds account for about 30–50% of the increase in productivity and enhancing profitability of farmers. The seed topic data can inform discussions on strengthening seed systems, indicating regulatory obstacles to the timely release of quality seed along with other factors, including limited public sector capacities and the socio-economic conditions of farmers.

Notes

1. Tripp 1998.

2. Langyintuo and others 2008.

3. *Enabling the Business of Agriculture 2015.*

4. *Breeder seed* is seed directly controlled by the originating or sponsoring plant breeding institution, firm or individual that is the source for the production of seed of the certified classes. *Foundation seed* is a progeny of breeder or foundation seed, handled to maintain specific

genetic purity and identity (USDA 2009, 1).

5. Fernandez-Cornejo 2004.

6. King and others 2012.

7. In Nicaragua no Plant Variety Protection title was approved in 2013 and a total of five Plant Variety Protection titles were in force at end of 2013; UPOV 2013.

8. Tripp 1997.

9. Rohrbach, Howard and Zulu 2004.

10. Aidoo and others 2014.

11. Gisselquist and Van Der Meer 2001.

References

Aidoo, R., J. Osei Mensah, B. Fenni Omono and V. Abankwah. 2014. "Factors Determining the Use of Certified Maize Seeds by Farmers in Ejura-Sekyedumasi Municipality in Ghana." *World Journal of Agricultural Sciences* 2 (5): 84–90.

Fernandez-Cornejo, J. 2004. "The Seed Industry in U.S. Agriculture: An Exploration of Data and Information on Crop Seed Markets, Regulation, Industry Structure, and Research and Development." Agriculture Information Bulletin 786, U.S. Department of Agriculture Economic Research Service, Washington, DC.

Gisselquist, D., and C. Van Der Meer. 2001. "Regulations for Seed and Fertilizer Markets: A Good Practice Guide for Policy Makers." Rural Development Working Paper 22817, World Bank, Washington, DC.

International Union for the Protection of New Varieties of Plants. 2013. *Plant Variety Protection Statistics for the Period 2009–2013. C/48/7* prepared by the Office of the Union.

King, J., A. Toole and K. Fuglie. 2012. "Complementary Roles of the Public and Private Sectors in U.S. Agricultural Research and Development." Economic Brief 19, U.S. Department of Agriculture Economic Research Service, Washington, DC.

Langyintuo, A.S., W. Mwangi, A.O. Diallo, J. MacRobert, J. Dixon and M. Bänziger. 2008. *An Analysis of the Bottlenecks Affecting the Production and Deployment of Maize Seed in Eastern and Southern Africa.* Harare, Zimbabwe: International Maize and Wheat Improvement Center.

Rohrbach, D., J. Howard and E. Zulu. 2004. "Harmonization of Seed Laws and Regulations in Southern Africa." In *Seed Trade Liberalization in Sub-Saharan Africa,* eds., David Rohrbach and Julie Howard. Michigan State University, International Crops Research Institute for the Semi-Arid Tropics (ICRISTAT).

Tripp, R. 1997. "Seed Regulatory Framework and the Availability of Crop Varieties." In *Easing Barriers to Movement of Plant Varieties for Agricultural Development,* eds., David Gisselquist and Jitendra Srivastava. Washington, DC: World Bank.

———. 1998. "Regulatory Issues: Varietal Registration and Seed Quality Control," In *Seed Industries in Developing Countries,* ed., M.L. Morris. Lynne Reinner Publishers, Boulder, Colorado, USA.

USDA (United States Department of Agriculture). 2009. "Understanding Seed Certification and Seed Labels." Plant Materials Technical Note 10, U.S. Department of Agriculture Natural Resources Conservation Service, Alexandria, LA.

3. FERTILIZER
IMPROVING SUPPLY AND QUALITY

A farmer wants to diversify her crops by growing different vegetable products. The fertilizer she has been using until now does not work well with this particular set of vegetables. The agro-input dealer in her village has told her that none of the fertilizers available provide the proper suite of nutrients for her vegetable crops. A fertilizer company is registering a new fertilizer product in the country suited for the vegetables she plans to grow, but burdensome regulations require the company to interact with multiple agencies to register the product and conduct fertilizer testing so that a national committee can approve the application. This whole process takes more than seven years and the farmer will have to wait until then before she can access this new fertilizer that can increase her yield.

EBA fertilizer indicators measure laws and regulations on the registration, import and quality control of fertilizer products. They address factors important to companies importing and selling fertilizer products, farmers using quality fertilizer products to increase their productivity and governments pursuing regulations that ensure the quality of products and effectiveness of fertilizer markets.

In many countries, fertilizer products must be registered before they can be sold commercially. Registration of fertilizer products is important because it brings new and innovative products to the market while ensuring safety and quality.

The first indicator, fertilizer registration, measures the requirements to register a fertilizer product for the first time and whether the registration is limited to a time period. Fertilizer registration ensures that governments have control over what types of fertilizers enter the market. It is important to provide market oversight through a registration scheme, since the effects of farm inputs may only become apparent long after they are used.[1] Inadequate nutrients, heavy metals or other residues found in fertilizer products can contaminate crops, animals and humans.[2] Farmers should be given assurance that the products they use will not contaminate their crops and the environment. But registration

procedures should be time- and cost-efficient to ensure that new products reach the market in a timely manner. If registration becomes lengthy and expensive, it can distort competition by limiting the number of players and products in the market. This indicator also measures the transparency of the registration system by examining catalogs listing registered fertilizer products and whether they are available online.

The second indicator, fertilizer import requirements, measures regulations for importing fertilizer. Import requirements are important because fertilizer production is concentrated only in a few countries, so most must rely on imports.[3] This is because fertilizer is subject to economies of scale at every stage of the supply chain, requiring vast amounts of capital and raw materials to produce.[4] Understanding import requirements and the associated time and costs allow for a better knowledge of the market. This indicator measures whether the private sector is allowed to import and sell fertilizer products. Allowing the private sector to engage in the domestic market for fertilizer can result in more efficient markets and lower prices.[5] More private sector participation in the market increases fertilizer access and use, which in turn raises crop yields and cuts reliance on heavy food imports.[6] This indicator also addresses the cost and time to obtain import registrations and permits. A quick and inexpensive import registration

process eases access to the market while informing the government of the players in the market within its borders.[7] But import permits obstruct trade by complicating the import process and increasing the required time and cost. This practice often creates bottlenecks between the companies and dealers supplying farmers.[8] Since import procedures vary across countries, this indicator aims to highlight the balance between control and efficiency needed to ensure a strong market for fertilizer.

The third indicator, fertilizer quality control, assesses government regulations and practices on preventing poor quality fertilizer products from reaching the market. Adulterated, low quality and counterfeit fertilizer products can stunt crop growth and development,[9] leading to lower crop yields, lower farmer incomes, increased food and income insecurities and even environmental problems. This indicator also addresses labeling requirements—important because labeling fertilizer bags increases market certainty (since consumers know what types of products they are buying). Labeling requirements give important information about a bag's contents and the name of its producer. In addition, the indicator looks at rules on the sale of open and mislabeled fertilizer containers. Governments should act to ensure that fertilizer labels correspond to the content inside their containers to guarantee trust between buyers and sellers.[10] Aside from mislabeling, the sale of open fertilizer bags can also be harmful to consumers, as they are susceptible to adulteration, hurting crop yields, reducing farmers' profits and increasing food insecurity.[11]

The *EBA* fertilizer data cover the following areas:

- **Fertilizer registration.** This indicator measures the requirements to register a fertilizer product for the first time, whether the registration is limited to a time period and the existence and accessibility of an official fertilizer catalog.

- **Fertilizer import requirements.** This indicator focuses on the private sector's role and the requirements for importing fertilizer, including the costs of registering as an importer of fertilizer and obtaining an import permit.

- **Fertilizer quality control.** This indicator measures labeling requirements, rules on the sale of open and mislabeled fertilizer containers and

practices for monitoring fertilizer quality.

Across the 40 countries surveyed, fertilizer regulations range from the more strict and highly protective, limiting market access, to the weaker or seemingly nonexistent; neither of the two extremes is desirable. Bosnia and Herzegovina, Poland, Greece, Colombia and Spain are the top 5 performers in the regulatory areas measured by the fertilizer topic (figure 3.1).

Bosnia and Herzegovina, Colombia, Greece and Poland have the strongest and most efficient regulations for fertilizer registration. In these countries, the private sector is required to register fertilizer products, registration of fertilizer products has no time limit and registered fertilizer products are listed in an official catalog that is accessible online. Thirty-three of the 40 countries surveyed require the private sector to register fertilizer. But only 17 of those have registrations that either have no time limit or have one that lasts at least 10 years. For fertilizer registration, the number of

procedures varies significantly across countries, with the time needed to register a new fertilizer product ranging between 15 and 1,125 calendar days, and the cost ranging from 0% to 1,064.5% of income per capita.

Bolivia, Bosnia and Herzegovina, Colombia, the EU countries (Denmark, Greece, Poland and Spain), Kenya, Turkey and Rwanda are the best performers in terms of the fertilizer import requirements measured. Regulatory bottlenecks for importing fertilizer, such as licensing requirements, are less costly and onerous in these countries than in the *EBA* 16 sample average. In Sub-Saharan Africa, both Kenya (a lower-middle-income country) and Rwanda (a low-income country) are among the best performers globally, offering good examples to other countries in the region that are not performing as well.

The differences among countries are less apparent in fertilizer quality control. Twelve of the 40 countries surveyed require labeling fertilizer containers and prohibit the sale of mislabeled and

FIGURE 3.1 Sixteen countries have overall fertilizer scores above the sample average

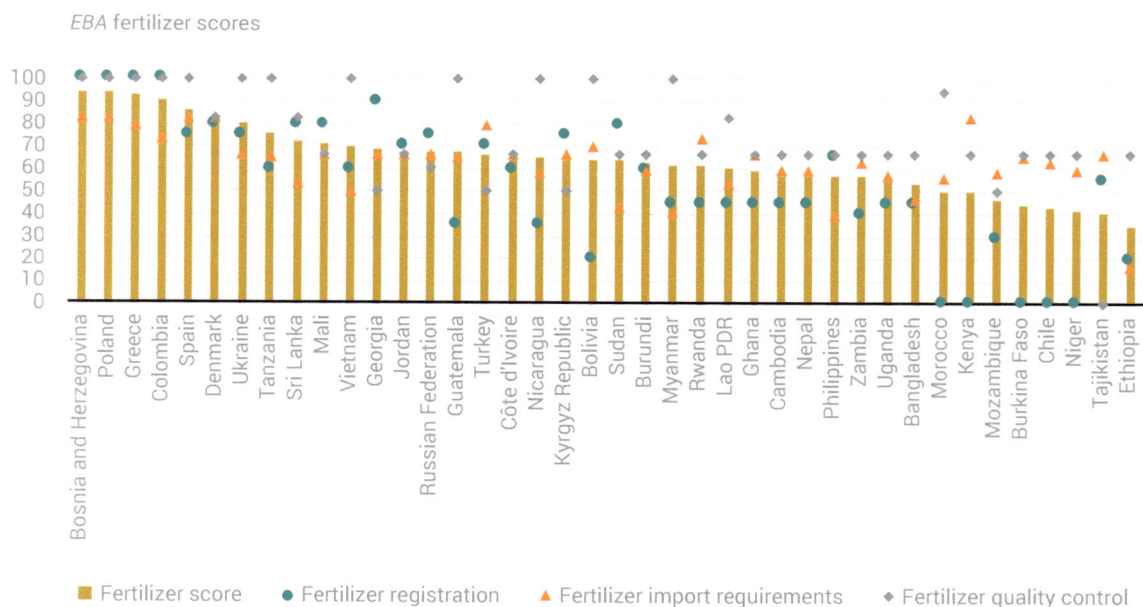

EBA fertilizer scores

Legend: ■ Fertilizer score   ● Fertilizer registration   ▲ Fertilizer import requirements   ◆ Fertilizer quality control

Source: EBA database.

opened fertilizer bags. All countries require labeling and most prohibit the sale of mislabeled products. But 22 of the 40 countries do not prohibit the sale of open fertilizer bags—a practice that is common because of affordability, but not recommended because it hampers the ability to ensure high-quality fertilizer.

Registration takes less time but is most costly in countries where it needs to be done only once

Registering new fertilizer products is a good practice because it ensures that a country has control over what fertilizers are used within its borders (box 3.1). Controls are necessary to prevent soil damage, environmental pollution or adulterated fertilizer use.[12] And product registration allows countries to increase market awareness, compile and share information with the public and guarantee human, animal and environmental safety.

Countries may require companies to register fertilizer products in three ways: once in a lifetime, re-applying for registration periodically or having the registration automatically renewed after a certain time. Having to register fertilizer products once in a lifetime or having the registration automatically renewed reduces the burden on companies by not requiring them to have to go through the process again.

It takes on average 258 calendar days to register a fertilizer product in the 40 countries sampled, ranging from 15 calendar days in Vietnam to 1,125 in Nepal (figure 3.2). Countries that take the least time usually require fewer procedures —usually an application for registration and a content verification report in the form of lab samples. Among these countries are Denmark, Guatemala, Nicaragua, Spain and Vietnam. Countries where fertilizer product registration takes the longest require several procedures, usually including an application for registration, content verification report in the form of lab samples, field testing, an environmental report, approval by a national committee and publication in the official gazette or journal. Of these procedures, field testing

> **BOX 3.1 Good practices for fertilizer registration**
>
> - Should require private companies to register fertilizer products. The registration would ideally be valid indefinitely.
>
>   - In countries where the registration is limited to a specific time period, the validity should be at least 10 years.
>
>   - In countries where the registration is limited to a specific time period, the renovation of application should be automatic.
>
> - Develop efficient and affordable fertilizer product registration.
>
> - Should list registered fertilizer products in an official catalog that is accessible online.

is the longest, as it can take place over many seasons, prolonging the registration process for several years.

The time it takes to register fertilizer products also depends on the type of registration. Registration takes less time but is most costly in countries where it needs to be done only once. Indeed, in countries where firms do not need to re-register fertilizer (once-in-a-lifetime registration), the registration of a new fertilizer product takes less time —on average 154.3 calendar days— ranging from 31 calendar days in Bosnia and Herzegovina to 578.5 in Tanzania. Registering a new fertilizer product for the first time takes on average 324.6 calendar days in countries where a new application is needed to re-register. And where re-registering is automatic, the time for registering a new fertilizer product is the highest—398 calendar days.

It is most expensive to register a fertilizer product in countries with once-in-a-lifetime registration, costing on average 179.7% of income per capita. Among countries with once-in-a-lifetime registration, Bosnia and Herzegovina is the least expensive, with a negligible cost. Tanzania is the most expensive, averaging 1,064.5% of income per capita, due to expensive costs for field testing, which alone costs 1,050% of income per capita and takes 570 calendar days (table 3.1). Countries where re-application

is necessary have a much lower cost to register a product for the first time (85.9% of income per capita), as do automatic-registration countries (3.7% of income per capita) (figure 3.3).

Only four countries require companies to register as an importer of fertilizer but do not require import permits

Registering import companies allows countries to monitor the supply of imported fertilizer products (box 3.2). Having simple and affordable registration processes is a good practice that allows competition and facilitates market access.[13] Import permits are primarily desirable for controlling potentially dangerous chemicals—such as ammonium nitrate, a chemical that can be used for producing explosives. But onerous requirements for obtaining import permits obstruct trade and create unnecessary burdens for importers.[14]

All studied countries except Ethiopia allow domestic companies to import fertilizer products for their sale. Ethiopia only allows domestic companies to import fertilizer products for self-consumption, a practice only carried out by large agro-industries. Bangladesh, Cambodia, Ethiopia, Myanmar, the Philippines and Sudan are the only countries that prohibit foreign companies from importing fertilizer products.

FIGURE 3.2 The time to register new fertilizer products ranges from 15 to 1,125 calendar days

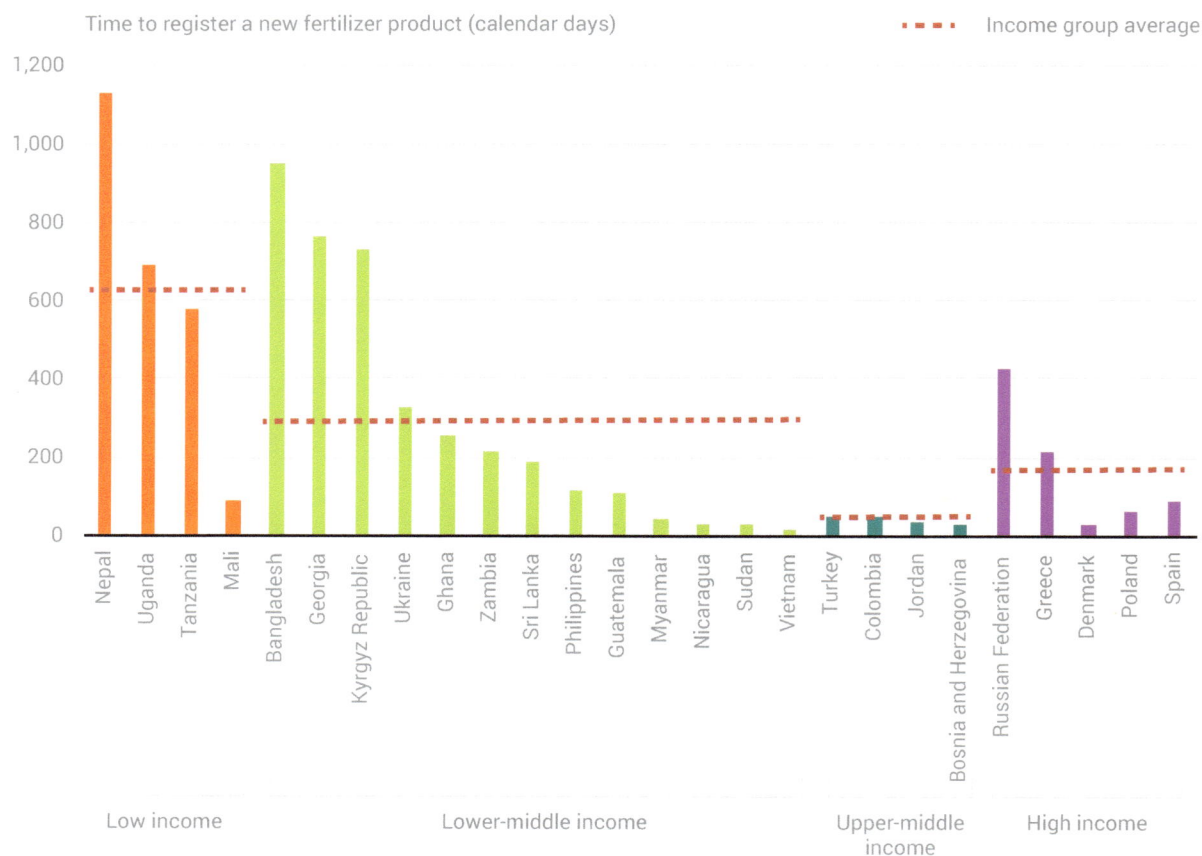

Source: EBA database.

TABLE 3.1 Cost and time to register a new fertilizer

COST TO REGISTER A NEW FERTILIZER (% OF GNI PER CAPITA)				TIME TO REGISTER A NEW FERTILIZER (DAYS)			
The least expensive...		... and the most expensive		The fastest...		... and the slowest	
Spain	0%	Tanzania	1,064.5%	Vietnam	15	Nepal	1,125
Jordan	0.3%	Ukraine	717.3%	Sudan	29	Bangladesh	951
Guatemala	0.4%	Uganda	258.9%	Nicaragua	30	Georgia	765
Denmark	0.4%	Zambia	241.5%	Bosnia and Herzegovina	31	Kyrgyz Republic	730
Bosnia and Herzegovina	0.5%	Ghana	89.2%	Denmark	31	Uganda	691

Source: EBA database.

FIGURE 3.3 Registration takes less time but is most costly in countries where it needs to be done only once

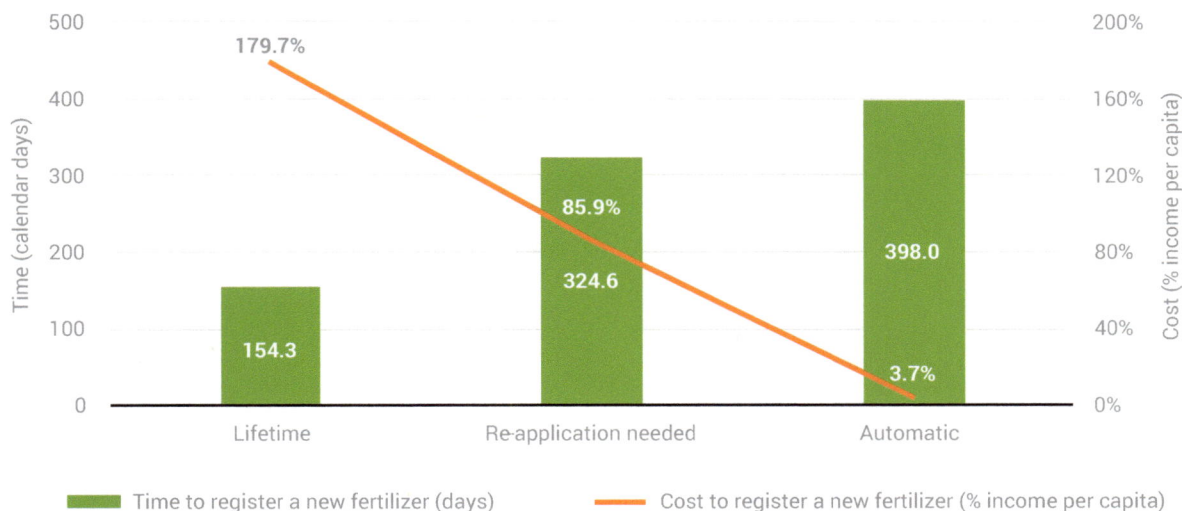

Source: EBA database.

BOX 3.2 Good practices for fertilizer import requirements

- Should allow fertilizer products already registered in another country (with good policies, regulations and quality and standards requirements) to be imported without needing to be re-registered in the importing country.

- Should allow private companies (including foreign ones) to import fertilizer for own use and sale.

- Should require private companies to register as importers of fertilizer in order to sell it. The registration would ideally not be limited to a specific time period.

- In countries where the registration is limited to a specific time period, the validity should be at least 10 years.

  - The cost of the registration should be affordable.

  - Should allow private companies to import fertilizer without needing to obtain a special permit.

- In countries where a permit is required, the permit should not be limited to a specific time period.

  - The cost of the permit should be affordable.

Twenty-five of the 40 countries studied require the private sector to register as an importer of fertilizer, and 12 of the 40 do not require companies to obtain import permits. Only 4 countries —Bosnia and Herzegovina, Côte d'Ivoire, Ghana and Kenya—follow both good practices. In countries where companies are required to register as fertilizer importers and obtain import permits, the cost varies substantially across countries. To register as a fertilizer importer, the cost ranges from free of charge to 57.5% of income per capita (figure 3.4). Bolivia, Bosnia and Herzegovina, Colombia, Mali, Nepal and Zambia are the six countries that require fertilizer importers to register and where the registration is free, which is considered a good practice. In import permits, the cost variation is smaller, ranging from no cost to 13% of income per capita.

A majority of countries prohibit mislabeled fertilizer containers and only one-third penalize the sale of open bags

Labeling fertilizer helps to ensure quality control (box 3.3).[15] All surveyed countries except Tajikistan require companies to label fertilizer containers

FIGURE 3.4 The cost to register as an importer ranges from 0 to 57.5% of income per capita

Cost to register as an importer of fertilizer by country   ▪▪▪▪ Income group average

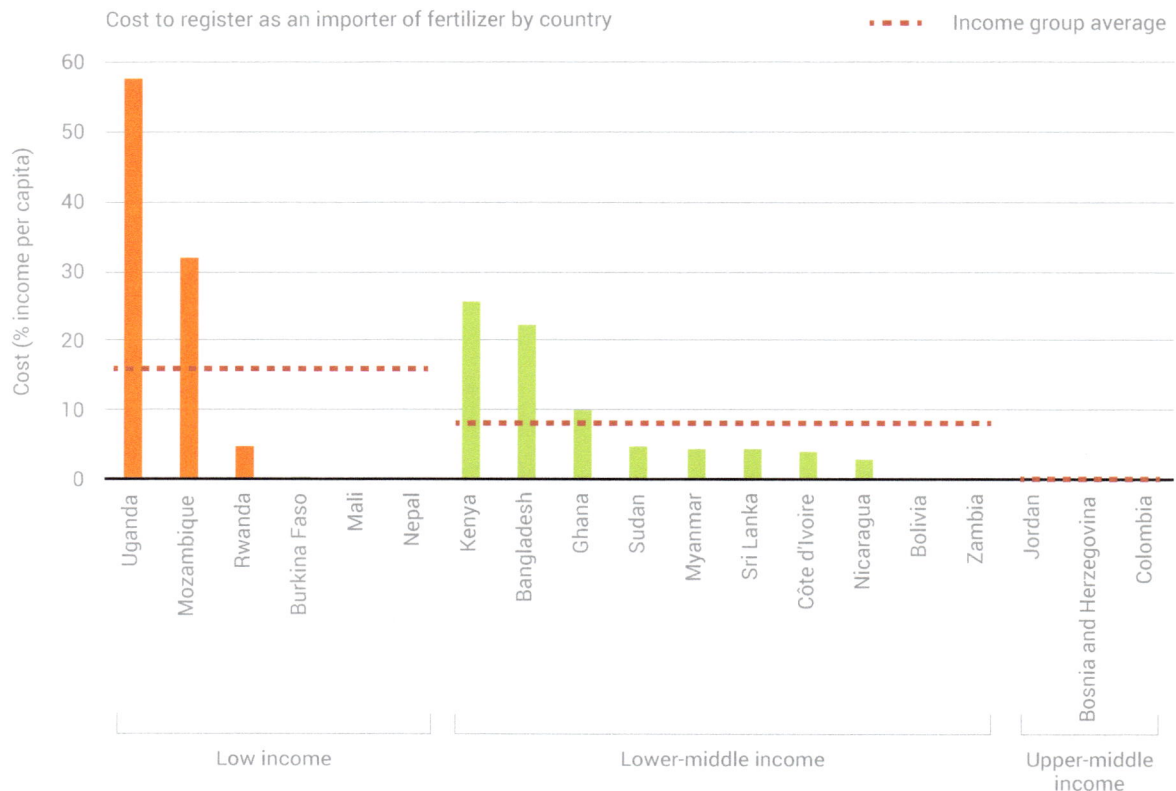

Source: EBA database.

BOX 3.3 Good practices for fertilizer quality control

- Should require labeling of fertilizer containers (bags, bottles).

  - The regulations should specify the requirement to include the fertilizer brand name, net weight or volume and a description of the content on the label.

- Should prohibit the sale of mislabeled fertilizers.

  - A penalty for the sale of mislabeled fertilizers should be established in the regulations.

- Should prohibit the sale of opened fertilizer containers.

  - A penalty for the sale of opened fertilizer containers/bags should be established in the regulations.

in order to sell them. And all surveyed countries except Turkey have laws prohibiting companies from selling mislabeled fertilizer. Allowing open fertilizer bags to be sold is not a good practice. Common in many counties where farmers cannot afford to purchase entire bags of fertilizer, the sale of fertilizers in open bags can be harmful since they are susceptible to adulteration—affecting crop yields, potentially reducing farmers' profits and leading to food insecurity.[16] Instead, markets should adapt to offer smaller bags. Over half the surveyed countries do not prohibit the sale of open fertilizer bags (figure 3.5). Of the countries that prohibit the sale of open fertilizer bags, only four —Denmark, Lao PDR, Sri Lanka and Turkey—do not establish penalties for companies that do so.

FIGURE 3.5 Over half of the surveyed countries do not prohibit the sale of open fertilizer bags—and those that do, do not always have a penalty for it

Percentages on the prohibition and penalties against the sale of open fertilizer bags
(number of countries)

■ Law prohibits the sale of opened fertilizer containers/bags

■ Law does not prohibit the sale of opened fertilizer containers/bags

■ Law establishes penalty for the sale of opened fertilizer containers/bags

■ Law does not establish penalty for the sale of opened fertilizer containers/bags

Source: EBA database.

Conclusion

A strong and competitive fertilizer market is extremely important to a country's agricultural sector since this input greatly influences farm productivity. Several external factors not measured by *EBA*, such as international commodity and shipping prices, have a strong influence on the industry. But the regulatory environment also determines the health of the fertilizer market. *EBA* aims to promote smart regulations that enable competitive markets in the fertilizer sector, such as:

- **Efficient and affordable fertilizer product registration for companies.** Colombia sets a good example with clear registration regulations and efficient procedures.

- **Streamlined import procedures for the private sector, which allow for timely availability of fertilizer.** Kenya's import regulations allow the private sector to import fertilizer products through an efficient import registration and licensing system.

- **Compulsory labeling and packaging requirements, which promote the sale of high-quality fertilizer.** Vietnam's exemplary regulations for ensuring quality fertilizer establish effective labeling mechanisms and penalize mislabeled and opened fertilizer bags.

Regulatory reforms are not easily accomplished and do not occur overnight. The complexity of the fertilizer sector demands smart regulations that balance the needs of a competitive sector while ensuring safety and quality for human health and the environment. The fertilizer topic measures regulations pertinent to companies and farmers in the areas of product registration, import and quality control. These indicators can be used by governments pursuing to improve their laws and regulations to enable a competitive fertilizer sector.

Notes

1. World Bank 2015.

2. Rutgers University 2006.

3. Hernandez and Torero 2011, 2013.

4. World Bank 2015.

5. Gisselquist and Van Der Meer 2001.

6. World Bank 2015.

7. Gisselquist and Van Der Meer 2001.

8. AGRA 2014; Keyser 2012; World Bank 2012.

9. Fintrac 2014; Liverpool-Tasie and others 2010; Mujeri and others 2012; Pullabhotla and Ganesh-Kumar 2012; Visker and others 1996.

10. Gisselquist and Van Der Meer 2001.

11. World Bank 2010.

12. Gisselquist and Van Der Meer 2001.

13. Gisselquist and Van Der Meer 2001.

14. AGRA 2014; Keyser 2012; World Bank 2012.

15. Gisselquist and Van Der Meer 2001.

16. World Bank 2010.

References

AGRA (Alliance for a Green Revolution in Africa). 2014. "Improving Fertilizer Supplies for African Farmers." Brief 2, AGRA, Nairobi, Kenya.

Fintrac. 2014. *Assessment of the Enabling Environment for Cross-Border Trade of Agricultural Inputs. Thailand, Vietnam and Cambodia*. Washington, DC: USAID/Enabling Agriculture Trade (EAT).

Gisselquist, D., and C. Van Der Meer. 2001. "Regulations for Seed and Fertilizer Markets: A Good Practice Guide for Policymakers." Rural Development Working Paper 22817, World Bank, Washington, DC.

Hernandez, M. A., and M. Torero. 2011. "Fertilizer Market Situation: Market Structure, Consumption and Trade Patterns, and Pricing Behavior." IFPRI Discussion Paper 01058, International Food Policy Research Institute (IFPRI), Washington, DC.

———. 2013. "Market Concentration and Pricing Behavior in the Fertilizer Industry: A Global Approach." *Agricultural Economics* 44 (6): 723–34.

Keyser, J. C., M. Elitta, G. Dimithe, G. Ayoola, and L. Sene. 2012. "Counting the Costs of Compliance with Trade Requirements from a Value Chain Perspective: Evidence from Southern Africa." Africa Trade Policy Notes 32, World Bank, Washington, DC.

Liverpool-Tasie, S. L.O., A. A. Auchan and A. B. Banful. 2010. "An Assessment of Fertilizer Quality Regulation in Nigeria." Nigeria Strategy Support Program Report 09, International Food Policy Research Institute (IFPRI), Abuja.

Mujeri, M. K., S. Shahana, T. T. Chowdhury and K. T. Haider. 2012. "Improving the Effectiveness, Efficiency and Sustainability of Fertilizer Use in South Asia." Policy Research Paper 08, Global Development Network, New Delhi.

Pullabhotla, H., and A. Ganesh-Kumar. 2012. "Review of Input and Output Policies for Cereal Production in Bangladesh." IFPRI Discussion Paper 01199, International Food Policy Research Institute (IFPRI), New Delhi.

Rutgers University. 2006. "Public Health Concerns with Hazardous Materials in Fertilizers." *The Soil Profile* 16. Rutgers, NJ: Rutgers University.

Visker, C., D. Rutland and K. Dahoui. 1996. *The Quality of Fertilizers in West Africa (1995)*. Muscle Shoals, Alabama: International Fertilizer Development Center (IFDC).

World Bank. 2010. *Africa Development Indicators 2010: Silent and Lethal: How Quiet Corruption Undermines Africa's Development Efforts*. Washington, DC: World Bank.

———. 2012. *Africa Can Help Feed Africa: Removing Barriers to Regional Trade in Food Staples*. Washington, DC: World Bank.

4. MACHINERY
EXPANDING MECHANIZATION WHILE ENSURING QUALITY AND SAFETY

Tractor accidents can be fatal and have direct economic consequences for poor farmers. Imagine a farmer who spends all of the family savings to buy a new tractor in hope of improving her farmland and increasing productivity. One day while working the field, she approaches a steep hill, and the tractor rolls over and fatally crushes her. Stricter quality control and safety regulations such as requiring roll-over protective structures and seatbelts on tractors could prevent these accidents and avoid the economic loss that her family must endure.

EBA machinery indicators measure obstacles facing dealers who import tractors for sale. Besides meeting the requirements for import and registration, the indicators also measure the regulations on standards and safety for operators of tractors. Regulations on imports, standards and safety and other requirements for introducing mechanical technology to the market affect the availability of appropriate machinery to farmers and agribusinesses. Agricultural machines can increase production since they are labor-saving and directly increase yields and production[1] with more efficient operations that can cultivate more land.[2] Agricultural mechanization spurs rural economic growth and ultimately improves rural livelihoods.

The *EBA* machinery indicators use agricultural tractors as a proxy to assess the regulations for agricultural machinery. Agricultural tractors are the most representative form of agricultural machinery and are used at different stages of agricultural production, from land preparation to harvest. The use of tractors around the globe make tractor-related indicators comparable across countries, unlike other forms of machinery specific to certain crops or regions.

Tractor dealer requirements, the first indicator for *EBA* machinery, was selected for study because there are a number

of prerequisites that must be ensured at the machinery dealer level that directly impact the availability of high-quality tractors. To enable the private machinery sector and promote farm mechanization services to farmers, appropriate government institutions responsible for standards, health and safety need to be in place.[3] Having national or regional centers for impartial testing and evaluation of agricultural machinery is a good practice. Conforming with established national or international standards, these tests ensure the quality of tractors and their suitability to country conditions. Tractor registration is another area where there are significant differences between countries. Lengthy and expensive procedural requirements stifle competition, limiting the players and products in the market. Providing after-sales services—sales of spare parts and training on how to use a tractor safely and correctly—are equally important. Having domestic support facilities that offer parts and repairs is an element of successful mechanization.[4]

Tractor standards and safety, the second *EBA* machinery indicator, addresses national and international standards on tractor performance and safety and how countries ensure that only high-quality machines enter their supply chain[5] and that consumers are given unbiased information about tractors. Given that the agricultural machinery industry is

a global industry, with tractors manufactured on one continent and sold on another,[6] international standards also help facilitate international trade.[7]

The third indicator for *EBA* machinery focuses on the requirements for importing agricultural tractors. Local manufacturing of agricultural tractors is concentrated in a few countries and the majority of countries rely on imports. Inefficient and costly import licensing obstructs trade in many countries, making it difficult for tractor importers to introduce their products in the market. Balancing control and efficiency requirements eases importing machinery.

Several other factors that are currently not measured—such as specific mechanization policies and market realities —also affect the agricultural machinery sector. Among the major constraints to increased levels of mechanization are the poor access of farmers to agricultural technologies (mainly as a result of the high cost of mechanization inputs) and the low purchasing power of smallholder farmers to acquire machinery. These factors limit both the demand by farmers and the supply of machinery, which, in turn, keeps prices high and stifles competition.[8] Also important, however, are the unfavorable regulations that machinery suppliers face in many countries and which is the main focus of the current indicators. The indicators encourage the adoption of smart regulations that enable competitive markets in the agricultural machinery sector while ensuring tractor quality and safety.

The data cover the following areas:

- **Tractor dealer requirements.** These indicators measure legal requirements for suitability testing of agricultural tractors, specific licensing required to operate a tractor, and warranties and post-sale services that must be provided at the retail level.

- **Tractor standards and safety.** These indicators look at legal requirements for operational safety and performance standards of tractors.

- **Tractor import requirements.** These indicators look at aspects of importing agricultural tractors,

including the private machinery sector's role and the required procedures to import.

For the machinery topic the laws and regulations appear strongest in EU countries (Denmark, Greece, Poland and Spain) and in the Philippines (figure 4.1). All five countries share a substantial number of good practices. Denmark, Greece and Spain have strong regulations related to tractor dealer and import requirements. The Philippines has strong regulations for tractor standards and safety. The Kyrgyz Republic is among the top performers in regulations for tractor import requirements but performs below average on standards and safety. The two countries surveyed in the Middle East and North Africa—Jordan and Morocco—score slightly better than the sample average, but vary on some indicators. Jordan has higher scores tractor import requirements but performs below average on standards and safety and on tractor dealer requirements, while Morocco has higher scores

on regulations for standards and safety but insufficient import requirements. The five countries with the lowest scores across all three indicators are Lao PDR, Myanmar, Nepal, Niger and Vietnam— each demonstrating room to adopt many of the good practices identified by *EBA*.

Most countries targeted require tractors to be registered, but the cost varies

Registering agricultural tractors is a good practice, among others, because it establishes ownership rights over the purchased tractor and facilitates the enforcement of road, safety and tax regulations. Many tractor manufacturers recommend that original equipment manufacturer (OEM) engines or drivetrain components be registered, and in doing so, provide tractor owners the opportunity to extend the standard warranty periods for their machine, but this procedure is not required in all surveyed

FIGURE 4.1 Denmark, Greece, Spain, the Philippines and Poland have the top five scores in the aspects measured by the machinery topic

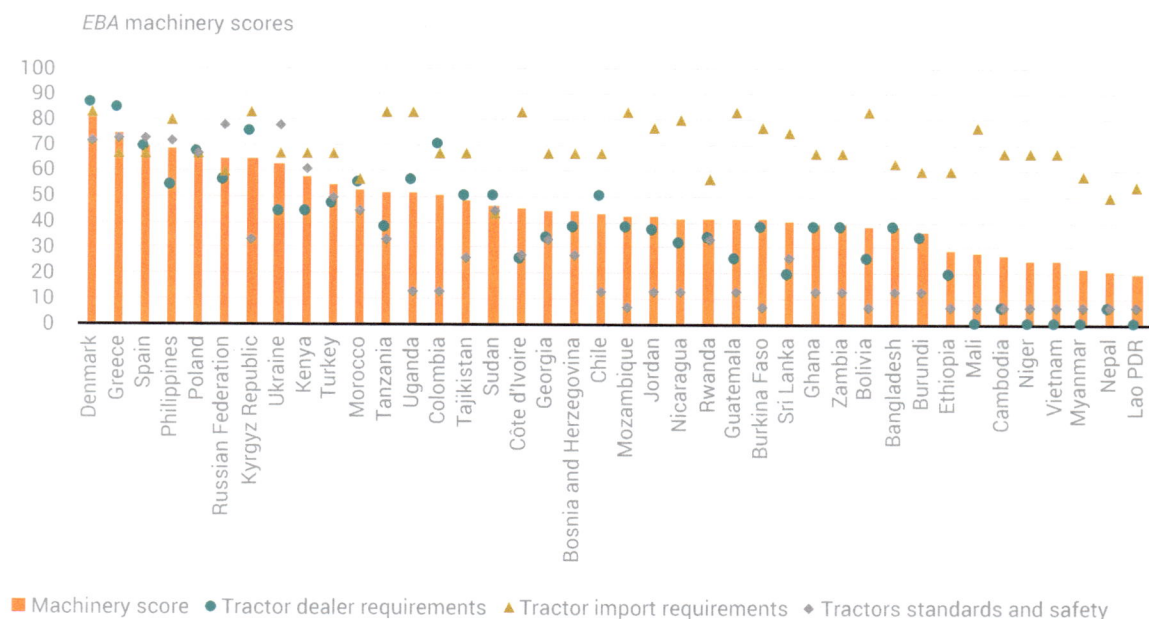

EBA machinery scores

■ Machinery score   ● Tractor dealer requirements   ▲ Tractor import requirements   ◆ Tractors standards and safety

Source: EBA database.

countries. Of the 40 countries, 27 require companies to register imported machinery, and only in Denmark is registration free. In the other 26 countries the registration cost for imported tractors ranges from 0.03% of average income per capita in the Philippines to 34.7% in Sudan (figure 4.2).

Few countries require importers to test machinery

Some countries have machinery testing and evaluation centers to determine what machinery is suited to country conditions and can enhance the productivity of farmers.[9] Typically carried out according to standards established by national authorities or international standardization organizations, these tests help farmers compare and select machinery. Of the 40 surveyed countries, 12 require

private companies to obtain proof of suitability of tractors, costing from 1.1% of income per capita in the Kyrgyz Republic to 765% in Tanzania.

Few countries studied require after-sales services by law

Farmers in many countries do not have access to machinery after-sales services, limiting their access to maintenance or spare parts. This is especially relevant in countries where there is little control on the quality of imported goods, which can lead to the import of substandard tractors.[10] Requiring that tractor dealers provide after-sales services is a good practice since it gives more security to buyers (box 4.1). Only seven of the countries studied legally require after-sales services. Five of them—Colombia, Denmark, Greece, the Philippines and

Turkey—require that dealers of agricultural tractors provide reparation services and supply spare parts if needed. Colombia also requires that machinery dealers provide training on how to use a tractor. None of the surveyed countries require that machinery dealers provide training on the maintenance of tractors (table 4.1).

Requirements for import licensing and permits and incurred costs vary significantly across countries

Few developing countries manufacture agricultural equipment and machines domestically. So machinery acquisitions rely on imports—usually handled by the private sector. Many countries require companies to register as machinery importers. This is a good practice because it gives public authorities a better understanding of trade flows in the country and

FIGURE 4.2 The cost to register imported tractors is highest in Sudan

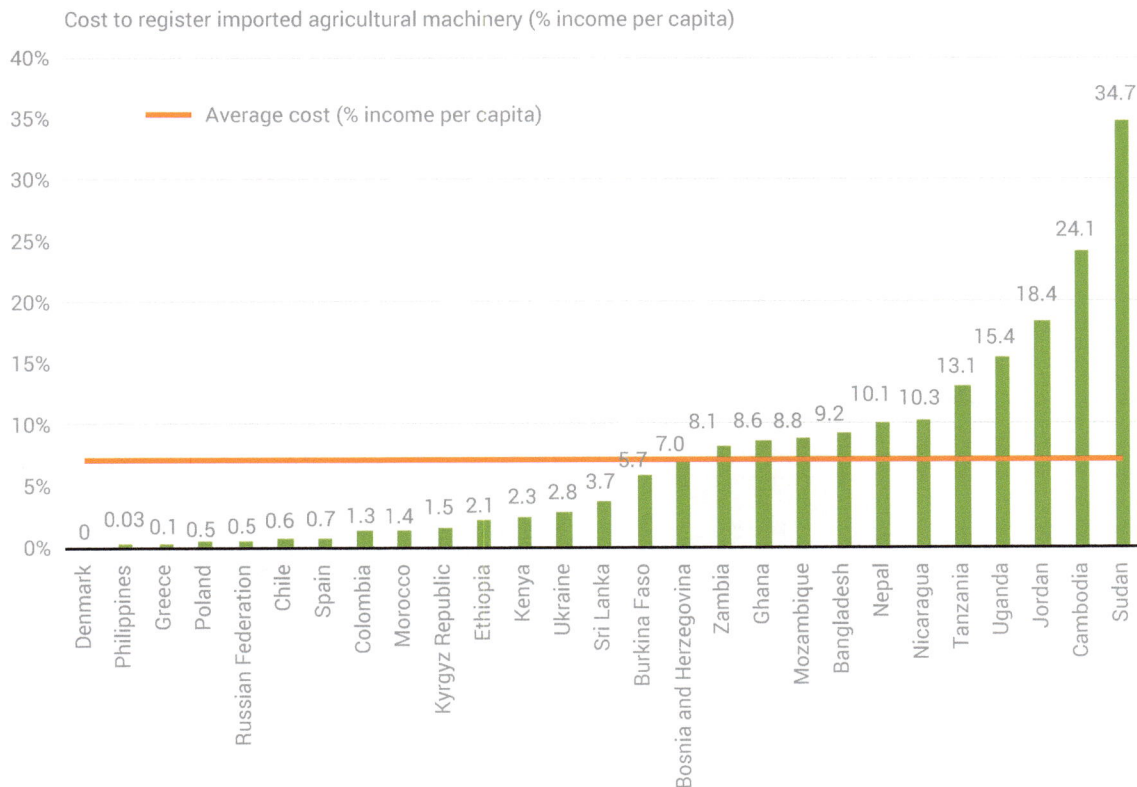

Cost to register imported agricultural machinery (% income per capita)

— Average cost (% income per capita)

Denmark 0, Philippines 0.03, Greece 0.1, Poland 0.5, Russian Federation 0.5, Chile 0.6, Spain 0.7, Colombia 1.3, Morocco 1.4, Kyrgyz Republic 1.5, Ethiopia 2.1, Kenya 2.3, Ukraine 2.8, Sri Lanka 3.7, Burkina Faso 5.7, Bosnia and Herzegovina 7.0, Zambia 8.1, Ghana 8.6, Mozambique 8.8, Bangladesh 9.2, Nepal 10.1, Nicaragua 10.3, Tanzania 13.1, Uganda 15.4, Jordan 18.4, Cambodia 24.1, Sudan 34.7

Source: EBA database.

BOX 4.1 Good practices for tractor dealer requirements

- Should require compulsory testing of tractors in conformity with established standards.

  - The test/proof of suitability should be affordable.

- Should require tractor registration.

  - The registration should be affordable and the process efficient.

- Should require tractor manufacturers or dealers to provide post-sale services, including:

  - repairing tractors.

  - replacing or returning poor quality tractors.

  - supplying spare parts.

  - training users in operating tractors.

ensures the quality of imported goods (box 4.2). In addition, importers may be required to obtain a permit each time they wish to import tractors. But import permits can often be used as trade barriers, creating costly burdens for importers. Among the 14 countries that require machinery importers to be registered, the incurred costs vary. They range from more than 35% of income per capita

in the Philippines to minimal or no cost in Sri Lanka (0.2% of income per capita), Jordan (0.3% of income per capita) and Bolivia, Mali and Nicaragua (free of charge). Mozambique levies a striking cost of 880.6% of income per capita on importer registration (figure 4.3).

Among the 13 countries that require import permits, the average cost is 4.6%

of income per capita. In Morocco and Rwanda, obtaining an import permit is free, while in Bangladesh the cost is over 40% of income per capita. Seven countries—Bangladesh, Burkina Faso, Ethiopia, Jordan, Myanmar, the Philippines[11] and Sudan—impose both the cost for registration as importer and the cost of import permit.

Most countries lack safety regulations that prevent injuries to machinery operators

Safety guidelines for machinery operators are a good practice because they can prevent or reduce worker injury and damage to machinery, saving lives and costs. Seat belts and roll-over protective structures have proven to be "99% effective in preventing death or serious injury in the event of tractor roll-overs" in the United States.[12] Since tractors often operate on uneven ground, a roll-over is a constant risk for workers.[13] But many safety measures are not required by law in most surveyed countries. Only nine countries require tractors to be equipped with roll-over protective structures: Denmark, Greece, Poland and Spain, Kenya, the Philippines, the Russia, Turkey and Ukraine.

Conclusion

Agricultural mechanization improves agricultural productivity, thereby enabling

TABLE 4.1 Countries where post-sale services are required by law

	REPAIR OF TRACTORS	WARRANTY ON TRACTORS	SUPPLY OF SPARE PARTS	TRAINING ON TRACTOR OPERATION
COLOMBIA	✔	✔	✔	✔
DENMARK	✔	✔	✔	
GREECE	✔	✔	✔	
JORDAN		✔		
MOROCCO		✔		
PHILIPPINES	✔		✔	
TURKEY	✔	✔	✔	

Source: EBA database.

- **Guarantee high-quality tractors by requiring compliance with national and international performance standards.** Fifteen of the 40 studied countries have established national standards for agricultural tractors, and 10 stipulate that imported tractors should conform to international standards.

- **Ensure safety of tractor operators by enforcing safety standards such as roll-over protective structures and seatbelts.** Regulations in Kenya stipulate that agricultural tractors must be fitted with a roll-over protection structure (ROPS) and require that seatbelts must be fitted where a ROPS structure is in use (box 4.3).

Laws and regulations that promote both control and efficiency requirements can help facilitate and ease the availability of machinery for agricultural production. The machinery topic identifies and measures several key regulatory constraints that can hinder farmers' access to appropriate machinery. The topic uses agricultural tractors as a proxy to assess the regulations for agricultural machinery. These actionable indicators are intended as a starting point for discussion with policymakers on possible ways to address regulatory constraints and inefficiencies that might obstruct the expansion of mechanization, the quality of imported tractors and safety of tractor operators.

markets for rural economic growth and improving rural livelihoods. There is still much to be done in countries to improve the enabling environment for successful agricultural mechanization and move toward the good practices identified, such as:

- **Safeguard availability and timely delivery of agricultural tractors through streamlining import procedures.** In Bolivia registering as a tractor importer has no cost, and importers are not required to get a permit each time they wish to import tractors.

- **Ensure that imported tractors suit country conditions by requiring testing of agricultural machinery.** In the Kyrgyz Republic regulations require that tractors be tested to ensure their suitability to country conditions, as well as their compliance with established performance standards. The cost of the test is minimal.

- **Facilitate tractor durability by requiring tractor registration and appropriate after-sales service.** In Colombia appropriate after-sales services must be provided at the tractor dealer level. It is also required that tractors must to be registered; the registration can be obtained within two days at a minimal cost.

FIGURE 4.3 Mozambique and Bangladesh impose high costs on importers of agricultural tractors

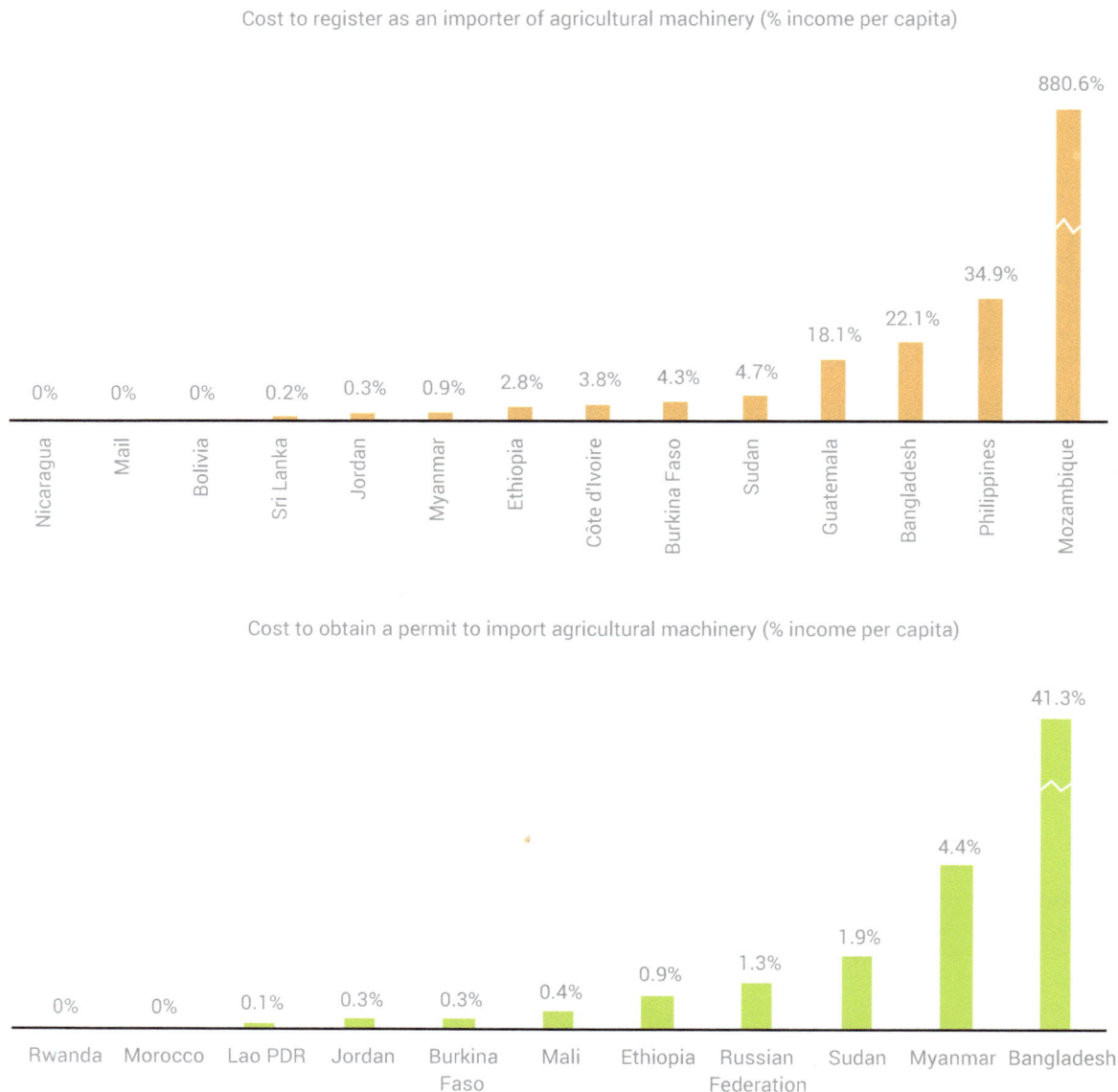

Cost to register as an importer of agricultural machinery (% income per capita)

Nicaragua	0%
Mali	0%
Bolivia	0%
Sri Lanka	0.2%
Jordan	0.3%
Myanmar	0.9%
Ethiopia	2.8%
Côte d'Ivoire	3.8%
Burkina Faso	4.3%
Sudan	4.7%
Guatemala	18.1%
Bangladesh	22.1%
Philippines	34.9%
Mozambique	880.6%

Cost to obtain a permit to import agricultural machinery (% income per capita)

Rwanda	0%
Morocco	0%
Lao PDR	0.1%
Jordan	0.3%
Burkina Faso	0.3%
Mali	0.4%
Ethiopia	0.9%
Russian Federation	1.3%
Sudan	1.9%
Myanmar	4.4%
Bangladesh	41.3%

Source: EBA database.

Note: Countries that require companies to register as an importer of agricultural machinery: Bangladesh, Bolivia, Burkina Faso, Côte d'Ivoire, Ethiopia, Guatemala, Jordan, Mali, Mozambique, Myanmar, Nicaragua, the Philippines, Sri Lanka and Sudan. Countries that require companies to obtain a permit to import agricultural machinery: Bangladesh, Bosnia and Herzegovina, Burkina Faso, Ethiopia, Jordan, Lao PDR, Mali, Morocco, Myanmar, the Philippines, Russian Federation, Rwanda and Sudan. Bosnia and Herzegovina and the Philippines were excluded from the lower figure because the price of the import permit for agricultural machinery is calculated as a percentage of the customs value.

Notes

1. Houmy and others 2013.

2. FAO and UNIDO 2008.

3. Sims and Kienzle 2009.

4. FAO and UNIDO 2008.

5. Sims and Kienzle 2009.

6. Ingle 2011.

7. OECD 2014.

8. Kienzle 2013.

9. Faleye and others 2014

10. Sims 2006.

11. The Philippines was excluded from the graph 4.3 because the price of the import permit for agricultural machinery is calculated as a percentage of the costumes value.

12. Murphy and Buckmaster 2015.

13. Springfeldt 1996.

References:

Faleye, T., A.J. Farounbi, O.S. Ogundipe and J.A. Adebija. 2014. "Testing and Evaluation of Farm Machines: An Essential Step for Developing Mechanization in Nigeria." *International Research Journal of Agricultural Science and Soil Science* 4 (2): 47–50.

FAO and UNIDO. 2008. "Agricultural Mechanization in Africa: Time for Action. Planning Investment for Enhanced Agricultural Productivity." Report of an Expert Group Meeting January 2008, Vienna, Austria: FAO and UNIDO.

Houmy, K., L. Clarke, J. Ashburner and J. Kienzle. 2013. "Agricultural Mechanization in Sub-Saharan Africa: Guidelines for Preparing a Strategy." *Integrated Crop Management* 22. Rome: FAO.

Ingle, C. 2011. *Agricultural Tractor Test Standards in America.* Washington, DC: The Catholic University of America.

Kienzle, J., J. Ashburner and B. Sims. 2013. "Mechanization for Rural Development: A review of patterns and progress from around the world." *Integrated Crop Management* 20.

Murphy, D., and D. Buckmaster. 2015. "Rollover Protection for Farm Tractor Operators." Cooperative Extension E-42, University Park, PA: Pennsylvania State University College of Agricultural Sciences, Agricultural and Biological Engineering.

OECD (Organisation for Economic Co-operation and Development). 2014. *OECD Standard Codes for the Official Testing of Agricultural and Forestry Tractors.* Paris: OECD.

Sims, B. 2006. "Addressing the Challenges Facing Agricultural Mechanization Input Supply and farm product processing." Agricultural and Food Engineering Technical Report 5, FAO, Rome.

Sims, B., and J. Kienzle. 2009. "Farm Equipment Supply Chains. Guidelines for Policymakers and Service Providers: Experiences from Kenya, Pakistan and Brazil." Agricultural and Food Engineering Technical Report 7, FAO, Rome.

Springfeldt, B. 1996. "Rollover of Tractors —International Experiences." *Safety Science* 24.

5. FINANCE
EXPANDING ACCESS TO FINANCIAL SERVICES

Imagine a successful farmer, Sophia, whose farm is in the Morogoro region of Tanzania. Sophia exercises great discipline by making sure she saved a substantial part of the money from selling her crops to pay for inputs and school fees as well as to deal with emergencies. But since there are no banks nearby in the Morogoro region, Sophia, like most farmers in the region, keeps her savings at home, where they are at risk of theft. This is about to change for Sophia and the other farmers since banks can now hire local agents that represent them where their branches fail to reach. Sophia will be able to deposit and withdraw cash, pay bills, transfer funds and obtain loans without needing to travel hours to the closest bank. And access to formal providers will offer a wider range of financial services as well as safer and less expensive transactions.

EBA finance indicators measure the quality of laws and regulations that promote access to financial services and support the development of agricultural enterprises. Regulations that ensure the stability of the financial system and protect customers while promoting innovative ways of delivering financial services help meet the financial needs of farmers and agribusinesses.[1] The finance indicators address factors important to customers excluded from traditional financial services due to their geographical location or the type of collateral they have available.

Regulation and supervision of microfinance institutions (MFIs) and credit unions, the first two indicators for *EBA* finance, were chosen for study because MFIs and credit unions are important providers of microcredit and other financial services to those who cannot access financial services through commercial banks.[2] They provide savings and credit for farmers and agribusinesses to purchase fertilizer and seed and pay for crop marketing, storage and transport. But many countries lack an appropriate legal framework to regulate and supervise those institutions.[3] While overly burdensome requirements on MFIs and credit unions drive up the cost of their

products, prudent regulations flexible to the different activities farmers engage in can cut the costs of financial services and foster financial inclusion.[4] Regulations also include consumer protection regulations that ensure that customers' savings are safely handled.

Formal financial markets fail to reach most smallholder farmers in developing countries[5] who live far from urban centers and cannot afford high transaction costs.[6] Agent banking and e-money, measured under the third and fourth indicators for *EBA* finance, offer farmers in rural locations access to financial services without needing to travel far to a bank. In agent banking agents provide financial services on behalf of a bank in areas where the bank's branches do not reach. Non-bank e-money issuers can provide payments, transfers and savings for those excluded from the formal financial system.[7] Regulation has not caught up with the rapid development of these new ways for delivering financial services. Legal uncertainty and nontransparency impede the growth of the market.[8] Regulators need to strike a balance between maximizing the opportunities for agent banking and e-money while minimizing the risks that they bring.[9]

The fifth indicator for *EBA* finance addresses warehouse receipt systems. Farmers often lack traditional collateral, such as houses or cars, required to obtain a loan. Warehouse receipt systems enable farmers to obtain financing by using their newly harvested crop as collateral. Strong regulations protect the interests of both depositors and lenders and help build trust in the system. They ensure transparency and predictability required to attract customers and financial institutions to use or accept the agricultural commodities as collateral.[10] The data[11] cover the following areas:

- **Microfinance institutions (MFIs).** This indicator covers the regulations for deposit-taking MFIs. It measures the requirements to establish an MFI, prudential regulations including minimum capital adequacy ratios and provisioning rules imposed on MFIs, as well as consumer protection requirements focusing on interest rate disclosure and enrollment in a deposit insurance system.

- **Credit unions.** This indicator measures the existence and content of credit union regulations including the minimum requirements to establish a credit union, prudential ratios and consumer protection requirements similar to those measured for MFIs.

- **Agent banking.** This indicator focuses on the regulations for allowing third party agents to provide financial services on behalf of commercial banks. It includes the minimum standards to qualify and operate as an agent, type of contract between commercial banks and agents, the range of financial services agents can provide and bank liability for agent actions.

- **Electronic money (e-money).** This indicator measures the regulations for the provision of e-money by non-bank issuers. It covers the licensing and operational standards, as well as requirements on safeguarding funds collected by non-bank e-money issuers.

- **Warehouse receipts.** This indicator covers the existence and scope of rules regulating warehouse receipt systems, including insurance and other performance guarantee requirements for warehouse operators and the form and content required for legally valid receipts.

Colombia has the highest score on *EBA* finance indicators, due to strong regulations on credit unions, e-money and warehouse receipts (figure 5.1).[12] Colombia's credit union regulations set minimum ratios to ensure financial stability and require transparency in loan pricing. E-money regulations set minimum standards for licensing and require issuers to safeguard customer funds and warehouse receipts regulations allow both paper and electronic receipts.

The Kyrgyz Republic is the only country that scores above average on all five indicators. Other countries in the top 10 show vast differences in their financial regulations. Kenya achieves the top score on electronic money but has no system for warehouse receipts. Although the Philippines scores 100 on credit unions, there is no regulation for agent banking.

Many countries impose overly strict regulations on microfinance institutions and lack regulations to ensure the financial stability of credit unions

MFIs and credit unions provide access to credit and savings for customers unable to obtain loans or open accounts at commercial banks—due to geographic location, a lack of credit history or low credit-worthiness. Whereas MFIs take deposits from the public, credit unions provide financial services to members and often at lower cost than banks and MFIs.[13] Both MFIs and credit unions reach customers in rural areas who are normally excluded from traditional banks.

MFI regulations have to be more stringent than those for banks.[14] MFIs have higher administrative costs for each dollar lent given the limited volume and value of microloans. And their portfolios tend to be confined to loan products with substantially similar risks, limiting the room for diversifying portfolio risk. Microloans have higher default risk since they are not secured by collateral and the

FIGURE 5.1 The Kyrgyz Republic is the only country that scores above average on all five indicators

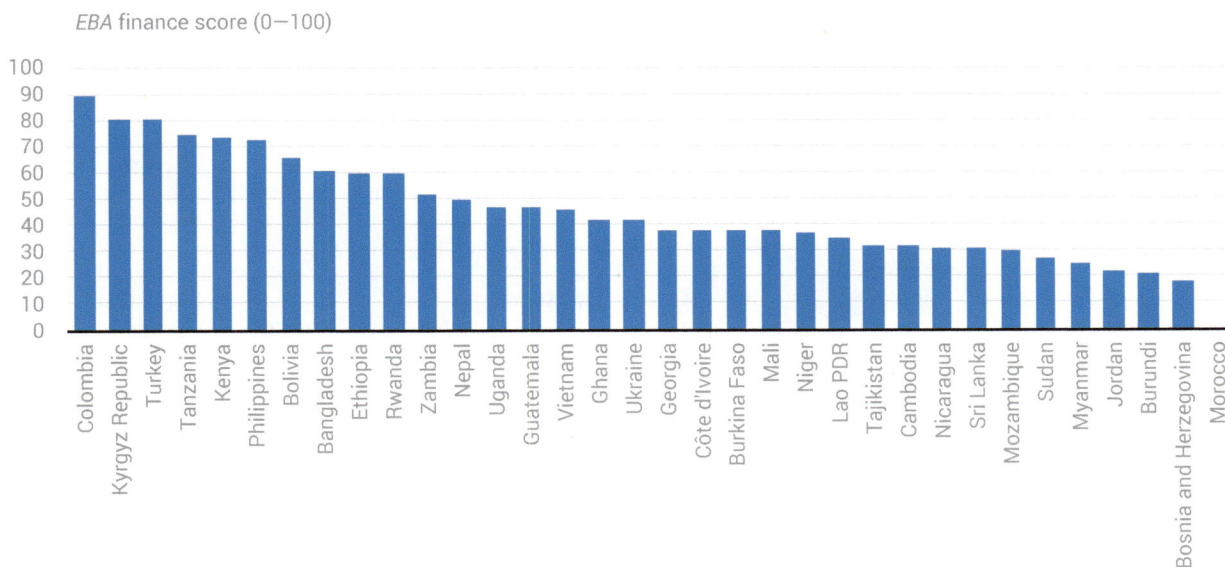

EBA finance score (0–100)

Source: EBA database.

Note: High-income countries—Chile, Denmark, Greece, Poland, Russian Federation and Spain—are not measured under *EBA* finance indicators.

BOX 5.1 Good practices for MFI regulations

- Should require MFIs to maintain a capital adequacy ratio (CAR) that is equal to or slightly higher than the CAR for commercial banks.

- Should require provisioning schedules for unsecured MFI loans to be similar to or slightly more aggressive than those for commercial banks.

- Should require MFIs to disclose the full cost of credit to loan applicants.

- Should require MFIs to participate in the deposit insurance system.

credit-worthiness of borrowers is hard to assess. But overly restrictive regulations can reduce loans to MFI customers, hindering access to financial services.[15] Smart MFI regulations should secure the financial stability of MFIs while protecting consumers, yet not be so restrictive as to reduce lending (box 5.1).

Among the 30 countries measured by the microfinance indicator, 24 allow MFIs to take deposits from the public while 6 do not.[16] MFIs that take deposits can offer more services to customers than credit-only institutions, such as savings accounts, which enable the poor to manage emergencies better, smooth consumption and take advantage of investment opportunities. Deposit mobilization also gives MFIs a stable channel to scale up operations and outreach.[17]

Once a loan becomes delinquent, financial institutions must set aside reserves ("provisions")—usually a percentage of the loan's value—in case the borrower is unable to repay. Although provisioning helps MFIs maintain stability in case of loan losses, requiring MFIs to provision too much too quickly leaves less money available to grant new loans. MFIs should be bound by similar or slightly more aggressive provisioning rules than commercial banks.[18] Of the 24 countries that allow MFIs to take deposits, 14 have similar provisioning rules for MFIs and commercial banks, while 9 overly burden MFIs.[19] In Ghana MFIs are required to reserve 100% of the value of an unsecured microfinance loan if the loan has been overdue for 150 days, while banks

are required to do so only when a loan has been overdue for one year.

A capital adequacy ratio (CAR) measures a financial institution's ability to withstand portfolio losses from nonperforming loans.[20] Regulators impose minimum CARs to protect depositors and promote the stability of financial institutions. Proportionately higher CARs should be required for deposit-taking MFIs given their riskier portfolios and higher operating costs. But CARs that are too high can reduce the number of loans granted.[21] Of the 24 countries where MFIs are allowed to take deposits, 8 require the same CARs for MFIs and commercial banks (figure 5.2). Nine countries impose discriminative rules against MFIs by requiring that minimum CARs be at least three percentage points higher than required for commercial banks. Three countries set lower CAR requirements for MFIs, putting MFIs at greater risk for financial instability.

Tajikistan scores the highest in this area, where minimum CAR requirements for MFIs are the same as for banks and both are bound by common provisioning rules. It also features strong consumer protection measures such as requiring MFIs to disclose the full cost of credit to loan applicants and requiring MFI participation in the deposit insurance system. These requirements promote customer confidence in microfinance institutions while ensuring financial stability.

Of the 6 lowest scoring countries on the MFI indicator, 5 are located in West

Africa. Regulations in these countries do not set a minimum capital requirement to establish an MFI and include overly restrictive provisioning schedules for them. These countries also have no mandatory deposit insurance systems.

While a majority of *EBA* countries that allow MFIs regulate them prudently, credit unions are not regulated to the same extent. Although credit unions take deposits from and lend to only their members, they should be subject to appropriate regulations to ensure financial stability and protect the deposits of their members (box 5.2).[22] Credit union regulations tend to have various financial stability requirements ranging from liquidity and reserve ratios to stable funding ratios—sometimes including a minimum CAR. Twenty-three of the 30 countries with credit unions regulate such ratios, and 8 require credit unions to adhere to a minimum CAR.

Transparent loan pricing helps customers determine whether they can afford a loan.[23] Requiring financial institutions to disclose a loan's effective interest rate to a borrower protects consumers from loans with unfair or abusive terms,[24] which is especially important for low-income and low-literate customers.[25] But of the 22 countries that have regulations for both MFIs and credit unions, only 11 require both types of institutions to disclose the effective interest rate to customers. Another 4 require only MFIs to disclose their effective interest rates, while 2 require only credit unions to disclose. The remaining 5 do not require either MFIs or credit unions to disclose the effective interest rate.

The Kyrgyz Republic, the Philippines and Tanzania score highest on the credit unions indicator. Regulations in these countries set prudent requirements that guarantee the financial stability of credit unions and include consumer protection measures. All require appropriate minimum capital requirements and a low minimum number of members to establish credit unions. And they set minimum ratios for financial stability for credit unions. Each ensures transparency in loan pricing by requiring that credit unions disclose loans' effective interest rates to prospective borrowers.

FIGURE 5.2 Almost half the countries that allow MFIs to take deposits require a higher capital adequacy ratio for MFIs than for commercial banks

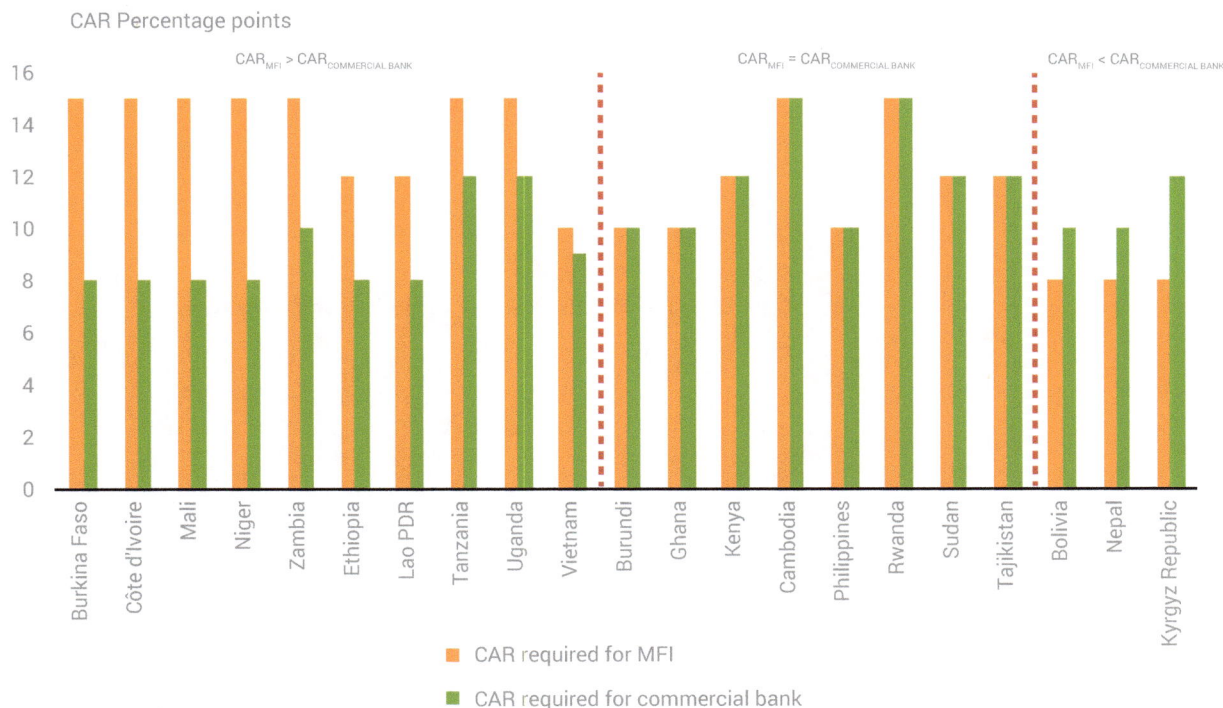

CAR Percentage points

CAR$_{MFI}$ > CAR$_{COMMERCIAL BANK}$ CAR$_{MFI}$ = CAR$_{COMMERCIAL BANK}$ CAR$_{MFI}$ < CAR$_{COMMERCIAL BANK}$

■ CAR required for MFI

■ CAR required for commercial bank

Source: EBA database.

Note: The capital adequacy ratio (CAR) is defined as an institution's total capital to risk weighted assets. It aims to prevent institutions from taking excess leverage and becoming insolvent in the process. International regulation recommendations encourage commercial banks to maintain a minimum CAR of 8% to safeguard against portfolio losses. Excessively high minimum CARs can reduce lending capacity and appetite of an institution. By contrast, a minimum CAR that is too low can result in financially unstable institutions. Therefore, a good practice is for MFIs to have equal to or slightly higher minimum CARs than commercial banks. There is no minimum CAR required for MFIs in Bangladesh, Mozambique and Myanmar.

BOX 5.2 Good practices for credit union regulations

- Establish appropriate minimum capital requirements to establish credit unions.

- Should define the minimum number of members to establish a credit union in regulations.

- Should require credit unions to adhere to minimum ratios for financial stability such as capital adequacy and liquidity ratios.

- Should require credit unions to disclose the full cost of credit to loan applicants.

The financial sector is more inclusive in countries with branchless banking laws

Few banks open branches in rural areas because population density is much lower than in cities and the limited customer base hardly justifies the costs of operating a new branch. Rapid ICT development has spurred new ways to deliver financial services without relying on a local bank. Agent banking, also called branchless banking, relies on agents that provide services to rural customers through retail points while remotely connected to a bank in a city. Alternatively, payments and deposits can be made electronically through mobile phones or debit cards (e-money). Both e-money and agent banking offer farmers more economical ways to access financial services so that they do not need to travel far to a bank branch.[26]

Of the low-income and lower-middle-income countries covered, only 11 regulate agent banking.[27] Among them, 7 adopt the good practice of allowing both exclusive and nonexclusive contracts between agents and financial institutions, while the remaining 4 prohibit exclusive contracts (figure 5.3). Exclusive contracts promote innovation by granting banks a monopoly over an agent. Nonexclusive contracts allow agents to provide services for multiple financial institutions, increasing access to financial services.[28]

It is good practice to allow agents to offer a wide variety of financial services (box 5.3).[29] Although most of the 11 countries measured allow agents to provide cash deposits, withdrawals, transfers and bill payments, only in Bangladesh and Ghana can clients open a deposit account through an agent.

Finally, it is good practice to hold commercial banks liable for the actions of their agents.[30] This ensures oversight of agents and increases customer confidence. Among the 11 countries measured, only Ghana and Ukraine do not hold commercial banks liable for the acts of their agents.

While both agent banking and e-money enable inexpensive and accessible financial services by lowering delivery costs, e-money allows customers to access savings, payments and transfers through mobile phones.[31]

Of the 28 countries that have regulations on e-money, 16 allow businesses to issue e-money without having to hold a banking license (box 5.4).[32] While these businesses still need adequate supervision, obtaining a banking license can be costly and is likely to deter innovative actors from entering the market.

Kenya's strong e-money regulations are reflected in the country's top score. Thanks to high standards for licensing

---

BOX 5.3 Good practices for agent banking regulations

- Should identify minimum standards to qualify and operate as an agent, such as real-time connectivity to the commercial bank.

- Should allow agents to enter both exclusive and nonexclusive contracts with financial institutions.

- Should allow agents to offer a wide range of services such as cash-in, cash-out, bill payment, account opening and processing of loan documents.

- Should hold commercial banks liable for the actions of their agents.

FIGURE 5.3 Countries are at different stages of developing legal frameworks to regulate agent banking activities

- Countries with a legal framework on agent banking
- Countries without a legal framework on agent banking
- Countries allow both exclusive and nonexclusive contracts
- Countries do not allow both exclusive and nonexclusive contracts

Source: EBA database.

Note: Thirty countries measured under the agent banking indicator include Bangladesh, Bolivia, Burkina Faso, Burundi, Cambodia, Côte d'Ivoire, Ethiopia, Georgia, Ghana, Guatemala, Kenya, Kyrgyz Republic, Lao PDR, Mali, Morocco, Mozambique, Myanmar, Nepal, Nicaragua, Niger, the Philippines, Rwanda, Sri Lanka, Sudan, Tajikistan, Tanzania, Uganda, Ukraine, Vietnam and Zambia.

BOX 5.4 Good practices for e-money regulations

- Should allow both banks and non-bank businesses to issue e-money.

- Should specify minimum licensing standards for non-bank e-money issuers, such as:

  - internal control mechanisms that comply with anti-money laundering and combating the financing of terrorism (AML/CFT) laws.

  - consumer protection measures and recourse mechanisms.

- Should require e-money issuers to safeguard and ring-fence customer funds by holding funds in a separate account at a regulated financial institution.

Performance guarantees—such as requirements that warehouse receipt operators file a bond with the regulator, pay into an indemnity fund and insure the warehouse and stored goods against theft, burglary and natural disasters—increase user confidence in the warehouse receipt system.[37] Furthermore, insuring a warehouse and the goods inside reduces a bank's risk in lending against a warehouse receipt, which may incentivize banks to extend credit.[38] Of the 15 countries with warehouse receipt laws, 12 require the warehouse operator to insure the warehouse and stored goods, but only 7 require that the operator file a bond or pay into an indemnity fund.

Of the 15 countries with laws regulating warehouse receipts, 5 score 100 on the warehouse receipt indicator, all having enacted specific warehouse receipt laws in the past 15 years. Three of the 5 are in Sub-Saharan Africa: Ethiopia, Uganda and Zambia.[39] Turkey and Ukraine also score full points.

Uganda's Warehouse Receipt System Act of 2006 and Warehouse Receipt Regulations of 2007 have created an enabling environment for the use of warehouse receipts as collateral for loans. The laws create licensing standards for warehouse operators, including a requirement to file a bond with the warehouse authority to ensure fulfillment of duties and a second

non-bank e-money issuers, regulations protect customers against fraud by imposing anti-money laundering and combating the financing of terrorism (AML/CFT) controls and require e-money issuers to have consumer protection measures, such as consumer recourse mechanisms. And they require issuers to safeguard customer funds by setting aside 100% of what is owed to customers, so that money is readily accessible when the customers want to convert their e-money back to cash.

The relevance of e-money for financial inclusion is shown by Global Findex data on the share of the poor population with an account at a financial institution.[33] This correlates positively with the licensing standards imposed on non-bank e-money providers as measured by the finance indicators, suggesting that in countries with strong e-money laws, a higher share of the population is financially included.[34] Regulations in these countries typically combine clear minimum capital requirements with internal AML/CFT controls and consumer protection measures.

Few countries regulate warehouse receipt systems

Many farmers in emerging economies lack traditional collateral required to access credit, so warehouse receipts can enable farmers and agricultural producers to use agricultural commodities as collateral for a loan.[35] And secure and reliable warehouse receipt systems can enable farmers to extend the sales period beyond the harvesting season (box 5.5).[36]

Comprehensive warehouse receipt regulations are still limited for the industry. Only 15 of the 34 countries measured under the warehouse receipts indicator have laws regulating warehouse receipt systems (figure 5.4).

BOX 5.5 Good practices for warehouse receipt systems

- Should require warehouse receipt operators to file a bond with the regulator or pay into an indemnity to secure performance of obligations as an operator.

- Should require that warehouse and stored goods be insured against fire, earthquakes, theft, burglary and other damage.

- Should require that both electronic and paper-based receipts be valid.

- Should define the information required to be stated on a receipt, including the location of storage, the quantity and quality of goods and the information on security interest over the goods, such as the certificate of pledge.

FIGURE 5.4 Three of the five top performers on regulations related to warehouse receipts are in Sub-Saharan Africa

Score on warehouse receipts (0—100)

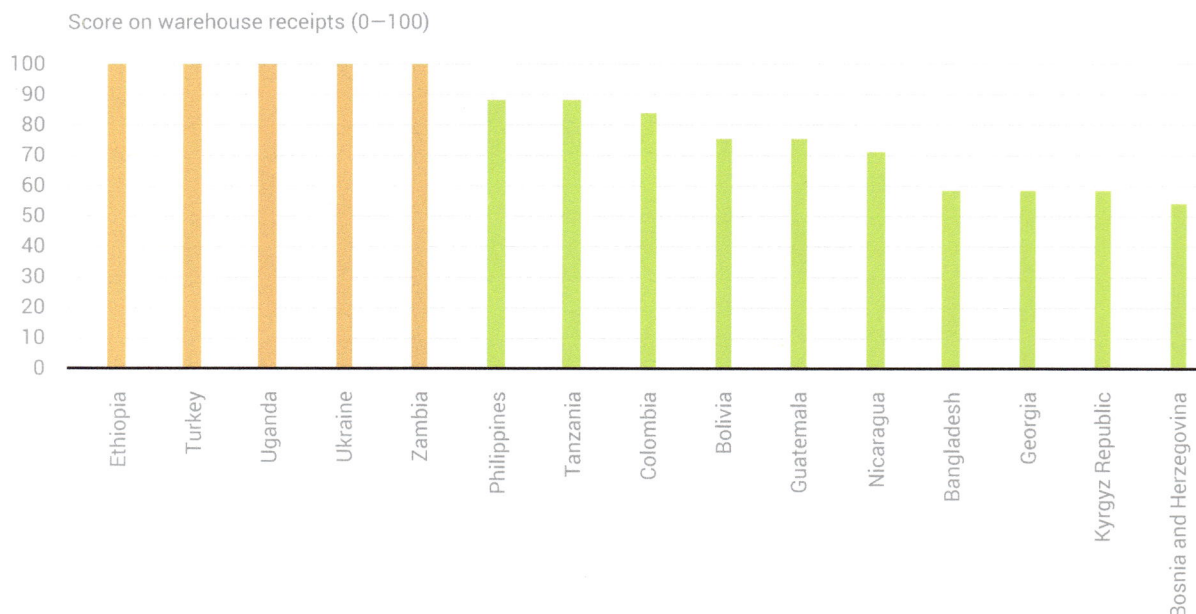

Source: EBA database.

Note: High-income countries—Chile, Denmark, Greece, Poland, Russian Federation and Spain are not measured under the warehouse receipts indicator. Burkina Faso, Burundi, Cambodia, Côte d'Ivoire, Ghana, Jordan, Kenya, Lao PDR, Mali, Morocco, Mozambique, Myanmar, Nepal, Niger, Rwanda, Sri Lanka, Sudan, Tajikistan and Vietnam do not have any regulations for warehouse receipts.

requirement that all stored goods are fully insured against loss by fire and other disasters. The law defines the content of a valid warehouse receipt and allows receipts to be negotiable.

Conclusion

Increasing access to financial services is key to helping farmers smooth volatile income flows, better allocate risk and increase production. The *EBA* finance results show that there is opportunity in many countries to improve laws and regulations and move towards good practices, such as:

- **Implementing standards for microfinance institutions that ensure stability and protect customers, yet are not so restrictive as to limit access to financial services.** Kenya's microfinance regulations set a loan provisioning schedule that is slightly more aggressive than that

for commercial banks and requires microfinance institutions to participate in a deposit insurance system.

- **Establishing minimum prudential and consumer protection standards for credit unions.** The Philippines' credit union regulations set a low minimum number of members to establish a credit union and require credit unions to disclose their effective interest rate to loan applicants.

- **Creating an enabling environment for commercial banks to hire agents to perform financial services.** The agent banking regulations in the Kyrgyz Republic require agents to have real-time connectivity to the commercial bank and hold commercial banks liable for the actions of their agents.

- **Allowing non-bank financial institutions to issue e-money.** Colombia

requires non-bank e-money issuers to have internal control mechanisms to comply with AML/CFT laws and standards and to safeguard 100% of customer funds.

- **Fostering a legal environment that raises confidence in the warehouse receipts system and the use of agricultural commodities as collateral for loans.** In Uganda warehouse operators must pay into an indemnity fund and insure the warehouse and stored goods against theft and damage.

An enabling regulatory environment can improve access to financial services for farmers and agribusinesses. The challenge is to strike a balance between stability of the financial sector and protecting customers, while increasing access to financial services. The finance topic focuses on a small set of regulatory indicators that measure lending constraints for microfinance institutions and credit unions, the entry and operational requirements for agent banking and non-bank e-money issuers and the regulations for using warehouse receipts as collateral. These indicators can help policymakers identify where regulatory reforms can improve access to finance for farmers and agribusinesses.

Notes

1. CABFIN 2001.

2. CGAP 2012.

3. Nair and Kloeppinger-Todd 2007.

4. IFC and GPFI 2011.

5. Besley 1998.

6. Poulton, Kydd and Doward 2006.

7. Lauer and Tarazi 2012.

8. Kumar and others 2006.

9. Alexandre, Mas and Radcliffe 2010.

10. Ammar and Ahmed 2014.

11. High-income countries—Chile, Denmark, Greece, Poland, Russia and Spain are not measured under the *EBA* finance indicators and data for those countries are shown as "N/A." The *EBA* finance indicators were designed to measure laws and regulations that promote access to financial services for potential customers that are partially or fully excluded from traditional financial services. This is not applicable to high-income countries whose agribusinesses and smallholder farmers have few obstacles accessing the formal financial sector. Data from the Global Findex database show that, on average, more than 80% of the population of high-income countries in the *EBA* sample have an account at a formal financial institution. In addition, high-income countries have developed alternative financial instruments to those covered by *EBA* finance indicators. For instance, instead of warehouse receipt financing, term financing and working capital financing are

widely used in high-income countries. Additional indicators will be designed to account for regulations governing relevant financial services in high-income countries next cycle.

12. Colombia, along with all high-income and upper-middle-income countries, is not measured under the MFI and agent banking subindicators.

13. WOCCU 2011.

14. CGAP 2012.

15. CGAP 2012; Cull, Demirgüç-Kunt and Morduch 2009.

16. High-income and upper-middle-income countries (Bosnia and Herzegovina, Chile, Colombia, Denmark, Greece, Jordan, Spain, Turkey, Poland and Russia) are not measured under the MFI subindicator since commercial banks serve the needs of the majority of the population in these countries.

17. CGAP 2003.

18. CGAP 2012.

19. Myanmar does not set a provisioning schedule for microfinance loans.

20. Capital adequacy ratio is defined as a financial institution's total capital to risk-weighted assets.

21. CGAP 2012.

22. Branch and Grace 2008.

23. Chien 2012.

24. The annual percentage rate (APR), an amortization table, or the total cost of credit including interest and other charges were used as proxies for the effective interest rate.

25. Chien 2012.

26. Jayanty 2012.

27. High-income and upper-middle-income countries (Bosnia and Herzegovina, Chile, Colombia, Denmark,

Greece, Jordan, Spain, Turkey, Poland and Russia) are not measured under the agent banking subindicator since bank branch penetration is high and branches are accessible in rural locations in those countries.

28. Muthiora 2015.

29. Tarazi and Breloff 2011.

30. *Ibid.*

31. Gutierrez and Singh 2013; Jack and Suri 2011.

32. High-income countries (Chile, Denmark, Greece, Poland, Russia and Spain) are not measured under the *EBA* finance indicators.

33. Demirgüç-Kunt and others 2014.

34. The correlation between the percentage of poor population having an account at a financial institution and the score on standards to be licensed as an e-money issuer is 0.35. The correlation is significant at the 5% level after controlling for income per capita.

35. Hollinger, Rutten and Kirakov 2009.

36. Lacroix and Varangis 1996.

37. Wehling and Garthwaite 2015.

38. *Ibid.*; Kiriakov and the QED Group, LLC 2007.

39. Only 4 of 14 Sub-Saharan African countries have laws regulating warehouse receipt systems.

References

Alexandre, C., I. Mas and D. Radcliffe. 2010. "Regulating New Banking Models that Can Bring Financial Services to All." *Challenge Magazine* 54 (3): 116–34.

Ammar, A., and E. M. Ahmed. 2014. *Microfinance and Mobile Banking Regulatory and Supervision Issues.* Melaka, Malaysia: Multimedia University.

Besley, T. 1998. "How Do Market Failures Justify Interventions in Rural Credit Markets?" In *International Agricultural Development,* eds., C.K. Eicher and J.M. Staatz.

CABFIN (Improving Capacity Building in Rural Finance). 2001. "An Analytical Framework for Regulation and Supervision of Agricultural Finance." Agricultural Finance Revisited Series 4, CABFIN, Rome.

CGAP (Consultative Group to Assist the Poor). 2003. *Microfinance Consensus Guidelines: Developing Deposit Services for the Poor.* Washington, DC: CGAP.

———. 2012. *A Guide to Regulation and Supervision of Microfinance.* Washington, DC: CGAP.

Chien, J. 2012. "Designing Disclosure Regimes for Responsible Financial Inclusion." Focus Note 78, CGAP, Washington, DC.

Cull, R., A. Demirgüç-Kunt and J. Morduch. 2009. "Does Regulatory Supervision Curtail Microfinance Profitability and Outreach?" Policy Research Working Paper 4748, World Bank, Washington, DC.

Demirgüç-Kunt, A., L. Klapper, D. Singer and P. Van Oudhuesden. 2014. "The Global Findex Database 2014: Measuring Financial Inclusion around the World." Policy Research Working Paper 7255, World Bank, Washington, DC.

Gutierrez, E., and S. Singh. 2013. "What Regulatory Frameworks Are More Conductive to Mobile Banking? Empirical Evidence from Findex Data." Policy Research Working Paper 6652, World Bank, Washington, DC.

IFC (International Finance Corporation) and GPFI (Global Partnership for Financial Inclusion). 2011. *Scaling up Finance for Agricultural SMEs.* Washington, DC: World Bank

Jack, W., and T. Suri. 2011. "Risk Sharing Benefits of Mobile Money." Georgetown University and Massachusetts Institute of Technology.

Jayanty, S.K. 2012. "Agency Banking: New Frontiers in Financial Inclusion." Infosys Finacle Thought Paper, Bangalore, India.

Kiriakov, K.D., and the QED Group, LLC. 2007. "Necessary Conditions for an Effective Warehouse Receipts Activity." United States Agency for International Development Concept Paper, USAID, Washington, DC.

Kumar, A., A. Nair, A. Parsons and E. Urdapilleta. 2006. "Expanding Bank Outreach through Retail Partnerships: Correspondent Banking in Brazil." Working Paper 85, World Bank, Washington, DC.

Hollinger, F., L. Rutten and K. Kiriakov. "The Use of Warehouse Receipt Finance in Agriculture in Transition Countries." FAO Working Paper presented at the World Grain Forum 2009, St. Petersburg, Russian Federation: FAO.

Lacroix, R., and P. Varangis. 1996. "Using Warehouse Receipts in Developing and Transition Economies." *Finance and Development* 33 (3): 36–39.

Lauer, K., and M. Tarazi. 2012. "Supervising Non-bank E-money Issuers." CGAP Brief, CGAP, Washington, DC.

Muthiora, B. 2015. *Enabling Mobile Money Policies in Kenya: Fostering a Digital Financial Revolution.* London: GSMA.

Nair, A., and R. Kloeppinger-Todd. 2007. "Reaching Rural Areas with Financial Services: Lessons from Financial Cooperatives in Brazil, Burkina Faso, Kenya, and Sri Lanka." Agricultural and Rural Development Discussion Paper 35, World Bank, Washington, DC.

Poulton, C., J. Kydd and A. Doward. 2006. "Overcoming Market Constraints on Pro-Poor Agricultural Growth in Sub-Saharan Africa." *Development Policy Review* 24 (3): 243–27.

Tarazi, M., and P. Breloff. 2011. "Regulating Banking Agents." Focus Note 68, CGAP, Washington, DC.

Wehling, P., and B. Garthwaite. 2015. "Designing Warehouse Receipt Legislation: Regulatory Options and Recent Trends." Prepared in collaboration with the Development Law Service of the FAO Legal Office. Rome: FAO.

World Council of Credit Unions (WOCCU). 2011. *Model Law for Credit Unions.* Madison, Wisconsin: WOCCU.

6. MARKETS
ENABLING ACCESS

Huy, a farmer in Vietnam's Mekong River Delta region, suspects a virus outbreak on his farm. If Huy reports the threat to the local plant protection authority, he can receive the necessary treatments to contain the outbreak and minimize the impact on his crop. So when the harvest comes he can fulfill his obligations as a member of an agricultural cooperative, pooling his production with other farms to sell to a local rice trader. Huy and his fellow farmers in the cooperative are interested in exporting to more profitable foreign markets, but they face several obstacles in the process. Besides preparing export documents and conducting expensive quality testing in order to sell in destination markets with more stringent product standards, they must first obtain a Certificate of Eligibility for the Rice Export Business issued by the Ministry of Industry and Trade—principally to state-owned enterprises and for a limited time only.

EBA markets indicators measure regulatory obstacles agribusinesses face in producing, marketing and exporting agricultural products, as well as the strength of plant protection measures.

Regulations on producers, buyers and exporters of agricultural goods can affect business growth and, in turn, the growth of the agricultural sector as a whole. Plant protection regulation, the first indicator for EBA markets, was selected for study because reliable pest management and robust pest control at the border go hand-in-hand with strong agricultural sectors.[1] Unmanaged and undocumented pest populations lead to crop failures, smaller harvests and contaminated products, hindering market access at home and abroad.[2] But where governments require pest surveillance activities by plant protection authorities and impose reporting obligations on the private sector, pest outbreaks can be dealt with promptly and crop damage minimized. Using this information to prepare pest lists and conduct pest risk analyses enables governments to regulate cross-border agricultural trade in a cost-effective manner, negotiate access to foreign markets for their producers and issue valid and reliable phytosanitary certificates for exports.[3] Producers and exporters rely on the guarantees of phytosanitary certificates to show that their products comply with

the plant health requirements in destination markets.

Production and sales, the second EBA markets indicator, is comprised of three components. The first component looks at the regulation of agricultural sales and purchases. Such regulations can take the form of licensing and registration requirements for the sale or purchase of certain agricultural products, or may involve special registration requirements for agricultural production contracts.[4] Such licenses can impose an additional regulatory hurdle and hinder market access opportunities for smallholder farmers. A second component analyzes the regulation of farmers' cooperatives. Farmers' cooperatives help producers overcome regulatory hurdles and achieve economies of scale.[5] Cooperatives allow members to access inputs at a lower cost through aggregate purchases of seeds and fertilizers and to use collectively owned equipment, such as tractors, harvesters and storage facilities. Farmers' cooperatives can also offer members services to facilitate sales, negotiate long-term agricultural contracts and enter lucrative and reliable value chains.[6] A final component of this second indicator addresses the enforceability of mediated settlement agreements and the ease of resolving contractual disputes outside traditional courts.

The third indicator for EBA markets addresses the requirements for exporting agricultural products. Regulatory bottlenecks—such as special licenses, registration and export documentation—can raise transaction costs associated specifically with exports and discourage private investment in marketing and storage capacity.[7] Delays in obtaining mandatory export documents can reduce overall export volumes due to damage or deterioration, especially for time-sensitive agricultural products.[8]

The data cover the following areas:

- **Plant protection.** This indicator measures key aspects of domestic plant protection regulations, including surveillance and pest reporting obligations, the existence and availability of quarantine pest lists, provision for pest risk analysis and risk-based border inspections, domestic containment and border quarantine procedures.

- **Production and sales.** This indicator addresses issues that can have an effect on the enabling environment for producers and other agribusinesses in a country. It considers (i) product-specific licenses to sell or purchase agricultural products, (ii) the ability of farmers cooperatives to establish, merge and take out loans and (iii) the enforceability of mediated settlement agreements, which is a preferred method of resolving disputes stemming from agricultural production contracts.

• **Agricultural exports.** This indicator, which is not scored, measures requirements on agricultural exports, including mandatory memberships, trader-level licenses and per-shipment documentary requirements, including the time and cost to obtain these documents.

Bosnia and Herzegovina, Chile, Colombia, Greece, Poland and Spain have the highest scores on markets indicators overall, with only minor differences observed with respect to regulations impacting agricultural production and sales (figure 6.1). Countries lagging behind on the overall score tend to have more divergent results with respect to each indicator, with the majority of countries receiving higher scores for the indicator on production

and sales than for plant protection. For example, Burkina Faso, Ethiopia, Mali, Myanmar, Rwanda and Uganda all have scores for production and sales that are 50 or more points higher than their scores for plant protection. Countries in Sub-Saharan Africa and East Asia and the Pacific have the lowest scores for plant protection. In Sub-Saharan Africa most countries do not have a list of regulated quarantine pests, which is a key element when negotiating with trading partners and for managing pests domestically. Countries in East Asia and the Pacific tend not to allow risk-based phytosanitary inspections on import consignments.

The strength of plant protection regulation varies greatly across countries. Denmark and Chile have robust plant protection regulations, including pest surveillance and reporting obligations, as well as pest containment and quarantine procedures in relevant laws. These countries carry out pest risk analyses and make pest lists publicly available.

Although the scores for production and sales do not vary as much across countries as for plant protection, differences exist. In Nepal there are no licensing requirements for potato production or purchase, while Sri Lanka requires coconut producers and buyers to register annually with the Coconut Development Authority. Some countries may impose potentially burdensome requirements on producers. Nicaragua requires coffee producers to be registered to produce and sell coffee. And in Morocco producers must meet certain minimum capital requirements to establish a farmers' cooperative. Imposing additional burdens and compliance costs can limit market access.

Roughly half of the countries surveyed impose at least one trader licensing or membership requirement on exporters and there is no significant variation among countries across income groups. Fourteen countries require one membership or license to export the selected product, while Kenya, Morocco and Sri

FIGURE 6.1 *EBA* markets scores overall and by indicator

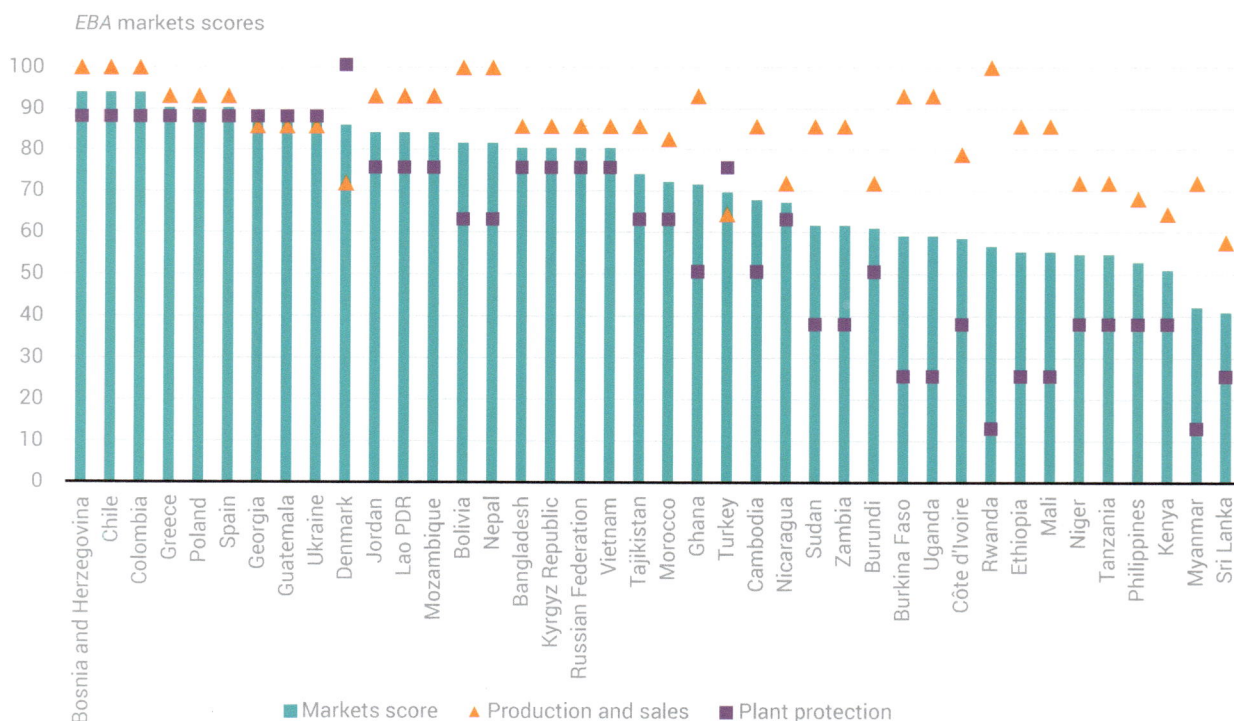

Source: EBA database.

Lanka require two and Ghana requires three.

In low-income and lower-middle-income countries, traders also face longer delays to obtain the documents required for each export shipment (figure 6.2). On average, it takes about twice as much time to obtain per-shipment export documents in low-income and lower-middle-income countries than in upper-middle-income and high-income countries. But significant variations exist within each income group. Obtaining the documents takes over 10 days in Tanzania (low income), Zambia (lower middle income) and the Russia (high income); it only takes 2 days in Burkina Faso, Mozambique and Nepal (all low income),

slightly below the average in upper-middle-income countries.

In some countries exporters face lengthy processes and high costs to obtain export documents, as in Zambia, where a cereal trader must spend roughly 11 days and 1,135 Zambian kwacha (10.8% of income per capita) to get all the required documents, including phytosanitary and fumigation certificates. Cambodian cereal traders face similar hurdles, spending about 7 days and over 350,000 Cambodian riels (8.6% of income per capita) to obtain a phytosanitary certificate, fumigation certificate and a quantity and weight certificate before they can export. But a fast process may also coincide with high costs. In Lao PDR a coffee trader has to spend more

than 1,200,000 Lao kip (9.4% of income per capita) to obtain the phytosanitary and fumigation certificates, although they are issued in just 3 days, below the average of lower-middle-income countries. Conversely, a Russian cereal trader spends only 1,190 Russian rubles (0.3% of income per capita) but waits about 12 days to obtain a phytosanitary certificate, a quality certificate, a fumigation certificate and a health certificate.

Strong plant protection frameworks correspond with low time and cost to obtain a phytosanitary certificate

Plant protection frameworks consist primarily of "phytosanitary measures,"

FIGURE 6.2 Time to obtain per-shipment export documents is greater in low-income and lower-middle-income countries on average, and it varies greatly within income group

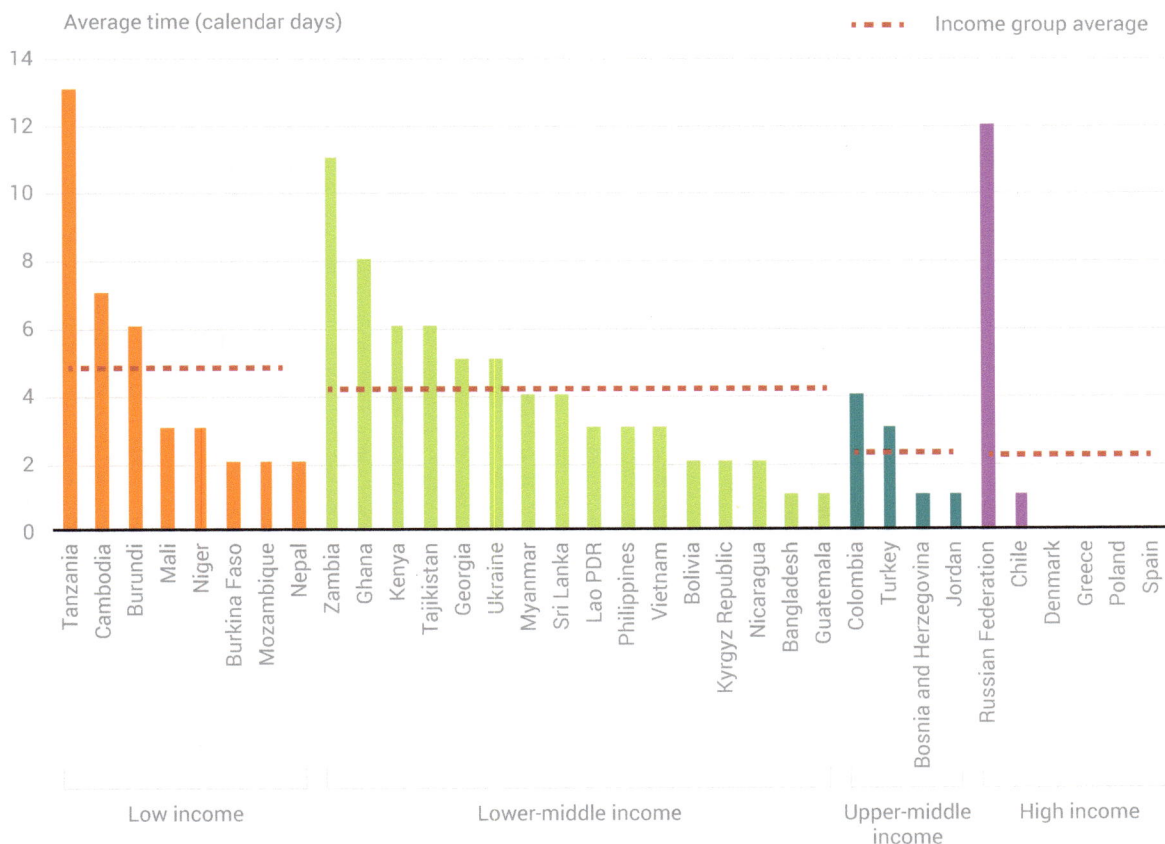

Source: EBA database.

Note: Data on time to obtain per-shipment export documents are not available for Côte d'Ivoire, Ethiopia, Morocco, Rwanda, Sudan and Uganda. These cases were excluded from the calculation of the averages by income group.

which refer to any legislation, regulation or official[9] procedure to protect plant health and prevent the introduction and spread of pests, diseases, or disease-carrying or disease-causing organisms and limit their economic impact.[10] Pest lists allow exporting countries to issue phytosanitary certificates tailored to foreign market requirements and facilitate trade negotiations by indicating whether specific pests are present in each country.[11] The list of regulated pests is publicly available for more than half the countries measured. Chile, Denmark and Spain have more advanced pest databases available online that list the status and geographic distribution of pests in the country.

Phytosanitary measures applied to imports of agricultural and other plant products at the border—such as inspections, sampling and laboratory testing and quarantine procedures—safeguard the domestic agricultural sector against the entry, establishment and spread of pests and diseases across borders. But since border agencies have limited resources to inspect and control every import consignment, pest risk analysis (PRA) can be used to differentiate between consignments based on risk and impose border controls accordingly at a higher or lower rate (box 6.1).[12] PRA evaluates biological or other scientific and economic evidence, often specific to a commodity or country of origin, to determine whether a pest should be regulated and the strength of any phytosanitary measures to be taken against it.[13] Of the 40 countries studied, 31 provide for a PRA procedure in legislation, or have a designated unit to carry out PRA. Seventeen countries allow phytosanitary import inspections to be carried out at a reduced frequency based on PRA: Bolivia, Bosnia and Herzegovina, Colombia, Denmark, Ethiopia, Georgia, Greece, Guatemala, Jordan, the Kyrgyz Republic, Mozambique, Poland, Russia, Spain, Tanzania, Turkey and Ukraine.

The strength of phytosanitary protection regulations can also affect whether agribusinesses meet phytosanitary requirements in destination markets, as they enable producers to meet certain minimum standards and demonstrate compliance.[14] Strong plant protection in high-income countries also corresponds

---

BOX 6.1 Good practices for phytosanitary regulation

- Should require plant protection agencies to conduct pest surveillance.

- Should require producers and land users to report outbreaks of pests.

- Should establish a publicly available pest database that lists pests present in the country and their current distribution and status to help land users to monitor and treat pests.

- Should establish a list of regulated quarantine pests and make available on the website of the International Plant Protection Convention.

- Should mandate pest risk analysis by law or officially task a unit to conduct it.

- Should allow phytosanitary import inspections on a risk-management basis.

- Should address both domestic containment and border quarantine procedures in relevant legislation.

---

with lower costs to obtain a phytosanitary certificate for export, while the certification process takes the least time to complete in upper-middle-income countries (figure 6.3).

The enabling environment for production and sales varies across countries

Many governments impose special licensing regimes on the domestic marketing of certain agricultural plant products. These requirements can determine whether farmers are permitted to sell regulated crops, or if those crops can be bought only by licensed buyers. Of the 40 countries covered, 9 require registration or licensing to sell or purchase agricultural products or enter agricultural production contracts.[15] In Tanzania, sweet potato producers must be registered with the authorities to sell their produce. In the Philippines, purchasers of coconut products need a license from the Philippine Coconut Authority. In Kenya, anyone engaged in collecting, transporting, storing, buying or selling potatoes for commercial ends must register with the Agriculture, Fisheries and Food Authority. And in Turkey, producers must register with the authorities to enter an agricultural production contract.

Agricultural production and marketing capacity can be improved through cooperative arrangements among farmers, but excessive initial capital requirements can make it harder for smallholder farmers to establish a cooperative in the first place (box 6.2).[16] Furthermore, limitations on the commercial operations of farmers' cooperatives—raising funds from third parties such as commercial banks, or merging with other farmers' cooperatives—hinder growth and marketing potential.[17] Of the 40 countries studied, most do not restrict third-party loans or mergers between farmers' cooperatives. But in Morocco, the Philippines and Turkey the law establishes a minimum capital requirement for the creation of a cooperative. This requirement is highest in Turkey, where shareholders are required to form a minimum capital of 50,000 Turkish lire, equivalent

FIGURE 6.3 Obtaining a phytosanitary certificate is less expensive in high-income countries, but takes less time in upper-middle-income countries

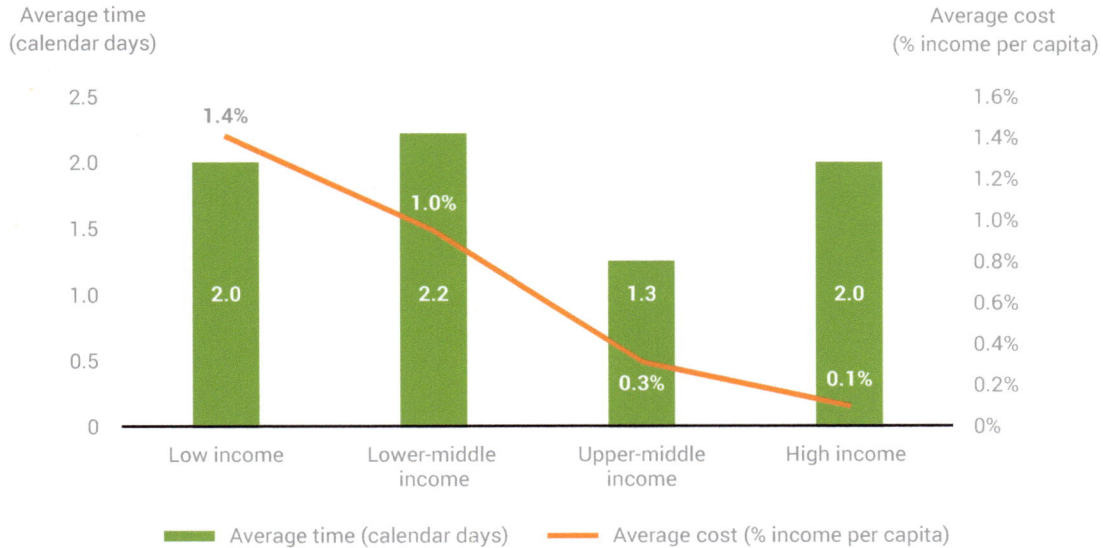

Average time (calendar days) — left axis
Average cost (% income per capita) — right axis

	Low income	Lower-middle income	Upper-middle income	High income
Average time (calendar days)	2.0	2.2	1.3	2.0
Average cost (% income per capita)	1.4%	1.0%	0.3%	0.1%

Legend: ■ Average time (calendar days) — Average cost (% income per capita)

Source: EBA database.

Note: The *EBA* sample covers high-income (6), upper-middle-income (4), lower-middle-income (19) and low-income (11) countries.

BOX 6.2 Good practices for regulations related to agricultural producers

- Should allow sales of plant products without product-specific licensing.

- Should allow farmers to establish cooperatives without minimum capital requirements.

- Should allow farmer' cooperatives to raise capital through loans from third-party sources.

- Should allow farmer' cooperatives to grow through mergers.

- Should enable prompt and effective dispute resolution through enforceable mediated settlement agreements.

---

to 219.2% of income per capita, just to register and establish a cooperative.[18]

In marketing agricultural products, disagreements may arise between farmers and buyers over prices, product quality or delays in delivery or payment. Disagreements can be potentially fatal for production contracts, which rely on long-term positive relationships and may account for all current and projected sales for farmers. Alternative dispute resolution (ADR) mechanisms, such as mediation, conciliation, expert determination and arbitration, offer means to resolve disputes more promptly and effectively than traditional court procedures, and as a result preserve business relationships and livelihoods.[19] Whereas the cost, length and complexity of traditional court procedures can heighten disagreements, ADR facilitated by a neutral third party is more consensual, collaborative and practical in nature.[20]

The legal force of any settlement agreement reached through ADR can be an important consideration for parties seeking dispute settlement. Of the 40 countries surveyed 22 allow settlement agreements reached through extrajudicial mediation to have the same enforceability as a court decision. In 8 of those countries a settlement agreement reached through extrajudicial mediation automatically has the same binding force as a court judgment. Four of those countries are located in Latin America and the Caribbean (Bolivia, Chile, Colombia and Nicaragua). In the remaining 14 the settlement agreement can be filed with a court or notarized to acquire the same enforceability as a court judgment and bind the parties accordingly. Six of those countries are located in Sub-Saharan Africa, 2 in East Asia and the Pacific, 2 in the Middle East and North Africa, 1 in Europe and Central Asia and the remaining 3 are OECD high-income countries. In 18 countries a successful extrajudicial mediation can result in a settlement agreement with the binding value of a contract between the parties. In case of a breach, enforcement would thus require civil litigation first to establish the validity of the agreement (or contract) and then to establish a breach. Thirty-eight countries offer the opportunity to seek mediation during the course of judicial proceedings upon a referral by the court or at the parties' own initiative.

More trader-level export requirements apply to cash crops than to other product groups

Many governments impose trader-level licensing regimes on the export of agricultural products. When analyzed by product type, cash crops stand out as being subject to more membership and licensing requirements to export, increasing the associated costs (figure 6.4).[21]

Similar trader-level licensing and membership requirements are imposed in the countries where cash crops were studied (figure 6.5). In Kenya, Rwanda and Sri Lanka, where tea was selected as the export product, exporters must maintain membership of and pay annual fees to a specific organization to source tea for export through an auction in the respective country. Exporters might also have to register or obtain an export license from a public agency responsible for affairs related to tea. In Kenya tea exporters must register annually with the Tea Directorate to obtain the right to export and be members of the East African Tea Trade Association to purchase tea at the Mombasa Tea Auction. In Sri Lanka both an annual export license issued by the Sri Lanka Tea Board and a pass to the Colombo Tea Auction from the Ceylon Chamber of Commerce are required

to export tea. The situation is similar in Rwanda, where the associated costs are equivalent to $1602.30 (246.5% of income per capita).

For coffee—the cash crop selected for Burundi, Colombia, Ethiopia, Lao PDR, Nicaragua and Uganda—all countries except Lao PDR impose an export license or its equivalent. Coffee exporters in Colombia must register with the Registro Nacional de Exportadores de Café. Exporters in Ethiopia must obtain a certificate of competence from the Ministry of Agriculture and Rural Development every year. Despite similarities in licensing regimes, the incurred costs vary greatly among countries. They range from greater than 85% of income per capita in Burundi and Uganda to minimal or no cost in Ethiopia (1.6% of income per capita), Colombia (free of charge) and Nicaragua (free of charge).

Between the two countries where *EBA* studied cocoa bean exports, Ghana has established more requirements for

FIGURE 6.4 Cash crops are subject to more trader licensing and membership requirements than other product groups and thus to higher costs

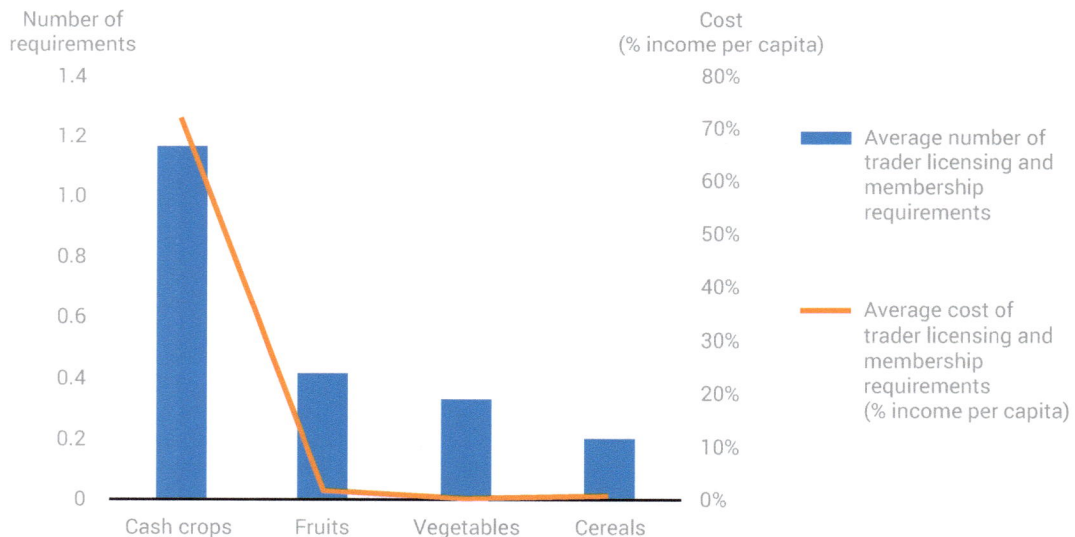

Source: *EBA* database.

Note: Cash crops were studied for Burundi (coffee), Colombia (coffee), Côte d'Ivoire (cocoa), Ethiopia (coffee), Ghana (cocoa), Kenya (tea), Lao PDR (coffee), Nepal (nutmeg, mace and cardamom), Nicaragua (coffee), Rwanda (tea), Sri Lanka (tea), Uganda (coffee). Data on cost of trader-level licensing and membership requirements are not available for Morocco and Tanzania, which were excluded from the calculation of the averages by product group.

FIGURE 6.5 Similar trader licensing and membership requirements are imposed in countries where cash crops are studied

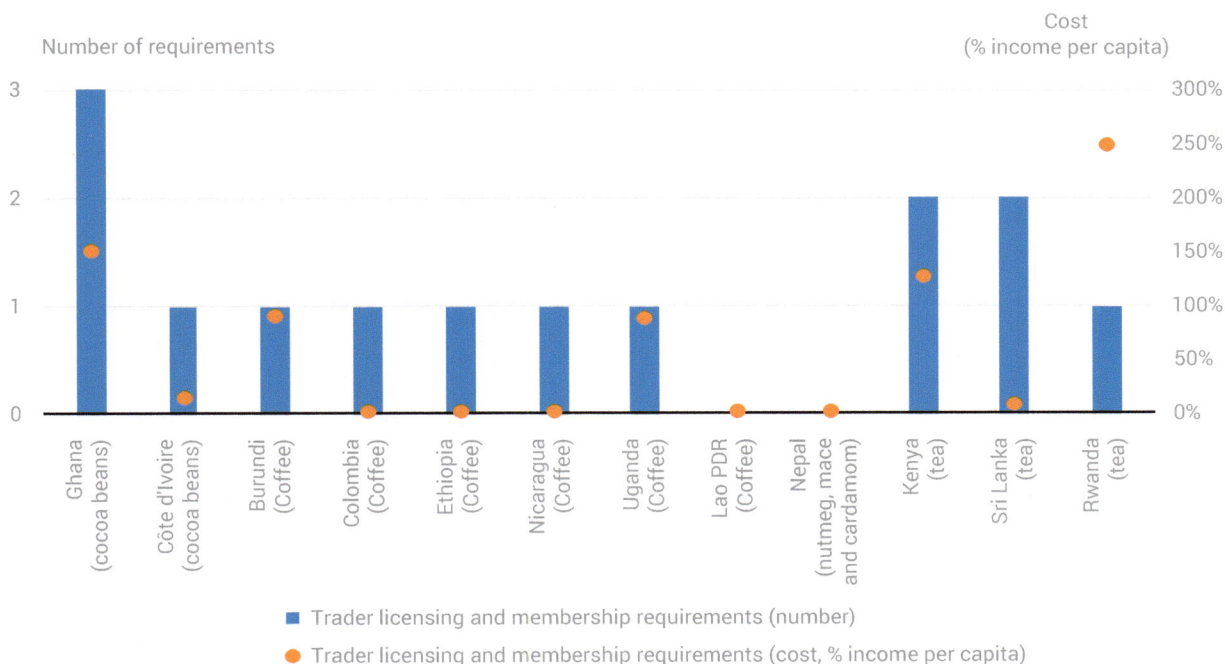

Source: *EBA* database.

exporters than Côte d'Ivoire. In Ghana cocoa exporters must be members of the Federation of Cocoa Commerce and are required to obtain an export license from the Ghana Cocoa Board as well as an annual accreditation by the Plant Protection and Regulatory Services Directorate, leading to a cumulative cost equivalent to approximately $2,345.60 or 150.3% of income per capita. In Côte d'Ivoire, by contrast, an export license granted by the Conseil du Café-Cacao costs roughly $198.30 or 12.8% of income per capita, and is the only requirement imposed on the trader level.

Per-shipment requirements have a lower time and cost under a bilateral or regional agreement

Regional and bilateral economic integration through preferential trade agreements (PTAs) typically reduces the number of per-shipment requirements to export. PTAs aim to reduce or remove tariff and non-tariff barriers to trade in goods, services and finances between participating countries.[22] They have grown in number and coverage in recent years and may extend to "the integration and improvement of transport and trade logistic systems, strengthening of infrastructure, harmonization of institutional arrangements and practices and improvement in behind-the-border policies and regulations that impose a burden on business activity."[23] They often streamline customs procedures and remove export licenses and other border measures; in complex arrangements they can facilitate harmonized and mutually recognized standards. As such, they can increase market access for agribusinesses in relevant countries and strengthen cross-border value chains.[24]

The EU countries measured (Denmark, Greece, Poland and Spain) illustrate this integration. While agribusinesses in these countries can export to other EU countries without special documentation, if they choose to export the same consignment to a non-EU country, it takes on average two days and 0.2% of income per capita to complete the required documents.[25] In other countries the time and cost associated with mandatory document requirements are generally lower when exporting agricultural products to regional or bilateral trading partners (figure 6.6).[26]

Conclusion

Improving access to markets for agricultural producers is crucial for developing a country's agricultural sector. The analysis shows that there is still plenty of room for countries to improve their laws and regulations and move towards good practices identified, such as:

- **Strong phytosanitary protection legislation governing national surveillance for pest lists, pest risk analysis and domestic and import**

FIGURE 6.6 It is on average faster and less expensive to complete per-shipment documents when exporting to regional or bilateral trading partners

Average time (calendar days)   Average cost (% income per capita)

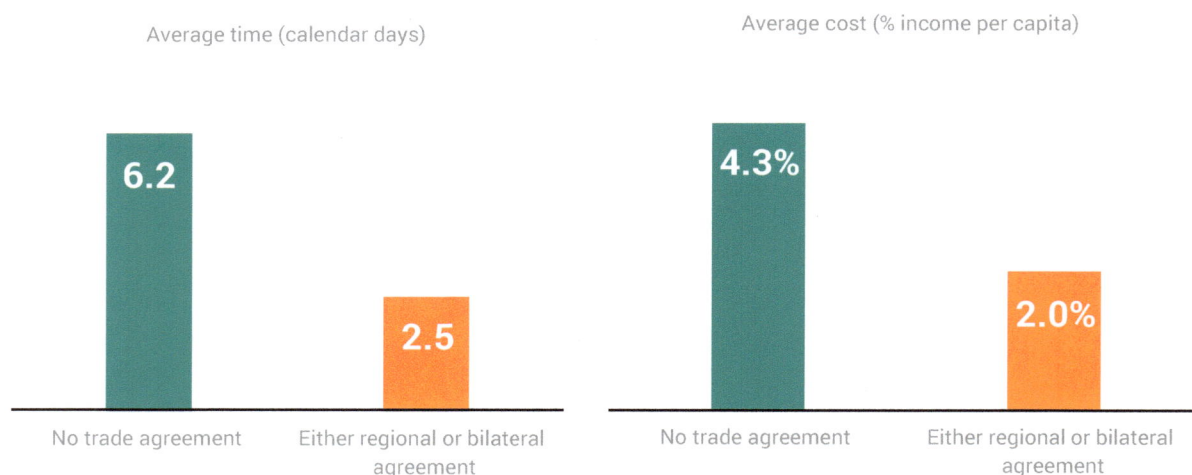

	No trade agreement	Either regional or bilateral agreement
Average time	6.2	2.5
Average cost	4.3%	2.0%

Source: EBA database.

Note: Relevant bilateral and regional trade agreements between studied countries and the selected trading partner were not identified for the following 14 countries: Bolivia, Burkina Faso, Burundi, Cambodia, Ethiopia, Ghana, Kenya, Russian Federation, Sri Lanka, Sudan, Tanzania, Turkey, Uganda and Ukraine. Data on time to obtain per-shipment export documents are not available for Côte d'Ivoire, Ethiopia, Morocco, Rwanda, Sudan and Uganda. Data on cost to obtain per-shipment export documents are not available for Colombia, Côte d'Ivoire, Morocco and Uganda. These cases were excluded from the calculation of the averages.

quarantine procedures. Plant protection laws and regulations in Nepal require the government to conduct pest surveillance and pest risk analysis and make a list of regulated quarantine pests publicly available.

- **Laws that do not obstruct the production or sale of agricultural goods domestically.** Thirty-one of the 40 countries studied do not require a product-specific license to engage in an agricultural production contract, or to sell or purchase the contracted product.

- **A legal environment that supports farmers' cooperatives.** In Zambia there is no minimum capital requirement to establish a farmers' cooperative, which facilitates farmer coordination activities and reduces the initial investment needed. Cooperatives are also allowed to merge and take out loans from third parties.

- **Efficient and affordable requirements to export major agricultural products, including membership, licensing and per-shipment documentation.** In Guatemala fruit exporters are not required to obtain a license or become a member of a specific organization before they can export and the process to obtain the per-shipment mandatory documents is efficient, costing only 0.2% of income per capita.

Identifying good regulatory practices is challenging when dealing with the agricultural sector because, besides facilitating production, market access and cross-border trade, regulation is also needed to protect domestic production and the environment from pests and diseases. The markets topic identifies certain regulatory constraints that can hinder agricultural production and sale. These indicators are a starting point for discussion with policymakers on addressing such regulatory constraints and working towards a more

streamlined, productive and profitable agricultural sector.

Notes

1. International Plant Protection Convention 2015; International Plant Protection Convention 2012; Lesser and Moïsé-Leeman 2009; World Bank 2012.

2. Murina and Nicita 2014.

3. International Plant Protection Convention 1997.

4. An agricultural production contract is a contract where "the producer undertakes to produce and deliver agricultural commodities in accordance with the contractor's specifications. The contractor, in turn, undertakes to acquire the product for a price and generally has some involvement in production activities through, for example, the supply of

inputs and provision of technical advice." See UNIDROIT, FAO and IFAD 2015.

5. Farmers' cooperatives are also known as agricultural cooperatives, farmers' cooperatives or producers' associations. A farmers' cooperative is defined as a voluntary, jointly-owned and democratically controlled association of farmers created to support and promote the economic interests of its members through joint economic activity, including, but not limited to, production, processing and marketing of agricultural products. If different types of farmers' organizations exist in a country, those that most closely adhere to this definition are selected for study.

6. Arias and others 2013; FAO 2013.

7. World Bank 2012; Pannhausen and Untied 2010; Comprehensive African Agriculture Development Programme (CAADP) 2009.

8. Djankov, Freund and Pham 2006.

9. "Established, authorized or performed by a National Plant Protection Organization." International Plant Protection Convention 2005.

10. International Plant Protection Convention 2005. Erratum. This definition should be understood to supersede and correct that in Enabling the Business of Agriculture 2015.

11. International Plant Protection Convention 2003.

12. International Plant Protection Convention 2004.

13. International Plant Protection Convention 2007.

14. Asian Development Bank 2013.

15. For each country, this finding is based on the most produced non-processed non-cereal product in terms of gross production value (current million US$). All data are sourced from FAOSTAT, using the production data of 2012 (the latest available year). Cereal crops are excluded from the analysis because they are less suitable for agricultural production contracts due to several characteristics, including high risk of side-selling given well-developed local or export markets, less need for technical assistance to meet market specifications and poor potential for price differentials.

16. For additional information on minimum capital requirements applicable to firms, please see Doing Business. http://www.doingbusiness .org/data/exploretopics/starting -a-business/good-practices.

17. FAO 1998; Von Pischke and Rouse 2004.

18. In the Philippines the minimum capital requirement is 60,000 Philippine peso (39.6% of income per capita), and in Morocco it is 700 Moroccan dirhams (2.7% of income per capita).

19. UNIDROIT, FAO and IFAD 2015.

20. Dixie and others 2014.

21. EBA defines and groups agricultural products as cash crops, cereals, fruits and vegetables according to the Harmonized Commodity Description and Coding System 1996 version (HS 96): cash crops (HS 09, HS 1201-HS 1206, HS 1210, HS 1212, HS 1801); cereals (HS 10); fruits (HS 08); vegetables (HS 07).

22. World Bank 2013.

23. World Bank 2013.

24. World Bank 2008.

25. Data for exports from European Union countries to third countries are available on the EBA website: eba.worldbank.org.

26. The bilateral and regional agreements included in our analysis are those covering agricultural trade and concluded between studied countries and their largest cross-border agricultural trading partner. Agricultural trade is defined as import and export of plant-based products, including cash crops, cereals, fruits and vegetables, according to the Harmonized Commodity Description and Coding System 1996 version (HS 96). All data are sourced from the UN Comtrade Database, using the import and export data from 2009-13. For each country, the cross-border partner country that represents the highest five-year average agricultural trade value (in US$) is selected.

References

Arias, P., D. Hallam, E. Krivonos and J. Morrison. 2013. Smallholder Integration in Changing Food Markets. Rome: FAO.

Asian Development Bank. 2013. Modernizing Sanitary and Phytosanitary Measures to Facilitate Trade in Agricultural and Food Products: Report on the Development of an SPS Plan for the CAREC Countries. Mandaluyong City, Manila, Philippines: Asian Development Bank.

Comprehensive African Agriculture Development Programme (CAADP). 2009. Framework for African Food Security. Midrand, South Africa: CAADP.

Dixie, G., M. Jonasova, L. Ronchi, A. Sergeant, P. Jaeger and J. Yap. 2014. "An Analytical Toolkit for Support to Contract Farming." Agriculture and Environmental Services Internal Paper, World Bank, Washington, DC.

Djankov, S., C. Freund and C. S. Pham. 2006. "Trading on Time." Policy Research Working Paper 3909, World Bank, Washington, DC.

———. 1998. "Agricultural Cooperative Development: A Manual for Trainers." Rome: FAO.

International Plant Protection Convention. 1997. "Guidelines for Surveillance." International Standard for Phytosanitary Measures No. 6. Rome: FAO.

——. 2003. "Guidelines on Lists of Regulated Pests." International Standard for Phytosanitary Measures No. 19. Rome: FAO.

——. 2004. "Guidelines for a Phytosanitary Import Regulatory System." International Standard for Phytosanitary Measures No. 20. Rome: FAO.

——. 2005. "Glossary of Phytosanitary Terms." International Standard for Phytosanitary Measures No. 5. Rome: FAO.

——. 2007. "Framework for Pest Risk Analysis." International Standards for Phytosanitary Measures No. 2. Rome: FAO.

——. 2012. "IPPC Strategic Framework 2012-2019: Celebrating 60 Years of Protecting Plant Resources from Pests." Rome: FAO.

——. 2015. "Plant Pest Surveillance." IPPC Technical Resources 7. Rome: FAO.

Lesser, C., and E. Moïsé-Leeman. 2009. "Informal Cross-Border Trade and Trade Facilitation Reform in Sub-Saharan Africa." OECD Trade Policy Working Paper 86, OECD, Paris.

Murina, M., and A. Nicita. 2014. "Trading With Conditions: The Effect of Sanitary and Phytosanitary Measures on Lower Income Countries' Agricultural Exports." Policy Issues in International Trade and Commodities Research Study Series 68, UNCTAD, Geneva.

Pannhausen, C, and B. Untied. 2010. *Regional Agricultural Trade for Economic Development and Food Security in Sub-Saharan Africa.* Eschborn, Germany: Deutsche Gesellschaft für Technische Zusammenarbeit (GTZ) mbH.

UNIDROIT, FAO and IFAD. 2015. "UNIDROIT/FAO/IFAD Legal Guide on Contract Farming." Rome: UNIDROIT, FAO and IFAD.

Von Pischke, J.D., and J. G. Rouse. 2004. *New Strategies for Mobilizing Capital in Agricultural Cooperatives.* Rome: FAO.

World Bank. 2008. *World Development Report 2009: Reshaping Economic Geography.* Washington, DC: World Bank.

——. 2012. *Africa Can Help Feed Africa: Removing Barriers to Regional Trade in Food Staples.* Washington, DC: World Bank.

7. TRANSPORT
MAKING TRANSPORTATION MORE RELIABLE AND AFFORDABLE

A young and dynamic entrepreneur, Guillaume, owns a truck and transports cereals for rural smallholder farmers to nearby markets. He is committed to provide reliable services to his clients by keeping his truck in good condition. He has the required truck-level transport license presenting his technical inspection and insurance certificates. But he finds it hard to expand his business with all the competition from formal and informal operators offering transport services below minimum quality and safety standards. As a certified driver and licensed truck operator, Guillaume would like his customers to be able to distinguish professional truckers ensuring certain standards from informal competitors. The government is aware of the situation and is working on improving the current licensing system to establish certain professional minimum standards.

EBA transport indicators measure laws and regulations that affect commercial road transport services. The indicators address factors that could potentially benefit farmers and agribusinesses through more competitive and better regulated services that enable the transport of agricultural products to the market.

With growing demand for food and increasing export opportunities in regional trade, farmers will need to transport their produce to these markets to benefit from their potential. High transport costs increase the price farmers pay for inputs and decrease their income, which decreases the incentive to invest in their farms.[1] Regulations affect the availability, efficiency, effectiveness, reliability and safety of transport services.[2]

Truck licenses, the first indicator for *EBA* transport, has been selected for study as licenses promote reliable and safe transport services. Truck licenses create a level playing field for road transport operators by regulating access to the profession and setting safety and environmental standards. Countries with few or no qualitative market entry criteria are dominated by many small, often informal businesses. Informality hampers the viability and efficiency of

formal road transport services, cutting the revenue collected from the transport sector. Smart regulations balance the need for safety and quality standards without becoming too burdensome and excessively restricting small and foreign companies in the market. The process for obtaining licenses or permits for transport equipment and operations should be clear, transparent and efficient. Making it easier to obtain licenses for transport equipment and operations is an important way to improve trade and transport.[3]

Cross-border transport, the second indicator for *EBA* transport, measures restrictions to foreign transport companies providing cross-border services. Permit and quota restrictions obstruct regional trade integration.[4] Increasing foreign participation in trucking and logistics is one way to improve the quality and competitiveness of transport services available to agribusinesses. Allowing foreign logistics services and foreign trucks to transport third-country cargo eases trade.[5] Backhauls and long travel times from waiting and idling during trips create inefficiencies that also raise transport prices.[6] Harmonizing and mutually recognizing technical and procedural standards between countries—such as axle load limits, technical inspections and

carrier liabilities—improves cross-border transport service quality and efficiency.

The data cover the following areas:

- **Truck licenses.** This indicator addresses the different licensing regimes for commercial road transport services in the domestic market, the extent to which license requirements and applications are available online, the additional legal requirements to obtain a license or permit and the price and freight allocation regulations affecting domestic road transport services. In addition, data has been collected on the time, cost and validity required for transport licenses and the cost and validity of mandatory technical inspections.

- **Cross-border transport.** This indicator measures restrictions to cross-border transport including the regulation of carrier's liabilities, rights of foreign trucking companies to transport agricultural goods in the country, and existence of quotas on number of transport rights granted.

Countries such as Denmark, Greece, Poland and Spain score better than most on both transport indicators, with regulations in place that lead to a more favorable enabling regulatory environments for transport operators (figure 7.1). They have transparent regulations and neither impose discriminatory criteria to obtain a license nor interfere with freight allocation and price setting—making it easier for foreign transport operators to enter and operate in the domestic market.

Countries that score poorly often struggle with the trade-off between the need for a more formal and professional sector and the availability of administrative and institutional resources. Transport regulators seek to promote the sector's professionalization by establishing quality standards and other requirements for obtaining a license. But limited enforcement and institutional capacity hinders progress. Low-income countries tend to have regulations with lower quality standards for operator licenses and more price-setting and freight allocation mechanisms, hurting their transport indicator scores. But some low-income countries perform better than

others—especially in cross border transport. For example, Kenya and Uganda are more open to foreign competition than Cambodia and Ethiopia.

Low-income countries have weaker regulations for cross-border transportation because they often grant fewer transport rights to trucking companies from their main neighboring trading partner, limiting foreign transport operators in the domestic market. But some countries are leveraging regional integration to gradually harmonize regional transport regulations and ease cross-border trade. Although Tanzania's transport license regulations restrict foreign transport operators, they allow transport companies from other East African Community (EAC) countries to offer more services.

Company road transport licensing promotes better transport operations

Introducing and enforcing quality criteria to enter the transport sector

should be a key objective of any transport regulation.[7] Regulation affects the competition and efficiency of transport services, as well as their availability, reliability and safety.[8] Competition improves service quality and lowers transport prices,[9] but imperfect competition accounts for 35% of national transport costs in Central America.[10] Lower prices and reliable services increase the profit margin for farmers, which they can reinvest in other production-related activities.

Company licenses promote more formal and professional transport sectors by regulating access to the profession, setting standards for transport operations, collecting revenue based on business profits, compiling more detailed data on the trucking industry and facilitating the enforcement of labor regulations (box 7.1).

They provide a level playing field to promote competition based on common criteria. They also ease establishing and enforcing certain minimum

FIGURE 7.1 High-income countries tend to have more regulations that promote market access and operations and cross-border transport

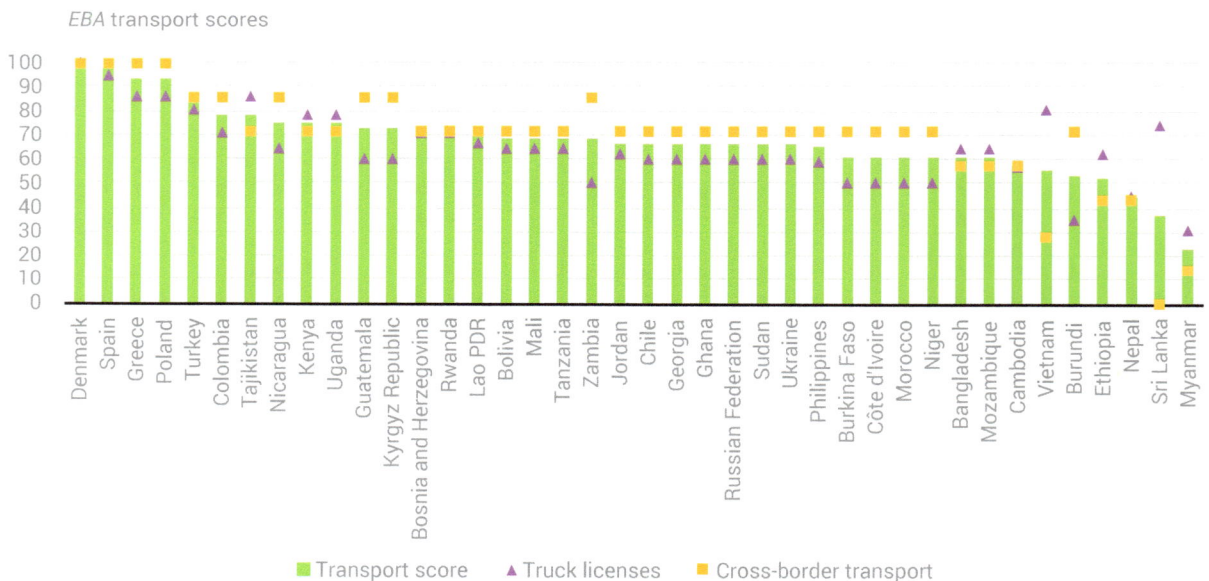

Source: EBA database.

Note: The EBA transport aggregate ranking is constructed by combining two subindicators: truck licenses and cross-border transport.

BOX 7.1 Good practices for road transport licensing systems

- Should require licenses to access the sector and provide truck services to establish minimum conditions and requirements such as technical inspection certificates.

- Should not include discriminatory requirements for licenses, such as nationality, membership in a trucking organization and minimum operational capacity.

- Should establish quality criteria such as good repute, financial standing and professional competence to obtain a transport license, preferably by implementing a company-level license.

- Should make licensing requirements transparent and accessible and collect and update road transport data.

- Should promote market-based price-setting mechanisms and freight allocation systems.

quality standards more than truck licenses,[11] which can be appropriate regulatory instruments to set basic trucking service standards, especially in more informal markets.

Licenses are also crucial to guarantee certain safety standards since trucking involves heavy and sophisticated machinery requiring training and regular maintenance.

Of the 40 countries measured, 12 require a company license only, 16 require a truck license only, 4 require both company and truck licenses and 8 require no company or truck licenses.

Company licenses are prevalent in OECD high-income countries, and truck licenses are mostly seen in Sub-Saharan Africa. Most countries in Europe and Central Asia do not require either a company or a truck license for domestic operations (figure 7.2).

High-income countries have the largest share of company-license regimes. Such licensing trends suggest that transitioning toward a company-license regime is not an easy task. Such systems may imply other regulatory reforms, such as labor law reforms that set standards for the access to the profession of licensed drivers or corporate tax code reforms associated with a company license. Another challenge for lower-income countries is the cost of investing in the enforcement of higher and more complex quality standards. But some low-income countries—such as Rwanda and Ethiopia—have company-license systems.

FIGURE 7.2 Transport license systems vary across regions

Share of total countries

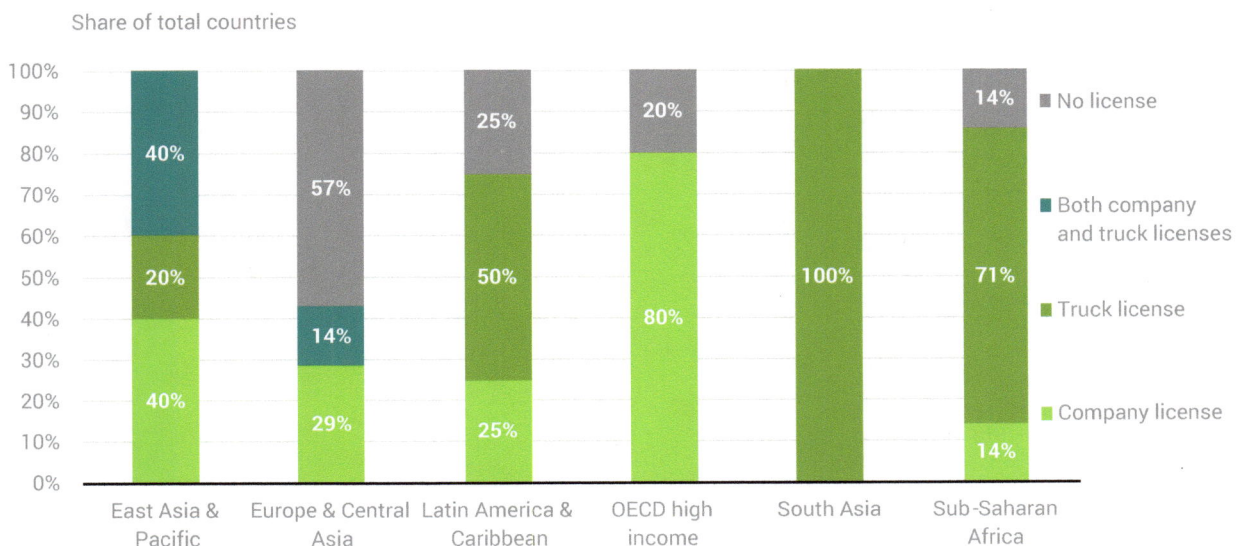

Source: EBA database.

Note: The Middle East and North Africa is excluded from the sample as *EBA* does not cover a representative number of countries (only Jordan and Morocco).

Online availability of transport regulations and license applications is not widespread

Transparency and information are crucial to enable citizens to monitor the quality of government services.[12] Accessing and understanding the requirements for a license ensures a predictable business environment for transport operators. It also enables them to demand better regulatory quality and reduces potential for discretionary practices by public officials. Evidence from the Asia-Pacific Economic Cooperation (APEC) suggests that increasing the transparency of transaction costs could raise intra-APEC trade by 7.5%.[13]

In many countries transport regulations are not easily accessible, evident in the number of countries still not publishing their transport regulations on government websites. And of the 24 countries publishing licensing requirements online, only 5 offer applicants an online platform to submit their license applications. Despite the costs and resources to set up such platforms, they can make licensing easy and accessible for applicants far from an application office. Greater transparency is also associated with less discrimination in entry. Countries that do not impose discriminatory requirements to obtain a license—such as nationality, mandatory association membership and minimum operational capacity criteria—also have the most transparency.[14]

Company licenses set higher standards for truck operators at no significantly higher cost

Transport regulations that strike the right balance between ensuring enforcement of essential safety and quality standards and avoiding excessive regulatory burdens for transport operators can lead to both better transport services and lower costs. Professional standards and certification for logistics service providers are important parts of an effective logistics sector. But quantitative and economic regulations of transport services that do not have an explicit and objective justification should be cut.[15]

Obtaining a company license takes longer than in other licensing systems such

as truck regimes.[16] But company licenses must comply with a wider number of technical and qualitative prerequisites such as applicant's proof of good repute, financial capacity, professional competence, operational capacity and fulfillment of tax obligations. So processing time in company systems tends to be longer than in truck systems—where technical and qualitative prerequisites are more limited (figure 7.3).

Countries with company-license systems record higher absolute costs than countries with truck-license systems. But relatively, company licenses are only slightly costlier than truck licenses (figure 7.4). And given that company licenses are valid longer than truck licenses, their yearly cost is considerably lower. Company-license systems strike a good balance between the standards of quality established and the efficiency of the issuance procedure.

FIGURE 7.3 Truck-level licenses are issued more expeditiously than other regulated systems

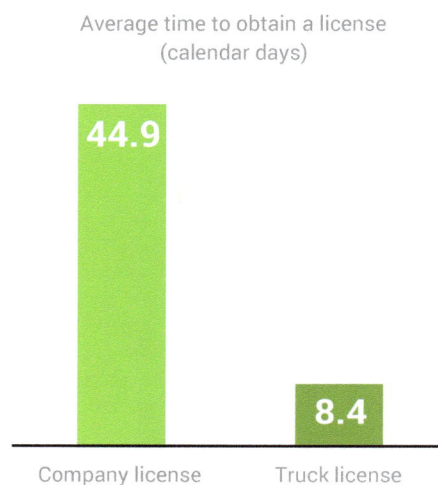

Average time to obtain a license
(calendar days)

Company license	44.9
Truck license	8.4

Source: EBA database.

FIGURE 7.4 Company licenses are more cost-effective than other licensing systems

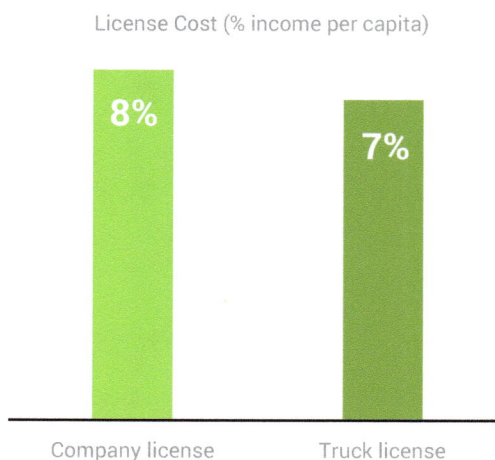

License Cost (% income per capita)

Company license	8%
Truck license	7%

Source: EBA database.

Linking Logistics Performance Index (LPI) data with *EBA* transport licensing categories reveals that countries with company-license systems record greater transport service satisfaction (as measured by perceptions of freight forwarders on the competence and quality of service provided by road transport service providers) than countries with other licensing systems (figure 7.5).[17] Truck licenses record the lowest satisfaction rates of any licensing regime (as measured by the percentage of respondents reporting high satisfaction), supporting the assumption that market entry quality criteria in company-license systems improve the professionalism of road transport operators.

The costs of technical inspections vary across countries

One of the key obstacles to an efficient road transport sector is the condition of vehicles, especially trucks. Trucks in poor condition lead to unreliable services and high operating costs from breakdowns and repair work. This affects road safety and the environment—for example, through higher emissions. For users of road transport services, reliable services

are important. Post-harvest losses due to transport conditions or accidents can cause a significant loss of income for farmers. To improve road safety and reliability of services, countries need an efficient system of technical inspections. Regular inspections can ensure that vehicles in operation are properly maintained to ensure their safety and durability.[18] Frequent and systematic vehicle tests make roads safer and reduce the number of accidents.[19]

Regular inspections are mandatory in all countries except Georgia, where technical inspections will become mandatory only in 2017. And in high-income countries such as EU members, the regulator monitors the quality of the technical inspection by introducing minimum standards and certifying centers that ensure compliance with the requirements. But in countries without such regulations, the technical inspection quality relies on each service provider, so the risk of a low-quality inspection is higher.

The average cost of a (first-time) technical inspection is 2.9% of income per capita, ranging between 0.1 and 13.9% (figure 7.6), and thus is not a constraining factor in most countries. But in

low-income countries it costs more of income per capita than in high-income countries. The average time to obtain a technical inspection certificate (a few hours) and the average validity of these certificates (six months) are similar across the 40 countries.

Few countries are truly open to international competition coming from their largest trading partner

Harmonizing and liberalizing regional road transport services exposes national service providers to wider regional competition. And that can lead to lower transport tariffs, higher efficiency and higher transport quality.[20] *EBA* transport indicators measure the number of transport rights granted to truck companies registered in the largest neighboring agricultural trading partner (box 7.2 and figure 7.7).

Additional transport rights denote an increased freedom of movements and operations allowed to foreign firms willing to do business in the domestic market. In spite of the efforts to facilitate cross-border transport, there is a wide disparity in actual openness to cross-border

FIGURE 7.5 Company-license systems record greater user satisfaction

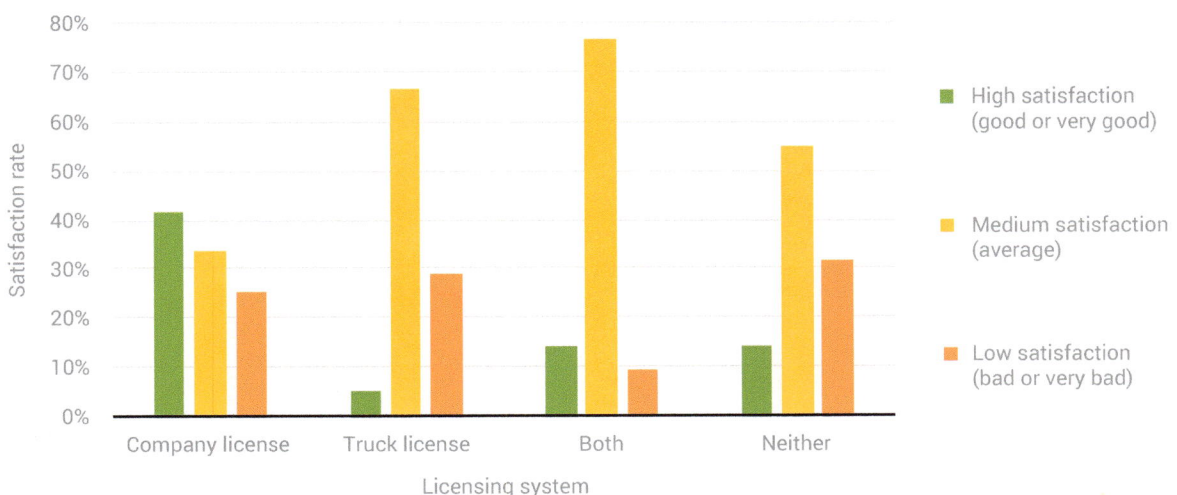

Sources: EBA database, LPI database.

Note: Graph developed based on question 19-1 of the 2014 LPI Survey. The LPI collects data in 33 of the 40 *EBA* countries.

FIGURE 7.6 The cost of technical inspection is not a constraint in most countries, but some disparity is observed in its relative cost

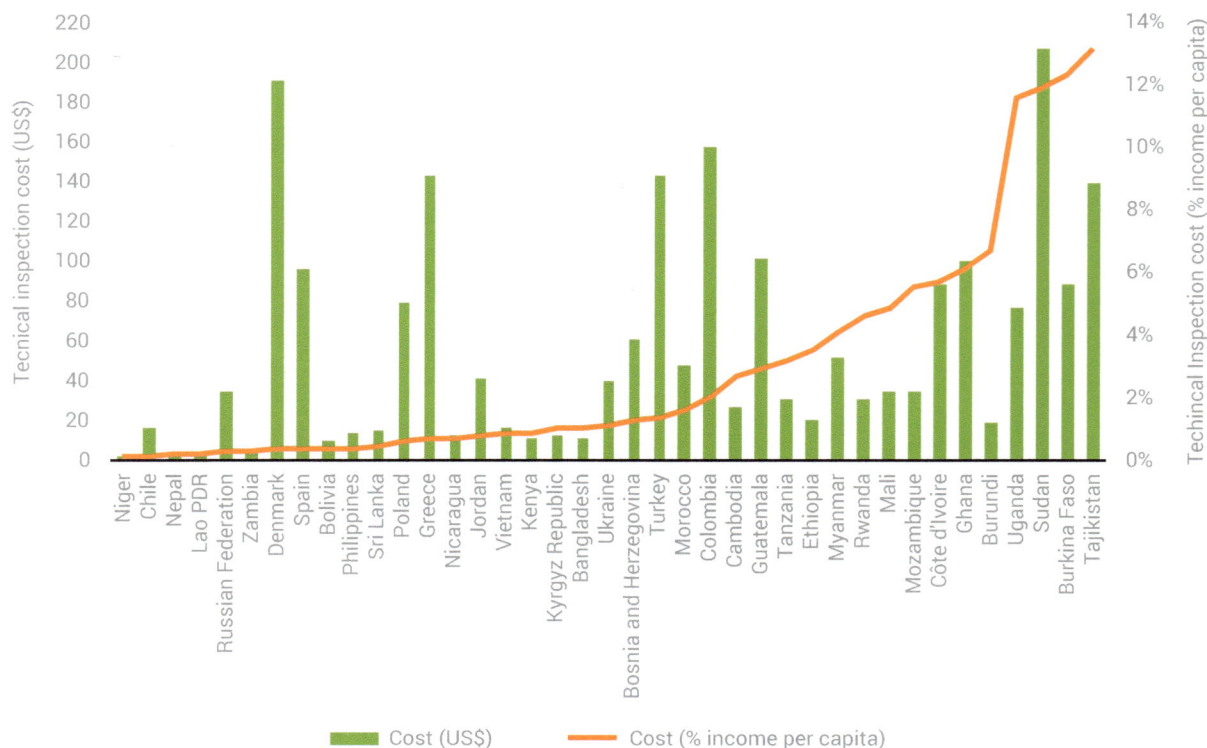

Source: EBA database.

Note: Regular vehicle inspections are mandatory in all countries except Georgia, where technical inspections will only become mandatory in 2017.

competition. Only four countries (Denmark, Greece, Poland and Spain) grant foreign companies the same transport entitlements as they do to domestic firms, and even in such cases there are limitations (figure 7.7).[21] But when granting transport rights to foreign companies governments should make sure that foreign trucks and transport firms comply with the same standards required to domestic operators. Only in such a way will licenses maintain minimum safety and quality service standards and provide a level playing field for competition.

The East African Community promotes cross-border transport openness by harmonizing standards on road transportation and standardizing license requirements. A larger market and greater competition benefit local producers by improving the quality and cutting the

price of transport services, prompting more producers to participate in regional value chains.

Regulations in the EU countries measured (Denmark, Greece, Spain and Poland) demonstrate greater openness to competition from truck operators from their largest neighboring agricultural trading partner as they grant on average all five transport rights measured by *EBA*. South Asia (Bangladesh, Nepal and Sri Lanka) is the least open region with an average of 1.3 rights granted (figure 7.8). Basic transport rights are granted in 38 of the 40 countries surveyed, except Myanmar and Sri Lanka.[22] But 18 countries have a quota on the number of permits granted. More open transport increases trade, as shown by the correlation between merchandise exports and regional liberalization as measured by the cross-border

transport indicator.[23] Granting foreign companies access to the domestic market—for example, by allowing importing and backhauling—increases cross-border trade and competition. But many obstacles to cross-border transport result from a lack of harmonization or lack of mutual recognition of a variety of technical standards, such as axle-load limits, truck dimensions and driver's licenses. So, bilateral and multilateral agreements granting transport rights should also address the harmonization and mutual recognition of transport standards that hinder cross-border transport. Public access to the respective information on transport rights and applied transport standards should be a fundamental part of harmonization.

Greater regional integration and easier trade and transit practices reduce entry

BOX 7.2 Transport rights definitions

- Transport rights: A truck registered in country A is allowed to transport goods produced in its country to country B for sale.

- Backhauling rights: A truck registered in country A is allowed to load goods in country B and transport them back to Country A.

- Transit rights: A truck registered in country A is allowed to travel through country B to deliver goods in country C.

- Triangular rights: A truck registered in country A is allowed to pick up goods in country B and transport them to country C.

- Cabotage rights: A truck registered in country A is allowed to pick up goods in country B and transport them to a different point in country B.

FIGURE 7.7 Only a few countries allow cabotage

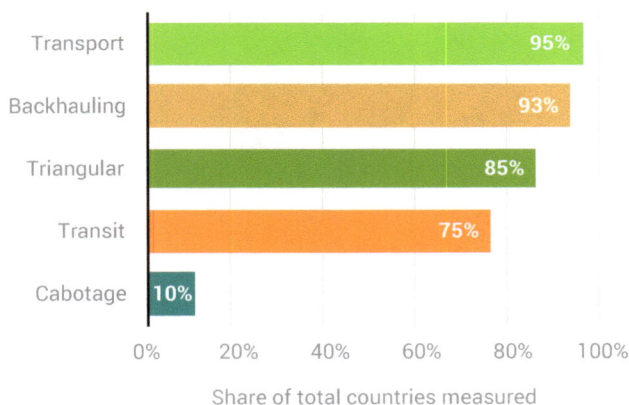

Share of total countries measured

Source: EBA database.

Note: Transport rights are entitlements granted by domestic transport authorities to trucking companies registered in the largest neighboring agricultural trading partner. For this study, transport rights are categorized along five basic rights or freedoms. Cabotage rights imply that foreign companies are granted treatment similar to domestic truck companies. Cabotage rights are only allowed in Denmark, Greece, Poland and Spain.

costs for transport service operators in landlocked countries.[24] So, achieving efficient cross border transport by reducing transit times and transport costs is another major objective for regional economic communities.[25] OECD countries that are also EU members are the only countries that allow cabotage, which the European Commission labels a free market essential. Allowing cabotage rights and optimizing capacity can improve efficiency and reduce environmental damage.[26]

Some regional economic communities also require contracting parties engaged in international transactions to sign a document acknowledging carrier liabilities or a waybill, as in ECOWAS and the European Union. Farmers can use such transport documents to claim losses from transport.

Conclusion

Improving access to reliable and affordable transport for agricultural producers is key to developing and strengthen a country's agricultural sector. There is still plenty of room for countries to improve their laws and regulations and move towards good practices identified, such as:

- **Strong licensing systems to access the road transport sector based on minimum requirements such as vehicle technical inspection certificates.** Tanzania's 2012 'Goods carrying vehicle' regulations establish clear binding principles to obtain and maintain a truck license, including valid vehicle registration cards, vehicle third-party liability insurance, vehicle inspection report from an authorized inspector or copy of employment contract between the driver and the licensee.

- **Eliminate discriminatory requirements to obtain road transport licenses, such as a certain nationality, membership in a trucking organization and minimum operational capacity.** Through its 2003

FIGURE 7.8 Regulations in OECD high-income countries demonstrate greater openness to cross-border competition, while countries in South Asia and East Asia and the Pacific tend to limit the scope of operations for foreign firms

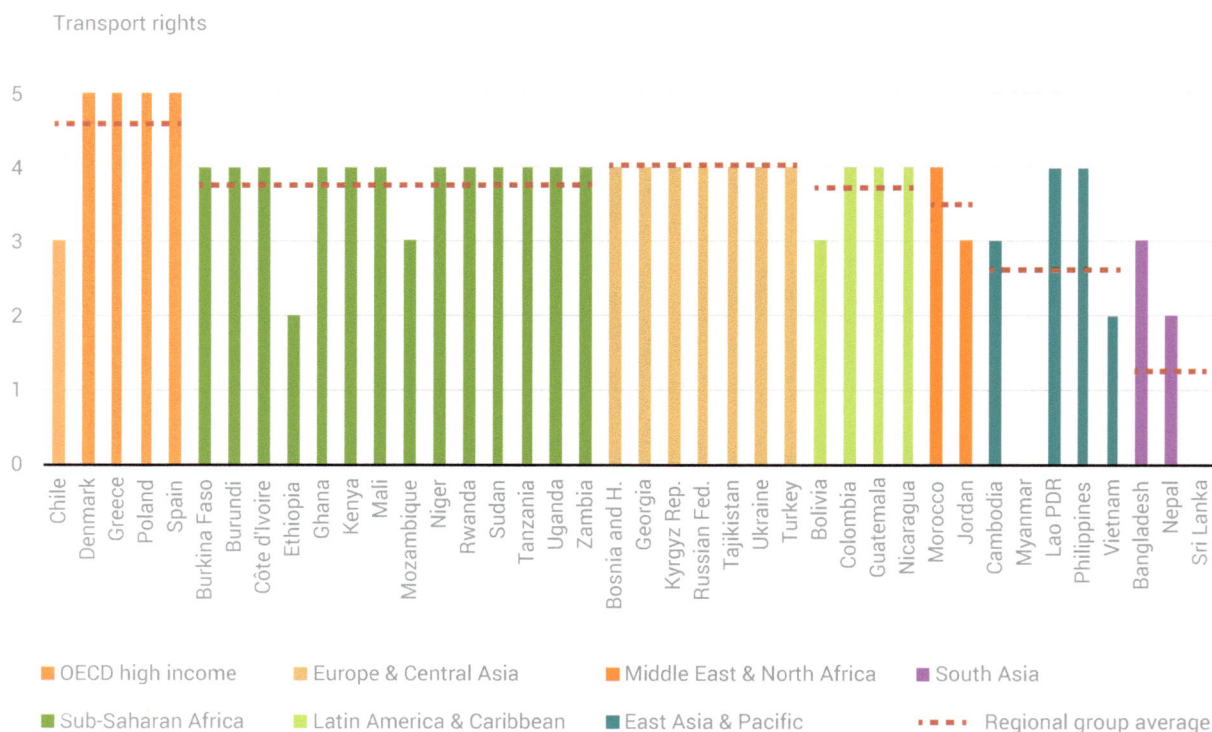

Transport rights

Legend:
- OECD high income
- Europe & Central Asia
- Middle East & North Africa
- South Asia
- Sub-Saharan Africa
- Latin America & Caribbean
- East Asia & Pacific
- Regional group average

Source: EBA database.

decree regulating merchandise road public transport, Morocco ensures any citizen with a nationally-constituted company can offer trucking services, ruling out the necessity to be a member of a transport association or to have a minimum fleet size.

- **Establish company licenses that enforce qualitative criteria such as good repute, financial standing and professional competence.** In 2014 Turkey reformed their transport regulations to create K1-type licenses requiring operators to provide proof of minimal working capital ($3,500), maximum fleet age (20 years) and national certification for managers.

- **Make licensing requirements more transparent and accessible, and collect and update road transport statistics.** Colombia's Ministry

of Transport consolidates all laws, regulations, directives, decrees, notifications or resolutions pertaining to road transport and makes them easily accessible on their governmental website.

- **Promote market-based price-setting mechanisms and freight allocation systems.** Nicaragua's 2005 'General road transport law' provides a solid legal foundation to guarantee that the conditions of carriage including pricing and cargo quantities are solely determined by the contracting parties without any external interference.

Reforming laws and regulations is a challenge for policymakers given the complexity of the transport sector. Identifying good regulatory practices is difficult when dealing with agricultural transport because besides ensuring efficiency,

laws and regulations are also needed to protect clients, consumers and the environment from unsafe, unreliable and polluting transport. The transport topic identifies and measures several key regulatory constraints that can hinder farmers and agribusiness firms from reaping the benefits of growing urban and rural markets in which to sale their production. These actionable indicators can be used as a starting point for discussion with policymakers on ways to address regulatory constraints that might obstruct efficient and quality transport for agricultural producers, buyers and exporters.

Notes

1.　Staatz and Dembélé 2007.

2.　Lema and others 2008.

3.　World Bank 2010.

4. World Bank 2010.

5. World Bank 2010.

6. Araya, Pachón and Saslavsky 2012.

7. International Road Transport Union 2007.

8. Lema, de Veen and Abukari 2008.

9. Teravaninthorn and Raballand 2009.

10. Osborne, Pachon and Araya 2014.

11. *Company license*: Specific licenses granted to established companies to legally offer domestic road transport services. For the purposes of this study general business registration licenses are not considered. Instead, a company-level license is a specific permit required exclusively for the provision of road transport services. A transport license at company level generally allows to operate several trucks under the same license. *Truck license*: Truck licenses are licenses granted to each truck to legally transport goods in the domestic market. For the purposes of this study vehicle registration certificates or road worthiness/technical inspection certificates are not considered, as these are usually not specific to the provision of road transport services.

12. Geginat and Saltane 2014.

13. Helble and others 2007.

14. Data analysis demonstrates a moderate positive correlation (0.27) between transparency (defined in this analysis by the scores obtained to the questions: "Are the license/permit requirements publicly available online?" and "Can the application for a license/permit or its renewal be submitted electronically?" Each country is ranked high, medium or low based on their scores in both questions) and additional requirements considered as discriminatory (mandatory association membership, minimum operational capacity or nationality criteria). This correlation is 5% significant when controlling for income per capita.

15. World Bank 2010; This is known as the 'regulatory guillotine' concept, in which all regulations affecting a certain sector or transaction are publicly listed and then automatically rescinded if an explicit justification for the regulation is not provided within a certain time frame. The 'economic regulations' mentioned in this context by the World Bank's Trade and Transportation Facilitation Assessment toolkit would include issues such as transportation price controls, quantitative limits on the provision of trucking services and so on.

16. *Company license*: Specific licenses granted to established companies to legally offer domestic road transport services. For the purposes of this study general business registration licenses are not considered. Instead, a company-level license is a specific permit required exclusively for the provision of road transport services. A transport license at company level generally allows to operate several trucks under the same license. *Truck-level license*: Truck-level licenses are licenses granted to each truck to legally transport goods in the domestic market. For the purposes of this study vehicle registration certificates or road worthiness/technical inspection certificates are not considered, as these are usually not specific to the provision of road transport services.

17. The LPI is a World Bank project published every two years since 2007 and measuring logistics performance or the on-the-ground efficiency of trade supply chains. The 2014 edition covers 160 countries and compiles information from approximately 1,000 respondents, providing a total of around 5,000 country assessments (website: http://lpi.worldbank.org/).

18. IRU 2011.

19. Cuerden, Edwards and Pittman 2011.

20. Raballand, Kunaka and Giersing 2008.

21. Granting cabotage rights to truck companies coming from the largest agricultural neighboring trading partner is equivalent to giving foreign transport firms national treatment with regard to transport operational freedom.

22. Sri Lanka transports goods internationally mostly by air or water.

23. *EBA* cross-border transport indicators measure the number of transport rights granted to the largest neighboring agricultural trading partner, including mandatory carrier's liabilities documents.

24. World Bank 2014.

25. Runji 2015.

26. European Commission 2006.

References

Araya, G., M. C. Pachón and D. Saslavsky 2012. "Road Freight in Central America: Five Explanations to High Costs of Service Provision." Background Paper, World Bank, Washington, DC.

Cuerden, R., M.J. Edwards and M.B. Pittman. 2011. "Effect of Vehicle Defects in Road Accidents." Transport Research Laboratory Limited. Published Project Report PPR565.

European Commission. 2006. *Road Transport Policy: Open Roads across Europe*. Brussels: European Commission.

Geginat, C., and V. Saltane. 2014. "Transparent Government and Business Regulation Open for Business?" Policy Research Working Paper 7132, World Bank, Washington, DC.

Helble, M., B. Shepherd and J. S. Wilson. 2007. "Transparency, Trade Costs, and Regional Integration in the Asia Pacific." Policy Research Working Paper 4401, World Bank, Washington, DC.

International Road Transport Union. 2007. "IRU Position on Access to the Profession of Road Passenger and

Goods Transport Operator." Position Paper, IRU, Geneva.

Lema, C., J. de Veen and M. Abukari. 2008. "Comprehensive Review of IFAD Rural Roads, Travel and Transport (RTT) Experiences, 1994–2007." International Fund for Agricultural Development.

Osborne, T., M. C. Pachón and G. E. Araya. 2014. "What Drives the High Price of Road Freight Transport in Central America?" Policy Research Working Paper 6844, World Bank, Washington, DC.

Raballand, G., C. Kunaka and B. Giersing. 2008. "The Impact of Regional Liberalization and Harmonization in Road Transport Services: A Focus on Zambia and Lessons for Landlocked Countries." Policy Research Working Paper 4482, World Bank, Washington, DC.

Runji, J. 2015. "Africa Transport Policy Performance Review: The Need for More Robust Transport Policies." Sub-Saharan Africa Transport Policy Program Discussion Paper 103, World Bank, Washington, DC.

Staatz, J., and N. Dembélé. 2007. "Agriculture for Development in Sub-Saharan Africa." Background Paper for the World Development Report 2008.

Teravaninthorn, S., and G. Raballand. 2009. "Transport Prices and Costs in Africa: A Review of the International Corridors." Policy Research Working Paper 46181, World Bank, Washington, DC.

World Bank. 2010. *Trade and Transport Facilitation Assessment: A Practical Toolkit for Country Implementation.* Washington, DC: World Bank.

———. 2014. "Improving Trade and Transport for Landlocked Developing Countries: A Ten-Year Review." World Bank–United Nations report in preparation for the 2nd United Nations Conference on Landlocked Developing Countries (LLDCs).

8. *EBA* TOPICS UNDER DEVELOPMENT

In this second year of the *EBA* project, some topics have been refined and restructured and several new topic areas added. The information and communication technology (ICT) topic area was piloted during the first year of the *EBA* project and restructured this year to include data about policies and regulations on mobile and internet services. The land topic was expanded to include new areas on tenure security, land sales and lease markets. Given the nature of the land topic and the legitimate interests involved, further consultations will be carried out and some new areas could be included next year, such as the cost of registering group rights, the time and cost of land surveying process, the procedural safeguards in case of expropriation and the management of land records. These developments will contribute to a more balanced scoring methodology.[1]

Two new topic areas were developed this year: water and livestock. Water is an essential input to agricultural production, and the security and proper management of water rights is essential to a well-functioning agricultural sector. Livestock is another area where governments design regulations to ensure the supply, safety and quality of animal production inputs. A scoring methodology for these two topic areas will be developed in the next *EBA* cycle.

Two cross-cutting themes were introduced and analyzed this year—gender and environmental sustainability. The gender analysis presented below shows how the data collected on several relevant indicators can be interpreted through the lens of gender. The environmental sustainability theme crosses several existing topics—mainly seed and water—to assess practices that protect natural resources for agricultural production.

Information and communication technology

Mobile phones and the internet are powerful tools for farmers today. When connecting to the internet from remote areas, farmers can access key resources such as real-time data on market and transport prices, information on seed varieties, pests and farming techniques as well as several tools for production and marketing. Better information and communication technologies facilitate farmers' access to markets, particularly to improved seed varieties and fertilizers.[2] So, many governments now disseminate information and provide extension services in rural areas using the internet, mobile applications and text and voice services, alongside more traditional channels of communication such as the radio and extension agents.

This multifaceted approach gives policymakers an opportunity to interact with the farming community and develop more targeted regulatory and policy interventions for agribusinesses. Appropriately designed ICT regulations can ensure market liberalization and competition in the ICT sector, leading to fair retail prices, more high-quality mobile services and greater mobile market penetration.[3] By contrast, burdensome licensing requirements can hinder competition and innovative mobile services solutions responsive to users' needs.

EBA ICT indicators measure laws, regulations and policies addressing ICT services in rural areas. The indicators focus on the institutional framework for service providers to operate and expand mobile networks and government strategies to improve farmers' access to ICT services and agricultural information.

- **Licensing regimes in the ICT sector.** These data measure countries' ICT licensing framework, validity and associated costs. The data also cover spectrum management, retail price regulations and quality standards, with a particular emphasis on standards in rural areas.

- **Government strategies to improve access to ICT services in rural areas.** These data describe government policies and measures to facilitate ICT in rural areas, including universal access and service funds, which use contributions from multiple sources to finance the expansion of network coverage and mobile services.

- **Agricultural e-extension services.** These data address how the government provides agricultural information, particularly on market prices and weather.

Licensing regimes in the ICT sector. Licenses are an effective tool for governments—not only to regulate competition and generate revenue, but also to define the obligations of market players on matters relevant to farmers and agribusinesses, such as rural coverage. Obtaining a license to offer telecommunication services is costly and may obstruct entry for mobile operators. *EBA* data on ICT collected this year show how licensing regimes vary among the 40 *EBA* countries. Individual licenses are most prevalent.[4] Only 7 countries have implemented a general authorization regime for mobile cellular services.[5] Compared with other licensing regimes, the general authorization regime has greater transparency and competition, as well as lower costs, since it creates a level playing field among providers and simplifies the regulatory process.[6] In all 7 countries costs are publicly available online.

Government strategies to improve access to ICT services in rural areas. The "last mile" of telecommunication infrastructure in rural areas is usually expensive, and the resulting benefits do not always make up for the costs.[7] Governments differ in how they address this. The solutions include tying coverage and quality requirements to licenses, offering tax breaks to providers that cover hard-to-reach areas, requiring mobile operators to offer social tariffs to eligible customers in rural areas and setting up universal access funds for infrastructure or other outreach projects.

Universal access funds are popular in developing countries since they generate funds from multiple sources, including contributions from mobile operators and international organizations, as well as direct funds from the government budget.[8] They help expand ICT coverage in otherwise commercially unviable areas.[9] But establishing the funds, collecting contributions, selecting projects, disbursing funds and monitoring and evaluating the impact of projects require capable administrators and transparent organizational structures.[10] Of the 40 countries studied, 24 have a universal access fund that has started collecting funds. Despite having a universal access fund in place, 4 countries (Bangladesh, Burkina Faso, Kenya and Niger) have never disbursed funds for ICT projects.

Agricultural e-extension services. Information asymmetries between participants in agricultural value chains can impede farmers' access to markets, especially in developing countries.[11] Access to information enables farmers to participate in value chains, scale up production and increase revenues.[12] E-extension services can address the information deficit farmers face in remote areas and empower them to engage more in agricultural production and marketing. In 22 of the countries studied, governments provide agricultural e-extension services, mainly for market prices and weather.

Land

Access to agricultural land and the legal and regulatory regimes underpinning that access are fundamental to economic

development.[13] Land is a key factor of agricultural production, and for many rural families it is the most valuable asset they possess. But in many countries the vast majority of agricultural land lies outside formal legal protection.[14] To encourage investments that can increase productivity, rights to land must be secure and transferable. Indeed, landowners will be willing to invest more to improve production, such as "planting perennials and establishing irrigation,"[15] when they believe their land will be protected from conflicting claims and expropriation.[16]

Security of tenure can be guaranteed through formal mechanisms, such as state-granted titles and state-backed legal enforcement. It can also be guaranteed through community-administered customary tenure, where the state recognizes customary rights as legitimate and protects them.[17] Legal frameworks must recognize all legitimate land rights (including informal and customary rights where applicable), enable their recordation and ensure their protection.[18] Customary land tenure continues to play a large role in agricultural production in many countries and statutory recognition of customary land tenure regimes can help protect agricultural producers from conflicting claims to customary land and government expropriation.[19] This is important as population growth, increased international investment and volatile commodity markets contribute to the scarcity of productive agricultural land, especially in Sub-Saharan Africa.[20]

Secure, transferable tenure enables the use of agricultural land as collateral, which can increase access to credit and agricultural investment.[21] Where markets operate smoothly, land transfers (through sale or lease) can operate to allocate land efficiently.[22] This is critical for skilled farmers seeking to expand and invest in more intensive production and for those seeking to exit farming to be able to invest the value of their land in other economic sectors.

EBA land indicators measure the rights of individuals and firms to register, use and transfer agricultural land and the administration of the procedures that give effect to these rights. Security of tenure[23] and transferability of rights[24] are important for increasing agricultural

productivity for different market actors at different levels of economic development. The administrative mechanisms that guide them must be transparent and easily navigable.[25]

- **Land tenure security.** These data include information on the types of land tenure granted by countries (private or public ownership), the formalization of informal rights of individuals and communities and the security that land registration provides.

- **Land sales and lease markets.** Impediments to transferring land and registering such transfers (whether leases or sales) reduce the likelihood of efficiency-enhancing exchanges. These data address how land sale and lease markets function, including government restrictions on land sales such as price controls, land ownership ceilings, minimum farm sizes and other restrictions on the ability of individuals and companies to buy, sell or lease land.

Land tenure security. Of the 40 countries surveyed, 32 recognize private ownership of land. In the remaining 8 countries all land is owned by the state, but the government allows for long-term leases or land use rights. The difference between the two is blurred by because not all leases are based on market rates and land use rights often come with an annual fee. Five of these 8 allow for perpetual land rights of some form: Ethiopia, Mozambique,[26] Myanmar, Lao PDR and Tajikistan. Of the remaining 3, Vietnam provides for use rights of up to 50 years (or 70 years for larger investments) and Tanzania[27] and Zambia both allow use rights of up to 99 years. Thirty-nine of 40 countries allow for land rights to be used as collateral for accessing credit.[28] In Ethiopia, while holders of perpetual use rights cannot mortgage them, those holding leases to land use rights can use them as collateral. In Zambia, too, leaseholders can use their lease rights as collateral.

First-time registration of informally held land rights is important to ensure land tenure security, particularly in developing countries. Thirty-one countries allow individuals to register agricultural land rights for the first time based solely on open, exclusive and notorious possession of the land.[29] Six countries in the study allow for registration of land use rights after possession for a statutorily stated period, even though they do not recognize private ownership. Of the 40 countries surveyed, 24 allow for the first-time registration of customary rights including 13 of 14 Sub-Saharan African countries. Three countries (Denmark, the Kyrgyz Republic and Rwanda) have registered all privately held land plots at the immovable property registry, and the first-time registration process is no longer applicable.[30]

Countries adopt different ways of addressing first time registrations of land rights, but the processes can generally be classified as either judicial or administrative, depending on which type of body does the formalization. Chile has both a judicial and an administrative process depending on the value of the land. The cost of first-time registration also follows one of two general regimes —a flat rate or a percentage of the land's value. Some countries have both. While collecting taxes is important, it can discourage the formalization of informal rights if it exceeds the actual cost of land registration.

Land sales and lease markets. Private ownership of land is not a requirement for land markets to operate efficiently. In 39 of 40 countries those who hold rights to agricultural land can lease those rights to other agricultural producers. For the 8 countries without private land ownership, 3 (Myanmar, Lao PDR and Tajikistan) allow buying and selling perpetual use rights. In Tanzania, Vietnam and Zambia no perpetual rights exist—only long-term use rights or leases, which can be subleased. In Ethiopia perpetual use rights exist but cannot be sold, though they can be leased for up to 15 years if the lessee engages in "mechanized agriculture." In Mozambique the constitution prohibits any dispossession of land whether sale, lease or mortgage. Although private property ownership is allowed in Ukraine, there has been a moratorium on sales of agricultural land since 2004.

Governments often restrict the sale and lease of land. Nineteen countries impose at least one restriction on the sale of land (minimum size of subdivision, maximum number of hectares, setting minimum or maximum prices) and 7 countries impose at least two of them. And 17 countries restrict registration to leases spanning a minimum number of years.

Water

Access to irrigation water is directly connected to the success of farmers and agribusinesses: a sufficient and stable water supply can lead to larger crop yields and more reliable production patterns. The highest crop yields from irrigation are more than twice those from rainfed agriculture, and the use of irrigation can increase crop yields by 100–400%.[31] Irrigation systems are thus critical to meeting the increasing global demand for food.[32]

Access to irrigation water can be constrained by its depletion and pollution. Insufficient or inappropriate regulation can also lead to the mismanagement of water resources and hamper access to irrigation water for both small and large agricultural producers.[33] For example, if legal rights surrounding the use of water are insecure, agribusinesses could reduce or forgo investments because of concerns that water supplies will be unreliable or insufficient to meet production targets. Similarly, the absence of decentralized governance mechanisms— such as water user associations (WUAs) to manage irrigation infrastructure—may prevent some farmers from securing equitable access to water and limit their ability to voice grievances and resolve water-related disputes.

EBA water indicators measure the quality of laws and regulations that affect the ability of both small and large commercial farms to get access to adequate quantities of water at the times and places needed for crop production, through appropriate irrigation infrastructure and decentralized institutions.

- **Permits for water use.** Effective water use permit systems provide secure rights to water users and allow resource managers to ensure sufficient water supply for future crop cycles. These data measure the legal security of water use permit systems by examining public notification requirements, permit duration and compensation for curtailment of rights, the scope of application of the permit system that exempts small-scale agriculture and the system's efficiency and sustainability by examining pricing water as a resource.

- **Decentralized irrigation management.** Decentralized mechanisms for the governance of water resources and infrastructure, such as WUAs, can improve system efficiencies and allow farms to have a greater role in the decisions affecting their access to water.[34] These data measure the extent to which the legal framework enables WUAs to manage irrigation infrastructure, by granting them the authority to decide on water allocations, set and collect fees and monitor and enforce rules. They also measure WUA membership restrictions and whether WUAs are included in broader decisions on basin planning and water resource management.

Permits for water use. For commercial farms of all sizes the security of water rights affects farmers' decisions for investing, producing crops and locating commercial operations.[35] A water use permit system either recognizes existing water use rights or creates new water use rights. Of the countries studied 35 have a permit system for both surface water and groundwater use.[36] Only Jordan and the Kyrgyz Republic require the permit system only for groundwater, and 3 countries have no formal permit system for water use. Such legal gaps could send negative signals to investors and commercial farms about a higher risk in securing enough water for planned crop production operations. Almost half the *EBA* countries (19) have a statutory obligation for the authority issuing permits to publicly announce new permit applications for both surface water and groundwater use, enhancing transparency for existing and potential water users on the allocation of water resources. The transparency of a permit system contributes to the security of water rights by sharing information of interest to water users and reducing the potential for disputes.

A long duration for water use permits can also enhance the security of water use rights. In *EBA* countries the duration of water use permits varies from 2 years in Burundi to 75 years in Spain. The average duration is approximately 20 years for both surface water and groundwater. Across regions, OECD high-income countries had the longest average permit duration, and Sub-Saharan Africa the shortest. Farmers are more likely to make bigger investments with long duration permits. But governments need to balance that incentive with the need to conserve and protect water resources.[37] Fourteen countries—including Ghana, the Philippines and Turkey—have legislation that gives the granting agency discretion to determine the duration at the time of issuance. While this gives the resource manager flexibility to set permit durations based on resource planning needs, it could reduce predictability and thus increase investment risks for commercial farms.

A formal permit requirement, despite its benefits, can impose a large burden on smallholder farmers and granting agencies alike. Formal permit requirements are not appropriate for all water users in all contexts.[38] Some countries exempt some categories of small-scale water users from the obligation to obtain a permit, based on specific thresholds or defining characteristics,[39] such as the volume of water used, land area, intended water use, means of water extraction and recognized customary water rights. Twelve *EBA* countries have exemptions that can facilitate water access for small commercial farms using surface water (16 for groundwater).[40]

In response to water scarcity concerns and increasing demand, many countries impose fees on the use of water resources. An appropriate fee structure is often considered to allocate water efficiently and promote water conservation,[41] though the specific systems vary significantly across countries.[42] Twenty-eight *EBA* countries allow authorities to charge permit holders for surface water used (29 for groundwater).[43]

Decentralized irrigation management. In recent decades many countries have taken steps to decentralize the governance of water resources

and infrastructure, implementing local participatory management systems,[44] mainly through WUAs, which should be supported by a strong legal framework.[45] Five *EBA* countries have introduced full specific legislation on WUAs. Another 26 countries have specific provisions for WUAs in their laws and regulations for sectors such as water, irrigation and agricultural development. The remaining 9 countries have no specific legal recognition of WUAs, which are subject to the general framework for associations or cooperatives.

Among the 31 countries that have specific provisions or full legislation on WUAs, several features have to do with the establishment and internal organization of WUAs.[46] In 16 countries the law explicitly permits WUAs to establish, monitor and enforce their own rules in areas such as water use, fee payment and infrastructure maintenance. Also in 16 countries (a different set) the law permits WUAs to directly collect irrigation fees for infrastructure maintenance; in 12 of them fees are freely set by the WUA to cover expenses. This legal autonomy and cost recovery ensure that WUAs have sufficient capacity and powers to improve and maintain the infrastructure that brings water to commercial farms. Despite sharing the previously mentioned good practices, Spain and Tanzania exclude leaseholders and other land users that are not registered owners from membership.

Livestock

Livestock production accounts for up to 40% of global agriculture GDP, trending toward 50–60%.[47] Fueled by a surge in global demand, livestock production is growing faster than any other agricultural production.[48] Over the last 30 years population growth, urbanization and rising incomes have steadily increased global consumption of animal protein. For example, global consumption of meat increased from 30 kg per capita in 1980 to 40 kg per capita in 2005[49] and to 42.9 kg per capita in 2012.[50] The fastest growth in production and consumption has been in developing countries, particularly in Asia.[51]

Such a steady increase in global livestock consumption, production and

trade offers substantial market opportunities for actors in the livestock value chains, including input suppliers. This calls for direct support of policymakers in designing and implementing regulations. Laws and regulations addressing the development and conservation of genetic resources, the availability and quality of veterinary medicinal products and the supply of safe feed resources can ensure production efficiency and create an environment for high-quality input throughout the livestock production process.[52] Regulations that encourage the genetic improvement of livestock breeds that are more efficient at converting feed to body mass can increase productivity and reduce feed expenditures, cutting production costs.[53] In this respect, gene banks are important for conserving genetic material for current and future breeding activities.[54]

EBA livestock indicators measure the supply, safety and quality of animal production inputs. Data also focus on the existence and quality of such infrastructure as databases, gene banks and testing laboratories.

- **Livestock genetic resources.** Regulating livestock genetic resources facilitates breeding by encouraging farmers to select for specific traits while ensuring the conservation of local animal breeds. The data describe the legislative framework for breed improvement (such as genetic evaluation), registration of new breeds and recognition of breeder organizations. Data also cover functioning gene banks for conserving livestock genetic material.

- **Animal disease prevention and veterinary inputs.** Prevention and control of animal diseases and availability of quality livestock medicinal inputs are key to a sustainable commercial livestock sector. The data collected cover accessibility to national databases on livestock diseases and registration of veterinary medicinal products and veterinary vaccines.

- **Safety of animal feed resources.** Safe livestock feed increases animal productivity and improves animal health, thus reducing production costs for livestock producers and contributing to the safety of food of animal origin. The data cover the regulation of feed resources, including standards for the production, composition and safety of feed. They also cover labeling requirements for animal feed and the accreditation of feed testing laboratories.

Livestock genetic resources. Only 23 countries regulate breeding activities, and fewer than half have a comprehensive breeding law that covers breed improvement (genetic evaluation and performance testing), new breed registration (herd bookkeeping and pedigree certificate) and recognition of breeding organizations (registration and accreditation). Of the 40 countries surveyed only 17 have a gene bank with functioning cryogenic storage capacity. Of the 23 countries that do not have a gene bank, 18 are low-income or lower-middle-income countries. Bosnia and Herzegovina, Chile, Greece, Jordan and the Russia are the only high-income and upper-middle-income countries without a national gene bank.

Animal disease prevention and veterinary inputs. The cost associated for submitting an application package for registration and market authorization is low in Nepal, at only $2, while in Greece it is high, at $16,500.[55] The time regulators take to review such applications and issue a decision also varies greatly. In the Kyrgyz Republic it takes only 3 days for authorities to review a dossier and issue a decision, whereas in West African Economic and Monetary Union (UEMOA) countries it can take up to 400 days and in Tanzania 548 days.

Safety of animal feed resources. While most *EBA* countries regulate feed resources, coverage of different focus areas prescribed by international guidelines is limited. Of the 35 countries that regulate animal feed resources, only 15 address all four areas included in the Codex Alimentarius Code of Practice for Good Animal Feeding, while 33 address at least one of the four areas. Burundi, Ghana, Lao PDR, Rwanda and Uganda are the five countries that do not regulate animal feed resources.

Environmental sustainability

Mitigating the negative effects of agricultural production on natural resources, such as soil, water and plant resources, is one of the biggest challenges facing agriculture today. Not only are these resources required for sustaining production, but their careful maintenance is essential for global food production to match population growth. So regulations that facilitate increased agricultural production while adhering to environmental good practices can enable farmers around the world to produce more without depleting resources.

As a result of the Green Revolution, plant genetic diversity has declined among domesticated species since 1960, particularly the intraspecies diversity in farmers' fields and farming systems. The main cause of this genetic erosion is the increased use of improved seed varieties instead of more genetically diverse local varieties.[56] But the development of improved seed varieties relies on the use of genes found in local varieties and wild relatives of domesticated crops. Without the genes from these crop wild relatives (CWRs), many useful traits would not exist in today's improved seed varieties.[57]

Water is another natural resource crucial to sustainable agricultural production but under increasing pressure from intensified agricultural production and the associated pollution.[58] By 2030 there will be a deficit of 40% between expected water withdrawals and existing supplies, and this will reach 50% for a third of the world's population, mostly in developing countries. Adopting policies and legislation that address growing water scarcity is essential for agriculture, which takes 85% of water withdrawals in developing countries.

EBA environment indicators measure laws and regulations that safeguard the long-term availability and use of natural resources for agricultural production.

- **Conservation of plant genetic resources.** These data measure the regulations and institutions for conserving plant genetic resources. *Ex situ* conservation conserves plant genetic resources outside their natural habitats, while *in situ*

conservation[59] is mainly used for wild species, including CWRs in wild habitats.[60]

- **Sustainable use of plant genetic resources.** These data measure the regulations that either promote or inhibit the increased use of genetically diverse plants, the possibility of commercializing seeds of landraces,[61] and the rights granted to farmers over farm-saved seeds.

- **Access to plant genetic resources.** These data measure the rules of access applicable to germplasm held publicly by gene banks or by communities.

- **Regulation of agricultural activities.** These data measure whether good agricultural practices are promoted through such laws and regulations as promoting cover crops, siting livestock operations relative to water sources and creating buffer zones between agricultural lands and water sources.

- **Integrated water resource management.** These data measure whether water resources are managed in an integrated way at the watershed level or, for transboundary water management, through bilateral or multilateral structures.

- **Monitoring water resources.** These data measure the quantity and quality of water monitoring for both surface and groundwater. Specifically, the data report on water resource inventories and water quality standards.

Some interesting results were collected this year in 29 *EBA* countries[62] to set the foundation for further indicator developments next year.

Conservation of plant genetic resources. All 29 countries have a national plan for the conservation and sustainable use of biological diversity, including plant genetic diversity.[63] Among them, only 13 have established a national plant inventory specifically documenting landraces or crop wild relatives of cultivated plants. For *ex situ* conservation, all countries studied report having functioning gene banks or collection systems. But while all *EBA* countries in East Asia and the Pacific, Europe and Central Asia and Latin America and the Caribbean regions have gene banks set by law, only one-third of the Sub-Saharan countries and none of the South Asian and Middle Eastern and North African countries do.

Sustainable use of plant genetic resources.

Informal seed systems must be retained alongside formal seed systems, given the significant contribution of informal seed systems to genetic diversity and the ability of both to complement each other.[64] All countries have seed laws that focus predominantly on formal seed systems and most are silent on the production and commercialization of landraces. One exception is the European Directive 2008/62 (for the protection of crops threatened by genetic erosion and adapted to regional and local conditions), implemented by Denmark, Greece and Spain, which formally establishes specific procedures to market landraces. Twenty-one countries have laws that allow farmers to save and use harvested seeds of an improved variety. Uganda also allows the exchange of those seeds among farmers. And four countries allow those seeds to be saved, used, exchanged and sold.

Access to plant genetic resources.

Breeders and farmers often rely on genetic material found in other countries to develop new varieties, so genetic resources must be shared to sustain food production and overcome diseases and climate change. Globally 18 countries have a law that regulates access to plant genetic resources. In Latin America and the Caribbean access is subject to the issuance of a permit. In 7 *EBA* countries the conditions applicable to the issuance of those permits differ for national and foreign applicants. The International Treaty on Plant Genetic Resources for Food and Agriculture requires its members to facilitate access to crops identified as the most relevant to human consumption.[65] Twenty-two *EBA* countries are signatories, but only Jordan, Kenya, Morocco, Poland, Spain, Tanzania and Zambia have satisfied this specific requirement.

Regulation of agricultural activities.

Regulation or policy guidance on good agricultural practices can transform production methods and contribute to a more environmentally sustainable agriculture in the long term. Among *EBA* countries 10 have laws or policies providing for a minimum distance of separation between any livestock facility and nearby surface water bodies. Sixteen address the establishment of buffer zones adjacent to agricultural land to prevent nutrient run-off into surface water bodies. And 15 regulate laws or policies addressing cultivation and irrigation on steeply sloping soils. Europe and Central Asia is the only region where more than half of the surveyed countries have policies or laws addressing the use of cover crops.[66]

Integrated water resource management.

Eighteen surveyed countries have laws establishing watershed commissions, which enable integrated management of the upper and lower parts of a watershed.[67] All mainland countries surveyed have transboundary water resources, and all are signatories to regional or bilateral agreements for their management and use. While most of the transboundary agreements establish authorities to address cost and benefit sharing,[68] Chile, Denmark and Turkey do not have a separate management authority for such waters.

Monitoring water resources.

Monitoring surface water and groundwater availability can avoid overexploitation and be used to develop early warning systems for shortfalls and to design mitigation measures. Nineteen *EBA* countries have laws that require monitoring both the quality and quantity of surface water and groundwater by a national authority. Most *EBA* countries (26 of 29) have national inventories for surface water and 21 for groundwater. In total, 14 countries (Bangladesh, Colombia, Denmark, Ethiopia, Greece, Jordan, Kenya, Mozambique, the Philippines, Poland, Russia, Uganda, Vietnam and Zambia) share all four good practices—laws requiring both surface water and groundwater monitoring and national inventories for both surface water and groundwater. Twenty-two *EBA* countries have laws that establish an authority to develop water quality standards, and 25 countries legally set these standards. But the standards typically

address the quality of water for domestic use rather than for irrigation (the case in only 11 of those countries).

Gender

Women make up 43% of the global agricultural workforce, with large regional and national variations.[69] Yet due to constraints that prevent them from fully participating in agricultural value chains, they continue to be unrecognized as farmers, producers and agropreneurs.[70] They have less decision-making power over basic assets, inputs and services, including land, livestock, labor, technology, education, extension and financial services. Due to their remote location and lack of formal education, they have less direct access to markets.

If women had the same access to productive resources as men, they could increase yields on their farms by 20–30%. That could raise total agricultural output in developing countries and reduce the number of hungry people in the world by 12–17%.[71] Yet recent studies in Africa have shown that, even with equal access to improved seed and fertilizer, yields of women farmers are lower than those of male farmers. So other factors beyond access can influence the effectiveness of these resources for women, such as legal restrictions, lack of information, social norms, market failures and institutional constraints.[72]

Reforming laws that directly affect women's capacity to own and manage property, conduct business, open accounts in own names and otherwise use public institutions and services increases women's economic empowerment and participation in agricultural value chains.[73] In 155 countries laws treat women differently from men, and in 100 countries women face gender-based job restrictions.[74] In Russia a woman cannot drive a truck carrying agricultural produce—a constraint relevant to *EBA* since one of the indicators looks at market access and operations for trucking service companies. Some countries restrict women's ability to be considered a head of household, which can prevent them from getting financial assistance or becoming part of decision-making bodies, like water user associations or farmer cooperative boards, two areas measured by *EBA* indicators. Not getting finance prevents women from overcoming the initial costs of entering certain value chains—the costs can be in money or time. Not being part of decision-making bodies means that policymakers may not address women's specific issues and constraints. In some countries laws restrict married women's ability to travel outside the home, register a business or open a bank account.[75]

Beyond direct legal discrimination some rules and regulations can hurt women more because they typically have less access to information, greater restrictions of time and capital and more constraints to institutional access.[76] High costs of market entry and burdensome

regulations to operate limit the products and services offered by agricultural resource and service providers leading to higher prices, again hurting women more because they have less capital and fewer assets. A lack of input dealers and financial services in remote locations can be a constraint for many women producers who want to engage in business activities but cannot afford to travel to major cities.

How can *EBA* indicators be used to regulate agribusiness inclusively?

EBA indicators address constraints women in agribusiness (table 8.1). Governments could implement laws and regulations to directly or indirectly enhance female participation in economic

activities—improving economic development and social welfare.[77]

Interesting insights can emerge by analyzing *EBA* data with other gender specific datasets. *EBA* data supports the finding that there is a positive relationship between regulations that allow bank agents and mobile money and increased account ownership among men and women in rural areas (figure 8.1).[101] Easing market entry and operation requirements for microfinance institutions and credit unions could help provide financial services to women without access due to bank lending policies. And expanding women's ability to use different types of movable goods as collateral, including warehouse receipts, could increase their chances to secure a loan.

TABLE 8.1 *EBA* **topic areas focus on constraints relevant to women's participation in agribusiness**

EBA TOPIC	SPECIFIC CONSTRAINT FOR WOMEN
LAND	Fewer than 20% of landholders worldwide are women. They often face legal constraints in owning and inheriting land, which often disadvantage them when claiming land after a divorce or the death of a husband or father. In 35 countries the law treats female surviving spouses differently from male spouses.[78] Beyond the direct legal discrimination, burdensome and opaque land administration procedures increase the cost and time to register transfers of ownership for both men and women—though this can be more prohibitive for women, who generally have less time and capital. In Ethiopia, Ghana and Rwanda women's lack of land tenure security could be one reason for the lower productivity of their agricultural plots.[79] *EBA* land indicators aim to improve regulations on tenure security and ease restrictions on land right transfers.
WATER	Women's limited access to water for agriculture is linked to their limited access to land and inheritance rights. As a result of insecure land rights, women can be marginalized in water user associations and farmers' organizations, which often formalize farmer access to water. In many instances restrictions for association membership are based on land ownership, and membership is limited to the head of the household only.[80] Such bylaws exclude women since many women do not own land and men are the heads of households. Women can also be barred from decision-making positions within such organizations, based on the same discriminatory restrictions. But it is important for women to be on the boards of user associations and farmers' organizations since they can inform gender-sensitive water management practices.[81] *EBA* water indicators address the legal frameworks that enable water user associations to make decisions affecting all users of water and irrigation in the country.

(continued)

TABLE 8.1 *EBA* **topic areas focus on constraints relevant to women's participation in agribusiness** *(continued)*

EBA TOPIC	SPECIFIC CONSTRAINT FOR WOMEN
SEED, FERTILIZER AND MACHINERY	Many countries struggle with low use of agricultural inputs, reducing farmers' productivity and livelihoods. But women face unequal access to inputs due to several factors, including a lack of credit, property ownership and appropriate extension services. In other words, gender differences in access to land and credit cause gender differences in access to inputs. Female-headed households are less likely to use fertilizer than male-headed households, with differences ranging from 25 percentage points to 3 percentage points. The same goes for machinery use between men and women, from 20 percentage points to less than 1 percentage point across countries.[82] In addition to using fewer inputs, women tend to use lower quality inputs, either due to capital constraints or a lack of information. And women tend to use inputs incorrectly more often than men do. This is partly due to the fact that extension services are tailored to men, and women often receive second-hand information or lack access to extension service providers due to cultural norms.[83] Insecure land rights and credit constraints mean that women seldom own the land they farm and generally have smaller plots than men. So they have fewer incentives to use agricultural inputs and technology.[84] *EBA* indicators of inputs measure the market constraints for seed, fertilizer and tractors. Regulations that ease the burden on importers and dealers of these inputs can make them more readily available and affordable in remote regions, and thus more accessible to women farmers. Improving the quality control of fertilizer, seeds and machinery is also key to ensuring that increased input use boosts women's productivity.
LIVESTOCK	It can be easier for women to acquire livestock than land, especially poultry and smaller ruminants.[85] Rural women account for two-thirds of livestock keepers.[86] But empirical evidence, national statistics and data on the role of women in livestock value chains are scarce, making it difficult to draw conclusions on the specific constraints women face in the livestock sector. Women have fewer rights of ownership over livestock and its means of production in Sub-Saharan Africa and the Middle East and North Africa regions. They have more control over animals in Latin America and the Caribbean and East Asia and the Pacific.[87] Other gender-specific concerns for women in livestock production or service provision include cultural norms, unequal control over production and access to information on disease prevention.[88] *EBA* livestock indicators measure factors affecting the supply, safety and quality of animal production inputs. They also focus on the existence and quality of specific infrastructure such as gene banks, testing laboratories and databases. The legal framework surrounding animal genetic resources and food security can benefit women livestock keepers.
FINANCE	The share of female farmers who have access to credit is, on average, 5 to 10 percentage points lower than for male farmers. Women face discriminatory legal provisions or bank practices dictated by cultural norms, which require women to seek the approval of a male guardian before their loan application can be processed. And when credit requires collateral, women are disadvantaged relative to men because they have less land to secure a loan.[89] In addition, delivery channels of financial services may inadequately serve women, especially in rural areas.[90] *EBA* finance indicators measure laws and regulations for microfinance institutions, credit unions and branchless banking such as agent banking and electronic money. The indicators account for alternative sources for movable collateral, such as warehouse receipts. All five can help improve financial inclusion and the access women have to financial resources.
TRANSPORT	Transport services and the quality of roads enable those in rural areas to reach markets, purchase inputs and sell goods. The cost of transport and lack of affordable options can be a particular constraint for women. In addition to their lack of capital to procure these services, the lack of service providers can also increase the time they have to spend working outside the home.[91] *EBA* transport indicators look at constraints on the market access and operation of trucking companies, including servicing demand using foreign-owned trucks. Removing or reducing these constraints could benefit women by reducing costs of transport and increasing the availability of transport services in a country.

(continued)

TABLE 8.1 *EBA* topic areas focus on constraints relevant to women's participation in agribusiness (*continued*)

EBA TOPIC	SPECIFIC CONSTRAINT FOR WOMEN
MARKETS	The participation of female producers in agricultural value chains depends on many factors.[92] Owning sufficiently large parcels of land, which women lack, is often a prerequisite to enter contract farming arrangements with buyers. Women make up a minority of participants in contracted production as diverse as barley and sugar in South Africa, tea and horticulture in Kenya, rice, sorghum and sunflower in Uganda and French beans in Senegal.[93] With limited access to credit, female producers can also be constrained in their capacity to invest in better inputs and equipment, which in turn affects their ability to upgrade processes and product to meet buyers' requirements for quantity and quality.[94] The benefits of social capital, such participation in farmers' cooperatives or professional associations range from facilitating access to inputs and equipment to sharing market information and to strengthening links with buyers.[95] Women are less likely to participate in farmer-based organizations and female leadership is even rarer.[96] Social norms, time constraints and high membership fees may limit women's willingness and capacity to participate. Reducing the transaction costs of obtaining the documents required for export, such as phytosanitary and quality certificates, can help resource-constrained producers, especially female farmers. Lowering the fees to join professional organizations such as commodity boards or acquire mandatory licenses can also facilitate female producers' access to social capital and marketing opportunities. And enabling regulations for cooperative creation and growth can help women leverage collective action in agricultural production and marketing.
ICT	The positive impact of ICTs on farmers' access to production and marketing information and services—potential and real—is well documented.[97] It also raises hope for addressing the information needs of women farmers for new farming practices, crop management, market prices and marketing opportunities.[98] But women are less likely than men to own a mobile phone, for example.[99] They have less access to ICTs because of illiteracy, cultural attitudes against women's access to technology and a reluctance to patronize cyber cafés, often owned and visited by men.[100] Rural women may also lack access to ICT infrastructure, such as mobile phone networks, outside the main urban centers. *EBA* ICT indicators investigate licensing regimes and regulations for service provider operations that affect the availability of ICT services in the country—and government strategies and initiatives to increase access and use of ICT services in rural areas. Indicators of e-extension services can help in analyzing the ICT-supported provision of agriculture-relevant information, such as weather forecasts and market prices, for the benefit of both women and men.

FIGURE 8.1 More people have bank accounts in countries that allow branchless banking

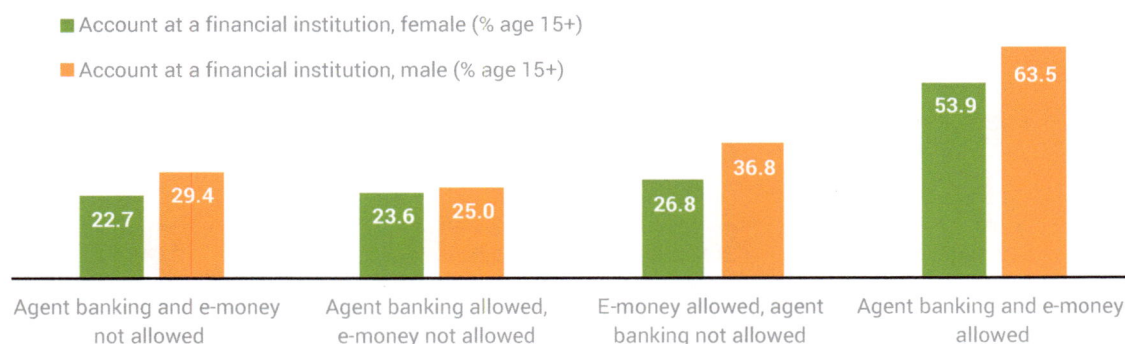

- Account at a financial institution, female (% age 15+)
- Account at a financial institution, male (% age 15+)

	Agent banking and e-money not allowed	Agent banking allowed, e-money not allowed	E-money allowed, agent banking not allowed	Agent banking and e-money allowed
Female	22.7	23.6	26.8	53.9
Male	29.4	25.0	36.8	63.5

Sources: EBA database; Global Findex Database 2014.

Notes

1. For information about areas covered by the ICT and land indicators during the first year of the *EBA* project please visit the website: http://eba.worldbank.org.

2. Ogutu, Okello and Otieno 2014.

3. The UN Broadband Commission study of 165 countries between 2001 and 2012 showed that countries with stronger competition had average broadband penetration 1.4% higher for fixed line broadband and up to 26.5% higher for mobile broadband than noncompetitive markets (Broadband Commission 2013).

4. Under an individual licensing regime every service provider is required to obtain a separate individual license in order to offer a specific service using specific technologies. Exact definitions vary across countries. Compare also with terminology in InfoDev and International Telecommunication Union 2015a.

5. General authorization regimes provide greater flexibility than individual licenses. They are technology and service neutral and providers meeting certain minimum requirements are permitted to offer a wide range of telecommunication services.

6. InfoDev and International Telecommunication Union 2015.

7. World Bank 2011.

8. Mobile operators typically contribute a percentage of their gross revenue to a universal access fund.

9. InfoDev and International Telecommunication Union 2015; International Telecommunication Union (ITU) 2013.

10. Ladcomm Corporation 2013.

11. Ogutu, Okello and Otieno 2014.

12. Qiang and others 2011.

13. Cotula, Quan and Toulmin 2006.

14. USAID Land Tenure and Resource Management Office 2013.

15. Coudouel and Paternostro 2006.

16. Besley 1995.

17. Coudouel and Paternostro 2006.

18. Committee on World Food Security 2012.

19. Knight 2010.

20. *Idem.*

21. Feder and Tongroj 1987.

22. Deininger 2003.

23. *Idem.*

24. Lerman, Csaki and Feder 2002.

25. Crabtree-Condor and Casey 2012.

26. DUATs obtained through occupancy are perpetual, while DUATs obtained by grant are limited to 50 years.

27. In Tanzania customary rights of occupancy can be perpetual, though they are customarily administered. Granted rights of occupancy are limited to 99 years. It should also be noted that a separate land governance regime exists in Zanzibar.

28. Land holders in Mozambique are prohibited by Article 109 of the Constitution from mortgaging land, though they can mortgage any improvements to the land.

29. When used in this context, "notorious" is a legal term of art. It means that it is well known that the person is in possession of the land. In the context of "adverse possession" in most legal systems the possession must fulfill five elements: 1. Open (not hidden) 2. Exclusive (others are not also in possession) 3. Notorious (well-known) 4. Adverse (contrary to the legal interests of a third party) 5. For a statutorily stated duration of time. Here, because the land does not belong to a third party the 4th element is dropped.

30. *Doing Business* database.

31. FAO 1996; FAO 2002.

32. FAO 2002; FAO 1996; Schoengold and Zilberman 2007.

33. Vapnek and others 2009.

34. Alternatively known as irrigation associations, user associations, or water user organizations, WUAs may be defined as "nongovernmental organizations that farmers and other water users form to manage an irrigation system at the local or regional level (Vapnek and others 2009).

35. Ausness 1983.

36. Many of these countries undertook reforms in the past 50 years to create formal permit systems (Van Koppen and others 2014).

37. Ausness 1983.

38. Van Koppen and others 2014.

39. Van Koppen and others 2014.

40. The case study used for purposes of data collection involved a mixed subsistence and commercial farm on a 2 hectare plot, with more than 30 years of similar use of water.

41. ICWE 1992.

42. Briscoe 1996; Johansson and others 2002; Rogers and others 1998.

43. Data on water fees were not collected this year.

44. Garces-Restrepo and others 2007; Groenfeldt 2000; Salman 1997; Vapnek and others 2009.

45. Vapnek and others 2009; Hodgson 2009.

46. Hodgson 2009.

47. Steinfeld and others 2006.

48. IAASTD 2009.

49. FAO 2009a.

50. FAO 2015.

51. Thornton 2010.

52. FAO 2010a.

53. Lamb and others 2013.

54. FAO 2012a, 2012b.

55. The World Organization for Animal Health (OIE) requires that countries provide information on animal diseases, but this is only for notifiable diseases.

56. FAO 1997.

57. Louwaars and de Boef 2012.

58. Resulting among others from the over-application of chemical or organic fertilizers.

59. FAO 2009b.

60. *In-situ* conservation also includes the conservation of traditional and locally adapted varieties of crops on farm (referred to as on-farm conservation).

61. Landraces and crop wild relatives are generally genetically diverse and therefore are important for plant genetic resources for food and agriculture. Landraces are domesticated plants that have developed unique characteristics through repeated *in situ* grower selection and thus are often closely associated with a specific geographical location and traditional farming systems. Crop wild relatives are undomesticated species that are closely related to crops and whose traits are of potential benefit for crop improvement (Maxted and others 2013).

62. The *EBA* country sample for environmental sustainability includes the following 29 countries: *East Asia and the Pacific*—Cambodia, Lao PDR, the Philippines, Vietnam; *Europe and Central Asia*—Denmark, Greece, Poland, Russia, Spain, Turkey; *Latin America and the Caribbean*—Bolivia, Chile, Colombia; *Middle East and North Africa*—Jordan, Morocco; *South Asia*—Bangladesh, Nepal, Sri Lanka; *Sub-Saharan Africa*—Burkina Faso, Burundi, Côte d'Ivoire, Ethiopia, Ghana, Kenya, Mali, Mozambique, Niger, Tanzania, Uganda, Zambia.

63. All 29 countries are parties to the Convention on Biological Diversity (CBD) and have adopted a National Biodiversity Strategy Plan (NBSAP). The CBD reports that most CBD member countries (94%) have adopted such plans; https://www.cbd.int/nbsap/.

64. Louwaars, de Boef and Edeme 2013.

65. The International Treaty on Plant Genetic Resources for Food and Agriculture facilitates the exchange and conservation of plant genetic materials, as well as the fair sharing of benefits from their use. To ensure easy access to those crops that are most relevant to human consumption, it created the Multilateral System (MLS) of Access and Benefit Sharing for seeds. Appendix 1 of the ITPGRFA identifies the priority crops that are important for food security and on which countries are interdependent (FAO 2009b).

66. FAO 2010b.

67. FAO 2007.

68. UN-Water 2008.

69. FAOSTAT database.

70. World Bank 2011a.

71. FAO 2011.

72. World Bank and ONE 2014.

73. FAO 2011; Quisumbing and others 2014; World Bank 2007.

74. For the latest data, see: http://wbl.worldbank.org.

75. World Bank 2015a.

76. Simavi, Maul and Blackden 2010.

77. World Development Report 2012; World Bank 2011; World Bank and ONE 2014.

78. *Women, Business and the Law* database.

79. World Bank and ONE 2014.

80. FAO 2002.

81. *Idem.*

82. World Bank 2011a.

83. World Bank and ONE 2014.

84. World Bank 2011a.

85. Njuki and Miller 2012.

86. FAO 2012c.

87. See "Women Livestock Managers in the Third World: a focus on technical knowledge" at http://www.ifad.org/gender/thematic/livestock/live_ap2.htm.

88. FAO 2012c.

89. Quisumbing and others 2014.

90. Dermish and others 2011

91. World Bank 2011a.

92. Rubin and Manfre 2014.

93. *Idem.*

94. *Idem.*

95. Meinzen-Dick and others 2014.

96. *Idem.*

97. World Bank 2011b.

98. World Bank 2015b.

99. Quisumbing and others 2014.

100. World Bank 2011b.

101. Allen and others 2012.

References

Allen, F., A. Demirgüç-Kunt, L. Klapper and M. S. Martinez Peria. 2012. "Foundations of Financial Inclusion." Policy Research Working Paper

6290, World Bank, Washington, DC.

Ausness, R. 1983. "Water Rights Legislation in the East: A Program for Reform." *William & Mary Law Review* 24: 547–90.

Besley, T. 1995. "Property Rights and Investment Incentives: Theory and Evidence from Ghana." *Journal of Political Economy*, 103 (5): 903–37.

Briscoe, J. 1996. "Water as an Economic Good: The Idea and What It Means in Practice." Proceedings of the Sixteenth Congress of the International Commission on Irrigation and Drainage, Cairo: 177–201.

Broadband Commission. 2013. *The State of Broadband 2013: Universalizing Broadband*. Annual Report. Broadband Commission: Geneva.

Committee on World Food Security. 2012. *Voluntary Guidelines on the Responsible Governance of Tenure of Land, Fisheries, and Forests*. Rome: FAO.

Cotula, L., J. Quan and C. Toulmin. 2006. "Better Land Access for the Rural Poor Lessons from Experience and Challenges Ahead." Paper presented at the conference "Agrarian Reform and Rural Development," Porto Alegre, Brazil, March 7–10.

Coudouel, A., and S. Paternostro. 2006. *Analyzing the Distributional Impact of Reforms*. Washington, DC: World Bank.

Crabtree-Condor, I., and L. Casey. 2012. *Lay of the Land*. ActionAid International: Johannesburg.

Deininger, K. 2003. "Land Policies for Growth and Poverty Reduction." Policy Research Report, World Bank, Washington, DC.

Dermish, A., C. Kneiding, P. Leishman and I. Mas. 2011. "Branchless and Mobile Banking Solutions for the Poor: A Survey of the Literature." *Innovations* 6 (4).

FAO (Food and Agriculture Organization). 1996. *World Food Summit:*

Rome Declaration on World Food Security. Rome: FAO.

———. 1997. *The State of the World's Plant Genetic Resources for Food and Agriculture*. Rome: FAO.

———. 2002. *Crops and Drops: Making the Best Use of Water for Agriculture*. Rome: FAO.

———. 2007. *Why Invest in Watershed Management?* Rome: FAO.

———. 2009a. *The State of Food and Agriculture 2009: Livestock in the Balance*. Rome: FAO.

———. 2009b. International Treaty on Plant Genetic Resources for Food and Agriculture (ITPGRFA): 2; 45–6. Rome: FAO.

———. 2010a. *Livestock Sector Policies and Programs in Developing Countries: A Menu for Practitioners*. Rome: FAO.

———. 2010b. "Green Manure/Cover Crops and Crop Rotation in Conservation Agriculture on Small Farms." Integrated Crop Management 12–2010. Rome: FAO.

———. 2011. *The State of Food and Agriculture 2010–11: Women in Agriculture: Closing the Gender Gap for Development*. Rome: FAO.

———. 2012a. "Cryoconservation of Animal Genetic Resources." Animal Production and Health Guidelines 12. Rome: FAO.

———. 2012b. *Conservation and Sustainable Use under the International Treaty*. Rome: FAO.

———. 2012c. *Passport to Mainstreaming Gender in Water Programmes: Key Questions for Interventions in the Agricultural Sector*. Rome: FAO.

———. 2015. "Meat Consumption." Rome. http://www.fao.org/ag/againfo /themes/en/meat/background.html.

Feder, G., and T. Onchan. 1987. "Land Ownership Security and Farm Investment in Thailand." *American Journal of Agricultural Economics* 69 (2): 311–20.

Garces-Restrepo, C., G. Muñoz and D. Vermillion. 2007. "Irrigation Management Transfer: Worldwide efforts and results." Water Report 32, FAO, Rome.

Groenfeldt, D. 2000. "A Global Consensus on Participatory Irrigation Management." In *Case Studies in Participatory Irrigation Management*, eds., David Groenfeldt and Mark Svendsen. Washington, DC: World Bank.

Hodgson, S. 2009. "Creating legal space for water user organizations: transparency, governance and the law." Legislative Study 100, FAO, Rome.

IAASTD (International Assessment of Agricultural Knowledge, Science and Technology for Development). 2009. "Agriculture at a Crossroads." Synthesis Report. Washington, DC: IAASTD.

ICWE (International Conference on Water and the Environment). 1992. *Dublin Statement on Water and Sustainable Development*. Dublin: ICWE.

InfoDev and International Telecommunication Union. 2015. *ICT Regulatory Toolkit*. Available at: http://www .ictregulationtoolkit.org.

ITU (International Telecommunication Union). 2013. "Universal Service Fund and Digital Inclusion for All Study." Universal Service Fund Study June 2013, ITU, Geneva.

Johansson, R. C., Y. Tsur, T. L. Roe, R. Doukkali and A. Dinar. 2002. "Pricing Irrigation Water: A Review of Theory and Practice." *Water Policy* 4: 173–99.

Knight, R. 2010. "Statutory Recognition of Customary Land Rights in Africa." Legislative Study 105, FAO Legal Office, Rome.

Ladcomm Corporation. 2013. "Universal Service Fund Study." Prepared for GSMA by Ladcomm Corporation: 237–8.

Lamb, C. G., T. E. Black, K. M. Bischoff and V. R.G. Mercadante. 2013. "The Importance of Feed Efficiency in the

Cow Herd." University of Florida—North Florida Research and Education Center, Marianna, FL, 106-7.

Lerman, Z., C. Csaki and G. Feder. 2002. "Land Policies and Evolving Farm Structures in Transition Countries." Policy Research Working Paper, World Bank, Washington, DC.

Louwaars, N. P. and W. S. de Boef. 2012. "Integrated Seed Sector Development in Africa: A Conceptual Framework for Creating Coherence Between Practices, Programs and Policies." *Journal of Crop Improvement* 26 (2012): 48.

Maxted, N., J. M. Brehm and S. Kell. 2013. *Resource Book for Preparation of National Plans for Conservation of Crop Wild Relatives and Landraces.* Birmingham, UK: University of Birmingham.

Meinzen-Dick, R., J.A. Behrman, L. Pandolfelli, A. Peterman and A. Quisumbing. 2014. "Gender and Social Capital for Agricultural Development." In *Gender in Agriculture, Closing the Knowledge Gap,* eds., Agnes R. Quisumbing, Ruth Meinzen-Dick, Terri L. Raney, André Croppenstedt, Julia Behram and Amber Peterman.

Njuki, J., and B. Miller. 2012. "Livestock and Gender; Achieving Poverty Alleviation and Food Security Through Livestock Policies that Benefit Women." GALVmed Economic Paper, University of London Royal Veterinary College, London.

Ogutu, S. O., J. J. Okello and D. J. Otieno. 2014. "Impact of Information and Communication Technology-based Market Information Services on Smallholder Farm Input Use and Productivity: The Case of Kenya." *World Development* 64 (December 2014): 311-21.

Qiang, C. Z., S. C. Kuek, A. Dymond and S. Esselaar. 2011. "Mobile Applications for Agriculture and Rural Development." ICT Sector Unit, World Bank, Washington, DC.

Quisumbing, A. R., R. Meinzen-Dick, T. L. Raney, A. Croppenstedt, J. Behram and A. Peterman. 2014. *Gender in Agriculture: Closing the Knowledge Gap.* Springer Netherlands.

Rogers, P., R. Bhatia and A. Huber. 1998. "Water as a Social and Economic Good: How to Put the Principle into Practice." Technical Advisory Committee Background Paper 2, Global Water Partnership, Stockholm.

Rubin, D., and C. Manfre. 2014. "Promoting Gender-Equitable Agricultural Value Chains: Issues, Opportunities and Next Steps." In *Gender in Agriculture, Closing the Knowledge Gap,* eds., Agnes R. Quisumbing, Ruth Meinzen-Dick, Terri L. Raney, André Croppenstedt, Julia Behram and Amber Peterman, 287-313.

Salman, S. M.A. 1997. "The Legal Framework for Water Users' Associations: A Comparative Study." World Bank Technical Paper 360, Washington, DC, World Bank.

Schoengold, K., and D. Zilberman. 2007. "The Economics of Water, Irrigation, and Development." In *Handbook of Agricultural Economics* 3, eds., Robert Evenson and Prabhu Pingali.

Simavi, S., C. Manuel and M. Blackden. 2010. *Gender Dimensions of Investment Climate Reform.* Washington, DC: World Bank.

Steinfeld, H., P. Gerber, T. Wassenaar, V. Castel, M. Rosales and C. de Haan. 2006. *Livestock's Long Shadow: Environmental Issues and Options.* Rome: FAO.

Thornton, P. 2010. "Livestock Production: Recent Trends and Future Prospects." *Philosophical Transactions of the Royal Society B* 365 (1554)

UN-Water. 2008. "Transboundary Waters: Sharing Benefits, Sharing Responsibilities." Thematic Paper. Zaragoza, Spain: United Nations Office to Support the International Decade for Action 'Water for Life' 2005-2015.

USAID Land Tenure and Resource Management Office. 2013. "Property Rights and Resource Governance Country Profile: Ghana." USAID Country Profile. Washington, DC: USAID.

Van Koppen, B., P. van der Zaag, E. Manzungu and B. Tapela. 2014. "Roman Water Law in Rural Africa: The Unfinished Business of Colonial Dispossession." *Water International* 39 (1): 49-62.

Vapnek, J., B. Aylward, C. Popp and J. Bartram. 2009. "Law for Water Management: A Guide to Concepts and Effective Approaches." Legislative Study 101, FAO, Rome.

World Bank. 2007. *World Development Report 2008: Agriculture for Development.* Washington, DC: World Bank.

———. 2011a. *World Development Report 2012: Gender Equality and Development.* Washington, DC: World Bank.

———. 2011b. *ICT in Agriculture: Connecting Smallholders to Knowledge, Networks, and Institutions. E- Sourcebook.* Report Number 64605. Washington, DC: World Bank.

———. 2015a. *Women, Business and the Law 2016.* Washington, DC: World Bank.

———. 2015b. *Supporting Women Agro-Enterprises in Africa with ICT. A Feasibility Study in Zambia and Kenya.* Report 93077-AFR. Washington, DC: World Bank.

World Bank and ONE. 2014. *Levelling the Field: Improving Opportunities for Women Farmers in Africa.* Washington, DC: World Bank.

APPENDIX A
METHODOLOGY

Enabling the Business of Agriculture measures regulations that can improve market access for producers, providing data and analysis that allow policymakers to compare their country's policies, regulations and market conditions with those of others. Data covers 40 countries in the following 11 areas: seed, fertilizer, machinery, finance, markets, transport, land, information and communication technology (ICT), water, livestock and environmental sustainability. Six of the topics were chosen for scoring and are presented below. The other 5 will go through further refinement and be scored next year.

The data for all sets of indicators presented are current as of March 31, 2015.

The report team welcomes feedback on the methodology. All the data and sources are publicly available at http://eba .worldbank.org.

Legal indicators

Legal indicators emerge from a reading of the laws and regulations. In this case, the team identified good regulatory practices for each topic area. The individual questions are assigned numerical scores ranging from 0 to 1 (see topic notes below for details). For each indicator developed, the scores of individual questions are averaged and multiplied by 100, resulting in a final score ranging from 0 to 100. The scores of the different indicators within one topic are also averaged into a topic score (0–100).

Most of the *EBA* topics constitute an individual *per se* market; the key actors in those markets are governed by a set of rules that facilitate or hinder their business activities as they affect their market entry and operations both locally and internationally. At the same time, those key actors need to respect the necessary safety standards and quality control in a sector as sensitive as agriculture

established by the relevant laws and regulations. Topics cover the following cross-cutting categories.

- **Operations** measures the requirements for local companies to enter the market (such as the registration of seeds and fertilizer products, licensing of trucking companies or requirements to start a MFI) and develop their respective agribusiness activities (such as the rules governing operations of producers and farmers organizations, activities allowed for agent banking or freight allocation for transportation of agricultural products);

- **Quality control** focuses on regulations governing plant protection, safety standards for users of machinery or quality control for seeds and fertilizer products.

- **Trade** looks into the trade restrictions for exporting agricultural

products, as well as importing fertilizer and tractors (given the lack of production in many countries) and cross-border transport rights;

Similar to the topic scores, each country has also a score for each cross-cutting category, averaging their scores in the specific indicators belonging to that category (table A.1).

Time and motion indicators

Time and motion data refer to the efficiency of the regulatory system—for example, the number of procedures and the time and cost to complete a process such as certifying seed for sale in the domestic market. Data of this type are built on legal requirements and cost measures are backed by official fee schedules when available. Time estimates often involve an element of judgment by respondents who routinely administer the relevant regulations or

Country assumptions and characteristics

Region and income group

Enabling the Business of Agriculture uses the World Bank regional and income group classifications, available at http://data.worldbank.org /about/country-and-lending-groups. While the World Bank does not assign regional classifications to high-income countries, regional averages presented in figures and tables in the report include countries from all income groups. For the report, high-income OECD countries are assigned the "regional" classification as OECD high income.

Gross national Income (GNI) per capita

Enabling the Business of Agriculture 2016 uses 2014 income per capita as published in the World Bank's *World Development Indicators 2015.* Income is calculated using the *Atlas* method (current U.S. dollars). For cost indicators expressed as percentage of income per capita, 2014 gross national income (GNI) in U.S. dollars us used as the denominator.

TABLE A.1 Legal indicators per topic and cross-cutting category

	OPERATIONS	QUALITY CONTROL	TRADE	
SEED	Seed registration (0–100) Seed development and certification (0–100)			**SEED SCORE (0–100)**
FERTILIZER	Fertilizer registration (0–100)	Fertilizer quality control (0–100)	Fertilizer Import requirements (0–100)	**FERTILIZER SCORE (0–100)**
MACHINERY	Tractor dealer requirements (0–100)	Tractor standards and safety (0–100)	Tractor import requirements (0–100)	**MACHINERY SCORE (0–100)**
FINANCE	Microfinance institutions (0–100) Credit unions (0–100) Agent banking (0–100) E-money (0–100) Warehouse receipts (0–100)			**FINANCE SCORE (0–100)**
MARKETS	Production and sales (0–100)	Plant protection (0–100)		**MARKETS SCORE (0–100)**
TRANSPORT	Truck licenses (0–100)		Cross-border transportation (0–100)	**TRANSPORT SCORE (0–100)**
	OPERATIONS SCORE (0–100)	**QUALITY CONTROL SCORE (0–100)**	**TRADE SCORE (0–100)**	

undertake the relevant transactions. To construct the time estimates for a particular regulatory process, such as completing the requirements to import fertilizer, the process is broken down into clearly defined steps and procedures. The time to complete these steps is verified with expert respondents—through conference calls, written correspondence and visits by the team—until there is convergence on a final answer. The specific rules followed by each topic on defining procedures, time and cost estimates is described in the following pages. Time and motion indicators are presented and analyzed in the report, but are not assigned a particular score (table A.2). The reason is that some

TABLE A.2 Time and motion indicators per topic and cross-cutting category

	OPERATIONS	QUALITY CONTROL	TRADE
SEED	Seed registration: procedures, time and cost		
FERTILIZER	Fertilizer registration: procedures, time and cost		Fertilizer import requirements: cost of import permit and importer registration for importers of fertilizer
MACHINERY			Tractor import requirements: cost of import permit and importer registration for importers of tractors
FINANCE			
MARKETS			Agricultural exports: documents, time and cost (per shipment)
TRANSPORT	Truck licenses: time, cost and validity of company licenses, truck permits and vehicle inspections		

processes follow good practices, such as the tests for evaluating and registering new seed varieties and the technical review by a variety release committee, while others may be redundant, such as an additional formal approval by a minister after the technical review. The individual good practices have been singled out and scored under the legal indicators. Since the time for taking the tests depends not only on regulations but also on the country's cropping seasons, it would be unfair to penalize countries for their specific geographical conditions. The methodology on time and motion indicators will be further developed next year.

The following assumptions and definitions were used to make the data comparable across countries.

APPENDIX B
TOPIC DATA NOTES

Seed

EBA seed indicators seek to identify the obstacles affecting the timely introduction and production of high-quality seed from formal sources, by examining availability of initial seed classes, requirements for the evaluation and registration of new varieties and seed quality control requirements.

Two sets of indicators have been developed:

- Seed registration.

- Seed development and certification.

Seed indicators have four main types of respondents: (i) seed producers and companies, (ii) seed associations, (iii) relevant government authorities (such as a ministry of agriculture seed authority) and (iv) academia. In addition, local and international technical experts from donor-funded seed programs and nongovernmental organizations were also consulted. Data were collected through interviews conducted during country visits directly with respondents as well as by email and teleconference calls from Washington, DC.

Responses from respondents were crosschecked by reading the applicable laws and regulations to the extent that these were available. Secondary research was also performed when necessary, such as the verification of information via recently published literature and online searches. In addition to the initial consultations with seed experts, the team received technical contributions on the methodology, data selection and the interpretation of the regulations from Joseph Cortes and Adelaida Harries. Lloyd Le Page also provided technical expertise on the indicator methodology.

To make the data comparable across countries, several assumptions about the evaluation and registration process are made.

Assumptions for evaluation and registration of new maize varieties

The variety:

- Is a maize variety that has been developed by the private sector.

- Is being registered for the first time in the entire country.

- Has not been registered in any other country.

- In exceptional cases when maize varieties are not being developed by the private sector in the country, is an imported maize variety, which may have been previously registered elsewhere.

Procedures

A procedure is defined as any interaction of the seed company's owner, manager, or employees with external parties, including any relevant government agencies, lawyers, committees, public and private inspectors and technical experts. All procedures that are legally or in practice required for the seed company to register a new seed variety are counted. Procedures are consecutive but can be simultaneous, such as the tests that need to be performed to evaluate the new variety.

Time

Time is recorded in calendar days and captures the median duration necessary to complete each procedure. It is assumed that the minimum time required for each procedure is one day. Although procedures such as testing may take place simultaneously, they cannot start on the same day (that is, simultaneous procedures start on consecutive days). A registration process is considered completed once the new variety has been released and commercial production can start. Any tests performed by the company prior to filling an application are not counted. It is assumed that the company's owners, managers or employees have had no prior contact with any of the officials.

In most countries, a new variety must pass standard tests in order to be released. Those tests are needed to evaluate the variety's distinctiveness, uniformity and stability (DUS tests) and its value for cultivation and use (VCU tests). The time required by law to perform these tests is often based on the number of cropping seasons required to test different aspects fully. This presents a methodological challenge in how the time is accounted and compared because countries can have one or two cropping seasons per calendar year depending on their geography. In addition, a cropping season in a country with one season per calendar year tends to last longer than one in a country with two seasons per year (estimated to 135 days in countries with one season and 182 days in countries with two seasons). So the time needed for the tests differs by climate.

The time for tests requiring a specified number of cropping seasons is measured in the following way:

Countries with two cropping seasons per calendar year (two testing seasons per year):

- If one season is required by law to perform the tests, 135 days are counted for the testing procedure.[1]

- If two seasons are required by law to perform the tests, 275 days are counted. This accounts for the 2 seasons of 135 days each and 5 days to account for the time needed to plow and prepare the land before the next cropping season (135 + 5 + 135 days)

- If three seasons are required by law to perform the test, 500 days are counted. This accounts for a full calendar year including two seasons (365 days) and an additional testing season (135 days).

Countries with one cropping season per calendar year (one testing season per year):

- If one season is required by law to perform the tests, 182 days are counted for the testing procedure.[2]

- If two seasons are required by law by law to perform the tests, 547 days are counted. This accounts for the full calendar year including one season (365 days) and an additional testing season (182 days).

- If three seasons are required by law to perform the test, 912 days are counted. This accounts for two full calendar years including one season (365 + 365 days) and an additional testing season (182 days).

Costs

Only official costs are recorded, including fees and taxes. In the absence of fee schedules, a government officer's estimate is taken as an official source. In the absence of a government officer's estimate, estimates by seed companies are used. If several seed companies provide different estimates, the median reported value is applied. Professional fees (notaries, lawyers or accountants) are only included if the company is required to use such services. All costs are indicated in U.S. dollars and as a percentage of the country's income per capita.

Specific terms

Basic/foundation seed has been produced under the responsibility of the maintainer according to the generally accepted practices for the maintenance of the variety and is intended for the production of

certified seed. Basic or foundation seed must conform to the appropriate conditions in the regulations and the fulfillment of these conditions must be confirmed by an official examination.

Breeder/pre-basic seed is directly controlled by the originating or sponsor plant breeding institution, firm or individual, and is the source for the production of seed of certified classes.

Distinctiveness, Uniformity and Stability (DUS) testing is a test performed to compare candidate varieties for registration with varieties already listed in seed register on these qualities:

- *Distinctness* (UPOV definition): A variety shall be deemed distinct if it is clearly distinguishable in at least one character from any other variety whose existence is a matter of common knowledge at the time of filing the application for registration.

- *Uniformity* (UPOV definition): A variety shall be deemed to be uniform if, subject to the variation that may be expected from the particular features of its propagation, it is sufficiently uniform in its relevant characteristics.

- *Stability* (UPOV definition): A variety shall be deemed stable if its relevant characteristics remain unchanged after repeated propagation by the method that is normally used for the particular variety.

Seed certification (OECD definition) is the quality assurance process during which seed intended for domestic or international markets is controlled and inspected by official sources to guarantee consistent high quality for consumers. This process involves: (i) controlling the seed in previous generations, (ii) conducting field inspections during the multiplication process to ensure there is little contamination and that the variety is true to type, (iii) growing samples of the known seed in control plots to ensure that the progeny is conform to the characteristics of the variety and (iv) testing the seed quality in laboratories.

UPOV is the International Union for the Protection of New Varieties of Plants, an intergovernmental organization based in Geneva, Switzerland. Its mission is to provide and promote an effective system of plant variety protection, with the aim of encouraging the development of new varieties of plants for the benefit of society. To be a member, the law of a country must conform to the standards of the 1991 Act of the UPOV Convention. The country can also have an observer status after having officially expressed an interest in becoming a member of UPOV and participating in the sessions of the Council. To date, 71 countries have a member status and 57 countries, an observer status.

Value for Cultivation and Use (VCU) is a test performed to assess whether a variety has characteristics and properties that affect improvement in cultivation or in the utilization of the harvest or its products in comparison to the existing listed varieties.

Variety (UPOV definition) is a plant grouping within a single botanical taxon of the lowest known rank, which, irrespective of whether the conditions for the grant of a breeder's right are fully met, can be:

- Defined by the expression of the characteristics resulting from a given genotype or combination of genotypes.

- Distinguished from any other plant grouping by the expression of at least one of the said characteristics.

- Considered as a unit with regard to its suitability for being propagated unchanged.

Variety catalog is a list of varieties that have been registered and released by a national authority and can be produced and marketed in a country or region as certified seed.

Variety release committee is the committee that decides whether a new variety can be registered and introduced on the domestic market.

TABLE B.1 Scoring methodology for seed

INDICATOR (CATEGORY)	DESCRIPTION	WHAT IS MEASURED	HOW IT IS SCORED
Seed registration (operations)	This indicator looks at the legally mandated processes and practices required to introduce a locally developed new maize variety into the domestic market	1. The law establishes a variety release committee (VRC) in the country	**A score of 1** if yes
		2. The composition of the legally mandated variety release committee includes the private sector	**A score of 1** if private and public sectors are equally represented (or if majority of private sector members) **A score of 0.75** if private sector representation between ½ and ¼ **A score of 0.5** if private sector representation between ¼ and $\frac{1}{8}$ **A score of 0.25** if private sector representation between $\frac{1}{8}$ and 0 **A score of 0** if no private sector representation or no variety release committee
		3. The variety release committee (VRC) meets regularly in practice	**A score of 1** if the VRC meets on demand, or at least twice a year in a country with 2 crop seasons or at least once a year in a country with 1 crop season **A score of 0** if the VRC meets once a year in a country with 2 crop seasons or less than once a year in a country with 1 crop season, or if the VRC does not exist or meet at all
		4. A variety can be commercialized immediately after the recommendation of the VRC	**A score of 1** if yes. *This question has double weight ($\frac{2}{8}$) with regard to the other questions of this indicator ($\frac{1}{8}$)*
		5. The country has a variety catalog listing new varieties and if it is available online	**A score of 1** if yes. **A score of ½** if a variety catalog exists but it is not available online
		6. The catalog specifies agro-ecological zones suitable for plantation of each listed variety	**A score of 1** if yes
		7. The variety catalog is updated frequently	**A score of 1** if the catalog is updated twice or more a year if the country has 2 crop seasons, or if the catalog is updated once a year if there is one crop season **A score of ½** if the catalog is updated once a year if the country has 2 crop seasons. **A score of 0** if the catalog is updated less than once a year irrespective of the number of crop seasons
		8. Total procedures to evaluate and register a new variety	**Not scored**
		9. Total time to evaluate and register a new variety	
		10. Total cost to evaluate and register a new variety	

(continued)

TABLE B.1 Scoring methodology for seed (continued)

INDICATOR (CATEGORY)	DESCRIPTION	WHAT IS MEASURED	HOW IT IS SCORED
Seed development and certification (operations)	This indicator measures the legal requirements for the production of initial seed classes and the certification of new varieties	1. The country currently implements regulation governing plant breeders' rights	**A score of 1** if yes
		2. Private enterprises are eligible to produce breeder/pre-basic seed of local public varieties for use in the domestic market	
		3. Private enterprises are eligible to produce foundation/basic seed of local public varieties for use in the domestic market	
		4. Private sector can access germplasm from the national gene bank	
		5. Materials for research and development of new varieties can be imported without further government field testing	
		6. There is an established system for licensing public varieties to private seed enterprises for production and sale in the domestic market	
		7. The regulations allow for a private institution or seed companies to be accredited to carry out the certification process	**A score of 1** if yes. For countries that do not allow this practice, this question is not counted when aggregating the indicator scores (bonus point)
		8. There is an official fee schedule established for seed certification activities carried out by the public sector	**A score of 1** if yes

Fertilizer

EBA fertilizer indicators measure laws and regulations on the registration, import and quality assurance of fertilizer products. The indicators focus on areas that are important for companies who want to import and sell fertilizer in a country.

Three sets of indicators have been developed:

- Fertilizer registration.

- Fertilizer quality control.

- Fertilizer import requirements.

Fertilizer indicators have three main types of respondents: (i) fertilizer companies, (ii) relevant government authorities (for example, the ministry of agriculture) and (iii) agricultural input dealer associations. The questionnaire targets all three groups of respondents, whereby the time and motion component is typically answered by the private sector. Data were collected through interviews conducted during country visits directly with respondents and also by email and teleconference calls from Washington, DC.

To make the data comparable across countries, several assumptions about the fertilizer company and the fertilizer product are used, as detailed below:

Assumptions about the business and registered fertilizer

The business:

- Is a fertilizer importer.

- Imports fertilizer to sell in the country.

- Has registered at least one new fertilizer product in the country.

- Does not operate in an export processing zone or an industrial estate with special import or export privileges.

The destination port for importation of fertilizers is the most used port in the country. If the country is landlocked, it is assumed that the most used border posts are employed.

The fertilizer:

- Is a new chemical fertilizer product that has not previously been registered in the country.

Procedures

A procedure is defined as any interaction of the company's owners, managers or employees with external parties, for example, government agencies, lawyers, auditors, notaries and customs or border authorities. It includes all procedures that are officially required for the business to legally perform its described activities, such as registering and importing fertilizer. Interactions among owners, managers and employees are not counted as procedures.

Time

Time is recorded in calendar days and captures the median duration of each procedure. The time span for each procedure starts with the first filing of the application or demand and ends once the company has received the final document, such as the fertilizer registration certificate. It is assumed that the company's owners, managers or employees have had no prior contact with any of the officials.

Costs

Only official costs required by law are recorded, including fees and taxes. If possible, the relevant fee schedule or calculation formula should be indicated (for example, as a percentage of the company's capital). Professional fees (notaries, lawyers or accountants) are only included if the company is required to use such services. All costs are indicated in U.S. dollars and as a percentage of the country's income per capita.

Specific terms

Blend is any combination or mixture of fertilizer products.

Fertilizer form is the form in which the fertilizer is presented, for example, liquid, granules, powder, spikes, tablets or pellets.

Fertilizer product is any product containing nitrogen, phosphorus, potassium, or any recognized plant nutrient element or compound that is used for its plant nutrient content.

Fertilizer types are as follows:

- NPK is composed of three main elements: Nitrogen (N), Phosphorus (P) and Potassium (K), each of these being essential in plant nutrition.

- Urea is a form of nitrogen fertilizer with an NPK (nitrogen-phosphorus-potassium) ratio of 46-0-0.

- DAP, diammonium phosphate, is the world's most widely used phosphorus (P) fertilizer.

- MAP (Monoammonium phosphate).

- MOP, Muriate of Potash, is the most common form of potash.

- Potash or fertilizer potassium (K), sometimes called "potash."

- Ammonium Nitrate is a salt of ammonia and nitric acid that is widely used in fertilizers. The substance can be used in explosive compounds, which is why many countries have imposed specific regulations for its transport, storage and handling.

TABLE B.2 Scoring methodology for fertilizer

INDICATOR (CATEGORY)	DESCRIPTION	WHAT IS MEASURED	HOW IT IS SCORED
Fertilizer registration (operations)	As many countries require fertilizer to be registered before they can be sold commercially, this indicator measures required procedures for fertilizer registration	1. The private sector is required to register fertilizer	**A score of 1** if yes
		1a. The registration is not limited to a specific time period or re-application is not needed	**A score of 1** if yes
		1b. If registration is limited to a specific time period, the following scores are assigned	**A score of 0.75** if equal to or greater than 10 years **A score of 0.5** if greater than or equal to 5 years, and less than 10 years **A score of 0.25** if greater than or equal to 2 years and less than 5 years **A score of 0** if less than 2 years
		1c. The renovation of application is automatic	**A score of 1** if yes, or if the renovation is not required
		2. There is an official fertilizer catalogue listing all registered fertilizer	**A score of 1** if yes
		3. The catalogue is accessible online	**A score of 1** if yes
		4. Total number of procedures legally required to register a new fertilizer product	**Not scored**
		5. Total time to register a new fertilizer product	**Not scored**
		6. Total cost to register a new fertilizer product	**Not scored**

(continued)

TABLE B.2 Scoring methodology for fertilizer (continued)

INDICATOR (CATEGORY)	DESCRIPTION	WHAT IS MEASURED	HOW IT IS SCORED
Fertilizer quality control (quality control)	This indicator focuses on labeling requirements, legislation on the sale of mislabeled and open fertilizer containers, and practices in monitoring fertilizer quality	1. The fertilizer law requires labeling of fertilizer containers (bags, bottles)	**A score of 1** if yes
		1a. The following scores are assigned with regard to the label content	**A score of ⅓** is assigned to each of the following elements: • Brand name • Net weight or volume • Content description
		2. The fertilizer law prohibits the sale of mislabeled fertilizer bags	**A score of 1** if yes
		2a. The fertilizer law establishes a penalty for the sale of mislabeled fertilizer	**A score of 1** if yes
		3. The fertilizer law prohibits the sale of opened fertilizer containers/bags	**A score of 1** if yes
		3a. The fertilizer law establishes a penalty for the sale of opened fertilizer containers/bags	**A score of 1** if yes

(continued)

TABLE B.2 Scoring methodology for fertilizer (continued)

INDICATOR (CATEGORY)	DESCRIPTION	WHAT IS MEASURED	HOW IT IS SCORED
Fertilizer import requirements (trade)	As fertilizer production is concentrated in only a few countries, requiring most others to rely on imports, this indicator focuses on the private sector's role and the requirements for importing fertilizer	1. A fertilizer product that has previously been registered in another country does not need to be re-registered in the country	**A score of 1** if yes
		2. The private sector is allowed to import fertilizer in the country for its own use	**A score of 1** if yes
		3. The private sector is allowed to import fertilizer in the country in order to sell it	**A score of 1** if yes
		4. Foreign firms are allowed to import fertilizer in order to sell it	**A score of 1** if yes
		5. The private sector is required to register as an importer of fertilizer in order to sell it. The registration is not limited to a specific time period	**A score of 1** if yes
		5a. If registration is limited to a specific time period, the following scores are assigned.	**A score of 0.75** if equal to or greater than 10 years **A score of 0.5** if greater than or equal to 5 years and less than 10 years **A score of 0.25** if greater than or equal to 2 years and less than 5 years **A score of 0** if less than 2 years or the importer registration is not required
		5b. Cost of the registration	**Not scored**
		6. The private sector is required to obtain an import permit to import fertilizer	**A score of 1** if no
		6a. If import permit is required, the following scores are assigned	**A score of 0.8** if permit is not limited to a specific time period **A score of 0.6** if valid for 12 months or longer **A score of 0.4** if valid for 6 months or longer and less than 12 months **A score of 0.2** if valid for longer than 1 month and less than 6 months **A score of 0** if valid for 1 month or less
		6b. Cost of the import permit	**Not scored**

Machinery

EBA machinery indicators measure obstacles facing tractor dealers wishing to import tractors for sale. Besides meeting the requirements for import and registration, the indicators also measure the regulations for standards and safety.

Three sets of indicators have been developed:

- Tractor dealer requirements.

- Tractor standards and safety.

- Tractor import requirements.

Machinery indicators have four main types of respondents: (i) agricultural machinery manufacturers, (ii) importers, (iii) machinery dealers and (iv) relevant government authorities (such as the ministry of agriculture). Data were collected through interviews conducted during country visits directly with respondents and also by email and teleconference calls from Washington, DC.

To make the data comparable across countries, several assumptions about the machinery company and the machinery product are used, as detailed below:

Assumptions about the business and the agricultural tractor

The business:

- Is an importer or dealer of agricultural tractors.

- Does not operate in an export processing zone or an industrial estate with special import or export privileges.

The destination port for importation of tractors is the most used port in the country. If the country is landlocked, it is assumed that the most used border posts are employed.

The tractor:

- Is a new or second-hand two-axle/four-wheel drive (4WD) tractor.

Costs

Only official costs required by law are recorded, including fees and taxes. If possible, the relevant fee schedule or calculation formula should be indicated (for example, as a percentage of the company's capital). In cases where no official costs are in place, the median of the responses from respondents is computed. Professional fees (notaries, lawyers or accountants) are only included if the company is required to use such services. All costs are indicated in U.S. dollars and as a percentage of the country's income per capita.

Specific terms

Agricultural tractor means a two- or four-wheel drive type vehicle or track vehicle of more than 20 engine horsepower, designed to furnish the power to pull, carry, propel or drive implements that are designed for agriculture. All self-propelled implements are excluded.

Roll-over protection structures (ROPS) are attached to the tractor frame and come as either two post fixed or foldable, four post, or as an integral part of a ROPS cab. They generally will limit a side overturn to ninety degrees (90°) and will provide an important safety zone for the operator provided the operator is wearing the seat belt.

TABLE B.3 Scoring methodology for machinery

INDICATOR (CATEGORY)	DESCRIPTION	WHAT IS MEASURED	HOW IT IS SCORED
Tractor dealer requirements (operations)	This indicator measures legal requirements with regard to suitability testing of agricultural tractors, specific licensing required to operate a tractor, as well as warranties and post-sale services that must be provided at the retail level	102. Requirement to obtain proof of suitability for the import of new agricultural tractors and associated cost.	**A score of 1** if proof of suitability is required and the cost is below 10% of GNI per capita **A score of 0.75** if proof of suitability is required and the cost is equal to or greater than 10% and less than 25% of GNI per capita **A score of 0.5** if proof of suitability is required and the cost is equal to or greater than 25% of GNI per capita and less than 50% of GNI per capita **A score of 0.25** if equal to or greater than 50% of GNI per capita **A score of 0** if proof of suitability is not required
		103. Requirement to register the tractor once the machine is imported and associated cost	**A score of 1** if registration is required and has no cost, or the cost is lower than 2% of GNI per capita **A score of 0.75** if registration is required and the cost is equal to or greater than 2% of GNI per capita and lower than 5% of GNI per capita **A score of 0.5** if registration is required and the cost is equal to or greater than 5% of GNI per capita and lower than 10% of GNI per capita **A score of 0.25** if registration is required and the cost is equal to or greater than 10% of GNI per capita **A score of 0** if registration is not required
		104. Requirement of a special operator's license in order to operate an agricultural tractor	**A score of 1** if yes
		105. Requirement that producers and sellers of agricultural tractors are responsible for providing post-sale services. The following scores are assigned with regard to the provision of post-sale services	**A score of 0.2** is assigned to each of the following post-sale services • Repair of tractors • Replace or return poor quality tractors • Supply of spare parts • Train users on the use of tractors • Train users on maintenance of tractors

(continued)

TABLE B.3 Scoring methodology for machinery (continued)

INDICATOR (CATEGORY)	DESCRIPTION	WHAT IS MEASURED	HOW IT IS SCORED
Tractor standards and safety (quality control)	These indicators look at legal requirements with regard to operational safety and performance standards of tractors. A score of 1 is assigned for each of the following 6 data points	106. Requirement that tractors must be equipped with a fixed roll-over protective structure (ROPS)	**A score of 1** if yes
		107. Exemption from this requirement if the owner provides proof by the tractor manufacturer that the tractor was not designed to be fitted with a ROPS	**A score of 1** if yes
		108. Requirement that tractors must be equipped with a seatbelt. The following scores are assigned	**A score of 1** if ROPS and seatbelts are required **A score of ⅔** if ROPS are required and seatbelts are not required **A score of ⅓** if neither ROPS nor seatbelts are required **A score of 0** if ROPS are not required and seatbelts are required
		109. Establishment of sanctions for owners of agricultural tractors that fail to comply with safety standards	**A score of ⅓** is assigned to each of the following • Establishment of sanctions for lack of seatbelts • Establishment of sanctions for lack of ROPS • Establishment of sanctions for not being in possession of an operator's license
		110. Requirement that manufacturers and sellers of agricultural tractors comply with national quality and performance standards	**A score of 1** if yes
		111. Requirement that tractor standards must be in accordance with international standards (e.g. International Organization for Standardization, ISO)	**A bonus point is assigned to those countries that have this requirement**

(continued)

TABLE B.3 Scoring methodology for machinery (continued)

INDICATOR (CATEGORY)	DESCRIPTION	WHAT IS MEASURED	HOW IT IS SCORED
Tractor import requirements (trade)	These indicators look at aspects of importing agricultural tractors and harvesters, including the private machinery sector's role and the required procedures to import	112. The private sector is allowed to import new agricultural tractors	**A score of 1** if yes
		113. The private sector is allowed to import second-hand agricultural tractors	**A score of 1** if yes
		114. The private sector is allowed to import spare parts for agricultural tractors	**A score of 1** if yes
		115. Requirement for pre-shipment inspections of new agricultural tractor	**A score of 1** if yes
		116. The private sector is required to register as an importer of agricultural tractors. The registration is not limited to a specific time period	**A score of 1** if yes
		117. If registration is limited to a specific time period, the following scores are assigned	**A score of 0.75** if equal to or greater than 10 years **A score of 0.5** if equal to or greater than 5 years and less than 10 years **A score of 0.25** if equal to or greater than 2 years and less than 5 years **A score of 0** if less than 2 years, or registration is not required
		118. Cost of the registration	**Not scored**
		119. The private sector is not required to obtain an import permit to import agricultural tractors	**A score of 1** if yes
		120. If import permit is required, the following scores are assigned	**A score of 0.8** if permit is not limited to a specific time period **A score of 0.6** if permit is valid for 12 months or longer **A score of 0.4** if permit is valid for 6 months or longer and less than 12 months **A score of 0.2** if permit is valid longer than 1 month and less than 6 months **A score of 0** if permit is valid for 1 month or less
		121. Cost of the import permit	**Not scored**

Finance

EBA finance indicators measure laws and regulations that promote access to a range of financial services, with focus on areas that are relevant for potential customers that are partially or fully excluded from traditional financial services due to factors such as their geographical location or available type of collateral.

Five sets of indicators have been developed:

- Microfinance institutions (MFIs).

- Credit unions.

- Agent banking.

- Electronic money (e-money).

- Warehouse receipts.

Finance indicators have three main types of respondents: financial sector supervisory authorities, financial lawyers and legal officers of financial institutions. Data collection includes interviews conducted during country visits directly with respondents, followed by rounds of follow-up communication via email and conference calls with respondents as well as with third parties. Data are also verified through analyses of laws and regulations, including review of public sources of information on banking law, warehouse receipt law, financial institutions law and others.

Assumptions about the financial institutions

Microfinance institutions (MFIs): MFIs are financial institutions that specialize in the provision of small-volume financial services (such as credit, deposits and loans) to low-income clients. MFIs can take deposits, lend and provide other financial services to the public and are licensed to operate and supervised by a public authority.

Credit unions: Credit unions are member-owned, not-for-profit financial cooperatives that provide savings, credit and other financial services to their members. There are typically two types of financial cooperatives: (i) small financial cooperatives that provide services only to their members and are typically supervised by either the central bank, the department of cooperatives, or the ministry of finance—they are referred to as savings and credit cooperatives (SACCOs) in some countries, and (ii) cooperative banks that take deposits from and lend to the public and are regulated under the main financial institution laws and supervised by the central bank. The credit union indicator measures small financial cooperatives to be consistent with the topic's emphasis on small-scale lending and financial inclusion.

Specific terms

Agent banking is the delivery of financial services through partnership with a retail agent (or correspondent) in order to extend financial services to locations where bank branches would be uneconomical.

Capital adequacy ratio is a measure of a bank's total capital expressed as a percentage of its risk-weighted assets.

Credit unions are member-owned, not-for-profit financial cooperatives that provide savings, credit and other financial services to their members.

Effective interest rate is the annual interest rate plus all fees associated with the administration of the loan to the client. It is a symbol of the total cost of the loan to the client. Proxies for the effective interest rate are the annual percentage rate or the amortization table/schedule for the loan.

E-money refers to money that is stored and exchanged through an electronic device and not associated with a deposit account at any financial institution.

Examples include electronic funds transfers and payments processed through mobile phones or prepaid cards.

Microfinance institutions (MFIs) are financial institutions specializing in the provision of small-volume financial services (credit, deposits, loans) to low-income clients, which can take deposits, lend and provide other financial services to the public and are licensed to operate and supervised by a public authority.

Negotiable receipts allow a transfer of ownership without having to physically deliver the commodity.

Non-bank businesses are those that do not hold a banking license, including telecoms, post offices or other businesses licensed by the central bank or financial supervisory authority to issue e-money.

Provisioning rules determine how much money banks must set aside as an allowance for bad loans in their portfolios. The share of a loan that must be covered by provisioning can either be the full loan amount or the part that is not secured by collateral (unsecured share).

Ratios to ensure financial stability can include liquidity ratio, capital adequacy ratio, solvency ratio, credit to deposit ratio, assets to liabilities ratio, stable funding ratio, net loan receivables to total assets and others. Countries address the issue of stability of credit unions using different criteria, therefore all the ratios above can be included in this measure.

Warehouse receipts are documents issued by warehouse operators as evidence that specified commodities are of stated quantity and quality, deposited or stored at particular locations by named depositors and owned by the beneficiary of the receipt issued. Where supported by an appropriate legal framework, warehouse receipts can serve as a form of collateral to obtain a loan from financial institutions and facilitate future sales.

TABLE B.4 Scoring methodology for finance

INDICATOR (CATEGORY)	DESCRIPTION	WHAT IS MEASURED	HOW IT IS SCORED
Microfinance institutions (operations)[3]	This indicator measures the regulations for deposit-taking MFIs	1. The economy allows and regulates deposit-taking MFIs 2. The regulated minimum capital adequacy ratio for MFIs is at least equal to, or no more than 2 percentage points higher, than the capital adequacy ratio for commercial banks 3. Loan sizes of MFIs are not limited to a specific amount or are greater than 10 times the GNI per capita if there is a specific amount[4] 4. The law requires MFIs to disclose the effective interest rate or a proxy to loan applicants 5. MFIs are required to fully provision a delinquent unsecured loan after the same number of days required for commercial banks, or within half the number of days required for commercial banks 6. The law requires MFIs to subscribe to a deposit insurance system	**A score of 1** if yes
		7. Minimum capital required to establish an MFI. Scores are divided into four groups (1, ⅔, ⅓ and 0) based on each country's minimum mandatory capital requirement as a multiple of GNI per capita. Threshold values are determined based on distribution	**A score of 1** if the mandatory capital requirement is greater than 0 but less than 201 times the GNI per capita of the country **A score of ⅔** (0.66) if the mandatory capital requirement is equal to or greater than 201 times, but less than 501 times the GNI per capita **A score is ⅓** (0.33) if the minimum mandatory capital requirement is equal to or greater than 501 times the GNI per capita, but less than 1001 times the GNI per capita **A score of 0** if the minimum mandatory capital requirement is equal to or greater than 1001 times the GNI per capita of the country or if there is no provisions on minimum capital requirement

(continued)

TABLE B.4 Scoring methodology for finance (continued)

INDICATOR (CATEGORY)	DESCRIPTION	WHAT IS MEASURED	HOW IT IS SCORED
Credit unions (operations)	This indicator measures the regulations for credit unions	1. The economy has a law regulating credit unions, or there is a specific section of a general cooperatives law that regulates the governance and operation of credit unions 2. 30 or fewer members are required to establish a credit union 3. The law defines ratios to ensure financial stability of credit unions 4. The law requires credit unions to disclose the effective interest rate or a proxy to loan applicants	**A score of 1** if yes for each question
		5. Minimum capital required to establish a credit union. The scores are divided into four groups (1, ⅔, ⅓ and 0) based on each country's minimum mandatory capital requirement as a multiple of GNI per capita. Threshold values are determined based on distribution	**A score of 1** if the mandatory capital requirement is greater than 0 but less than 11 times the GNI per capita of the country **A score of ⅔** if the mandatory capital requirement is equal to or greater than 11 times, but less than 51 times the GNI per capita **A score of ⅓** if the minimum mandatory capital requirement is equal to or greater than 51 times the GNI per capita, but less than 101 times the GNI per capita **A score is 0** if the minimum mandatory capital requirement is equal to or greater than 101 times the GNI per capita of the country or if there is no provisions on minimum capital requirement

(continued)

TABLE B.4 Scoring methodology for finance (continued)

INDICATOR (CATEGORY)	DESCRIPTION	WHAT IS MEASURED	HOW IT IS SCORED
Agent banking (operations)[5]	This indicator measures the entry and operational requirements for agent banking	1. There exists a legal framework to regulate agent banking activities	**A score of 1** if yes
		2. Whether there are minimum standards in order to qualify and operate as an agent in the following areas: 1) has to be an operating/established business, 2) has to have positive financial records, 3) has to have real-time connectivity to a commercial bank. Each standard is weighted equally with a score of $1/3$	**A score of $1/3$** for each standard **For example: A score of 1** if the law states all three of the minimum standards as requirements to qualify and operate as an agent. If the law states only two out of three of the minimum standards, the score is $2/3$
		3. Type of contracts that agents can enter with financial institutions	**A score of 1** is assigned if agents are allowed to enter both exclusive and nonexclusive contracts **A score of ½** is assigned if only nonexclusive contracts are allowed **A score of 0** is assigned if only exclusive contracts are allowed
		4. The types of services agents can offer on behalf of a bank. This data point looks at 7 services: cash deposits, cash withdrawals, transfer of funds to other customers' accounts, bill payments, balance inquiry, opening a deposit account and collection/processing of loan application documents. Each of the above services is equally weighted and worth $1/7$ of a point	**A score of $1/7$** for each service
		5. Whether commercial banks are liable for the acts of commission and omission of agents providing financial services on their behalf	**A score of 1** if the legislation states that commercial banks are liable **A score of 0** if they are not liable

(continued)

TABLE B.4 Scoring methodology for finance (continued)

INDICATOR (CATEGORY)	DESCRIPTION	WHAT IS MEASURED	HOW IT IS SCORED
Electronic money (e-money) (operations)	This indicator measures the legal framework for e-money, in particular the entry and operational requirements for non-bank e-money issuers	1. E-money is allowed 2. Non-bank businesses are allowed to issue e-money 3. Non-bank e-money issuers are required to keep a minimum of liquid assets to safeguard customer funds	**A score of 1** if yes for each question
		4. The requirements for non-bank businesses to receive a license to issue e-money. The four requirements are: • an initial capital requirement; for the initial capital requirement, countries are divided into four groups (1, $^2/_3$, $^1/_3$, 0) based on the country's capital requirement as a multiple of its GNI per capita	**A score of "1 * ¼"** if the capital requirement is less than 101 times the GNI per capita but greater than 0 **A score of "$^2/_3$ * ¼"** if the minimum capital is equal to or greater than 101 times the GNI per capita but less than 501 **A score of "$^1/_3$ * ¼"** if the minimum capital is equal to or greater than 501 times the GNI per capita but less than 901 **A score of 0** if the minimum capital requirement is equal to or greater than 901 times the GNI per capita or if there is no provisions on minimum capital requirement
		• interoperability with other existing electronic money payment/transfer systems • existence of internal control mechanisms to comply with Anti-Money Laundering and Combatting Financing of Terrorism (AML/CFT) laws, standards and measures • consumer protection measures such as consumer recourse mechanisms, consumer awareness programs, etc. Each of the above services is equally weighted with a score of ¼.	**A score of ¼ if the law states the requirement and 0** if it does not

(continued)

TABLE B.4 Scoring methodology for finance (continued)

INDICATOR (CATEGORY)	DESCRIPTION	WHAT IS MEASURED	HOW IT IS SCORED
Warehouse receipts (operations)	This indicator measures the regulations facilitating the use of agricultural commodities as collateral	1. The economy has a law regulating the operation of warehouse receipts, or the regulation of warehouse receipts is included in other general legislation 2. Warehouse operators are required to file a bond with the regulator or pay into an indemnity fund to secure performance by him of his obligations as a warehouse operator 3. Warehouse operators are required to insure the warehouse or the stored goods against fire, earthquakes, theft, burglary or other damage 4. Warehouse receipts are negotiable	**A score of 1** if yes for each question
		5. Types of warehouse receipts that are legally valid: paper-based, electronic or both	**A score of 1** is assigned if the law allows both paper-based and electronic warehouse receipts and if electronic warehouse receipts are explicitly mentioned in the regulation **A score of ½** is assigned if the law allows only paper-based receipts **A score of 0** is assigned if warehouse receipt is not recognized or used
		6. Information that must be listed on a warehouse receipt for it to be valid. There are 4 details measured: location of storage, amount in storage, description of goods (type, quality and harvest) and information on security interest over the goods (certificate of pledge)	**Each piece of information counts for ¼ of a point** **For example, a score of 1** is assigned if all 4 pieces of information are required to be listed on the receipt for it to be legally valid **A score of ¾** is assigned if only 3 above the pieces of information are required to be listed on the receipt, and so on

Markets

EBA markets indicators measure obstacles faced by agribusinesses in the production and marketing of agricultural products and when accessing foreign markets. Phytosanitary regulations that favor agricultural trade through the promotion of plant and crop health are also assessed.

Three sets of indicators have been developed:

- Plant protection.

- Production and sales.

- Agricultural exports.

Markets indicators have six main types of respondents: (i) government agencies (responsible for trade, customs, plant protection and cash crops), (ii) private producers, processors and exporters of agricultural products (both domestic and multinational companies) and related trade/export associations, (iii) farmers' organizations, including unions, federations, cooperatives and other similar entities; (iv) chambers of commerce, (v) lawyers and (vi) freight forwarders and customs brokers. Data were collected from these respondents using four different surveys: two for the public sector and two for the private sector. Data were collected through interviews conducted during country visits directly with respondents and also by email and teleconference calls from Washington, DC.

To render data on production and sales as well as agricultural export more comparable across countries, several assumptions about the business, the agricultural products and the trading partner are used, as detailed below:

Assumptions about the contracted product

The contracted product is defined as the most produced non-processed non-cereal product in terms of gross production value (current million U.S. dollars). All data are sourced from FAOSTAT, using the production data of 2012 (the latest available year). Cereal crops are excluded from the analysis because they are less suitable for agricultural production contracts due to high risks of side-selling in well-developed local or export markets,

the reduced need for technical assistance to meet market specifications and reduced price differentials at each point in the supply chain.

Assumptions about the business

The business:

- Performs general agricultural trading activities.

- Does not operate in a special export processing zone.

Assumptions about the export product and trading partner

The export products are defined and grouped as cash crops, cereals, fruits and vegetables according to the Harmonized Commodity Description and Coding System 1996 version (HS 96). All data are sourced from the UN Comtrade Database, using the export data from 2009–13. For each country, the combination of the product and the partner country that represents the highest five-year average export value (in U.S. dollars) is selected. For example, cereal export to Zimbabwe is selected for Zambia. In addition, for countries where cash crops are selected as the export product, the HS 4-digit product within the category that is exported the most to the partner country is used for studying the legal and regulatory requirements. For example, coffee export to the United States is selected for Colombia since coffee is the top product in the cash crop category and the United States is Colombia's main trading partner.

Assumptions about the shipment

- Is transported via a 20-foot full container-load.

- Weighs 10 metric tons.

- All packing material that requires fumigation (such as wood pallets) is assumed to be treated and marked with an approved international mark certifying that treatment.

Requirements to export

A "requirement" for purposes of the study is any legally required qualification

or document that must be obtained by the exporter (Company A) in order to export the selected product to the trading partner. These requirements may apply to the trader (annual export license or mandatory memberships) or to the consignment on a per shipment basis (phytosanitary certificate or fumigation certificate). These requirements involve interactions with external parties, including government agencies, inspectors, laboratories and other relevant institutions. All requirements mandated in the law in order to complete the export transaction outlined by the case study are taken into account, even if they may be avoided in certain cases. Buyer-driven requirements or documents are not considered for purposes of the study. The following principles apply to the requirements recorded:

- Only requirements specific to the export product group (or the top exported subproduct within that group) and agricultural products more generally are captured. Customs procedures or documentary requirements that are not specific in this way are not measured (certificate of origin, generalized system of preferences (GSP) certificate, export declaration, commercial, shipping or transport documents, letter of credit and so on).

- Mandatory membership of a public or private entity is included if it is required to obtain and exercise the right to export the selected product or agricultural products more generally.

- Trader-level export licenses include any document or action that is required to obtain and exercise the right to export, including registration or accreditation requirements, or traditional licenses.

- Documents are collected on a per shipment basis and one document includes both application and completion of the process (phytosanitary certificate, quality certificate from a private laboratory).

- Where multiple documents are obtained simultaneously, they are recorded as separate documents but time is adjusted to reflect their simultaneity.

- The mandatory documents required by both the country studied and the selected trading partner are included.

- Both public and private fumigation certificates are excluded if they are not required by the laws of either the country studied or the select-ed trading partner. Only fumigation that is required for the product itself is captured and separate fumigation for packaging prior to its purchase and use is not included.

Time

Time is recorded in calendar days and captures the median duration to obtain each mandatory document to export on a per shipment basis. Time to complete membership requirements or to obtain trader-level licenses is not captured. The time span for each document starts with the first filing of the application or demand and ends once the company has received the final document, such as the phytosanitary certificate. It is assumed that the company's owners, managers or employees have had no prior con-tact with any of the officials and that the company completes each procedure to obtain the document without delay on its side. The following principles apply to the documents coded:

- It is assumed that the minimum time required for each document is 1 day, except for documents that can be fully obtained online, for which the time required is recorded as half a day.

- Although multiple documents may be obtained (and related process-es completed) simultaneously, the process to obtain each document cannot start on the same day (that is, simultaneous processes start on consecutive days).

- If the process to obtain a document can be accelerated for an additional cost and is available to all types of companies, the fastest legal pro-cess is chosen and the related costs are recorded. Fast-track options

applying only to firms located in an export processing zone or to certain accredited firms under authorized economic operator programs are not taken into account.

Costs

The costs include all official fees and fees for legal or professional services if such services are required by law to complete the qualification requirement or obtain a document. Service fees (charged by fumigation companies or private labora-tories) are only included if the company is required by law to use such services. Traditional (scheduled) border taxes and tariffs are not captured. Other spe-cial charges or taxes that apply to the export product or subproduct, or the export of agricultural products general-ly, are included only where they result in the issuance of a stand-alone mandato-ry document to export or are needed to obtain another mandatory document to export.

Where possible, laws, regulations and fee schedules are used as sources for calculating costs. In the absence of fee schedules, estimates by public and pri-vate sector respondents are used. If several respondents provide different estimates, the median reported value is applied. In all cases the cost excludes bribes. All costs are indicated in U.S. dol-lars and as a percentage of the country's income per capita.

Specific terms

Alternative Dispute Resolution (ADR) is any litigation process or procedure, other than adjudication by a presiding judge in court, in which a neutral third party assists in or decides on the resolution of the issues in dispute.

Farmers' cooperatives are also known as agricultural cooperatives, farmers' orga-nizations, or producers' associations. A farmers' cooperative is defined as a voluntary, jointly-owned and democrat-ically controlled association of farmers created to support and promote the eco-nomic interests of its members through joint economic activity, including, but not limited to, production, processing and marketing of agricultural products. If different types of farmers' organizations

exist in a country's laws, that which most closely adheres to this definition is selected for study.

Inspections on a risk-management basis involve an import monitoring programme where the monitoring (the number of consignments inspected) is established on the basis of predicted risk through pest risk analysis (PRA).

Mediation is an ADR process in which a neutral mediator helps the parties discuss and find a mutually acceptable solution. The mediator's role is strictly facilitative; he or she does not decide in favor of one party or another, but guides the parties toward a consensual resolution.

Pest risk analysis (PRA) is defined as "[t]he process of evaluating biological or other scientific and economic evidence to determine whether a pest should be regulated and the strength of any phyto-sanitary measures to be taken against it."[6] It consists of three stages: initiating the process for analyzing risk, assessing pest risk and managing pest risk.

Phytosanitary measures include "[a]ny legislation, regulation or official proce-dure having the purpose to prevent the introduction and/or spread of quarantine pests, or to limit the economic impact of regulated non-quarantine pests."[7]

Plant protection encompasses regula-tions, policies and institutional frame-works that affect plant health in a country, including domestic pest man-agement measures as well as phyto-sanitary controls at the border.

Production and sales encompasses regu-lations, policies and institutional frame-works that impact the production, processing, marketing and sales of agri-cultural products in a country.

Regulated quarantine pest refers to "[a] pest of potential economic importance to the area endangered thereby and not yet present there, or present but not widely distributed and being officially controlled."[8]

Settlement agreement is a mutually acceptable solution found by the parties upon conciliation or mediation.

TABLE B.5 Scoring methodology for markets

INDICATOR (CATEGORY)	DESCRIPTION	WHAT IS MEASURED	HOW IT IS SCORED
Plant protection (quality control)	This indicator looks at the strength of the domestic plant protection framework by considering the legal obligations applicable to domestic pest management	1. There is an obligation on the national plant protection agency or another government agency to carry out pest surveillance activities on plants in your country 2. There is an obligation on producers/land owners to monitor and report outbreaks of pests to the government 3. The government or national plant protection agency maintains a list of regulated quarantine pests that is accessible to the public 4. The list of regulated quarantine pests is uploaded to the IPPC website 5. A pest database that contains details on the pests present in your country, such as their current status, geographical distribution and/or treatment, is available on a government website 6. Pest risk analysis (PRA) is provided for in the law OR there is a designated unit in the government to carry out PRA 7. Phytosanitary inspections on imports of plant products may be carried out on a risk basis 8. Phytosanitary legislation covers both domestic containment and import/export quarantine procedures at the border	**A score of 1** if yes

(continued)

TABLE B.5 Scoring methodology for markets (continued)

INDICATOR (CATEGORY)	DESCRIPTION	WHAT IS MEASURED	HOW IT IS SCORED
Production and sales (operations)	This indicator measures legal requirements with regard to the establishment and activities of farmers' cooperatives, the ease of engaging in contract farming arrangements and resolving related disputes	Please note that questions 1 and 2 on licenses are based on the selected contracted product: 1. The producer or seller requires a license to sell the contracted product or to engage in an agricultural production contract 2. The contractor needs a license to purchase the contracted product or engage in an agricultural production contract	**A score of 1** if no
		3. Farmers' cooperatives can seek loans or lines of credits provided by non-members 4. Farmers' cooperatives can merge	**A score of 1** if yes
		5. Minimum capital requirement to establish a farmers' cooperative	**A score of 1** if there is no minimum capital requirement **A score of 0.25** if the minimum capital requirements is equal to or less than 1 times the income per capita **A score of 0** if the minimum capital requirement is greater than 1 times the income per capita
		6. Mediation/conciliation can be attempted after the start of judicial proceedings upon either court-referral or application of the parties	**A score of 1** if yes
		7. Enforceability of a settlement agreement reached through an extra-judicial and/or extra-arbitral negotiation, conciliation or mediation	**A score of 1** if the settlement agreement has the same enforceability as a court decision **A score of 0.5** if the settlement agreement can acquire the same enforceability as a court decision upon submission to a judicial body or upon notarization **A score of 0** if the settlement agreement is enforceable only under the laws of contract

(continued)

TABLE B.5 Scoring methodology for markets (continued)

INDICATOR (CATEGORY)	DESCRIPTION	WHAT IS MEASURED	HOW IT IS SCORED
Agricultural export (trade)	This indicator looks at the mandatory requirements to export the selected product to the selected trading partner at the trader level and per shipment	1. Exporters do or do not have to be a member of a specific association or organization in order to obtain the right to export the selected product or agricultural products more generally 2. Exporters do or do not have to obtain a trader-level export license in order to export the selected product or agricultural products more generally to the selected trading partner 3. Total number of mandatory documents required to export 4. Total time to obtain mandatory documents required to export 5. Total cost to obtain mandatory documents required to export	**Not scored**

Transport

EBA transport indicators measure regulatory and administrative constraints affecting the market access and operations of reliable and sustainable commercial road transport services and the regulatory requirements for cross-border transportation.

Two sets of indicators have been developed:

- Truck licenses.

- Cross-border transportation.

Transport indicators used two different questionnaire versions targeting: (i) private sector respondents—mainly trucking associations, trucking companies, freight forwarders, lawyers; and (ii) public sector respondents—mainly ministries of transport, road transport regulatory authorities and ministries of infrastructure. Data were collected through interviews conducted during country visits directly with respondents, by email and teleconference calls from Washington, DC and by local staff in the different target countries.

To make the data comparable across countries, several assumptions about the trucking company and its environment were made, as detailed below:

Assumptions about the business

The business:

- Is a limited liability company.

- Is 100% domestically owned.

- Has between five and 10 employees.

- Owns a maximum of five trucks; each truck has two axles and a loading capacity of 20 metric tons.[9]

- Rents a garage.

- Transports agricultural products within the country, including perishable goods.

- Does not transport fertilizers, pesticides or any hazardous products.

The information on transport licenses and permits refers exclusively to domestic operations. The section on cross-border transportation assumes trade is undertaken with the largest neighboring agricultural trading partner.

Time

Time is recorded in calendar days and captures the median duration of obtaining the required company or truck license. The timespan starts once all required documents have been submitted to the relevant authority and ends once the company has received the final document. The minimum time to obtain a company or truck license is one day. It is assumed that the company's owners, managers or employees have had no prior contact with any of the officials.

Cost

Costs capture only official costs required by law, including fees and taxes. Transport laws and regulations have been used as legal basis when available, and an estimation from respondents have been used when not. In such cases where no official costs are in place, the median of responses is computed. This section assumes all documents have been submitted correctly. All costs are indicated in U.S. dollars and as a percentage of the country's income per capita.

Validity

Validity is measured for company and truck licenses and for technical inspections. Validity is expressed in years.

Specific terms

Freight allocation:

- *Deregulated market*: Market actors can freely interact with each other.

  - Freight allocation occurs through direct contracting between a producer or trader and a trucking company.

  - Direct contracting is facilitated by a "freight exchange" (platform in which freight supply and demand are made public to all actors).

- *Regulated market*: Freight allocation is influenced or organized by a third party.

  - *Queuing system ("tour de rôle")*: freight allocation practice by which freight is sequentially allocated by trucking associations, unions or the government.

Cross-border transportation:

- *Transport rights*: A truck registered in Country A is able to transport agricultural goods produced in its country into Country B for sale.

- *Backhauling rights*: A truck registered in Country A is able to transport agricultural goods into Country B for sale, load other goods in Country B and carry them back to Country A.

- *Transit rights*: A truck registered in Country A is able to travel through Country B to deliver agricultural goods into Country C.

- *Triangular rights*: A truck registered in Country A is able to pick up agricultural goods in Country B and transport them to be delivered into Country C.

- *Cabotage rights*: A truck registered in Country A is able to pick up agricultural goods in Country B and deliver them to a different point in Country B.

TABLE B.6 Scoring methodology for transport

INDICATOR (CATEGORY)	DESCRIPTION	WHAT IS MEASURED	HOW IT IS SCORED
Truck licenses (operations)	This indicator categorizes the different licensing regimes to provide commercial road transport services in the domestic market. It also measures the extent to which license requirements and application submissions are available online, additional legal requirements to obtain a license/permit and price and freight allocation regulations affecting road transport services in the domestic market	1. Type of licensing regime required for a company to legally transport agricultural products in the domestic market	**A score of 1** if only company license required **A score of 0.5** if both company and truck licenses are required **A score of 0.25** if only registry, franchise/public concession or truck license is required **A score of 0** if no license is required *This question has double weight ($^2/_7$) with regard to the other questions of this indicator ($^1/_7$)*
		2. Online availability of license or permit requirements	**A score of 1** if yes *This question is not scored for countries without a license or permit*
		3. Availability of an electronic submission platform for license or permit application or renewal	**A score of 1** if yes *This question is not scored for countries without a license or permit*
		4. Additional requirements for obtaining the relevant licenses, permits, inspections and certificates with regard to nationality, membership with a trucking association or operational size	**A score of 1** if none of the following is a requirement to obtain a license / permit: (a) membership to an association, (b) being of a specific nationality and (c) certain operational size (number of trucks) **A score of $^2/_3$** if one is required **A score of $^1/_3$** if two are required **A score of 0** if all three are required to obtain a license or permit
		5. Government regulation of prices for agricultural road transport service	**A score of 1** if no
		6. Presence of a queuing system (also known as a "tour de rôle") binding for all trucking companies and used to access or allocate freight in the country	**A score of 1** if no
	Licenses and permits	1. Total time to obtain a license at company level to transport agricultural products by truck 2. Total cost to obtain a license at company level 3. Validity of the license at company level 4. Total time to obtain a permit or license at truck level 5. Total cost to obtain a license or permit at truck level 6. Validity of the permit or license at truck level 7. Total cost of a vehicle technical inspection 8. Validity of vehicle technical inspection	**Not scored**

(continued)

TABLE B.6 Scoring methodology for transport (continued)

INDICATOR (CATEGORY)	DESCRIPTION	WHAT IS MEASURED	HOW IT IS SCORED
Cross-border transportation (trade)	This indicator measures the restrictions to cross-border transport including the regulation of carrier's liabilities	1. Requirement of a written contract acknowledging carrier's liabilities in cross-border transportation transactions	**A score of 1** if yes
		2. The right of foreign trucking companies registered in the largest agricultural trading partner to transport goods into the country	**A score of 1** if yes
		3. Existence of quotas on the number of transport right permits granted	**A score of 1** if no **A score of 0** if yes or if no transport rights granted
		4. The right of foreign trucking companies registered in the largest agricultural trading partner to transport goods back from the country (backhauling)	**A score of 1** if yes
		5. The right of foreign trucking companies registered in the largest agricultural trading partner to transport goods from the country into a third country (triangular rights)	**A score of 1** if yes
		6. The right of foreign trucking companies registered in the largest agricultural trading partner to transit through the country	**A score of 1** if yes
		7. The right of foreign trucking companies registered in the largest agricultural trading partner to transport goods between two points within the country (cabotage)	**A score of 1** if yes

Notes

1. Based on the average growing time for medium-maturing varieties of maize.

2. Seasons in countries with one season per calendar year tend to last longer.

3. High-income and upper-middle-income countries are not measured under the MFI indicator.

4. In some countries, the maximum loan an MFI can extend is limited to a percentage of deposits or a percentage of core capital. This language is included in regulations for risk management, intended to limit the exposure of the institution to a single borrower. For countries with this type of loan limitation, *EBA* considers it "no limit" because the currency value corresponding to that percentage is so high as to present no effective limit to borrowers.

5. High-income and upper-middle-income countries are not measured under the agent banking indicator.

6. International Plant Protection Convention 2005. p. 16.

7. International Plant Protection Convention 2005. p. 17.

8. International Plant Protection Convention 2005. p. 18.

9. A truck is defined as one tractor unit, excluding the trailer.

Reference

2005. "Glossary of Phytosanitary Terms." International Standard for Phytosanitary Measures No. 5. Rome: FAO.

APPENDIX C
ALTERNATIVE WAYS OF PRESENTING THE DATA

The following are two alternative ways of presenting *EBA* data. The questions used to build the accessibility of agribusiness regulatory information and discrimination of agribusiness regulations scores are questions also used to build the topics and cross-cutting categories scores. For example, a seed variety catalogue (within accessibility of agribusiness regulatory information) also belongs to the seed registration (operations) indicator, so it is part of the seed score and the operations score. Similarly, the eligibility of the foreign firms to import fertilizer (within discrimination of agribusiness regulations) belongs to the fertilizer import requirements (trade) indicator, so it is part of the fertilizer score and the trade score.

Discrimination of agribusiness regulations

The data on discrimination of agribusiness regulations were collected across six *EBA* topics (table C.1). For each question, countries where the nondiscriminatory feature under study is in place are assigned a score of 1; those without such features are assigned a score of 0. The total score of the 18 questions reflects the number of good practices related to nondiscrimination. These questions are also part the corresponding topic and score.

TABLE C.1 Discrimination of agribusiness regulations data by topic

GOOD PRACTICES BY TOPICS		
SEED	1.	The mandatory participation of private sector representatives in seed variety release committee
	2.	The eligibility of private enterprises to produce breeder/pre-basic seed of local public varieties for use in the domestic market
	3.	The eligibility of private enterprises to produce foundation/basic seed of local public varieties for use in the domestic market
	4.	The accessibility of germplasm from the national gene bank for the private sector
	5.	The existence of a system for licensing public varieties to private seed enterprises for production and sale in the domestic market
	6.	The eligibility of the private sector to be accredited to carry out the certification process
FERTILIZER	7.	The eligibility of the private sector to register fertilizer
	8.	The eligibility of the domestic firms to import fertilizer in order to sell it
	9.	The eligibility of the foreign firms to import fertilizer in order to sell it
MACHINERY	10.	The eligibility of the private sector to import new agricultural tractors and harvesters
	11.	The eligibility of the private sector to import second-hand agricultural tractors and harvesters
	12.	The eligibility of the private sector to import spare parts for agricultural tractors and harvesters
FINANCE	13.	The eligibility of non-bank businesses (businesses that do not hold any financial institution license) to issue e-money
MARKETS	14.	The absence of minimum capital requirements to establish a farmers' cooperative
TRANSPORT	15.	In addition to company and/or truck level licenses as well as technical inspections, the absence of other requirements regarding nationality, membership with a trucking association or operational size for a transport operator to offer commercial road transport services in the domestic market
	16.	The eligibility of foreign trucking companies registered in the country's largest agricultural trading partner to transport goods into the country
	17.	The eligibility of foreign trucking companies registered in the country's largest agricultural trading partner to transport goods back from the country (backhauling)
	18.	The eligibility of foreign trucking companies registered in the country's largest agricultural trading partner to transport goods between two points within the country (cabotage)

Accessibility of agribusiness regulatory information

The data on accessibility of agribusiness regulatory information were collected across five *EBA* topics (table C.2). For each question, countries where the information accessibility feature under study is in place are assigned a score of 1; those without such features are assigned a score of 0. The total score of the 10 questions reflects the number of good practices related to access to information. These questions are also part the corresponding topic and score.

TABLE C.2 Accessibility of agribusiness regulatory information data by topic

GOOD PRACTICES BY TOPICS		
SEED	1.	The existence of a seed variety catalog listing new varieties
	2.	The online availability of the seed variety catalog
	3.	The existence of an official fee schedule for seed certification activities carried out by the public sector
FERTILIZER	4.	The existence of an official catalog listing all registered fertilizer
	5.	The online availability of the fertilizer catalog
FINANCE	6.	The legal requirement for credit unions to disclose their effective interest rate or the annual percentage rate to loan applicants
MARKETS	7.	The existence of a list of regulated pests
	8.	The availability of a database on a government website that lists pests present in the country, their current distribution and/or status
TRANSPORT	9.	The online availability of the transport license/permit requirements
	10.	The existence of an electronic procedure to apply and/or renew the transport license/permit

COUNTRY TABLES

The team collected data in 40 countries in the following 11 areas: seed, fertilizer, machinery, finance, markets, transport, land, information and communications technology (ICT), water, livestock and environmental sustainability. Six of the topics were chosen for scoring and are presented in this section.

BANGLADESH

70.8	52.8	38.1	60.1	80.4	60.7
SEED	FERTILIZER	MACHINERY	FINANCE	MARKETS	TRANSPORT

70.8 SEED
84.4 Δ Seed registration (0–100)
2[a] Procedures (number)
3[a] Time (days)
0.0[a] Cost in US$ (% income per capita)
57.1 Δ Seed development and certification (0–100)

52.8 FERTILIZER
45.0 Δ Fertilizer registration (0–100)
7 Procedures (number)
951 Time (days)
702.6 (65.1) Cost in US$ (% income per capita)
66.7 ∂ Fertilizer quality control (0–100)
46.7 ◊ Fertilizer import requirements (0–100)
238.2 (22.1) Cost to register as an importer of fertilizer in US$ (% income per capita)
0 Cost to obtain an import permit for fertilizer in US$ (% income per capita)

38.1 MACHINERY
37.5 Δ Tractor dealer requirements (0–100)
13.3 ∂ Tractor standards and safety (0–100)
63.3 ◊ Tractor import requirements (0–100)
238.2 (22.1) Cost to register as an importer of tractors in US$ (% income per capita)
446.6 (41.3) Cost to obtain an import permit for tractors in US$ (% income per capita)

60.1 FINANCE
57.1 Δ Microfinance institutions (0–100)
60.0 Δ Credit unions (0–100)
100 Δ Agent banking (0–100)
25.0 Δ Electronic money (0–100)
58.3 Δ Warehouse receipts (0–100)

80.4 MARKETS
85.7 Δ Production and sales (0–100)
75.0 ∂ Plant protection (0–100)
1 Export documents per shipment (number)
1 Time to prepare export documents (days)
6.0 (0.6) Cost of export documents in US$ (% income per capita)
0 Trader licensing and membership requirements (number)
N/A Cost of licenses and membership in US$ (% income per capita)

60.7 TRANSPORT
64.3 Δ Truck licenses (0–100)
N/A Time to obtain company license (days)
N/A Cost to obtain company license in US$ (% income per capita)
N/A Validity of company license (years)
3.5 Time to obtain truck permit (days)
30.0 (2.8) Cost to obtain truck permit in US$ (% income per capita)
3 Validity of truck permit (years)
10.7 (1.0) Cost to obtain vehicle technical inspection in US$ (% income per capita)
1 Validity of vehicle inspection (years)
57.1 ◊ Cross-border transportation (0–100)

60.6	51.7	55.7
OPERATIONS (Δ)	QUALITY CONTROL (∂)	TRADE (◊)

The operations score is an average of seed, fertilizer, machinery, finance, markets and transport indicator scores indicated with a Δ. The quality control score is an average of seed, fertilizer, machinery and markets indicator scores indicated with a ∂. The trade score is an average of fertilizer, machinery and transport indicator scores indicated with a ◊.
a. Registration is not available for maize varieties. Private companies can, at their discretion and at no cost, list maize varieties in the national catalogue. This is what the procedures and time capture.

84.4 SEED	63.3 FERTILIZER	38.3 MACHINERY	65.3 FINANCE	81.3 MARKETS	67.9 TRANSPORT

84.4 SEED
81.3 Δ Seed registration (0−100)
5 Procedures (number)
517 Time (days)
711.3 (25.1) Cost in US$ (% income per capita)
87.5 Δ Seed development and certification (0−100)

63.3 FERTILIZER
20.0 Δ Fertilizer registration (0−100)
N/Aᵃ Procedures (number)
N/Aᵃ Time (days)
N/Aᵃ Cost in US$ (% income per capita)
100 ∂ Fertilizer quality control (0−100)
70.0 ◊ Fertilizer import requirements (0−100)
0 Cost to register as an importer of fertilizer in US$ (% income per capita)
No data Cost to obtain an import permit for fertilizer in US$ (% income per capita)

38.3 MACHINERY
25.0 Δ Tractor dealer requirements (0−100)
6.7 ∂ Tractor standards and safety (0−100)
83.3 ◊ Tractor import requirements (0−100)
0 Cost to register as an importer of tractors in US$ (% income per capita)
N/A Cost to obtain an import permit for tractors in US$ (% income per capita)

65.3 FINANCE
66.7 Δ Microfinance institutions (0−100)
93.3 Δ Credit unions (0−100)
0 Δ Agent banking (0−100)
91.7 Δ Electronic money (0−100)
75.0 Δ Warehouse receipts (0−100)

81.3 MARKETS
100 Δ Production and sales (0−100)
62.5 ∂ Plant protection (0−100)
1 Export documents per shipment (number)
2 Time to prepare export documents (days)
54.0 (1.9) Cost of export documents in US$ (% income per capita)
0 Trader licensing and membership requirements (number)
N/A Cost of licenses and membership in US$ (% income per capita)

67.9 TRANSPORT
64.3 Δ Truck licenses (0−100)
N/A Time to obtain company license (days)
N/A Cost to obtain company license in US$ (% income per capita)
N/A Validity of company license (years)
4.5 Time to obtain truck permit (days)
10.0 (0.4) Cost to obtain truck permit in US$ (% income per capita)
1 Validity of truck permit (years)
10 (0.4) Cost to obtain vehicle technical inspection in US$ (% income per capita)
1 Validity of vehicle inspection (years)
71.4 ◊ Cross-border transportation (0−100)

59.8 OPERATIONS (Δ)	56.4 QUALITY CONTROL (∂)	74.9 TRADE (◊)

The operations score is an average of seed, fertilizer, machinery, finance, markets and transport indicator scores indicated with a Δ. The quality control score is an average of seed, fertilizer, machinery and markets indicator scores indicated with a ∂. The trade score is an average of fertilizer, machinery and transport indicator scores indicated with a ◊.
a. The private sector is not required to register fertilizer.

BOSNIA AND HERZEGOVINA

42.0 SEED	94.4 FERTILIZER	44.0 MACHINERY	18.1 FINANCE	93.8 MARKETS	71.4 TRANSPORT

42.0 SEED
- 12.5 Δ Seed registration (0–100)
- *No practice* Procedures (number)
- *No practice* Time (days)
- *No practice* Cost in US$ (% income per capita)
- 71.4 Δ Seed development and certification (0–100)

94.4 FERTILIZER
- 100 Δ Fertilizer registration (0–100)
- 2 Procedures (number)
- 31 Time (days)
- 23.3 (0.5) Cost in US$ (% income per capita)
- 100 ∂ Fertilizer quality control (0–100)
- 83.3 ◊ Fertilizer import requirements (0–100)
- 0 Cost to register as an importer of fertilizer in US$ (% income per capita)
- N/A Cost to obtain an import permit for fertilizer in US$ (% income per capita)

44.0 MACHINERY
- 37.5 Δ Tractor dealer requirements (0–100)
- 27.8 ∂ Tractor standards and safety (0–100)
- 66.7 ◊ Tractor import requirements (0–100)
- N/A Cost to register as an importer of tractors in US$ (% income per capita)
- N/A[a] Cost to obtain an import permit for tractors in US$ (% income per capita)

18.1 FINANCE
- N/A[b] Δ Microfinance institutions (0–100)
- 0 Δ Credit unions (0–100)
- N/A[b] Δ Agent banking (0–100)
- 0 Δ Electronic money (0–100)
- 54.2 Δ Warehouse receipts (0–100)

93.8 MARKETS
- 100 Δ Production and sales (0–100)
- 87.5 ∂ Plant protection (0–100)
- 1 Export documents per shipment (number)
- 1 Time to prepare export documents (days)
- 26.7 (0.6) Cost of export documents in US$ (% income per capita)
- 0 Trader licensing and membership requirements (number)
- N/A Cost of licenses and membership in US$ (% income per capita)

71.4 TRANSPORT
- 71.4 Δ Truck licenses (0–100)
- 60 Time to obtain company license (days)
- 266.7 (5.6) Cost to obtain company license in US$ (% income per capita)
- 10 Validity of company license (years)
- 30 Time to obtain truck permit (days)
- 33.3 (0.7) Cost to obtain truck permit in US$ (% income per capita)
- 10 Validity of truck permit (years)
- 60.0 (1.3) Cost to obtain vehicle technical inspection in US$ (% income per capita)
- 1 Validity of vehicle inspection (years)
- 71.4 ◊ Cross-border transportation (0–100)

61.5 OPERATIONS (Δ)	71.8 QUALITY CONTROL (∂)	73.8 TRADE (◊)

The operations score is an average of seed, fertilizer, machinery, finance, markets and transport indicator scores indicated with a Δ. The quality control score is an average of seed, fertilizer, machinery and markets indicator scores indicated with a ∂. The trade score is an average of fertilizer, machinery and transport indicator scores indicated with a ◊.
a. 10% of customs value. b. Upper-middle-income countries are not measured under the microfinance institutions indicator and agent banking indicator.

BURKINA FASO

54.2 SEED	43.9 FERTILIZER	40.6 MACHINERY	37.2 FINANCE	58.9 MARKETS	60.7 TRANSPORT

54.2 SEED
65.6	Δ Seed registration (0–100)
No practice	Procedures (number)
No practice	Time (days)
No practice	Cost in US$ (% income per capita)
42.9	Δ Seed development and certification (0–100)

43.9 FERTILIZER
0	Δ Fertilizer registration (0–100)
N/Aª	Procedures (number)
N/Aª	Time (days)
N/Aª	Cost in US$ (% income per capita)
66.7	∂ Fertilizer quality control (0–100)
65.0	◊ Fertilizer import requirements (0–100)
2.0 (0.3)	Cost to register as an importer of fertilizer in US$ (% income per capita)
2.0 (0.3)	Cost to obtain an import permit for fertilizer in US$ (% income per capita)

40.6 MACHINERY
37.5	Δ Tractor dealer requirements (0–100)
6.7	∂ Tractor standards and safety (0–100)
77.5	◊ Tractor import requirements (0–100)
30.4 (4.3)	Cost to register as an importer of tractors in US$ (% income per capita)
2.0 (0.3)	Cost to obtain an import permit for tractors in US$ (% income per capita)

37.2 FINANCE
42.9	Δ Microfinance institutions (0–100)
60.0	Δ Credit unions (0–100)
0	Δ Agent banking (0–100)
83.3	Δ Electronic money (0–100)
0	Δ Warehouse receipts (0–100)

58.9 MARKETS
92.9	Δ Production and sales (0–100)
25.0	∂ Plant protection (0–100)
2	Export documents per shipment (number)
2	Time to prepare export documents (days)
19.2 (2.7)	Cost of export documents in US$ (% income per capita)
0	Trader licensing and membership requirements (number)
N/A	Cost of licenses and membership in US$ (% income per capita)

60.7 TRANSPORT
50.0	Δ Truck licenses (0–100)
N/A	Time to obtain company license (days)
N/A	Cost to obtain company license in US$ (% income per capita)
N/A	Validity of company license (years)
1	Time to obtain truck permit (days)
21.0 (3.0)	Cost to obtain truck permit in US$ (% income per capita)
0.5	Validity of truck permit (years)
87.0 (12.3)	Cost to obtain vehicle technical inspection in US$ (% income per capita)
0.5	Validity of vehicle inspection (years)
71.4	◊ Cross-border transportation (0–100)

45.3 OPERATIONS (Δ)	32.8 QUALITY CONTROL (∂)	71.3 TRADE (◊)

The operations score is an average of seed, fertilizer, machinery, finance, markets and transport indicator scores indicated with a Δ. The quality control score is an average of seed, fertilizer, machinery and markets indicator scores indicated with a ∂. The trade score is an average of fertilizer, machinery and transport indicator scores indicated with a ◊.
a. The private sector is not required to register fertilizer.

53.8	62.2	35.6	21.3	60.7	53.6
SEED	FERTILIZER	MACHINERY	FINANCE	MARKETS	TRANSPORT

SEED — 53.8

21.9	Δ Seed registration (0–100)
No practice	Procedures (number)
No practice	Time (days)
No practice	Cost in US$ (% income per capita)
85.7	Δ Seed development and certification (0–100)

FERTILIZER — 62.2

60.0	Δ Fertilizer registration (0–100)
No practice	Procedures (number)
No practice	Time (days)
No practice	Cost in US$ (% income per capita)
66.7	∂ Fertilizer quality control (0–100)
60.0	◊ Fertilizer import requirements (0–100)
N/A	Cost to register as an importer of fertilizer in US$ (% income per capita)
No data	Cost to obtain an import permit for fertilizer in US$ (% income per capita)

MACHINERY — 35.6

33.3	Δ Tractor dealer requirements (0–100)
13.3	∂ Tractor standards and safety (0–100)
60.0	◊ Tractor import requirements (0–100)
N/A	Cost to register as an importer of tractors in US$ (% income per capita)
No data	Cost to obtain an import permit for tractors in US$ (% income per capita)

FINANCE — 21.3

66.7	Δ Microfinance institutions (0–100)
40.0	Δ Credit unions (0–100)
0	Δ Agent banking (0–100)
0	Δ Electronic money (0–100)
0	Δ Warehouse receipts (0–100)

MARKETS — 60.7

71.4	Δ Production and sales (0–100)
50.0	∂ Plant protection (0–100)
3	Export documents per shipment (number)
6	Time to prepare export documents (days)
3.0 (1.1)	Cost of export documents in US$ (% income per capita)
1	Trader licensing and membership requirements (number)
240.7 (89.2)	Cost of licenses and membership in US$ (% income per capita)

TRANSPORT — 53.6

35.7	Δ Truck licenses (0–100)
N/A	Time to obtain company license (days)
N/A	Cost to obtain company license in US$ (% income per capita)
N/A	Validity of company license (years)
1	Time to obtain truck permit (days)
12.0 (4.5)	Cost to obtain truck permit in US$ (% income per capita)
0.5	Validity of truck permit (years)
18.1 (6.7)	Cost to obtain vehicle technical inspection in US$ (% income per capita)
0.5	Validity of vehicle inspection (years)
71.4	◊ Cross-border transportation (0–100)

45.9	43.3	63.8
OPERATIONS (Δ)	QUALITY CONTROL (∂)	TRADE (◊)

The operations score is an average of seed, fertilizer, machinery, finance, markets and transport indicator scores indicated with a Δ. The quality control score is an average of seed, fertilizer, machinery and markets indicator scores indicated with a ∂. The trade score is an average of fertilizer, machinery and transport indicator scores indicated with a ◊.

CAMBODIA

68.8	57.2	26.5	32.0	67.9	57.1
SEED	**FERTILIZER**	**MACHINERY**	**FINANCE**	**MARKETS**	**TRANSPORT**

68.8	**SEED**	
37.5	Δ Seed registration (0–100)	
6	*Procedures (number)*	
407	*Time (days)*	
187.0 (18.5)	*Cost in US$ (% income per capita)*	
100	Δ Seed development and certification (0–100)	

57.2	**FERTILIZER**	
45.0	Δ Fertilizer registration (0–100)	
3	*Procedures (number)*	
No data [a]	*Time (days)*	
506.5 (50.1)	*Cost in US$ (% income per capita)*	
66.7	∂ Fertilizer quality control (0–100)	
60.0	◊ Fertilizer import requirements (0–100)	
No data	*Cost to register as an importer of fertilizer in US$ (% income per capita)*	
No data	*Cost to obtain an import permit for fertilizer in US$ (% income per capita)*	

26.5	**MACHINERY**	
6.3	Δ Tractor dealer requirements (0–100)	
6.7	∂ Tractor standards and safety (0–100)	
66.7	◊ Tractor import requirements (0–100)	
N/A	*Cost to register as an importer of tractors in US$ (% income per capita)*	
N/A	*Cost to obtain an import permit for tractors in US$ (% income per capita)*	

32.0	**FINANCE**	
85.7	Δ Microfinance institutions (0–100)	
0	Δ Credit unions (0–100)	
74.3	Δ Agent banking (0–100)	
0	Δ Electronic money (0–100)	
0	Δ Warehouse receipts (0–100)	

67.9	**MARKETS**	
85.7	Δ Production and sales (0–100)	
50.0	∂ Plant protection (0–100)	
3	*Export documents per shipment (number)*	
7	*Time to prepare export documents (days)*	
86.6 (8.6)	*Cost of export documents in US$ (% income per capita)*	
0	*Trader licensing and membership requirements (number)*	
N/A	*Cost of licenses and membership in US$ (% income per capita)*	

57.1	**TRANSPORT**	
57.1	Δ Truck licenses (0–100)	
10	*Time to obtain company license (days)*	
365.2 (36.2)	*Cost to obtain company license in US$ (% income per capita)*	
2	*Validity of company license (years)*	
3.5	*Time to obtain truck permit (days)*	
11.0 (1.1)	*Cost to obtain truck permit in US$ (% income per capita)*	
1	*Validity of truck permit (years)*	
26.8 (2.7)	*Cost to obtain vehicle technical inspection in US$ (% income per capita)*	
1	*Validity of vehicle inspection (years)*	
57.1	◊ Cross-border transportation (0–100)	

49.1	41.1	61.3
OPERATIONS (Δ)	**QUALITY CONTROL (∂)**	**TRADE (◊)**

The operations score is an average of seed, fertilizer, machinery, finance, markets and transport indicator scores indicated with a Δ. The quality control score is an average of seed, fertilizer, machinery and markets indicator scores indicated with a ∂. The trade score is an average of fertilizer, machinery and transport indicator scores indicated with a ◊.
a. No data on application for registration, but approval by committee takes 56 days.

CHILE

93.8	43.3	43.3	N/A[b]	93.8	65.7
SEED	FERTILIZER	MACHINERY	FINANCE	MARKETS	TRANSPORT

93.8 SEED
87.5	Δ Seed registration (0–100)
5	*Procedures (number)*
848	*Time (days)*
920.8 (6.2)	*Cost in US$ (% income per capita)*
100	Δ Seed development and certification (0–100)

43.3 FERTILIZER
0	Δ Fertilizer registration (0–100)
N/A[a]	*Procedures (number)*
N/A[a]	*Time (days)*
N/A[a]	*Cost in US$ (% income per capita)*
66.7	∂ Fertilizer quality control (0–100)
63.3	◊ Fertilizer import requirements (0–100)
N/A	*Cost to register as an importer of fertilizer in US$ (% income per capita)*
20.1 (0.1)	*Cost to obtain an import permit for fertilizer in US$ (% income per capita)*

43.3 MACHINERY
50.0	Δ Tractor dealer requirements (0–100)
13.3	∂ Tractor standards and safety (0–100)
66.7	◊ Tractor import requirements (0–100)
N/A	*Cost to register as an importer of tractors in US$ (% income per capita)*
N/A	*Cost to obtain an import permit for tractors in US$ (% income per capita)*

N/A[b] FINANCE
-	Δ Microfinance institutions (0–100)
-	Δ Credit unions (0–100)
-	Δ Agent banking (0–100)
-	Δ Electronic money (0–100)
-	Δ Warehouse receipts (0–100)

93.8 MARKETS
100	Δ Production and sales (0–100)
87.5	∂ Plant protection (0–100)
1	*Export documents per shipment (number)*
1	*Time to prepare export documents (days)*
0[c]	*Cost of export documents in US$ (% income per capita)*
0	*Trader licensing and membership requirements (number)*
N/A	*Cost of licenses and membership in US$ (% income per capita)*

65.7 TRANSPORT
60.0	Δ Truck licenses (0–100)
N/A	*Time to obtain company license (days)*
N/A	*Cost to obtain company license in US$ (% income per capita)*
N/A	*Validity of company license (years)*
N/A	*Time to obtain truck permit (days)*
N/A	*Cost to obtain truck permit in US$ (% income per capita)*
N/A	*Validity of truck permit (years)*
15.4 (0.1)	*Cost to obtain vehicle technical inspection in US$ (% income per capita)*
0.5	*Validity of vehicle inspection (years)*
71.4	◊ Cross-border transportation (0–100)

60.8	55.8	67.1
OPERATIONS (Δ)	QUALITY CONTROL (∂)	TRADE (◊)

The operations score is an average of seed, fertilizer, machinery, finance, markets and transport indicator scores indicated with a Δ. The quality control score is an average of seed, fertilizer, machinery and markets indicator scores indicated with a ∂. The trade score is an average of fertilizer, machinery and transport indicator scores indicated with a ◊.
a. The private sector is not required to register fertilizer. b. High-income countries are not measured under the finance topic. c. The cost is 0.002 US$ (0.0001% of income per capita)

COLOMBIA

75.0 SEED	91.1 FERTILIZER	50.0 MACHINERY	89.4 FINANCE	93.8 MARKETS	78.6 TRANSPORT

75.0 — SEED
50.0	Δ Seed registration (0–100)
5	Procedures (number)
591	Time (days)
4,526.4 (58.2)	Cost in US$ (% income per capita)
100	Δ Seed development and certification (0–100)

91.1 — FERTILIZER
100	Δ Fertilizer registration (0–100)
3	Procedures (number)
48	Time (days)
No data	Cost in US$ (% income per capita)
100	∂ Fertilizer quality control (0–100)
73.3	◊ Fertilizer import requirements (0–100)
0	Cost to register as an importer of fertilizer in US$ (% income per capita)
31.3 (0.4)	Cost to obtain an import permit for fertilizer in US$ (% income per capita)

50.0 — MACHINERY
70.0	Δ Tractor dealer requirements (0–100)
13.3	∂ Tractor standards and safety (0–100)
66.7	◊ Tractor import requirements (0–100)
No data	Cost to register as an importer of tractors in US$ (% income per capita)
N/A	Cost to obtain an import permit for tractors in US$ (% income per capita)

89.4 — FINANCE
N/A[a]	Δ Microfinance institutions (0–100)
93.3	Δ Credit unions (0–100)
N/A[a]	Δ Agent banking (0–100)
91.7	Δ Electronic money (0–100)
83.3	Δ Warehouse receipts (0–100)

93.8 — MARKETS
100	Δ Production and sales (0–100)
87.5	∂ Plant protection (0–100)
2	Export documents per shipment (number)
4	Time to prepare export documents (days)
No data [b]	Cost of export documents in US$ (% income per capita)
1	Trader licensing and membership requirements (number)
0	Cost of licenses and membership in US$ (% income per capita)

78.6 — TRANSPORT
71.4	Δ Truck licenses (0–100)
57	Time to obtain company license (days)
268 (3.4)	Cost to obtain company license in US$ (% income per capita)
Indefinite [c]	Validity of company license (years)
N/A	Time to obtain truck permit (days)
N/A	Cost to obtain truck permit in US$ (% income per capita)
N/A	Validity of truck permit (years)
156.4 (2.0)	Cost to obtain vehicle technical inspection in US$ (% income per capita)
2	Validity of vehicle inspection (years)
85.7	◊ Cross-border transportation (0–100)

84.3 OPERATIONS (Δ)	66.9 QUALITY CONTROL (∂)	75.2 TRADE (◊)

The operations score is an average of seed, fertilizer, machinery, finance, markets and transport indicator scores indicated with a Δ. The quality control score is an average of seed, fertilizer, machinery and markets indicator scores indicated with a ∂. The trade score is an average of fertilizer, machinery and transport indicator scores indicated with a ◊.
a. Upper-middle-income countries are not measured under the microfinance institutions indicator and agent banking indicator. b. The cost of document 1 (phytosanitary certificate) is $33.9 (0.4% of income per capita). The cost of document 2 (quality certificate) could not be obtained. c. Has to be validated every year.

54.7	64.4	45.4	37.7	58.0	60.7
SEED	FERTILIZER	MACHINERY	FINANCE	MARKETS	TRANSPORT

54.7 SEED

59.4	Δ Seed registration (0–100)
6	*Procedures (number)*
368	*Time (days)*
2,082.2 (134.2)	*Cost in US$ (% income per capita)*
50.0	Δ Seed development and certification (0–100)

64.4 FERTILIZER

60.0	Δ Fertilizer registration (0–100)
No practice	*Procedures (number)*
No practice	*Time (days)*
No practice	*Cost in US$ (% income per capita)*
66.7	∂ Fertilizer quality control (0–100)
66.7	◊ Fertilizer import requirements (0–100)
59.5 (3.8)	*Cost to register as an importer of fertilizer in US$ (% income per capita)*
N/A	*Cost to obtain an import permit for fertilizer in US$ (% income per capita)*

45.4 MACHINERY

25.0	Δ Tractor dealer requirements (0–100)
27.8	∂ Tractor standards and safety (0–100)
83.3	◊ Tractor import requirements (0–100)
59.5 (3.8)	*Cost to register as an importer of tractors in US$ (% income per capita)*
N/A	*Cost to obtain an import permit for tractors in US$ (% income per capita)*

37.7 FINANCE

42.9	Δ Microfinance institutions (0–100)
60.0	Δ Credit unions (0–100)
0	Δ Agent banking (0–100)
85.4	Δ Electronic money (0–100)
0	Δ Warehouse receipts (0–100)

58.0 MARKETS

78.6	Δ Production and sales (0–100)
37.5	∂ Plant protection (0–100)
3	*Export documents per shipment (number)*
No data	*Time to prepare export documents (days)*
No data	*Cost of export documents in US$ (% income per capita)*
1	*Trader licensing and membership requirements (number)*
198.3 (12.8)	*Cost of licenses and membership in US$ (% income per capita)*

60.7 TRANSPORT

50.0	Δ Truck licenses (0–100)
N/A	*Time to obtain company license (days)*
N/A	*Cost to obtain company license in US$ (% income per capita)*
N/A	*Validity of company license (years)*
1	*Time to obtain truck permit (days)*
49.6 (3.2)	*Cost to obtain truck permit in US$ (% income per capita)*
2	*Validity of truck permit (years)*
87.1 (5.6)	*Cost to obtain vehicle technical inspection in US$ (% income per capita)*
0.5	*Validity of vehicle inspection (years)*
71.4	◊ Cross-border transportation (0–100)

51.0	44.0	73.8
OPERATIONS (Δ)	QUALITY CONTROL (∂)	TRADE (◊)

The operations score is an average of seed, fertilizer, machinery, finance, markets and transport indicator scores indicated with a Δ. The quality control score is an average of seed, fertilizer, machinery and markets indicator scores indicated with a ∂. The trade score is an average of fertilizer, machinery and transport indicator scores indicated with a ◊.

DENMARK

87.5 SEED	82.2 FERTILIZER	80.7 MACHINERY	N/Aª FINANCE	85.7 MARKETS	100 TRANSPORT

87.5 SEED

87.5	Δ Seed registration (0–100)	
6	Procedures (number)	
690	Time (days)	
4,640.5 (7.6)	Cost in US$ (% income per capita)	
87.5	Δ Seed development and certification (0–100)	

82.2 FERTILIZER

80.0	Δ Fertilizer registration (0–100)
2	Procedures (number)
31	Time (days)
267.7 (0.4)	Cost in US$ (% income per capita)
83.3	∂ Fertilizer quality control (0–100)
83.3	◊ Fertilizer import requirements (0–100)
N/A	Cost to register as an importer of fertilizer in US$ (% income per capita)
N/A	Cost to obtain an import permit for fertilizer in US$ (% income per capita)

80.7 MACHINERY

86.7	Δ Tractor dealer requirements (0–100)
72.2	∂ Tractor standards and safety (0–100)
83.3	◊ Tractor import requirements (0–100)
N/A	Cost to register as an importer of tractors in US$ (% income per capita)
N/A	Cost to obtain an import permit for tractors in US$ (% income per capita)

N/Aª FINANCE

-	Δ Microfinance institutions (0–100)
-	Δ Credit unions (0–100)
-	Δ Agent banking (0–100)
-	Δ Electronic money (0–100)
-	Δ Warehouse receipts (0–100)

85.7 MARKETS

71.4	Δ Production and sales (0–100)
100	∂ Plant protection (0–100)
0	Export documents per shipment (number)
0	Time to prepare export documents (days)
0	Cost of export documents in US$ (% income per capita)
1	Trader licensing and membership requirements (number)
667.5 (1.1)	Cost of licenses and membership in US$ (% income per capita)

100 TRANSPORT

100	Δ Truck licenses (0–100)
27	Time to obtain company license (days)
0	Cost to obtain company license in US$ (% income per capita)
10	Validity of company license (years)
N/A	Time to obtain truck permit (days)
N/A	Cost to obtain truck permit in US$ (% income per capita)
N/A	Validity of truck permit (years)
190.5 (0.3)	Cost to obtain vehicle technical inspection in US$ (% income per capita)
1	Validity of vehicle inspection (years)
100	◊ Cross-border transportation (0–100)

85.1 OPERATIONS (Δ)	85.2 QUALITY CONTROL (∂)	88.9 TRADE (◊)

The operations score is an average of seed, fertilizer, machinery, finance, markets and transport indicator scores indicated with a Δ. The quality control score is an average of seed, fertilizer, machinery and markets indicator scores indicated with a ∂. The trade score is an average of fertilizer, machinery and transport indicator scores indicated with a ◊.
a. High-income countries are not measured under the finance topic.

58.9	34.4	28.5	59.8	55.4	52.4
SEED	FERTILIZER	MACHINERY	FINANCE	MARKETS	TRANSPORT

58.9 SEED
75.0	Δ Seed registration (0–100)
4	*Procedures (number)*
620	*Time (days)*
488.9 (88.9)	*Cost in US$ (% income per capita)*
42.9	Δ Seed development and certification (0–100)

34.4 FERTILIZER
20.0	Δ Fertilizer registration (0–100)
N/A[a]	*Procedures (number)*
N/A[a]	*Time (days)*
N/A[a]	*Cost in US$ (% income per capita)*
66.7	∂ Fertilizer quality control (0–100)
16.7	◊ Fertilizer import requirements (0–100)
N/A	*Cost to register as an importer of fertilizer in US$ (% income per capita)*
N/A	*Cost to obtain an import permit for fertilizer in US$ (% income per capita)*

28.5 MACHINERY
18.8	Δ Tractor dealer requirements (0–100)
6.7	∂ Tractor standards and safety (0–100)
60.0	◊ Tractor import requirements (0–100)
15.3 (2.8)	*Cost to register as an importer of tractors in US$ (% income per capita)*
5.2 (0.9)	*Cost to obtain an import permit for tractors in US$ (% income per capita)*

59.8 FINANCE
47.6	Δ Microfinance institutions (0–100)
60.0	Δ Credit unions (0–100)
91.4	Δ Agent banking (0–100)
0	Δ Electronic money (0–100)
100	Δ Warehouse receipts (0–100)

55.4 MARKETS
85.7	Δ Production and sales (0–100)
25.0	∂ Plant protection (0–100)
3	*Export documents per shipment (number)*
No data[b]	*Time to prepare export documents (days)*
80.9 (14.7)	*Cost of export documents in US$ (% income per capita)*
1	*Trader licensing and membership requirements (number)*
9.0 (1.6)	*Cost of licenses and membership in US$ (% income per capita)*

52.4 TRANSPORT
61.9	Δ Truck licenses (0–100)
1	*Time to obtain company license (days)*
34.6 (6.3)	*Cost to obtain company license in US$ (% income per capita)*
1	*Validity of company license (years)*
N/A	*Time to obtain truck permit (days)*
N/A	*Cost to obtain truck permit in US$ (% income per capita)*
N/A	*Validity of truck permit (years)*
19.4 (3.5)	*Cost to obtain vehicle technical inspection in US$ (% income per capita)*
1	*Validity of vehicle inspection (years)*
42.9	◊ Cross-border transportation (0–100)

50.9	32.8	39.8
OPERATIONS (Δ)	QUALITY CONTROL (∂)	TRADE (◊)

The operations score is an average of seed, fertilizer, machinery, finance, markets and transport indicator scores indicated with a Δ. The quality control score is an average of seed, fertilizer, machinery and markets indicator scores indicated with a ∂. The trade score is an average of fertilizer, machinery and transport indicator scores indicated with a ◊.
a. The private sector is not required to register fertilizer. b. The time to obtain document 1 (phytosanitary certificate) is 1 day, and the time to obtain document 3 (fumigation certificate) is 1 day. The time to obtain document 2 (quality certificate) could not be obtained.

GEORGIA

75.0	68.9	44.4	37.7	86.6	65.7
SEED	FERTILIZER	MACHINERY	FINANCE	MARKETS	TRANSPORT

75.0 — **SEED**
62.5 — Δ Seed registration (0–100)
6 — *Procedures (number)*
534 — *Time (days)*
No data — *Cost in US$ (% income per capita)*
87.5 — Δ Seed development and certification (0–100)

68.9 — **FERTILIZER**
90.0 — Δ Fertilizer registration (0–100)
5 — *Procedures (number)*
765 — *Time (days)*
260.6 (7.0) — *Cost in US$ (% income per capita)*
50.0 — ∂ Fertilizer quality control (0–100)
66.7 — ◊ Fertilizer import requirements (0–100)
N/A — *Cost to register as an importer of fertilizer in US$ (% income per capita)*
N/A — *Cost to obtain an import permit for fertilizer in US$ (% income per capita)*

44.4 — **MACHINERY**
33.3 — Δ Tractor dealer requirements (0–100)
33.3 — ∂ Tractor standards and safety (0–100)
66.7 — ◊ Tractor import requirements (0–100)
N/A — *Cost to register as an importer of tractors in US$ (% income per capita)*
N/A — *Cost to obtain an import permit for tractors in US$ (% income per capita)*

37.7 — **FINANCE**
0 — Δ Microfinance institutions (0–100)
80.0 — Δ Credit unions (0–100)
0 — Δ Agent banking (0–100)
50.0 — Δ Electronic money (0–100)
58.3 — Δ Warehouse receipts (0–100)

86.6 — **MARKETS**
85.7 — Δ Production and sales (0–100)
87.5 — ∂ Plant protection (0–100)
2 — *Export documents per shipment (number)*
5 — *Time to prepare export documents (days)*
95.6 (2.6) — *Cost of export documents in US$ (% income per capita)*
0 — *Trader licensing and membership requirements (number)*
N/A — *Cost of licenses and membership in US$ (% income per capita)*

65.7 — **TRANSPORT**
60.0 — Δ Truck licenses (0–100)
N/A — *Time to obtain company license (days)*
N/A — *Cost to obtain company license in US$ (% income per capita)*
N/A — *Validity of company license (years)*
N/A — *Time to obtain truck permit (days)*
N/A — *Cost to obtain truck permit in US$ (% income per capita)*
N/A — *Validity of truck permit (years)*
N/A — *Cost to obtain vehicle technical inspection in US$ (% income per capita)*
N/A — *Validity of vehicle inspection (years)*
71.4 — ◊ Cross-border transportation (0–100)

63.6	56.9	68.3
OPERATIONS (Δ)	QUALITY CONTROL (∂)	TRADE (◊)

The operations score is an average of seed, fertilizer, machinery, finance, markets and transport indicator scores indicated with a Δ. The quality control score is an average of seed, fertilizer, machinery and markets indicator scores indicated with a ∂. The trade score is an average of fertilizer, machinery and transport indicator scores indicated with a ◊.

GHANA

40.6	59.4	39.2	41.7	71.4	65.7
SEED	FERTILIZER	MACHINERY	FINANCE	MARKETS	TRANSPORT

40.6 SEED
43.8 Δ Seed registration (0–100)
6 *Procedures (number)*
757 *Time (days)*
No data *Cost in US$ (% income per capita)*
37.5 Δ Seed development and certification (0–100)

59.4 FERTILIZER
45.0 Δ Fertilizer registration (0–100)
4 *Procedures (number)*
255 *Time (days)*
1,445.4 (89.2) *Cost in US$ (% income per capita)*
66.7 ∂ Fertilizer quality control (0–100)
66.7 ◊ Fertilizer import requirements (0–100)
158.4 (9.8) *Cost to register as an importer of fertilizer in US$ (% income per capita)*
N/A *Cost to obtain an import permit for fertilizer in US$ (% income per capita)*

39.2 MACHINERY
37.5 Δ Tractor dealer requirements (0–100)
13.3 ∂ Tractor standards and safety (0–100)
66.7 ◊ Tractor import requirements (0–100)
N/A *Cost to register as an importer of tractors in US$ (% income per capita)*
N/A *Cost to obtain an import permit for tractors in US$ (% income per capita)*

41.7 FINANCE
42.9 Δ Microfinance institutions (0–100)
80.0 Δ Credit unions (0–100)
60.5 Δ Agent banking (0–100)
25.0 Δ Electronic money (0–100)
0 Δ Warehouse receipts (0–100)

71.4 MARKETS
92.9 Δ Production and sales (0–100)
50.0 ∂ Plant protection (0–100)
3 *Export documents per shipment (number)*
8 *Time to prepare export documents (days)*
5.9 (0.4) *Cost of export documents in US$ (% income per capita)*
3 *Trader licensing and membership requirements (number)*
2,435.6 (150.3) [a] *Cost of licenses and membership in US$ (% income per capita)*

65.7 TRANSPORT
60.0 Δ Truck licenses (0–100)
N/A *Time to obtain company license (days)*
N/A *Cost to obtain company license in US$ (% income per capita)*
N/A *Validity of company license (years)*
N/A *Time to obtain truck permit (days)*
N/A *Cost to obtain truck permit in US$ (% income per capita)*
N/A *Validity of truck permit (years)*
99 (6.1) *Cost to obtain vehicle technical inspection in US$ (% income per capita)*
1 *Validity of vehicle inspection (years)*
71.4 ◊ Cross-border transportation (0–100)

52.9	43.3	68.3
OPERATIONS (Δ)	QUALITY CONTROL (∂)	TRADE (◊)

The operations score is an average of seed, fertilizer, machinery, finance, markets and transport indicator scores indicated with a Δ. The quality control score is an average of seed, fertilizer, machinery and markets indicator scores indicated with a ∂. The trade score is an average of fertilizer, machinery and transport indicator scores indicated with a ◊.
a. The total cost excludes the cost of Ghana's Cocoa Export License, which could not be quantified and was recorded as "variable" based on contributor responses and the applicable regulations.

GREECE

73.4 SEED	**93.3** FERTILIZER	**74.6** MACHINERY	**N/A**[a] FINANCE	**90.2** MARKETS	**92.9** TRANSPORT

73.4	**SEED**	
46.9	Δ Seed registration (0–100)	
6	*Procedures (number)*	
729	*Time (days)*	
1,911.4 (8.7)	*Cost in US$ (% income per capita)*	
100	Δ Seed development and certification (0–100)	
93.3	**FERTILIZER**	
100	Δ Fertilizer registration (0–100)	
7	*Procedures (number)*	
211	*Time (days)*	
1,282.4 (5.8)	*Cost in US$ (% income per capita)*	
100	∂ Fertilizer quality control (0–100)	
80.0	◊ Fertilizer import requirements (0–100)	
N/A	*Cost to register as an importer of fertilizer in US$ (% income per capita)*	
135.0 (0.6)	*Cost to obtain an import permit for fertilizer in US$ (% income per capita)*	
74.6	**MACHINERY**	
83.8	Δ Tractor dealer requirements (0–100)	
73.3	∂ Tractor standards and safety (0–100)	
66.7	◊ Tractor import requirements (0–100)	
N/A	*Cost to register as an importer of tractors in US$ (% income per capita)*	
N/A	*Cost to obtain an import permit for tractors in US$ (% income per capita)*	
N/A[a]	**FINANCE**	
-	Δ Microfinance institutions (0–100)	
-	Δ Credit unions (0–100)	
-	Δ Agent banking (0–100)	
-	Δ Electronic money (0–100)	
-	Δ Warehouse receipts (0–100)	
90.2	**MARKETS**	
92.9	Δ Production and sales (0–100)	
87.5	∂ Plant protection (0–100)	
0	*Export documents per shipment (number)*	
0	*Time to prepare export documents (days)*	
0	*Cost of export documents in US$ (% income per capita)*	
1	*Trader licensing and membership requirements (number)*	
809.9 (3.7)	*Cost of licenses and membership in US$ (% income per capita)*	
92.9	**TRANSPORT**	
85.7	Δ Truck licenses (0–100)	
60	*Time to obtain company license (days)*	
674.9 (3.1)	*Cost to obtain company license in US$ (% income per capita)*	
10	*Validity of company license (years)*	
N/A	*Time to obtain truck permit (days)*	
N/A	*Cost to obtain truck permit in US$ (% income per capita)*	
N/A	*Validity of truck permit (years)*	
141.7 (0.6)	*Cost to obtain vehicle technical inspection in US$ (% income per capita)*	
1	*Validity of vehicle inspection (years)*	
100	◊ Cross-border transportation (0–100)	

87.2 OPERATIONS (Δ)	**86.9** QUALITY CONTROL (∂)	**82.2** TRADE (◊)

The operations score is an average of seed, fertilizer, machinery, finance, markets and transport indicator scores indicated with a Δ. The quality control score is an average of seed, fertilizer, machinery and markets indicator scores indicated with a ∂. The trade score is an average of fertilizer, machinery and transport indicator scores indicated with a ◊.
a. High-income countries are not measured under the finance topic.

GUATEMALA

71.0	66.9	40.6	46.3	86.6	72.9
SEED	FERTILIZER	MACHINERY	FINANCE	MARKETS	TRANSPORT

71.0 SEED
56.3	Δ Seed registration (0–100)
4	Procedures (number)
166	Time (days)
67.5 (2.0)	Cost in US$ (% income per capita)
85.7	Δ Seed development and certification (0–100)

66.9 FERTILIZER
35.0	Δ Fertilizer registration (0–100)
2	Procedures (number)
105	Time (days)
12.5 (0.4)	Cost in US$ (% income per capita)
100	∂ Fertilizer quality control (0–100)
65.8	◊ Fertilizer import requirements (0–100)
No data	Cost to register as an importer of fertilizer in US$ (% income per capita)
No data	Cost to obtain an import permit for fertilizer in US$ (% income per capita)

40.6 MACHINERY
25.0	Δ Tractor dealer requirements (0–100)
13.3	∂ Tractor standards and safety (0–100)
83.3	◊ Tractor import requirements (0–100)
622.6 (18.1)	Cost to register as an importer of tractors in US$ (% income per capita)
N/A	Cost to obtain an import permit for tractors in US$ (% income per capita)

46.3 FINANCE
0	Δ Microfinance institutions (0–100)
40.0	Δ Credit unions (0–100)
91.4	Δ Agent banking (0–100)
25.0	Δ Electronic money (0–100)
75.0	Δ Warehouse receipts (0–100)

86.6 MARKETS
85.7	Δ Production and sales (0–100)
87.5	∂ Plant protection (0–100)
1	Export documents per shipment (number)
1	Time to prepare export documents (days)
6.3 (0.2)	Cost of export documents in US$ (% income per capita)
0	Trader licensing and membership requirements (number)
N/A	Cost of licenses and membership in US$ (% income per capita)

72.9 TRANSPORT
60.0	Δ Truck licenses (0–100)
N/A	Time to obtain company license (days)
N/A	Cost to obtain company license in US$ (% income per capita)
N/A	Validity of company license (years)
N/A	Time to obtain truck permit (days)
N/A	Cost to obtain truck permit in US$ (% income per capita)
N/A	Validity of truck permit (years)
100 (2.9)	Cost to obtain vehicle technical inspection in US$ (% income per capita)
1	Validity of vehicle inspection (years)
85.7	◊ Cross-border transportation (0–100)

53.8	66.9	78.3
OPERATIONS (Δ)	QUALITY CONTROL (∂)	TRADE (◊)

The operations score is an average of seed, fertilizer, machinery, finance, markets and transport indicator scores indicated with a Δ. The quality control score is an average of seed, fertilizer, machinery and markets indicator scores indicated with a ∂. The trade score is an average of fertilizer, machinery and transport indicator scores indicated with a ◊.

71.0 SEED	67.8 FERTILIZER	42.1 MACHINERY	21.7 FINANCE	83.9 MARKETS	66.7 TRANSPORT

71.0 SEED
56.3 Δ Seed registration (0–100)
No practice — Procedures (number)
No practice — Time (days)
No practice — Cost in US$ (% income per capita)
85.7 Δ Seed development and certification (0–100)

67.8 FERTILIZER
70.0 Δ Fertilizer registration (0–100)
3 — Procedures (number)
36 — Time (days)
15.0 (0.3) [a] — Cost in US$ (% income per capita)
66.7 ∂ Fertilizer quality control (0–100)
66.7 ◊ Fertilizer import requirements (0–100)
13.6 (0.3) — Cost to register as an importer of fertilizer in US$ (% income per capita)
13.6 (0.3) — Cost to obtain an import permit for fertilizer in US$ (% income per capita)

42.1 MACHINERY
36.3 Δ Tractor dealer requirements (0–100)
13.3 ∂ Tractor standards and safety (0–100)
76.7 ◊ Tractor import requirements (0–100)
13.6 (0.3) — Cost to register as an importer of tractors in US$ (% income per capita)
13.6 (0.3) — Cost to obtain an import permit for tractors in US$ (% income per capita)

21.7 FINANCE
N/A [b] Δ Microfinance institutions (0–100)
40.0 Δ Credit unions (0–100)
N/A [b] Δ Agent banking (0–100)
25.0 Δ Electronic money (0–100)
0 Δ Warehouse receipts (0–100)

83.9 MARKETS
92.9 Δ Production and sales (0–100)
75.0 ∂ Plant protection (0–100)
1 — Export documents per shipment (number)
1 — Time to prepare export documents (days)
2.7 (0.1) — Cost of export documents in US$ (% income per capita)
0 — Trader licensing and membership requirements (number)
N/A — Cost of licenses and membership in US$ (% income per capita)

66.7 TRANSPORT
61.9 Δ Truck licenses (0–100)
3 — Time to obtain company license (days)
203.3 (3.9) — Cost to obtain company license in US$ (% income per capita)
1 — Validity of company license (years)
1 — Time to obtain truck permit (days)
521.7 (10.1) — Cost to obtain truck permit in US$ (% income per capita)
1 — Validity of truck permit (years)
40.7 (0.8) — Cost to obtain vehicle technical inspection in US$ (% income per capita)
1 — Validity of vehicle inspection (years)
71.4 ◊ Cross-border transportation (0–100)

58.9 OPERATIONS (Δ)	51.7 QUALITY CONTROL (∂)	71.6 TRADE (◊)

The operations score is an average of seed, fertilizer, machinery, finance, markets and transport indicator scores indicated with a Δ. The quality control score is an average of seed, fertilizer, machinery and markets indicator scores indicated with a ∂. The trade score is an average of fertilizer, machinery and transport indicator scores indicated with a ◊.
a. Cost of application for registration is $15, but cost of lab report is unknown. Approval by the National Committee is free. b. Upper-middle-income countries are not measured under the microfinance institutions indicator and agent banking indicator.

90.6 SEED	**50.0** FERTILIZER	**57.2** MACHINERY	**72.9** FINANCE	**50.9** MARKETS	**75.0** TRANSPORT

90.6 SEED
93.8	Δ Seed registration (0–100)
6	Procedures (number)
321	Time (days)
1,798.5 (140.5)	Cost in US$ (% income per capita)
87.5	Δ Seed development and certification (0–100)

50.0 FERTILIZER
0	Δ Fertilizer registration (0–100)
N/A[a]	Procedures (number)
N/A[a]	Time (days)
N/A[a]	Cost in US$ (% income per capita)
66.7	∂ Fertilizer quality control (0–100)
83.3	◊ Fertilizer import requirements (0–100)
327.0 (25.5)	Cost to register as an importer of fertilizer in US$ (% income per capita)
N/A	Cost to obtain an import permit for fertilizer in US$ (% income per capita)

57.2 MACHINERY
43.8	Δ Tractor dealer requirements (0–100)
61.1	∂ Tractor standards and safety (0–100)
66.7	◊ Tractor import requirements (0–100)
N/A	Cost to register as an importer of tractors in US$ (% income per capita)
N/A	Cost to obtain an import permit for tractors in US$ (% income per capita)

72.9 FINANCE
90.5	Δ Microfinance institutions (0–100)
86.7	Δ Credit unions (0–100)
87.1	Δ Agent banking (0–100)
100	Δ Electronic money (0–100)
0	Δ Warehouse receipts (0–100)

50.9 MARKETS
64.3	Δ Production and sales (0–100)
37.5	∂ Plant protection (0–100)
4	Export documents per shipment (number)
6	Time to prepare export documents (days)
130.8 (10.2) [b]	Cost of export documents in US$ (% income per capita)
2	Trader licensing and membership requirements (number)
1,602.3 (125.2)	Cost of licenses and membership in US$ (% income per capita)

75.0 TRANSPORT
78.6	Δ Truck licenses (0–100)
N/A	Time to obtain company license (days)
N/A	Cost to obtain company license in US$ (% income per capita)
N/A	Validity of company license (years)
1	Time to obtain truck permit (days)
32.7 (2.6)	Cost to obtain truck permit in US$ (% income per capita)
1	Validity of truck permit (years)
10.9 (0.9)	Cost to obtain vehicle technical inspection in US$ (% income per capita)
1	Validity of vehicle inspection (years)
71.4	◊ Cross-border transportation (0–100)

58.3 OPERATIONS (Δ)	**55.1** QUALITY CONTROL (∂)	**73.8** TRADE (◊)

The operations score is an average of seed, fertilizer, machinery, finance, markets and transport indicator scores indicated with a Δ. The quality control score is an average of seed, fertilizer, machinery and markets indicator scores indicated with a ∂. The trade score is an average of fertilizer, machinery and transport indicator scores indicated with a ◊.
a. The private sector is not required to register fertilizer. b. The total cost excludes the cost of document 4 (export release order), which requires payment of an ad valorem levy (1% of ex-warehouse price for tea exports sold at the tea auction).

KYRGYZ REPUBLIC

48.9	63.9	63.9	79.8	80.4	72.9
SEED	FERTILIZER	MACHINERY	FINANCE	MARKETS	TRANSPORT

48.9 SEED
40.6	Δ Seed registration (0–100)
5	Procedures (number)
970	Time (days)
2,850.7 (228.1)	Cost in US$ (% income per capita)
57.1	Δ Seed development and certification (0–100)

63.9 FERTILIZER
75.0	Δ Fertilizer registration (0–100)
5	Procedures (number)
730	Time (days)
277.9 (22.2)	Cost in US$ (% income per capita)
50.0	∂ Fertilizer quality control (0–100)
66.7	◊ Fertilizer import requirements (0–100)
N/A	Cost to register as an importer of fertilizer in US$ (% income per capita)
N/A	Cost to obtain an import permit for fertilizer in US$ (% income per capita)

63.9 MACHINERY
75.0	Δ Tractor dealer requirements (0–100)
33.3	∂ Tractor standards and safety (0–100)
83.3	◊ Tractor import requirements (0–100)
N/A	Cost to register as an importer of tractors in US$ (% income per capita)
N/A	Cost to obtain an import permit for tractors in US$ (% income per capita)

79.8 FINANCE
61.9	Δ Microfinance institutions (0–100)
100	Δ Credit unions (0–100)
91.4	Δ Agent banking (0–100)
87.5	Δ Electronic money (0–100)
58.3	Δ Warehouse receipts (0–100)

80.4 MARKETS
85.7	Δ Production and sales (0–100)
75.0	∂ Plant protection (0–100)
1	Export documents per shipment (number)
2	Time to prepare export documents (days)
10.1 (0.8)	Cost of export documents in US$ (% income per capita)
0	Trader licensing and membership requirements (number)
N/A	Cost of licenses and membership in US$ (% income per capita)

72.9 TRANSPORT
60.0	Δ Truck licenses (0–100)
N/A	Time to obtain company license (days)
N/A	Cost to obtain company license in US$ (% income per capita)
N/A	Validity of company license (years)
N/A	Time to obtain truck permit (days)
N/A	Cost to obtain truck permit in US$ (% income per capita)
N/A	Validity of truck permit (years)
12.4 (1.0)	Cost to obtain vehicle technical inspection in US$ (% income per capita)
1	Validity of vehicle inspection (years)
85.7	◊ Cross-border transportation (0–100)

70.7	52.8	78.6
OPERATIONS (Δ)	QUALITY CONTROL (∂)	TRADE (◊)

The operations score is an average of seed, fertilizer, machinery, finance, markets and transport indicator scores indicated with a Δ. The quality control score is an average of seed, fertilizer, machinery and markets indicator scores indicated with a ∂. The trade score is an average of fertilizer, machinery and transport indicator scores indicated with a ◊.

LAO PDR

45.5	60.6	20.0	34.3	83.9	69.0
SEED	FERTILIZER	MACHINERY	FINANCE	MARKETS	TRANSPORT

SEED — 45.5

45.5	SEED
62.5	Δ Seed registration (0–100)
No practice	Procedures (number)
No practice	Time (days)
No practice	Cost in US$ (% income per capita)
28.6	Δ Seed development and certification (0–100)

FERTILIZER — 60.6

60.6	FERTILIZER
45.0	Δ Fertilizer registration (0–100)
4	Procedures (number)
No data	Time (days)
7.9 (0.5)	Cost in US$ (% income per capita)
83.3	∂ Fertilizer quality control (0–100)
53.3	◊ Fertilizer import requirements (0–100)
N/A	Cost to register as an importer of fertilizer in US$ (% income per capita)
3.1 (0.2)	Cost to obtain an import permit for fertilizer in US$ (% income per capita)

MACHINERY — 20.0

20.0	MACHINERY
0	Δ Tractor dealer requirements (0–100)
6.7	∂ Tractor standards and safety (0–100)
53.3	◊ Tractor import requirements (0–100)
N/A	Cost to register as an importer of tractors in US$ (% income per capita)
1.2 (0.1)	Cost to obtain an import permit for tractors in US$ (% income per capita)

FINANCE — 34.3

34.3	FINANCE
66.7	Δ Microfinance institutions (0–100)
80.0	Δ Credit unions (0–100)
0	Δ Agent banking (0–100)
25.0	Δ Electronic money (0–100)
0	Δ Warehouse receipts (0–100)

MARKETS — 83.9

83.9	MARKETS
92.9	Δ Production and sales (0–100)
75.0	∂ Plant protection (0–100)
2	Export documents per shipment (number)
3	Time to prepare export documents (days)
151.0 (9.4)	Cost of export documents in US$ (% income per capita)
0	Trader licensing and membership requirements (number)
N/A	Cost of licenses and membership in US$ (% income per capita)

TRANSPORT — 69.0

69.0	TRANSPORT
66.7	Δ Truck licenses (0–100)
30	Time to obtain company license (days)
24.4 (1.5)	Cost to obtain company license in US$ (% income per capita)
1	Validity of company license (years)
7	Time to obtain truck permit (days)
67.2 (4.2)	Cost to obtain truck permit in US$ (% income per capita)
1	Validity of truck permit (years)
2.4 (0.2)	Cost to obtain vehicle technical inspection in US$ (% income per capita)
1	Validity of vehicle inspection (years)
71.4	◊ Cross-border transportation (0–100)

47.4	55.0	59.4
OPERATIONS (Δ)	QUALITY CONTROL (∂)	TRADE (◊)

The operations score is an average of seed, fertilizer, machinery, finance, markets and transport indicator scores indicated with a Δ. The quality control score is an average of seed, fertilizer, machinery and markets indicator scores indicated with a ∂. The trade score is an average of fertilizer, machinery and transport indicator scores indicated with a ◊.

MALI

56.0 SEED	71.1 FERTILIZER	27.8 MACHINERY	37.2 FINANCE	55.4 MARKETS	67.9 TRANSPORT

SEED — 56.0
40.6	Δ Seed registration (0–100)
No practice	Procedures (number)
No practice	Time (days)
No practice	Cost in US$ (% income per capita)
71.4	Δ Seed development and certification (0–100)

FERTILIZER — 71.1
80.0	Δ Fertilizer registration (0–100)
4	Procedures (number)
90	Time (days)
No data	Cost in US$ (% income per capita)
66.7	∂ Fertilizer quality control (0–100)
66.7	◊ Fertilizer import requirements (0–100)
0	Cost to register as an importer of fertilizer in US$ (% income per capita)
3.0 (0.4)	Cost to obtain an import permit for fertilizer in US$ (% income per capita)

MACHINERY — 27.8
0	Δ Tractor dealer requirements (0–100)
6.7	∂ Tractor standards and safety (0–100)
76.7	◊ Tractor import requirements (0–100)
0	Cost to register as an importer of tractors in US$ (% income per capita)
3.0 (0.4)	Cost to obtain an import permit for tractors in US$ (% income per capita)

FINANCE — 37.2
42.9	Δ Microfinance institutions (0–100)
60.0	Δ Credit unions (0–100)
0	Δ Agent banking (0–100)
83.3	Δ Electronic money (0–100)
0	Δ Warehouse receipts (0–100)

MARKETS — 55.4
85.7	Δ Production and sales (0–100)
25.0	∂ Plant protection (0–100)
1	Export documents per shipment (number)
3	Time to prepare export documents (days)
19.8 (2.7)	Cost of export documents in US$ (% income per capita)
0	Trader licensing and membership requirements (number)
N/A	Cost of licenses and membership in US$ (% income per capita)

TRANSPORT — 67.9
64.3	Δ Truck licenses (0–100)
N/A	Time to obtain company license (days)
N/A	Cost to obtain company license in US$ (% income per capita)
N/A	Validity of company license (years)
3	Time to obtain truck permit (days)
31.6 (4.4)	Cost to obtain truck permit in US$ (% income per capita)
1	Validity of truck permit (years)
34.6 (4.8)	Cost to obtain vehicle technical inspection in US$ (% income per capita)
0.5	Validity of vehicle inspection (years)
71.4	◊ Cross-border transportation (0–100)

53.9 OPERATIONS (Δ)	32.8 QUALITY CONTROL (∂)	71.6 TRADE (◊)

The operations score is an average of seed, fertilizer, machinery, finance, markets and transport indicator scores indicated with a Δ. The quality control score is an average of seed, fertilizer, machinery and markets indicator scores indicated with a ∂. The trade score is an average of fertilizer, machinery and transport indicator scores indicated with a ◊.

85.9	50.4	52.0	0	72.3	60.7
SEED	FERTILIZER	MACHINERY	FINANCE	MARKETS	TRANSPORT

85.9 — SEED
71.9	Δ Seed registration (0–100)	
6	Procedures (number)	
585	Time (days)	
469.9 (15.6)	Cost in US$ (% income per capita)	
100	Δ Seed development and certification (0–100)	

50.4 — FERTILIZER
0	Δ Fertilizer registration (0–100)
N/A[a]	Procedures (number)
N/A[a]	Time (days)
N/A[a]	Cost in US$ (% income per capita)
94.4	∂ Fertilizer quality control (0–100)
56.7	◊ Fertilizer import requirements (0–100)
N/A	Cost to register as an importer of fertilizer in US$ (% income per capita)
0	Cost to obtain an import permit for fertilizer in US$ (% income per capita)

52.0 — MACHINERY
55.0	Δ Tractor dealer requirements (0–100)
44.4	∂ Tractor standards and safety (0–100)
56.7	◊ Tractor import requirements (0–100)
N/A	Cost to register as an importer of tractors in US$ (% income per capita)
0	Cost to obtain an import permit for tractors in US$ (% income per capita)

0 — FINANCE
0	Δ Microfinance institutions (0–100)
0	Δ Credit unions (0–100)
0	Δ Agent banking (0–100)
0	Δ Electronic money (0–100)
0	Δ Warehouse receipts (0–100)

72.3 — MARKETS
82.1	Δ Production and sales (0–100)
62.5	∂ Plant protection (0–100)
2	Export documents per shipment (number)
No data[b]	Time to prepare export documents (days)
No data[c]	Cost of export documents in US$ (% income per capita)
2	Trader licensing and membership requirements (number)
No data	Cost of licenses and membership in US$ (% income per capita)

60.7 — TRANSPORT
50.0	Δ Truck licenses (0–100)
3	Time to obtain company license (days)
0	Cost to obtain company license in US$ (% income per capita)
Indefinite[d]	Validity of company license (years)
N/A	Time to obtain truck permit (days)
N/A	Cost to obtain truck permit in US$ (% income per capita)
N/A	Validity of truck permit (years)
47 (1.6)	Cost to obtain vehicle technical inspection in US$ (% income per capita)
1	Validity of vehicle inspection (years)
71.4	◊ Cross-border transportation (0–100)

45.5	67.1	61.6
OPERATIONS (Δ)	QUALITY CONTROL (∂)	TRADE (◊)

The operations score is an average of seed, fertilizer, machinery, finance, markets and transport indicator scores indicated with a Δ. The quality control score is an average of seed, fertilizer, machinery and markets indicator scores indicated with a ∂. The trade score is an average of fertilizer, machinery and transport indicator scores indicated with a ◊.
a. The private sector is not required to register fertilizer. b. The time to obtain document 1 (phytosanitary certificate) is 3 days. The time to obtain document 2 (inspection certificate) could not be obtained. c. The cost of document 1 (phytosanitary certificate) is $17.6 (0.6% of income per capita). The cost of document 2 (inspection certificate) could not be obtained. d. License is revoked if any of the pre-requirements are not fullfiled.

MOZAMBIQUE

90.6 SEED	46.1 FERTILIZER	42.5 MACHINERY	29.8 FINANCE	83.9 MARKETS	60.7 TRANSPORT

90.6 SEED
- 81.3 Δ Seed registration (0–100)
- 7 Procedures (number)
- 582 Time (days)
- 500.0 (79.4) Cost in US$ (% income per capita)
- 100 Δ Seed development and certification (0–100)

46.1 FERTILIZER
- 30.0 Δ Fertilizer registration (0–100)
- No practice Procedures (number)
- No practice Time (days)
- No practice Cost in US$ (% income per capita)
- 50.0 ∂ Fertilizer quality control (0–100)
- 58.3 ◊ Fertilizer import requirements (0–100)
- 200.0 (31.7) Cost to register as an importer of fertilizer in US$ (% income per capita)
- 81.6 (13) Cost to obtain an import permit for fertilizer in US$ (% income per capita)

42.5 MACHINERY
- 37.5 Δ Tractor dealer requirements (0–100)
- 6.7 ∂ Tractor standards and safety (0–100)
- 83.3 ◊ Tractor import requirements (0–100)
- 5548.1 (880.6) Cost to register as an importer of tractors in US$ (% income per capita)
- N/A Cost to obtain an import permit for tractors in US$ (% income per capita)

29.8 FINANCE
- 57.1 Δ Microfinance institutions (0–100)
- 66.7 Δ Credit unions (0–100)
- 0 Δ Agent banking (0–100)
- 25.0 Δ Electronic money (0–100)
- 0 Δ Warehouse receipts (0–100)

83.9 MARKETS
- 92.9 Δ Production and sales (0–100)
- 75.0 ∂ Plant protection (0–100)
- 1 Export documents per shipment (number)
- 2 Time to prepare export documents (days)
- 13.4 (2.1) Cost of export documents in US$ (% income per capita)
- 0 Trader licensing and membership requirements (number)
- N/A Cost of licenses and membership in US$ (% income per capita)

60.7 TRANSPORT
- 64.3 Δ Truck licenses (0–100)
- N/A Time to obtain company license (days)
- N/A Cost to obtain company license in US$ (% income per capita)
- N/A Validity of company license (years)
- 2.5 Time to obtain truck permit (days)
- 130.5 (20.7) Cost to obtain truck permit in US$ (% income per capita)
- 5 Validity of truck permit (years)
- 34.4 (5.5) Cost to obtain vehicle technical inspection in US$ (% income per capita)
- 0.5 Validity of vehicle inspection (years)
- 57.1 ◊ Cross-border transportation (0–100)

57.5 OPERATIONS (Δ)	43.9 QUALITY CONTROL (∂)	66.3 TRADE (◊)

The operations score is an average of seed, fertilizer, machinery, finance, markets and transport indicator scores indicated with a Δ. The quality control score is an average of seed, fertilizer, machinery and markets indicator scores indicated with a ∂. The trade score is an average of fertilizer, machinery and transport indicator scores indicated with a ◊.

MYANMAR

53.6	61.9	21.4	24.6	42.0	22.6
SEED	FERTILIZER	MACHINERY	FINANCE	MARKETS	TRANSPORT

53.6 SEED
50.0	Δ Seed registration (0–100)
6	*Procedures (number)*
306	*Time (days)*
445.1 (35.1)	*Cost in US$ (% income per capita)*
57.1	Δ Seed development and certification (0–100)

61.9 FERTILIZER
45.0	Δ Fertilizer registration (0–100)
3	*Procedures (number)*
42	*Time (days)*
122.4 (9.6)	*Cost in US$ (% income per capita)*
100	∂ Fertilizer quality control (0–100)
40.8	◊ Fertilizer import requirements (0–100)
55.6 (4.4)	*Cost to register as an importer of fertilizer in US$ (% income per capita)*
55.6 (4.4)	*Cost to obtain an import permit for fertilizer in US$ (% income per capita)*

21.4 MACHINERY
0	Δ Tractor dealer requirements (0–100)
6.7	∂ Tractor standards and safety (0–100)
57.5	◊ Tractor import requirements (0–100)
11.1 (0.9)	*Cost to register as an importer of tractors in US$ (% income per capita)*
55.6 (4.4)	*Cost to obtain an import permit for tractors in US$ (% income per capita)*

24.6 FINANCE
42.9	Δ Microfinance institutions (0–100)
80.0	Δ Credit unions (0–100)
0	Δ Agent banking (0–100)
0	Δ Electronic money (0–100)
0	Δ Warehouse receipts (0–100)

42.0 MARKETS
71.4	Δ Production and sales (0–100)
12.5	∂ Plant protection (0–100)
2	*Export documents per shipment (number)*
4	*Time to prepare export documents (days)*
20.3 (1.6)	*Cost of export documents in US$ (% income per capita)*
0	*Trader licensing and membership requirements (number)*
N/A	*Cost of licenses and membership in US$ (% income per capita)*

22.6 TRANSPORT
31.0	Δ Truck licenses (0–100)
N/A	*Time to obtain company license (days)*
N/A	*Cost to obtain company license in US$ (% income per capita)*
N/A	*Validity of company license (years)*
11.5	*Time to obtain truck permit (days)*
2.2 (0.2)	*Cost to obtain truck permit in US$ (% income per capita)*
1	*Validity of truck permit (years)*
51.7 (4.1)	*Cost to obtain vehicle technical inspection in US$ (% income per capita)*
1	*Validity of vehicle inspection (years)*
14.3	◊ Cross-border transportation (0–100)

37.6	39.7	37.5
OPERATIONS (Δ)	QUALITY CONTROL (∂)	TRADE (◊)

The operations score is an average of seed, fertilizer, machinery, finance, markets and transport indicator scores indicated with a Δ. The quality control score is an average of seed, fertilizer, machinery and markets indicator scores indicated with a ∂. The trade score is an average of fertilizer, machinery and transport indicator scores indicated with a ◊.

NEPAL

55.8 SEED	57.2 FERTILIZER	21.0 MACHINERY	50.0 FINANCE	81.3 MARKETS	44.0 TRANSPORT

55.8 SEED
68.8	Δ Seed registration (0−100)
5	Procedures (number)
611	Time (days)
0	Cost in US$ (% income per capita)
42.9	Δ Seed development and certification (0−100)

57.2 FERTILIZER
45.0	Δ Fertilizer registration (0−100)
3	Procedures (number)
1125	Time (days)
49.4 (6.8)	Cost in US$ (% income per capita)
66.7	∂ Fertilizer quality control (0−100)
60.0	◊ Fertilizer import requirements (0−100)
0	Cost to register as an importer of fertilizer in US$ (% income per capita)
83.9 (11.5)	Cost to obtain an import permit for fertilizer in US$ (% income per capita)

21.0 MACHINERY
6.3	Δ Tractor dealer requirements (0−100)
6.7	∂ Tractor standards and safety (0−100)
50.0	◊ Tractor import requirements (0−100)
N/A	Cost to register as an importer of tractors in US$ (% income per capita)
N/A	Cost to obtain an import permit for tractors in US$ (% income per capita)

50.0 FINANCE
57.1	Δ Microfinance institutions (0−100)
93.3	Δ Credit unions (0−100)
74.3	Δ Agent banking (0−100)
25.0	Δ Electronic money (0−100)
0	Δ Warehouse receipts (0−100)

81.3 MARKETS
100	Δ Production and sales (0−100)
62.5	∂ Plant protection (0−100)
2	Export documents per shipment (number)
2	Time to prepare export documents (days)
5.3 (0.7)	Cost of export documents in US$ (% income per capita)
0	Trader licensing and membership requirements (number)
N/A	Cost of licenses and membership in US$ (% income per capita)

44.0 TRANSPORT
45.2	Δ Truck licenses (0−100)
N/A	Time to obtain company license (days)
N/A	Cost to obtain company license in US$ (% income per capita)
N/A	Validity of company license (years)
2	Time to obtain truck permit (days)
303.7 (41.6)	Cost to obtain truck permit in US$ (% income per capita)
0.3	Validity of truck permit (years)
1.0 (0.1)	Cost to obtain vehicle technical inspection in US$ (% income per capita)
0.5	Validity of vehicle inspection (years)
42.9	◊ Cross-border transportation (0−100)

50.4 OPERATIONS (Δ)	45.3 QUALITY CONTROL (∂)	51.0 TRADE (◊)

The operations score is an average of seed, fertilizer, machinery, finance, markets and transport indicator scores indicated with a Δ. The quality control score is an average of seed, fertilizer, machinery and markets indicator scores indicated with a ∂. The trade score is an average of fertilizer, machinery and transport indicator scores indicated with a ◊.

NICARAGUA

54.9	64.4	41.5	31.2	67.0	75.0
SEED	FERTILIZER	MACHINERY	FINANCE	MARKETS	TRANSPORT

54.9 — SEED
81.3	Δ Seed registration (0–100)
6	*Procedures (number)*
650	*Time (days)*
15,265.0 (834.2)	*Cost in US$ (% income per capita)*
28.6	Δ Seed development and certification (0–100)

64.4 — FERTILIZER
35.0	Δ Fertilizer registration (0–100)
2	*Procedures (number)*
30	*Time (days)*
1,600.0 (87.4)	*Cost in US$ (% income per capita)*
100	∂ Fertilizer quality control (0–100)
58.3	◊ Fertilizer import requirements (0–100)
50.0 (2.7)	*Cost to register as an importer of fertilizer in US$ (% income per capita)*
25.0 (1.4)	*Cost to obtain an import permit for fertilizer in US$ (% income per capita)*

41.5 — MACHINERY
31.3	Δ Tractor dealer requirements (0–100)
13.3	∂ Tractor standards and safety (0–100)
80.0	◊ Tractor import requirements (0–100)
0	*Cost to register as an importer of tractors in US$ (% income per capita)*
No data	*Cost to obtain an import permit for tractors in US$ (% income per capita)*

31.2 — FINANCE
0	Δ Microfinance institutions (0–100)
60.0	Δ Credit unions (0–100)
0	Δ Agent banking (0–100)
25.0	Δ Electronic money (0–100)
70.8	Δ Warehouse receipts (0–100)

67.0 — MARKETS
71.4	Δ Production and sales (0–100)
62.5	∂ Plant protection (0–100)
2	*Export documents per shipment (number)*
2	*Time to prepare export documents (days)*
28.9 (1.6)	*Cost of export documents in US$ (% income per capita)*
1	*Trader licensing and membership requirements (number)*
0	*Cost of licenses and membership in US$ (% income per capita)*

75.0 — TRANSPORT
64.3	Δ Truck licenses (0–100)
N/A	*Time to obtain company license (days)*
N/A	*Cost to obtain company license in US$ (% income per capita)*
N/A	*Validity of company license (years)*
7.5	*Time to obtain truck permit (days)*
94.3 (5.2)	*Cost to obtain truck permit in US$ (% income per capita)*
5	*Validity of truck permit (years)*
12.1 (0.7)	*Cost to obtain vehicle technical inspection in US$ (% income per capita)*
0.5	*Validity of vehicle inspection (years)*
85.7	◊ Cross-border transportation (0–100)

48.0	58.6	74.7
OPERATIONS (Δ)	QUALITY CONTROL (∂)	TRADE (◊)

The operations score is an average of seed, fertilizer, machinery, finance, markets and transport indicator scores indicated with a Δ. The quality control score is an average of seed, fertilizer, machinery and markets indicator scores indicated with a ∂. The trade score is an average of fertilizer, machinery and transport indicator scores indicated with a ◊.

43.8	42.2	24.4	36.8	54.5	60.7
SEED	FERTILIZER	MACHINERY	FINANCE	MARKETS	TRANSPORT

43.8 SEED
37.5 Δ Seed registration (0–100)
No practice — Procedures (number)
No practice — Time (days)
No practice — Cost in US$ (% income per capita)
50.0 Δ Seed development and certification (0–100)

42.2 FERTILIZER
0 Δ Fertilizer registration (0–100)
N/Aᵃ Procedures (number)
N/Aᵃ Time (days)
N/Aᵃ Cost in US$ (% income per capita)
66.7 ∂ Fertilizer quality control (0–100)
60.0 ◊ Fertilizer import requirements (0–100)
N/A Cost to register as an importer of fertilizer in US$ (% income per capita)
39.9 (9.3) Cost to obtain an import permit for fertilizer in US$ (% income per capita)

24.4 MACHINERY
0 Δ Tractor dealer requirements (0–100)
6.7 ∂ Tractor standards and safety (0–100)
66.7 ◊ Tractor import requirements (0–100)
N/A Cost to register as an importer of tractors in US$ (% income per capita)
N/A Cost to obtain an import permit for tractors in US$ (% income per capita)

36.8 FINANCE
42.9 Δ Microfinance institutions (0–100)
60.0 Δ Credit unions (0–100)
0 Δ Agent banking (0–100)
81.3 Δ Electronic money (0–100)
0 Δ Warehouse receipts (0–100)

54.5 MARKETS
71.4 Δ Production and sales (0–100)
37.5 ∂ Plant protection (0–100)
1 Export documents per shipment (number)
3 Time to prepare export documents (days)
10 (2.3) Cost of export documents in US$ (% income per capita)
0 Trader licensing and membership requirements (number)
N/A Cost of licenses and membership in US$ (% income per capita)

60.7 TRANSPORT
50.0 Δ Truck licenses (0–100)
N/A Time to obtain company license (days)
N/A Cost to obtain company license in US$ (% income per capita)
N/A Validity of company license (years)
1 Time to obtain truck permit (days)
39.9 (9.3) Cost to obtain truck permit in US$ (% income per capita)
0.5 Validity of truck permit (years)
0.3 (0.1) Cost to obtain vehicle technical inspection in US$ (% income per capita)
0.5 Validity of vehicle inspection (years)
71.4 ◊ Cross-border transportation (0–100)

33.7	36.9	66.0
OPERATIONS (Δ)	QUALITY CONTROL (∂)	TRADE (◊)

The operations score is an average of seed, fertilizer, machinery, finance, markets and transport indicator scores indicated with a Δ. The quality control score is an average of seed, fertilizer, machinery and markets indicator scores indicated with a ∂. The trade score is an average of fertilizer, machinery and transport indicator scores indicated with a ◊.
a. The private sector is not required to register fertilizer.

92.2	57.2	68.7	72.6	52.7	65.5
SEED	FERTILIZER	MACHINERY	FINANCE	MARKETS	TRANSPORT

92.2 SEED
84.4	Δ Seed registration (0–100)
6 [a]	Procedures (number)
571 [a]	Time (days)
0.0 [a]	Cost in US$ (% income per capita)
100	Δ Seed development and certification (0–100)

57.2 FERTILIZER
65.0	Δ Fertilizer registration (0–100)
3	Procedures (number)
114	Time (days)
108.9 (6.0) [b]	Cost in US$ (% income per capita)
66.7	∂ Fertilizer quality control (0–100)
40.0	◊ Fertilizer import requirements (0–100)
No data	Cost to register as an importer of fertilizer in US$ (% income per capita)
No data	Cost to obtain an import permit for fertilizer in US$ (% income per capita)

68.7 MACHINERY
53.8	Δ Tractor dealer requirements (0–100)
72.2	∂ Tractor standards and safety (0–100)
80.0	◊ Tractor import requirements (0–100)
1200 (34.9)	Cost to register as an importer of tractors in US$ (% income per capita)
N/A [c]	Cost to obtain an import permit for tractors in US$ (% income per capita)

72.6 FINANCE
85.7	Δ Microfinance institutions (0–100)
100	Δ Credit unions (0–100)
0	Δ Agent banking (0–100)
89.6	Δ Electronic money (0–100)
87.5	Δ Warehouse receipts (0–100)

52.7 MARKETS
67.9	Δ Production and sales (0–100)
37.5	∂ Plant protection (0–100)
2	Export documents per shipment (number)
3	Time to prepare export documents (days)
97.3 (2.8)	Cost of export documents in US$ (% income per capita)
1	Trader licensing and membership requirements (number)
113.5 (3.3)	Cost of licenses and membership in US$ (% income per capita)

65.5 TRANSPORT
59.5	Δ Truck licenses (0–100)
235	Time to obtain company license (days)
136.1 (4)	Cost to obtain company license in US$ (% income per capita)
5 [d]	Validity of company license (years)
N/A	Time to obtain truck permit (days)
N/A	Cost to obtain truck permit in US$ (% income per capita)
N/A	Validity of truck permit (years)
12.8 (0.4)	Cost to obtain vehicle technical inspection in US$ (% income per capita)
1	Validity of vehicle inspection (years)
71.4	◊ Cross-border transportation (0–100)

68.5	58.8	63.8
OPERATIONS (Δ)	QUALITY CONTROL (∂)	TRADE (◊)

The operations score is an average of seed, fertilizer, machinery, finance, markets and transport indicator scores indicated with a Δ. The quality control score is an average of seed, fertilizer, machinery and markets indicator scores indicated with a ∂. The trade score is an average of fertilizer, machinery and transport indicator scores indicated with a ◊.
a. Registration is not mandatory, therefore we do not account for non-mandatory costs. b. The cost of application for registration and field testing is $108.9 but there is no data on the lab reports. c. 10–20% of import value. d. Licenses can be issued with varying validity from a minimum of 1 year up to a maximum of 5 years.

POLAND

78.1 SEED	94.4 FERTILIZER	66.7 MACHINERY	N/Aª FINANCE	90.2 MARKETS	92.9 TRANSPORT

78.1 SEED
56.3	Δ Seed registration (0–100)
6	Procedures (number)
699	Time (days)
979.2 (7.1)	Cost in US$ (% income per capita)
100	Δ Seed development and certification (0–100)

94.4 FERTILIZER
100	Δ Fertilizer registration (0–100)
4	Procedures (number)
60	Time (days)
219.8 (1.6)	Cost in US$ (% income per capita)
100	∂ Fertilizer quality control (0–100)
83.3	◊ Fertilizer import requirements (0–100)
N/A	Cost to register as an importer of fertilizer in US$ (% income per capita)
N/A	Cost to obtain an import permit for fertilizer in US$ (% income per capita)

66.7 MACHINERY
66.7	Δ Tractor dealer requirements (0–100)
66.7	∂ Tractor standards and safety (0–100)
66.7	◊ Tractor import requirements (0–100)
N/A	Cost to register as an importer of tractors in US$ (% income per capita)
N/A	Cost to obtain an import permit for tractors in US$ (% income per capita)

N/Aª FINANCE
-	Δ Microfinance institutions (0–100)
-	Δ Credit unions (0–100)
-	Δ Agent banking (0–100)
-	Δ Electronic money (0–100)
-	Δ Warehouse receipts (0–100)

90.2 MARKETS
92.9	Δ Production and sales (0–100)
87.5	∂ Plant protection (0–100)
0	Export documents per shipment (number)
0	Time to prepare export documents (days)
0	Cost of export documents in US$ (% income per capita)
0	Trader licensing and membership requirements (number)
N/A	Cost of licenses and membership in US$ (% income per capita)

92.9 TRANSPORT
85.7	Δ Truck licenses (0–100)
90	Time to obtain company license (days)
249.5 (1.8)	Cost to obtain company license in US$ (% income per capita)
15	Validity of company license (years)
N/A	Time to obtain truck permit (days)
N/A	Cost to obtain truck permit in US$ (% income per capita)
N/A	Validity of truck permit (years)
78 (0.6)	Cost to obtain vehicle technical inspection in US$ (% income per capita)
1	Validity of vehicle inspection (years)
100	◊ Cross-border transportation (0–100)

84.7 OPERATIONS (Δ)	84.7 QUALITY CONTROL (∂)	83.3 TRADE (◊)

The operations score is an average of seed, fertilizer, machinery, finance, markets and transport indicator scores indicated with a Δ. The quality control score is an average of seed, fertilizer, machinery and markets indicator scores indicated with a ∂. The trade score is an average of fertilizer, machinery and transport indicator scores indicated with a ◊.
a. High-income countries are not measured under the finance topic.

RUSSIAN FEDERATION

67.0 SEED	67.6 FERTILIZER	64.7 MACHINERY	N/A[b] FINANCE	80.4 MARKETS	65.7 TRANSPORT

67.0 SEED
62.5	Δ Seed registration (0–100)	
5	Procedures (number)	
716	Time (days)	
0[a]	Cost in US$ (% income per capita)	
71.4	Δ Seed development and certification (0–100)	

67.6 FERTILIZER
75.0	Δ Fertilizer registration (0–100)
5	Procedures (number)
424	Time (days)
9,059.9 (68.6)	Cost in US$ (% income per capita)
61.1	∂ Fertilizer quality control (0–100)
66.7	◊ Fertilizer import requirements (0–100)
N/A	Cost to register as an importer of fertilizer in US$ (% income per capita)
N/A	Cost to obtain an import permit for fertilizer in US$ (% income per capita)

64.7 MACHINERY
56.3	Δ Tractor dealer requirements (0–100)
77.8	∂ Tractor standards and safety (0–100)
60.0	◊ Tractor import requirements (0–100)
N/A	Cost to register as an importer of tractors in US$ (% income per capita)
168.3 (1.3)	Cost to obtain an import permit for tractors in US$ (% income per capita)

N/A[b] FINANCE
-	Δ Microfinance institutions (0–100)
-	Δ Credit unions (0–100)
-	Δ Agent banking (0–100)
-	Δ Electronic money (0–100)
-	Δ Warehouse receipts (0–100)

80.4 MARKETS
85.7	Δ Production and sales (0–100)
75.0	∂ Plant protection (0–100)
4	Export documents per shipment (number)
12	Time to prepare export documents (days)
33.4 (0.3)	Cost of export documents in US$ (% income per capita)
0	Trader licensing and membership requirements (number)
N/A	Cost of licenses and membership in US$ (% income per capita)

65.7 TRANSPORT
60.0	Δ Truck licenses (0–100)
N/A	Time to obtain company license (days)
N/A	Cost to obtain company license in US$ (% income per capita)
N/A	Validity of company license (years)
N/A	Time to obtain truck permit (days)
N/A	Cost to obtain truck permit in US$ (% income per capita)
N/A	Validity of truck permit (years)
34.6 (0.3)	Cost to obtain vehicle technical inspection in US$ (% income per capita)
1	Validity of vehicle inspection (years)
71.4	◊ Cross-border transportation (0–100)

68.8 OPERATIONS (Δ)	71.3 QUALITY CONTROL (∂)	66.0 TRADE (◊)

The operations score is an average of seed, fertilizer, machinery, finance, markets and transport indicator scores indicated with a Δ. The quality control score is an average of seed, fertilizer, machinery and markets indicator scores indicated with a ∂. The trade score is an average of fertilizer, machinery and transport indicator scores indicated with a ◊.
a. Registering up to five varieties in a year is free of charge. b. High-income countries are not measured under the finance topic.

RWANDA

27.7 SEED	61.7 FERTILIZER	41.1 MACHINERY	59.1 FINANCE	56.3 MARKETS	71.4 TRANSPORT

27.7 SEED
12.5 Δ Seed registration (0–100)
No practice — Procedures (number)
No practice — Time (days)
No practice — Cost in US$ (% income per capita)
42.9 Δ Seed development and certification (0–100)

61.7 FERTILIZER
45.0 Δ Fertilizer registration (0–100)
5 Procedures (number)
No data Time (days)
14.9 (2.3) Cost in US$ (% income per capita)
66.7 ∂ Fertilizer quality control (0–100)
73.3 ◊ Fertilizer import requirements (0–100)
29.8 (4.6) Cost to register as an importer of fertilizer in US$ (% income per capita)
0 Cost to obtain an import permit for fertilizer in US$ (% income per capita)

41.1 MACHINERY
33.3 Δ Tractor dealer requirements (0–100)
33.3 ∂ Tractor standards and safety (0–100)
56.7 ◊ Tractor import requirements (0–100)
N/A Cost to register as an importer of tractors in US$ (% income per capita)
0 Cost to obtain an import permit for tractors in US$ (% income per capita)

59.1 FINANCE
61.9 Δ Microfinance institutions (0–100)
73.3 Δ Credit unions (0–100)
87.1 Δ Agent banking (0–100)
72.9 Δ Electronic money (0–100)
0 Δ Warehouse receipts (0–100)

56.3 MARKETS
100 Δ Production and sales (0–100)
12.5 ∂ Plant protection (0–100)
1 Export documents per shipment (number)
No data [a] Time to prepare export documents (days)
0.3 (0.0) Cost of export documents in US$ (% income per capita)
1 Trader licensing and membership requirements (number)
1,602.3 (246.5) Cost of licenses and membership in US$ (% income per capita)

71.4 TRANSPORT
71.4 Δ Truck licenses (0–100)
7 Time to obtain company license (days)
158.5 (24.4) Cost to obtain company license in US$ (% income per capita)
1 Validity of company license (years)
N/A Time to obtain truck permit (days)
N/A Cost to obtain truck permit in US$ (% income per capita)
N/A Validity of truck permit (years)
29.8 (4.6) Cost to obtain vehicle technical inspection in US$ (% income per capita)
1 Validity of vehicle inspection (years)
71.4 ◊ Cross-border transportation (0–100)

56.1 OPERATIONS (Δ)	37.5 QUALITY CONTROL (∂)	67.1 TRADE (◊)

The operations score is an average of seed, fertilizer, machinery, finance, markets and transport indicator scores indicated with a Δ. The quality control score is an average of seed, fertilizer, machinery and markets indicator scores indicated with a ∂. The trade score is an average of fertilizer, machinery and transport indicator scores indicated with a ◊.
a. The time to obtain document 1 (phytosanitary certificate) is 2 days. The time to obtain document 2 (quality certificate) could not be obtained.

SPAIN

81.3	86.1	69.6	N/Aª	90.2	97.6
SEED	FERTILIZER	MACHINERY	FINANCE	MARKETS	TRANSPORT

81.3 **SEED**
62.5 Δ Seed registration (0–100)
6 *Procedures (number)*
598 *Time (days)*
2,841 (9.6) *Cost in US$ (% income per capita)*
100 Δ Seed development and certification (0–100)

86.1 **FERTILIZER**
75.0 Δ Fertilizer registration (0–100)
1 *Procedures (number)*
90 *Time (days)*
0 *Cost in US$ (% income per capita)*
100 ∂ Fertilizer quality control (0–100)
83.3 ◊ Fertilizer import requirements (0–100)
N/A *Cost to register as an importer of fertilizer in US$ (% income per capita)*
N/A *Cost to obtain an import permit for fertilizer in US$ (% income per capita)*

69.6 **MACHINERY**
68.8 Δ Tractor dealer requirements (0–100)
73.3 ∂ Tractor standards and safety (0–100)
66.7 ◊ Tractor import requirements (0–100)
N/A *Cost to register as an importer of tractors in US$ (% income per capita)*
N/A *Cost to obtain an import permit for tractors in US$ (% income per capita)*

N/Aª **FINANCE**
- Δ Microfinance institutions (0–100)
- Δ Credit unions (0–100)
- Δ Agent banking (0–100)
- Δ Electronic money (0–100)
- Δ Warehouse receipts (0–100)

90.2 **MARKETS**
92.9 Δ Production and sales (0–100)
87.5 ∂ Plant protection (0–100)
0 *Export documents per shipment (number)*
0 *Time to prepare export documents (days)*
0 *Cost of export documents in US$ (% income per capita)*
1 *Trader licensing and membership requirements (number)*
0 *Cost of licenses and membership in US$ (% income per capita)*

97.6 **TRANSPORT**
95.2 Δ Truck licenses (0–100)
3.5 *Time to obtain company license (days)*
50.9 (0.2) *Cost to obtain company license in US$ (% income per capita)*
Indefinite [b] *Validity of company license (years)*
N/A *Time to obtain truck permit (days)*
N/A *Cost to obtain truck permit in US$ (% income per capita)*
N/A *Validity of truck permit (years)*
94.9 (0.3) *Cost to obtain vehicle technical inspection in US$ (% income per capita)*
1 *Validity of vehicle inspection (years)*
100 ◊ Cross-border transportation (0–100)

82.6	86.9	83.3
OPERATIONS (Δ)	QUALITY CONTROL (∂)	TRADE (◊)

The operations score is an average of seed, fertilizer, machinery, finance, markets and transport indicator scores indicated with a Δ. The quality control score is an average of seed, fertilizer, machinery and markets indicator scores indicated with a ∂. The trade score is an average of fertilizer, machinery and transport indicator scores indicated with a ◊.
a. High-income countries are not measured under the finance topic. b. Has to be validated every 2 years. License is revoked if any of the pre-requirements are not fulfilled.

SRI LANKA

53.6 SEED	72.2 FERTILIZER	40.1 MACHINERY	30.3 FINANCE	41.1 MARKETS	36.9 TRANSPORT

53.6 SEED
50.0 Δ Seed registration (0–100)
4 Procedures (number)
298 Time (days)
0 Cost in US$ (% income per capita)
57.1 Δ Seed development and certification (0–100)

72.2 FERTILIZER
80.0 Δ Fertilizer registration (0–100)
3 Procedures (number)
187 Time (days)
73.5 (2.2) Cost in US$ (% income per capita)
83.3 ∂ Fertilizer quality control (0–100)
53.3 ◊ Fertilizer import requirements (0–100)
147.0 (4.3) Cost to register as an importer of fertilizer in US$ (% income per capita)
0 Cost to obtain an import permit for fertilizer in US$ (% income per capita)

40.1 MACHINERY
18.8 Δ Tractor dealer requirements (0–100)
26.7 ∂ Tractor standards and safety (0–100)
75.0 ◊ Tractor import requirements (0–100)
7.4 (0.2) Cost to register as an importer of tractors in US$ (% income per capita)
N/A Cost to obtain an import permit for tractors in US$ (% income per capita)

30.3 FINANCE
0 Δ Microfinance institutions (0–100)
60.0 Δ Credit unions (0–100)
0 Δ Agent banking (0–100)
91.7 Δ Electronic money (0–100)
0 Δ Warehouse receipts (0–100)

41.1 MARKETS
57.1 Δ Production and sales (0–100)
25.0 ∂ Plant protection (0–100)
3 Export documents per shipment (number)
4 Time to prepare export documents (days)
273.2 (8) Cost of export documents in US$ (% income per capita)
2 Trader licensing and membership requirements (number)
222 (6.5) Cost of licenses and membership in US$ (% income per capita)

36.9 TRANSPORT
73.8 Δ Truck licenses (0–100)
N/A Time to obtain company license (days)
N/A Cost to obtain company license in US$ (% income per capita)
N/A Validity of company license (years)
1.5 Time to obtain truck permit (days)
101.1 (3.0) Cost to obtain truck permit in US$ (% income per capita)
1 Validity of truck permit (years)
15.1 (0.4) Cost to obtain vehicle technical inspection in US$ (% income per capita)
1 Validity of vehicle inspection (years)
0 ◊ Cross-border transportation (0–100)

52.3 OPERATIONS (Δ)	45.0 QUALITY CONTROL (∂)	42.8 TRADE (◊)

The operations score is an average of seed, fertilizer, machinery, finance, markets and transport indicator scores indicated with a Δ. The quality control score is an average of seed, fertilizer, machinery and markets indicator scores indicated with a ∂. The trade score is an average of fertilizer, machinery and transport indicator scores indicated with a ◊.

76.6	63.3	45.9	27.1	61.6	65.7
SEED	FERTILIZER	MACHINERY	FINANCE	MARKETS	TRANSPORT

76.6   **SEED**
53.1   Δ Seed registration (0–100)
5   *Procedures (number)*
654   *Time (days)*
12,554.3 (721.5)   *Cost in US$ (% income per capita)*
100   Δ Seed development and certification (0–100)

63.3   **FERTILIZER**
80.0   Δ Fertilizer registration (0–100)
4   *Procedures (number)*
29   *Time (days)*
65.9 (3.8)   *Cost in US$ (% income per capita)*
66.7   ∂ Fertilizer quality control (0–100)
43.3   ◊ Fertilizer import requirements (0–100)
82.4 (4.7)   *Cost to register as an importer of fertilizer in US$ (% income per capita)*
33.0 (1.9)   *Cost to obtain an import permit for fertilizer in US$ (% income per capita)*

45.9   **MACHINERY**
50.0   Δ Tractor dealer requirements (0–100)
44.4   ∂ Tractor standards and safety (0–100)
43.3   ◊ Tractor import requirements (0–100)
82.4 (4.7)   *Cost to register as an importer of tractors in US$ (% income per capita)*
33.0 (1.9)   *Cost to obtain an import permit for tractors in US$ (% income per capita)*

27.1   **FINANCE**
85.7   Δ Microfinance institutions (0–100)
0   Δ Credit unions (0–100)
0   Δ Agent banking (0–100)
50.0   Δ Electronic money (0–100)
0   Δ Warehouse receipts (0–100)

61.6   **MARKETS**
85.7   Δ Production and sales (0–100)
37.5   ∂ Plant protection (0–100)
2   *Export documents per shipment (number)*
No data [a]   *Time to prepare export documents (days)*
41.9 (2.4)   *Cost of export documents in US$ (% income per capita)*
0   *Trader licensing and membership requirements (number)*
N/A   *Cost of licenses and membership in US$ (% income per capita)*

65.7   **TRANSPORT**
60.0   Δ Truck licenses (0–100)
N/A   *Time to obtain company license (days)*
N/A   *Cost to obtain company license in US$ (% income per capita)*
N/A   *Validity of company license (years)*
N/A   *Time to obtain truck permit (days)*
N/A   *Cost to obtain truck permit in US$ (% income per capita)*
N/A   *Validity of truck permit (years)*
205.9 (11.8)   *Cost to obtain vehicle technical inspection in US$ (% income per capita)*
1   *Validity of vehicle inspection (years)*
71.4   ◊ Cross-border transportation (0–100)

63.2	49.5	52.7
OPERATIONS (Δ)	QUALITY CONTROL (∂)	TRADE (◊)

The operations score is an average of seed, fertilizer, machinery, finance, markets and transport indicator scores indicated with a Δ. The quality control score is an average of seed, fertilizer, machinery and markets indicator scores indicated with a ∂. The trade score is an average of fertilizer, machinery and transport indicator scores indicated with a ◊.
a. The time to obtain document 1 (phytosanitary certificate) is 7 days. The time to obtain document 2 (fumigation certificate) could not be obtained.

TAJIKISTAN

56.7	40.6	47.8	32.0	74.1	78.6
SEED	FERTILIZER	MACHINERY	FINANCE	MARKETS	TRANSPORT

56.7 SEED
56.3	Δ Seed registration (0–100)
No data	Procedures (number)
No data	Time (days)
No data	Cost in US$ (% income per capita)
57.1	Δ Seed development and certification (0–100)

40.6 FERTILIZER
55.0	Δ Fertilizer registration (0–100)
No data	Procedures (number)
No data	Time (days)
No data	Cost in US$ (% income per capita)
0ª	∂ Fertilizer quality control (0–100)
66.7	◊ Fertilizer import requirements (0–100)
N/A	Cost to register as an importer of fertilizer in US$ (% income per capita)
N/A	Cost to obtain an import permit for fertilizer in US$ (% income per capita)

47.8 MACHINERY
50.0	Δ Tractor dealer requirements (0–100)
26.7	∂ Tractor standards and safety (0–100)
66.7	◊ Tractor import requirements (0–100)
N/A	Cost to register as an importer of tractors in US$ (% income per capita)
N/A	Cost to obtain an import permit for tractors in US$ (% income per capita)

32.0 FINANCE
95.2	Δ Microfinance institutions (0–100)
40.0	Δ Credit unions (0–100)
0	Δ Agent banking (0–100)
25.0	Δ Electronic money (0–100)
0	Δ Warehouse receipts (0–100)

74.1 MARKETS
85.7	Δ Production and sales (0–100)
62.5	∂ Plant protection (0–100)
2	Export documents per shipment (number)
6	Time to prepare export documents (days)
62.9 (5.9)	Cost of export documents in US$ (% income per capita)
0	Trader licensing and membership requirements (number)
N/A	Cost of licenses and membership in US$ (% income per capita)

78.6 TRANSPORT
85.7	Δ Truck licenses (0–100)
30	Time to obtain company license (days)
111.0 (10.5)	Cost to obtain company license in US$ (% income per capita)
5.0 ᵇ	Validity of company license (years)
N/A	Time to obtain truck permit (days)
N/A	Cost to obtain truck permit in US$ (% income per capita)
N/A	Validity of truck permit (years)
138.8 (13.1)	Cost to obtain vehicle technical inspection in US$ (% income per capita)
1	Validity of vehicle inspection (years)
71.4	◊ Cross-border transportation (0–100)

60.9	29.7	68.3
OPERATIONS (Δ)	QUALITY CONTROL (∂)	TRADE (◊)

The operations score is an average of seed, fertilizer, machinery, finance, markets and transport indicator scores indicated with a Δ. The quality control score is an average of seed, fertilizer, machinery and markets indicator scores indicated with a ∂. The trade score is an average of fertilizer, machinery and transport indicator scores indicated with a ◊.
a. According to the Law On Production and Safe Use of Pesticides and Agrochemicals (03/07/2012), quality control is not regulated. b. Not less than 5 years.

71.9	75.0	51.4	74.2	54.5	67.9
SEED	FERTILIZER	MACHINERY	FINANCE	MARKETS	TRANSPORT

71.9 SEED
56.3 Δ Seed registration (0–100)
6 Procedures (number)
333 Time (days)
652.1 (70.1) Cost in US$ (% income per capita)
87.5 Δ Seed development and certification (0–100)

75.0 FERTILIZER
60.0 Δ Fertilizer registration (0–100)
5 Procedures (number)
578.5 Time (days)
9,899.5 (1,064.5) Cost in US$ (% income per capita)
100 ∂ Fertilizer quality control (0–100)
65.0 ◊ Fertilizer import requirements (0–100)
No data Cost to register as an importer of fertilizer in US$ (% income per capita)
No data Cost to obtain an import permit for fertilizer in US$ (% income per capita)

51.4 MACHINERY
37.5 Δ Tractor dealer requirements (0–100)
33.3 ∂ Tractor standards and safety (0–100)
83.3 ◊ Tractor import requirements (0–100)
N/A Cost to register as an importer of tractors in US$ (% income per capita)
N/A Cost to obtain an import permit for tractors in US$ (% income per capita)

74.2 FINANCE
71.4 Δ Microfinance institutions (0–100)
100 Δ Credit unions (0–100)
87.1 Δ Agent banking (0–100)
25.0 Δ Electronic money (0–100)
87.5 Δ Warehouse receipts (0–100)

54.5 MARKETS
71.4 Δ Production and sales (0–100)
37.5 ∂ Plant protection (0–100)
4 Export documents per shipment (number)
13 Time to prepare export documents (days)
39 (4.2) [a] Cost of export documents in US$ (% income per capita)
1 Trader licensing and membership requirements (number)
No data Cost of licenses and membership in US$ (% income per capita)

67.9 TRANSPORT
64.3 Δ Truck licenses (0–100)
N/A Time to obtain company license (days)
N/A Cost to obtain company license in US$ (% income per capita)
N/A Validity of company license (years)
3 Time to obtain truck permit (days)
47.4 (5.1) Cost to obtain truck permit in US$ (% income per capita)
1 Validity of truck permit (years)
29.6 (3.2) Cost to obtain vehicle technical inspection in US$ (% income per capita)
1 Validity of vehicle inspection (years)
71.4 ◊ Cross-border transportation (0–100)

63.2	56.9	73.3
OPERATIONS (Δ)	QUALITY CONTROL (∂)	TRADE (◊)

The operations score is an average of seed, fertilizer, machinery, finance, markets and transport indicator scores indicated with a Δ. The quality control score is an average of seed, fertilizer, machinery and markets indicator scores indicated with a ∂. The trade score is an average of fertilizer, machinery and transport indicator scores indicated with a ◊.
a. The total cost excludes the cost of document 3 (radioactivity analysis certificate), which is approximately 0.3% of the FOB value of the goods exported.

TURKEY

76.6	66.7	54.3	79.7	69.6	83.3
SEED	FERTILIZER	MACHINERY	FINANCE	MARKETS	TRANSPORT

SEED — 76.6
78.1	Δ Seed registration (0–100)
6	Procedures (number)
646	Time (days)
3,367.3 (31.0)	Cost in US$ (% income per capita)
75	Δ Seed development and certification (0–100)

FERTILIZER — 66.7
70.0	Δ Fertilizer registration (0–100)
3	Procedures (number)
50	Time (days)
180.7 (1.7)	Cost in US$ (% income per capita)
50.0	∂ Fertilizer quality control (0–100)
80.0	◊ Fertilizer import requirements (0–100)
No data	Cost to register as an importer of fertilizer in US$ (% income per capita)
No data	Cost to obtain an import permit for fertilizer in US$ (% income per capita)

MACHINERY — 54.3
46.3	Δ Tractor dealer requirements (0–100)
50.0	∂ Tractor standards and safety (0–100)
66.7	◊ Tractor import requirements (0–100)
N/A	Cost to register as an importer of tractors in US$ (% income per capita)
N/A	Cost to obtain an import permit for tractors in US$ (% income per capita)

FINANCE — 79.7
N/A [a]	Δ Microfinance institutions (0–100)
60.0	Δ Credit unions (0–100)
N/A [a]	Δ Agent banking (0–100)
79.2	Δ Electronic money (0–100)
100	Δ Warehouse receipts (0–100)

MARKETS — 69.6
64.3	Δ Production and sales (0–100)
75.0	∂ Plant protection (0–100)
3	Export documents per shipment (number)
3	Time to prepare export documents (days)
19 (0.2)	Cost of export documents in US$ (% income per capita)
1	Trader licensing and membership requirements (number)
0	Cost of licenses and membership in US$ (% income per capita)

TRANSPORT — 83.3
81.0	Δ Truck licenses (0–100)
4	Time to obtain company license (days)
4280.5 (39.5)	Cost to obtain company license in US$ (% income per capita)
5	Validity of company license (years)
N/A	Time to obtain truck permit (days)
N/A	Cost to obtain truck permit in US$ (% income per capita)
N/A	Validity of truck permit (years)
142.7 (1.3)	Cost to obtain vehicle technical inspection in US$ (% income per capita)
1	Validity of vehicle inspection (years)
85.7	◊ Cross-border transportation (0–100)

69.6	58.3	77.5
OPERATIONS (Δ)	QUALITY CONTROL (∂)	TRADE (◊)

The operations score is an average of seed, fertilizer, machinery, finance, markets and transport indicator scores indicated with a Δ. The quality control score is an average of seed, fertilizer, machinery and markets indicator scores indicated with a ∂. The trade score is an average of fertilizer, machinery and transport indicator scores indicated with a ◊.
a. Upper-middle-income countries are not measured under the microfinance institutions indicator and agent banking indicator.

44.2	56.4	51.0	46.3	58.9	75.0
SEED	FERTILIZER	MACHINERY	FINANCE	MARKETS	TRANSPORT

44.2 SEED

31.3	Δ Seed registration (0–100)
5	Procedures (number)
523	Time (days)
0[a]	Cost in US$ (% income per capita)
57.1	Δ Seed development and certification (0–100)

56.4 FERTILIZER

45.0	Δ Fertilizer registration (0–100)
5	Procedures (number)
691	Time (days)
1,708.9 (258.9)	Cost in US$ (% income per capita)
66.7	∂ Fertilizer quality control (0–100)
57.5	◊ Fertilizer import requirements (0–100)
379.8 (57.5)	Cost to register as an importer of fertilizer in US$ (% income per capita)
0	Cost to obtain an import permit for fertilizer in US$ (% income per capita)

51.0 MACHINERY

56.3	Δ Tractor dealer requirements (0–100)
13.3	∂ Tractor standards and safety (0–100)
83.3	◊ Tractor import requirements (0–100)
N/A	Cost to register as an importer of tractors in US$ (% income per capita)
N/A	Cost to obtain an import permit for tractors in US$ (% income per capita)

46.3 FINANCE

66.7	Δ Microfinance institutions (0–100)
40.0	Δ Credit unions (0–100)
0	Δ Agent banking (0–100)
25.0	Δ Electronic money (0–100)
100	Δ Warehouse receipts (0–100)

58.9 MARKETS

92.9	Δ Production and sales (0–100)
25.0	∂ Plant protection (0–100)
4	Export documents per shipment (number)
No data	Time to prepare export documents (days)
No data	Cost of export documents in US$ (% income per capita)
1	Trader licensing and membership requirements (number)
569.6 (86.3)	Cost of licenses and membership in US$ (% income per capita)

75 TRANSPORT

78.6	Δ Truck licenses (0–100)
N/A	Time to obtain company license (days)
N/A	Cost to obtain company license in US$ (% income per capita)
N/A	Validity of company license (years)
1	Time to obtain truck permit (days)
41.8 (6.3)	Cost to obtain truck permit in US$ (% income per capita)
1	Validity of truck permit (years)
76 (11.5)	Cost to obtain vehicle technical inspection in US$ (% income per capita)
1	Validity of vehicle inspection (years)
71.4	◊ Cross-border transportation (0–100)

60.5	35.0	70.8
OPERATIONS (Δ)	QUALITY CONTROL (∂)	TRADE (◊)

The operations score is an average of seed, fertilizer, machinery, finance, markets and transport indicator scores indicated with a Δ. The quality control score is an average of seed, fertilizer, machinery and markets indicator scores indicated with a ∂. The trade score is an average of fertilizer, machinery and transport indicator scores indicated with a ◊.
a. In practice, the National Agriculture Research Organization (NARD), which is in charge of registration, has not been charging fees for these procedures.

UKRAINE

74.1	80.6	62.7	41.6	86.6	65.7
SEED	FERTILIZER	MACHINERY	FINANCE	MARKETS	TRANSPORT

74.1	**SEED**	
62.5	Δ Seed registration (0–100)	
6	*Procedures (number)*	
714	*Time (days)*	
1,136.4 (31.9)	*Cost in US$ (% income per capita)*	
85.7	∂ Seed development and certification (0–100)	
80.6	**FERTILIZER**	
75.0	Δ Fertilizer registration (0–100)	
5	*Procedures (number)*	
325	*Time (days)*	
25,537.2 (717.3)	*Cost in US$ (% income per capita)*	
100	∂ Fertilizer quality control (0–100)	
66.7	◊ Fertilizer import requirements (0–100)	
N/A	*Cost to register as an importer of fertilizer in US$ (% income per capita)*	
N/A	*Cost to obtain an import permit for fertilizer in US$ (% income per capita)*	
62.7	**MACHINERY**	
43.8	Δ Tractor dealer requirements (0–100)	
77.8	∂ Tractor standards and safety (0–100)	
66.7	◊ Tractor import requirements (0–100)	
N/A	*Cost to register as an importer of tractors in US$ (% income per capita)*	
N/A	*Cost to obtain an import permit for tractors in US$ (% income per capita)*	
41.6	**FINANCE**	
0	Δ Microfinance institutions (0–100)	
40.0	Δ Credit unions (0–100)	
42.9	Δ Agent banking (0–100)	
25.0	Δ Electronic money (0–100)	
100	Δ Warehouse receipts (0–100)	
86.6	**MARKETS**	
85.7	Δ Production and sales (0–100)	
87.5	∂ Plant protection (0–100)	
3	*Export documents per shipment (number)*	
5	*Time to prepare export documents (days)*	
31.2 (0.9)	*Cost of export documents in US$ (% income per capita)*	
0	*Trader licensing and membership requirements (number)*	
N/A	*Cost of licenses and membership in US$ (% income per capita)*	
65.7	**TRANSPORT**	
60.0	Δ Truck licenses (0–100)	
N/A	*Time to obtain company license (days)*	
N/A	*Cost to obtain company license in US$ (% income per capita)*	
N/A	*Validity of company license (years)*	
N/A	*Time to obtain truck permit (days)*	
N/A	*Cost to obtain truck permit in US$ (% income per capita)*	
N/A	*Validity of truck permit (years)*	
39.3 (1.1)	*Cost to obtain vehicle technical inspection in US$ (% income per capita)*	
1	*Validity of vehicle inspection (years)*	
71.4	◊ Cross-border transportation (0–100)	

63.4	88.4	68.3
OPERATIONS (Δ)	QUALITY CONTROL (∂)	TRADE (◊)

The operations score is an average of seed, fertilizer, machinery, finance, markets and transport indicator scores indicated with a Δ. The quality control score is an average of seed, fertilizer, machinery and markets indicator scores indicated with a ∂. The trade score is an average of fertilizer, machinery and transport indicator scores indicated with a ◊.

VIETNAM

62.5	70.0	24.4	45.3	80.4	54.8
SEED	FERTILIZER	MACHINERY	FINANCE	MARKETS	TRANSPORT

62.5 SEED
62.5	Δ Seed registration (0–100)
6	*Procedures (number)*
901	*Time (days)*
8,050.8 (426.0)	*Cost in US$ (% income per capita)*
62.5	Δ Seed development and certification (0–100)

70.0 FERTILIZER
60.0	Δ Fertilizer registration (0–100)
3	*Procedures (number)*
15	*Time (days)*
50.0 (2.6)	*Cost in US$ (% income per capita)*
100	∂ Fertilizer quality control (0–100)
50.0	◊ Fertilizer import requirements (0–100)
N/A	*Cost to register as an importer of fertilizer in US$ (% income per capita)*
20.0 (1.1)	*Cost to obtain an import permit for fertilizer in US$ (% income per capita)*

24.4 MACHINERY
0	Δ Tractor dealer requirements (0–100)
6.7	∂ Tractor standards and safety (0–100)
66.7	◊ Tractor import requirements (0–100)
N/A	*Cost to register as an importer of tractors in US$ (% income per capita)*
N/A	*Cost to obtain an import permit for tractors in US$ (% income per capita)*

45.3 FINANCE
71.4	Δ Microfinance institutions (0–100)
80.0	Δ Credit unions (0–100)
0	Δ Agent banking (0–100)
75.0	Δ Electronic money (0–100)
0	Δ Warehouse receipts (0–100)

80.4 MARKETS
85.7	Δ Production and sales (0–100)
75.0	∂ Plant protection (0–100)
2	*Export documents per shipment (number)*
3	*Time to prepare export documents (days)*
38.5 (2.0)	*Cost of export documents in US$ (% income per capita)*
1	*Trader licensing and membership requirements (number)*
0	*Cost of licenses and membership in US$ (% income per capita)*

54.8 TRANSPORT
81.0	Δ Truck licenses (0–100)
3	*Time to obtain company license (days)*
9.2 (0.5)	*Cost to obtain company license in US$ (% income per capita)*
7	*Validity of company license (years)*
N/A	*Time to obtain truck permit (days)*
N/A	*Cost to obtain truck permit in US$ (% income per capita)*
N/A	*Validity of truck permit (years)*
16.1 (0.9)	*Cost to obtain vehicle technical inspection in US$ (% income per capita)*
0.5	*Validity of vehicle inspection (years)*
28.6	◊ Cross-border transportation (0–100)

55.7	60.6	48.4
OPERATIONS (Δ)	QUALITY CONTROL (∂)	TRADE (◊)

The operations score is an average of seed, fertilizer, machinery, finance, markets and transport indicator scores indicated with a Δ. The quality control score is an average of seed, fertilizer, machinery and markets indicator scores indicated with a ∂. The trade score is an average of fertilizer, machinery and transport indicator scores indicated with a ◊.

ZAMBIA

70.3 SEED	**56.7** FERTILIZER	**39.2** MACHINERY	**51.3** FINANCE	**61.6** MARKETS	**67.9** TRANSPORT

70.3 SEED
53.1	Δ Seed registration (0–100)
5	Procedures (number)
544	Time (days)
1,045.0 (59.4)	Cost in US$ (% income per capita)
87.5	Δ Seed development and certification (0–100)

56.7 FERTILIZER
40.0	Δ Fertilizer registration (0–100)
4	Procedures (number)
211	Time (days)
4,249.8 (241.5)	Cost in US$ (% income per capita)
66.7	∂ Fertilizer quality control (0–100)
63.3	◊ Fertilizer import requirements (0–100)
0	Cost to register as an importer of fertilizer in US$ (% income per capita)
183.0 (10.4)	Cost to obtain an import permit for fertilizer in US$ (% income per capita)

39.2 MACHINERY
37.5	Δ Tractor dealer requirements (0–100)
13.3	∂ Tractor standards and safety (0–100)
66.7	◊ Tractor import requirements (0–100)
N/A	Cost to register as an importer of tractors in US$ (% income per capita)
N/A	Cost to obtain an import permit for tractors in US$ (% income per capita)

51.3 FINANCE
66.7	Δ Microfinance institutions (0–100)
40.0	Δ Credit unions (0–100)
0	Δ Agent banking (0–100)
50.0	Δ Electronic money (0–100)
100	Δ Warehouse receipts (0–100)

61.6 MARKETS
85.7	Δ Production and sales (0–100)
37.5	∂ Plant protection (0–100)
5	Export documents per shipment (number)
11	Time to prepare export documents (days)
190.6 (10.8)	Cost of export documents in US$ (% income per capita)
0	Trader licensing and membership requirements (number)
N/A	Cost of licenses and membership in US$ (% income per capita)

67.9 TRANSPORT
50.0	Δ Truck licenses (0–100)
N/A	Time to obtain company license (days)
N/A	Cost to obtain company license in US$ (% income per capita)
N/A	Validity of company license (years)
90	Time to obtain truck permit (days)
17.6 (1.0)	Cost to obtain truck permit in US$ (% income per capita)
1	Validity of truck permit (years)
5.2 (0.3)	Cost to obtain vehicle technical inspection in US$ (% income per capita)
1	Validity of vehicle inspection (years)
85.7	◊ Cross-border transportation (0–100)

55.8 OPERATIONS (Δ)	**39.2** QUALITY CONTROL (∂)	**71.9** TRADE (◊)

The operations score is an average of seed, fertilizer, machinery, finance, markets and transport indicator scores indicated with a Δ. The quality control score is an average of seed, fertilizer, machinery and markets indicator scores indicated with a ∂. The trade score is an average of fertilizer, machinery and transport indicator scores indicated with a ◊.

LOCAL EXPERTS

GLOBAL RESPONDENTS

Africa Legal Network (ALN)

AGCO

Baker & McKenzie

Bayer Animal Health

Bayer CropScience

Ceva Santé Animale

Clifford Chance

Colibri Law Firm

DFDL

FINCA

GALVmed

Hester Biosciences Limited

IFDC

John Deere

KWS

Merial

Monsanto

OLAM

One Acre Fund

Pioneer

SQM

Syngenta

Syngenta Foundation

Tilleke & Gibbins

VimpelCom

Vodafone Group Plc

Yara

BANGLADESH

Bangladesh Agricultural Research Institute

Hatim Industries Ltd.

Karnaphuli Fertilizer Co. Ltd (KAFCO)

Microcredit Regulatory Authority (MRA)

Md. Joynal Abedin, Ministry of Local Government, Rural Development and Cooperatives

Rozina Afroz, Bangladesh Agricultural Research Institute

Iftekhar Ahmed, Bangladesh Agricultural Research Institute

Vinay Ahuja, DFDL

Shahid Akbar, Bangladesh Institute of ICT in Development (BIID)

Lamisa Alam, Kamal Hossain & Associates

S. M. Khorshed Alam, Bangladesh Agricultural Research Council

Saiful Alam, Ministry of Water Resources

Mohsin Ali, WAVE Foundation

Shah Mohammad Arefin, Lal Teer Seed Limited

Jennifer Ashraf, Legacy Legal Corporate Law firm

Mohammed Ayub, Rural Development Academy (RDA)

Abdul Halim Bhuiyan, Bangladesh Agricultural Development Corporation (BADC)

Sharif Bhuyian, Kamal Hossain & Associates

Ahnaf Chowdhury, Kamal Hossain & Associates

Md. Mozammel Ali Chowdhury, Young Power in Social Action

Ahmed Zaker Chowdhury, Kamal Hossain & Associates

Subrato Dey, ADESH

Chowdhury Md. Feroz Bin Alam, Bangladesh Bank

Rajiv Ghandi, Hester Biosciences Ltd

Bishwojit Ghosh, Jagorani Chakra Foundation (JCF)

Golam Zilani, Milky Way Shipping Lines (Pvt.) Limited

Md. Osman Goni, OGR Legal

Aminul Haque, Advance Animal Science Co. Ltd.

Aminul Haque, Come To Save Cooperative (CTS)

Altaf Hossain, Directorate General of Drug Administration (DGDA)

Amjad Hossain, Bangladesh Agricultural Research Institute

Anwar Hossain, WAVE Foundation

Israil Hossain, Bangladesh Agricultural Research Institute

Md. Sanwar Hossain, S Hossain & Associates

Mohammad Iqbal Hossain

Shahadat Hossain, ACDI/VOCA

S. M. Jahangir Hossain

Nazmul Huda, Bangladesh Society of Seed Technology

Arif Imtiaz, OGR Legal

Mohammad Iqbal, Bangladesh Chemical Industries Corporation

M. Amir-Ul Islam, Amir & Amir Law Associates, member of Lex Mundi

Md. Monjurul Islam

Md. Nazrul Islam, Bangladesh Bank

Raisul Islam, Kamal Hossain & Associates

Md. Tariqul Islam, Bangladesh Agricultural Research Institute

Mohammed Khairul Islam, Jagorani Chakra Foundation (JCF)

Towhidul Islam, Legacy Legal Corporate Law firm

Ishrat Jahan, International Fertilizer Development Center (IFDC)

Md. Abdul Jalil, Land Records and Survey Department, Ministry of Land

Ahmed Kafiluddin, Bangladesh Fertilizer Association

A. Z. M. Momtazul Karim, Department of Agricultural Extension (DAE)

Abu Raihan Muhammed Khalid, Raihan Khalid & Associates

Md. Anwar Hossain Khan, Department of Agricultural Extension (DAE)

Munzur Murshid Khan, Advance Animal Science Co. Ltd.

Md. Abdul Malek, Bangladesh Agricultural Research Institute

Moin Ghani, Kamal Hossain & Associates

Ahmed Moinuddin, Advance Animal Science Co. Ltd.

Md. Rezwan Molla, Bangladesh Agricultural Research Institute

Mohamm Monsured

Md. Abu Fazal Munif, Legacy Legal Corporate Law firm

Nujhat Naeem, Banglalink Digital Communications Ltd.

Afrina Naznin, Legacy Legal Corporate Law firm

Md. Aminur Rahman, Ministry of Local Government, Rural Development and Cooperatives

Md. Mizanur Rahman, Ministry of Local Government, Rural Development and Cooperatives

Md. Moshiar Rahman, Bangladesh Road Transport Authority

Pulak Rangan Shaha, Ministry of Agriculture

Bazlur Rashid, Department of Agricultural Extension (DAE)

Md. Abdur Razzaque, Ministry of Agriculture

Quazi Rezaul Islam, Ministry of Local Government, Rural Development and Cooperatives

Durlave Roy, Northern Agro Services Ltd

Sheikh Saiful Rajib, S Hossain & Associates

Kalidas Sarkar, Department of Livestock Services (DLS), Ministry of Fisheries and Livestock

Shafique Shafiquzzaman, Maxwell Stamp Ltd

Sreekanta Sheel

Kuri Siddique, Kamal Hossain & Associates

S. K. Sinha, ASA

Mashrufa Tanzin, Rural Development Academy (RDA)

Ashraf Uddin, Pedrollo nk Ltd.

Md. Amir Uddin, Bangladesh Bank

Nashir Uddin, Biswas Agrovet Ltd.

Read Uddin, Jus Counsel

Md. Wahiduzzaman, Jagorani Chakra Foundation (JCF)

Quazi Ludmila Zaman, Amir & Amir Law Associates, member of Lex Mundi

BOLIVIA

Instituto Nacional de Innovación Agropecuaria y Forestal (INIAF)

La Autoridad de Supervisión del Sistema Financiero (ASFI)

Ministerio de Desarrollo Rural y Tierras

Nibol Ltd.

Sociedad Anónima Comercial Industrial (SACI)

Servicio Nacional de Sanidad Agropecuaria e Inocuidad Alimentaria (SENASAG)

Viceministerio de Desarrollo Rural y Agropecuario

Yara

Mauricio Becerra de la Roca Donoso, Becerra de la Roca Donoso & Asociados SRL

José Campero, Instituto Nacional de Innovación Agropecuaria y Forestal (INIAF)

Magaly Castillo Tamayo, Naandanjain

Remi Castro Ávila, SENASAG

Maritza Céspedes, Biogénesis-Bagó

Gonzalo Colque, Taller de Iniciativas en Estudios Rurales y Reforma Agraria (TIERRA)

Sergio José Dávila Zeballos, C.R.&F. Rojas Abogados

Diego Fernando Rojas Moreno, C.R.&F. Rojas Abogados

Úrsula Font, Indacochea & Asociados

Humberto Gandarillas, Deutsche Gesellschaft für Internationale Zusammenarbeit (GIZ) GmbH

Carlos L. Gerke, Estudio Jurídico Gerke, Soc. Civ.

Alberto Guzmán, AGC Consultora

Jorge Guzmán, Banco Prodem S.A.

Alonso Indacochea, Indacochea & Asociados

Cesar Iriarte, Sociedad Industrial y Comercial de Riego y Agricultura Sicra Ltda.

Jose Nelson Joaquin, Universidad Autónoma Gabriel René Moreno

Fabrizio Leigue Rioja, AG Logistics

Ichín Ma, Indacochea & Asociados

Sergio Diego Martínez Calbimonte, Marcal Consultores

Marco Antonio Torrico Navia, Viceministerio de Telecomunicaciones

Álvaro Otondo Maldonado, Instituto Nacional de Innovación Agropecuaria y Forestal (INIAF)

Jaime Alfredo Palenque Quintanilla, Association of Agricultural Input Suppliers (APIA)

María Laura Paz G., Indacochea & Asociados

Rodrigo Peña

Gustavo Pozo Vargas, Viceministerio de Telecomunicaciones

Silvia Quevedo, AG Logistics

Pablo Quispe, Trucks Logistics

Carlos Quitón

Blanca Roca, CTG Andrea (Genética Líquida) PIC

Carlos Saavedra, HELVETAS Swiss Intercooperation

Carlos Sanabria, ATT Bolivia

Gabriela Santucho, SUR CARGO S.R.L.

Larry Serrate, AgroNáyade

Pablo Stejskal, Stejskal & Asociados

Alvaro Tufiño

Marcos Vargas Caravallo, Instituto Nacional de Reforma Agraria

David Wilson, Instituto Nacional de Reforma Agraria

José Noel Zamora, Banco Prodem S.A.

BOSNIA AND HERZEGOVINA

Banking Agency of the Republic of Srpska

Banking Agency of the Federation of Bosnia and Herzegovina (FBA)

MCO EKI

AgroDar s.p.z.

State Veterinary Office of Bosnia-Herzegovina

Snežana Akulović, Direction for the Plant Protection

Eldin Alikadić, Ministry of Agriculture, Water Management and Forestry of the Federation of Bosnia and Herzegovina

Marina Antić, University of Banja Luka

Sadina Bina, MCO EKI

Stevan Dimitrijević, Karanović & Nikolić

Amina Djugum, Marić & Co. Law Firm

Dražen Marić, Euro Part HB d.o.o

Nusmir Huskić, Huskić Law Office

Jesenka Jahić, Ministry of Agriculture, Water Management and Forestry of the Federation of Bosnia and Herzegovina

Ljubiša Kačavenda, InfoMap Novi Grad

Kenan Karahasanović, Ministry of Agriculture, Water Management and Forestry of the Federation of Bosnia and Herzegovina

Almin Karamehić, EKO-BeL Laktaši

Ivana Karanović, Karanović & Nikolić

Smiljana Knežević, Plant Health Protection Administration of Bosnia and Herzegovina

Danijela Kondić, University of Banja Luka

Meliha Kovačević, Communications Regulatory Agency

Smiljana Kraljević, Ministry of Agriculture, Water Management and Forestry of the Federation of Bosnia and Herzegovina

Tarik Kupusović, Hydro-Engineering Institute Sarajevo

Dajana Legin-Dedić, Microcredit Foundation Sunrise

Branko Marić, Marić & Co. Law Firm

Vladimir Markuš, Karanović & Nikolić

Dragan Mataruga, Republic of Srpska Inspectorate

Dragana Mehmedović, AMFI Association

Ena Mesihović, Huskić Law Office

Ensar Osmić, Ziraat Bank

Enida Pecikoza, Ministry of Agriculture, Water Management and Forestry of the Federation of Bosnia and Herzegovina

Amer Ramić, Advokatska kancelarija Ramić Amer

Adela Rizvić, Advokatska kancelarija Tkalčić-Đulić, Prebanić, Rizvić, Jusufbašić-Goloman

Philippe Sabot, Merial

Aleksandar Sajić, Sajić Advokatska Firma

Zlatan Salihović, Communications Regulatory Agency

Emina Saračević, Saračević and Gazibegović Lawyers (SGL)

Nadžida Sarić, Communications Regulatory Agency

Tanja Savičić, Karanović & Nikolić

Selim Škaljić, University of Sarajevo

Mehmed Spaho, Spaho Law Office

Dragan Stijak, Sajić Law Office

Vladimir Šušnjar, EKO-BeL Laktaši

Bojana Tkalčić – Đulić, Advokatska kancelarija Tkalčić-Đulić, Prebanić, Rizvić, Jusufbašić-Goloman

Vojislav Trkulja, University of Banja Luka

Ismet Velić, Ismet Velić Law Firm

Larisa Velić, High Judicial and Prosecutorial Council of Bosnia and Herzegovina (HJPC)

Željko Žepić, Transkop Tuzla

BURKINA FASO

ACFIME-CREDO

Centre International de Recherche-Développement sur l'Elevage en Zone Subhumide

Chambre d'Agriculture du Burkina Faso

Ministère de l'Agriculture

Valentin Akue, United Bank for Africa Burkina (UBA Burkina)

Sienou Al Hassan, Tropic Agro Chem

Laeticia Aoue/Some, Juris-Gouv International Consulting SARL

Diallo Ali Badara, Union Nationale des Producteurs de Coton du Burkina

Léon Badiara, Genetic Center

Boureima Bado, GRAINE sarl

Didier Balma, Institut de l'Environnement et Recherches Agricoles (INERA)

Theodore Bele, Direction Générale des Aménagements et du Développement de l'Irrigation (MAH)

Frédéric Belem, United Bank for Africa Burkina (UBA Burkina)

Patinde Marie Louise Eléonore Bélemlilga, The Volta Basin Authority

Boukaré Bikienga, Comité Interprofessionnel du Riz du Burkina (CIRB)

Mamoudou Birba, Le Cadre d'Action des Juristes de l'Environnement

Adama Bitie, Fisconsult-Bitié & Associés

Boukary Boly, Société d'Exportation du Faso (SEFA)

Issaka Bougoum, SN Ranch du Koba BF

Mamadou Boukouma, Ministère des Infrastructures, du Désenclavement et des Transports

Yves Bertrand Capo-Chichi, Agriculture et Artisanat, Agence pour la promotion de la Petite et Moyenne Entreprise

Halidou Compaoré, Institut de l'Environnement et des Recherches Agricoles (INERA)

Arnaud Chabanne, CB Énergie

Laurent Compaoré

Konkourou Coulibaly, AGRIMOTOR

Gertrude Marie Mathilda Coulibaly/ Zombré, Millénium Challenge Account

Yempabou Coulidiati, Association TIN BA

Amadou Dao

Philippe d'Arondel de Hayes, Houet Select

Jean de Foucauld, Ceva Santé Animale

Mamadou Cellou Diallo, Bagrépôle

Amidou Garane, Université de Ouagadougou

Henri Girard, Terre Verte

Philippe Goabga, Telecel Faso

Michel Havard, CIRAD

Dioyel Laeticia Hetie, Juris-Gouv International Consulting SARL

Innocent Hien, United Bank for Africa Burkina (UBA Burkina)

Etienne Kabore, Bagrépôle

Félicité Kaboré, Maison de l'Entreprise du Burkina Faso

Lassiné Kaboré, Ministère des Infrastructures, du Désenclavement et des Transports

Saidou Kabré, AGRODIA

Issaka Kanazoe, Airtel Burkina Faso S.A.

Bonaventure Kéré, Syndicat National des Transporteurs Routiers de Voyageurs du Burkina (SNTRV-B)

Georges Kiénou, Union Nationale des Producteurs de Riz du Burkina Faso (UNPR-B)

Lancina Ki, West African Economic and Monetary Union (UEMOA)

Diara Kocty/Thiombiano, Centre National de Multiplication des Animaux Performants (CMAP)

Amoulyakar Arnaud Koné, United Bank for Africa Burkina (UBA Burkina)

Joachim Koné, Cyfu Agro

Mahamane Miampo, Agence pour la promotion des exportations du Burkina (APEX)

Issoufou Maïga, Organisation des Transporteurs Routiers du Faso (OTRAF)

Dibi Millogo, Partnenariat National de l'Eau

Charles Adolphe Nanema, Ministère de l'Agriculture de l'Hydraulique et des Recherches Halieutiques

Nadine Naré, Ministère de l'Agriculture de l'Hydraulique et des Recherches Halieutiques

Aristide Ongone Obame

Ochuko Patrick Otoba, Saso Industries

Abou Simbel Ouattara, Moablaou S.A.

Laurent Ouedraogo, Direction de la modernisation et de la mécanisation agricole (DMMA)

Mahamadi Ouedraogo, Ministère de la Recherche scientifique et de l'Innovation

Maïmouna Ouedraogo, Union Nationale des Producteurs de Riz du Burkina Faso (UNPR-B)

Modibo Ouedraogo, Agriculture et Artisanat, Agence pour la promotion de la Petite et Moyenne Entreprise

Mohamed Ouedraogo, Sudconseil

T. Jeremy Ouedraogo, Ministère de la Recherche scientifique et de l'Innovation

Yassia Ouedraogo, UCOBAM

Emma Palm, Ministère de l'Agriculture de l'Hydraulique et des Recherches Halieutiques

Souleymane Pindé, Ministère des Ressources Animales (MRA)

Brahima Rabo, Union des Chauffeurs Routiers du Burkina (UCRB)

Bationo Rakissiwinde, Conseil Burkinabé des Chargeurs (CBC)

Philippe Sabot, Merial

Adaman Sanfo, MCA

Pierre Sanon, Société Nationale d'aménagement du Territoire et de l'Equipement Rurale

Daouda Sanou, Airtel Burkina Faso S.A.

Issouf Sanou, Fédération Nationale des Organisations Paysannes (FENOP)

Jacob Sanou, Institut de l'Environnement et de Recherches Agricoles (INERA)

Irene Sare/Kanzie, Autorité de Régulation des Communications Electroniques et des Postes (ARCEP)

Moumini Savadogo, Union Internationale pour la Conservation de la Nature (UICN)

Aoua Sawadogo, Réseau des caisses populaires du Burkina Faso (RCPB)

Daouda Sawadogo, Réseau des caisses populaires du Burkina Faso (RCPB)

Maliki Sawadogo, Ministère des Infrastructures, du Désenclavement et des Transports

Neerbewendin G. Sawadogo, Agence pour la Promotion de la Petite et Moyenne Entreprise Agriculture et Artisanat (APME2A)

Saïdou Sawadogo

Abdoulaye R Semdé, Ministère des Ressources Animales (MRA)Ministère des Ressources Animales (MRA)

El Hadj Kassoum K. Simpore, Organisation des Transporteurs Routiers du Faso (OTRAF)

Ansenekoun Désiré Some, Ministère des Ressources Animales (MRA)

François Some, Bolloré Africa Logistics

Albert Soudre, Ministère des Ressources Animales (MRA)

Roland A. Sow, Bolloré Africa Logistics

Laurent Stravato, iDE

Kalga Tanga, Saso Industries

Yamine Tangongosse, AGRODIA

Evariste Tapsoba, Ministère de l'Agriculture de l'Hydraulique et des Recherches Halieutiques

Issaka Tapsoba, GGTI Motors

Assiongbon Têko-Agbo, Commission de l'Union Economique et Monétaire Ouest Africaine (UEMOA)

Salif Tentica, Ministère de l'Agriculture de l'Hydraulique et des Recherches Halieutiques

Ali Traoré, Conseil Burkinabé des Chargeurs (CBC)

Ibrahima Traoré, Ministère des Infrastructures, du Désenclavement et des Transports

Karim Traoré, Monsanto

Hamma Yacouba, Institut International d'Ingénierie de l'Eau et de l'Environnement

Jean Pierre Yaméogo, ETY-GTZ

Blaise Yoda, Ministère de l'Agriculture de l'Hydraulique et des Recherches Halieutiques

Jonas Yogo, Agro Productions

Roger Zangré, Ministère de la Recherche scientifique et de l'Innovation

Rufive Zougrana, Conseil Burkinabé des Chargeurs (CBC)

BURUNDI

Banque de la République du Burundi

NAHA S.U.

PPFO Fertilizer

Rubeya & Co Advocates

Daudi Amani, African Promotion Company (APROCO)

Albert Arakaza

Donatien Bahimenda, Collectif des Producteurs des Semences du Burundi (COPROSEBU)

Jean-Claude Barakamfitiye, Muyango Law Firm

Leger Bruggeman

Marius Bucumi, Autorité de Régulation de la Filière Café (ARFIC)

Ménard Bucumi, CRDB Bank

François Butoke

Leone Comin, International Fertilizer Development Center (IFDC)

Christophe Gahungu, Water, Climate and Development Programme for Africa

Fidèle Gahungu, Office national de contrôle et de certification des semences (ONCCS)

Paul Gatin, SHER Ingénieurs-conseil

Hakizimana Anselme, ATRIDA

Richard Havyarimana, Forum des Organisations des Producteurs Agricoles du Burundi (FOPABU)

Clodette Inarukundo, Inarukundo Claudette

Boris Ininahazwe, Banque de Crédit de Bujumbura

Desire Irakoze, Leo (U-Com)

Flora Irakoze, Banque Nationale de Développement Économique

Patrick Itangishaka, SDV Transami - Bolloré Africa Logistics

Richard Kaderi, African Promotion Company (APROCO)

Louise Kamikazi, WISE

Ferdinand Kantungeko

Béatrice Kanyange, Ministère de l'Eau, de l'Environnement, de l'Aménagement du Territoire et de l'Urbanisme

Emmanuel Karikurubu, Ministère du Transport

Arnaud Kimana, Ministère de l'Agriculture et de l'Élevage

Bernard Kinyata, Receka Inking

Festus Ciza alias Kigazi, Association pour la promotion des Palmiculteurs du Burundi (APROPABU)

Ida Marie Mabushi, Diamond Trust Bank Burundi (DTB)

Damien Macumi, Programme National Foncier

René Madebari, ENSafrica

Béatrice Moregeya, Ministère de l'Agriculture et de l'Élevage

Renilde Masunku, African Promotion Company (APROCO)

Deusdedit Mchomba, CRDB Bank

Jean Marie Vianney Musangwa, Turame Community Finance S.A.

Astère Muyango, Muyango Law Firm

Bruce Mwile, CRDB Bank

Leopold Nahawenimana, Direction des Titres fonciers et du Cadastre national

Dieudonne Nahimana, Institut des Sciences Agronomiques du Burundi (ISABU)

Jonathan Nahimana, Econet

Joseph Nahayo, Forum des Organisations de Producteurs Agricoles du Burundi (FOPABU)

Gérard Ndabemeye, Ministère de l'Agriculture et de l'Élevage

Cyprien Ndayishimiye, Réseau des institutions de microfinance au Burundi-RIM

Prosper Ndihokubwayo, Deutsche Gesellschaft für Internationale Zusammenarbeit (GIZ) GmbH

Emmanuel Ndorimana, Ministère de l'Eau, de l'Environnement, de l'Aménagement du Territoire et de l'Urbanisme

Christian Nduwayo, Cabinet de Maître Placide Gatoto

Gilbert Nibigirwe, Gilbert & Partners

Cyriaque Nibitegeka, Nibitegeka Advocates

Claver Nigarura, Rubeya & Co Advocates

Alice Nijimbere, Mkono & Co

Fiston Nikiza, Société de Commercialisation des Intrants Agricoles et des Services Divers (SOCEASED)

Emery Ninganza, Christian Aid

Pascal Niyingabo, Direction des Titres fonciers et du Cadastre national

Alfred Niyokwishimira, Ministère de l'Agriculture et de l'Élevage

Régine Mireille Niyongabo, Muyango Law Firm

Célestin Niyongere, Institut des Sciences Agronomiques du Burundi (ISABU)

Fortunate Niyonkuru, Muyango Law Firm

Emmanuel Niyonzima

Melchiade Niyonzima, General Trading and Transport (GTT)

Grégoire Nkeshimana, Direction des Titres fonciers et du Cadastre national

Albert Nkunumana, Direction des Titres fonciers et du Cadastre national

Pierre Claver Nkunzabagenzi, Hope Fund

Laurent Nkurikiye, BUCOFCO

Eric Nkurunziza, Université Lumière de Bujumbura

François Nkurunziza, Armajaro Burundi S.U.R.L.

M. Louise Nsabiyumva, Caisse Coopérative d'Epargne et de Crédit Mutuelle (CECM)

Emmanuel Nshimirimana, BIRATURABA

Eric Ntangaro, Association des transporteurs internationaux du Burundi (ATIB)

Daniel Ntawurishira, SODETRA Ltd.

Philomène Ntiharirizwa, Twitezimbere

Adelin Ntungumburanye, Chambre Fédérale de Commerce et d'Industrie du Burundi

Jean Claude Ntwari, Office national de contrôle et de certification des semences (ONCCS)

Emery Nukuri, Université du Burundi

Boland Rasquinha, Pharma Bolena

Ena Rasquinha, Pharma Bolena

Roland Brian Rasquinha, Alchem

Alice Remezo, Milk Chel

Théodomir Rishirumuhirwa, Agrobiotec

Lauren Rosenberg, Long Miles Coffee

Prosper Ruberintwari, Food and Agriculture Organization of the United Nations (FAO)

Déogratias Rurimunzu, Agence de Régulation et de Contrôle des Télécommunications (ARCT)

Salvator Ruzima

Philippe Sabot, Merial

Steve Sahabo, CofiCo s.a.

Eliakim Sakayoya, Ministère de l'Agriculture et de l'Élevage

Annick Sezibera, Confédération des associations des producteurs agricoles pour le développement (CAPAD)

Alexis Sinarinzi, Agence de Régulation et de Contrôle des Télécommunications (ARCT)

Alexandre Sindayigaya, Diamond Trust Bank Burundi (DTB)

CAMBODIA

Boost Riche (Cambodia) Co., Ltd

Chuan Wei (Cambodia) Co. Ltd.

DFDL

Heifer International

Ministry of Agriculture, Forestry and Fisheries

P&A Asia

Sithisak Law office

Telecommunication Regulator of Cambodia (TRC)

Lotfi Allal, Food and Agriculture Organization of the United Nations (FAO)

Maros Apostol, Thaneakea Phum Limited (TKL)

Ravindranath Balakrishnan

Sopheak Chan, Angkor Green Investment and Development Co., Ltd

Sam Ol Chhim, Central Law Firm

Martin Desautels, DFDL

H. Naryth Hem, BNG Legal

Kimsreng Kong, Ministry of Environment

Kundi Lay, Co-operative Association of Cambodia (CAC)

Hun Lak, Mekong Oryza Trading Co., Ltd

Andy Lay, City Rice Import Export Co., Ltd

Robert Lay, City Rice Import Export Co., Ltd

Joseph Lovell, BNG Legal

Menghak Phem, Royal University of Agriculture

Sokla San, P&A Asia Law Firm

Buon Sarakmony, SETHAVITOU Notary Public of The Kingdom of Cambodia

Vong Sarinda, Co-operative Association of Cambodia (CAC)

Saruth Chan, Ministry of Agriculture, Forestry and Fisheries

Chanvireak Seng, DFDL

Leanhour Seng, Kong Hour Rice Mill Import Export Co., Ltd

Thyse Seng, Kong Hour Rice Mill Import Export Co., Ltd

Say Sony, PRASAC Microfinance Institution Ltd

Sovan Meas, BNG Legal

Yon Sovann, Bayon Cereal Co., Ltd

Tayseng Ly, HBS Law Firm & Consultants

Yap Thoeurn, Cambodian Farmer Association Federation of Agricultural Producers

Hartono Tiodora, Multico MS (Cambodia) Co Ltd

CHILE

Centro Latinoamericano para el Desarrollo Rural (RIMISP)

Fondo Esperanza

National Customs Service

Oficina de Estudios y Políticas Agrarias (ODEPA)

Salinas y Fabres S.A

Servicio Agrícola y Ganadero (SAG)

Soquimich Comercial S.A. SQM

Maria Fernanda Almendras Arriagada, Elecnor Chile S.A

Edmundo Araya, Asociación de Exportadores de Frutas de Chile A.G. (ASOEX)

Matías Araya, Araya & Cía Abogados

Rodrigo Astete Rocha, Servicio Agrícola y Ganadero (SAG)

Pedro Pablo Ballivian, Barros & Errázuriz Abogados

Andres Bittner, Chilolac

Marlene Brokering, Brokering & Luarte Abogados

Carlos Browne, Brokering & Luarte Abogados

Carlos Bustos, Quinzio Abogados

Miguel Canala-Echeverria, Asociación de Exportadores de Frutas de Chile A.G. (ASOEX)

Maricela Canto, National Association of Seed Producers of Chile (ANPROS)

Alberto Cardemil, Carey Lawyers

Claudia Castillo, Quinzio Abogados

Magaly Castillo Tamayo, Naandanjain

Lohengrin Cortés Cea

Inés De Ros Casacuberta, Araya & Cía Abogados

Tamara Del Río

Sebastián R. Donoso, Sebastián Donoso y Asociados Abogados

Patricio Gajardo, Gajardo & Rodríguez Law Firm

Enrique Garcés B., R&Q Ingeniería S.A.

Pamela Grandon

Hermes Guerrero, Ministerio de Bienes Nacionales

Nelson Gutierrez Gonzalez, Conservador de Bienes Raíces de Coronel

Marcelo Huenchuñir Gómez, Fundación Banigualdad

Camila Lavin, Carey Lawyers

Alejandro León, Universidad de Chile

Francisco Lobos, Asociación Gremial Chilena de Empresarios del Transporte Internacional de Cargas por Carretera

Ivan Marambio

Eduardo Martin, Carey Lawyers

Raul Mazzarella, Carey Lawyers

Felipe Meneses, Carey Lawyers

Sebastián Norris, Araya & Cía Abogados

Mario Olivares, Cooprinsem

Carolina Olivares Agurto, Transportes Olivares

Matias Orfali

Rodrigo Orlandi Arrate, Boreal Gestión Inmobiliaria Limitada

René Pinochet Chateau, Novafeed

Loreto Poblete F., Quinzio Abogados

Sebastian Querol Rodriguez, Ministerio de Bienes Nacionales

Maria Teresa Quirke Arrau, Quirke & Cia

Julio Recordon, Carey Lawyers

Roberto Saelzer, Universidad de Concepción

Miguel Saldivia, Carey Lawyers

Alfonso Silva, Carey Lawyers

José Miguel Stegmeier Schmidlin, Sociedad Agrícola de Bio Bio AG.

Rodrigo Benitez Ureta, Baker & McKenzie

Álvaro Varas, Araya & Cía Abogados

Rafael Vergara, Carey Lawyers

Jaime Zaldumbide, Carey Lawyers

COLOMBIA

Asociación Nacional de Médicos Veterinarios de Colombia (AMEVEC)

Centro Nacional de Investigaciones de Café - Cenicafé

Federación Nacional de Cafeteros de Colombia

Financiera América

Instituto Colombiano Agropecuário (ICA)

Instituto Colombiano de Desarrollo Rural (INCODER)

Yara

Andrew Abela, Abela Maldonado & Asociados Abodagos

Miguel Achury Jimenez, Bancamía S.A., Banco de las Microfinanzas

Massiel Alvarez Alarcón, Bancamía S.A., Banco de las Microfinanzas

Felipe Ardila, Comercial de Riegos

Luis Fernando Cataño Córdoba, Federación de Empresas Transportadoras de Carga de Colombia (FEDETRANSCOL)

Juan Fernando Cifuentes, Ministerio de Agricultura y Desarrollo Rural

Miguel Cortés Mendieta, Asociación Nacional De Empresas Transportadoras De Carga Por Carretera (ASECARGA)

Julián Camilo Cruz González, Cruz & Asociados

Freddy Diez, Procam SA

Diego Escobar, Abonamos

Pedro Fuentes, Ministerio de Agricultura y Desarrollo Rural

P. German Dario Arias

Alberto Gomez Mejia, Red Nacional de Jardines Botánicos de Colombia

Ana Patricia Heredia Vargas, Ministerio de Salud y Protección Social

Jairo Herrera Murillo, Asociación Nacional De Empresas Transportadoras De Carga Por Carretera (ASECARGA)

Martha Jama, Operadores del Campo, S.A

Juan Nicolas Laverde, Brigard & Urrutia

Luis Fernando Macías Gómez, Macías Gómez Asociados Abogados

Jairo Alonso Mesa Guerra, Superintendencia de Notariado y Registro

Juana Micán, Brigard & Urrutia

Sergio Michelsen Jaramillo, Brigard & Urrutia

Julieth Andrea Navarrete Fernández, Corpoica

Camilo Pardo, Unidad de Restitución de Tierras

Jorge Alejandro Pinzon

Dora Inés Rey Martínez, Unidad de Planificación de Tierras Rurales (UPRA)

Jackeline Rincón C., Bancamía S.A., Banco de las Microfinanzas

Andrés Ramón Rodríguez, Gómez-Pinzón Zuleta

Bernardo Rodriguez Ossa, Parra Rodríguez Sanín SAS

Juan Pablo Rodríguez Suárez, Bancamía S.A., Banco de las Microfinanzas

Carlos Ignacio Rojas Gaitán, Asociación Nacional de Exportadores de Café de Colombia (ASOEXPORT)

Oscar Romero Guevara, Unidad de Planificación de Tierras Rurales (UPRA)

Esteban Rubio, Brigard & Urrutia

Ricardo Sabogal, Unidad de Restitución de Tierras

Amparo Scorcia

Guillermo Tejeiro, Brigard & Urrutia

Carlos Umaña Trujillo, Brigard & Urrutia

Camilo Valencia, Camilo Valencia Abogados

Jorge Vargas, Invasa Maquinaria S.A.S.

Irene Velandia, Brigard & Urrutia

Juan Hernando Velasco Lozano, Unidad de Planificación de Tierras Rurales (UPRA)

Jorge Enrique Vélez García, Superintendencia de Notariado y Registro

CÔTE D'IVOIRE

Callivoire

Chambre de Commerce & d'Industrie de Côte d'Ivoire

Ministère de l'Agriculture

MTN

Office National de Développement de la Riziculture (ONDR)

Syndicat National des Transporteurs de Côte d'Ivoire

Audrey Abouo, SCPA Bilé-Aka, Brizoua-Bi & Associés

Allouko Aka Alexandre, PolyPompes Ivoire

Fataye Akamou, Ministère de l'Agriculture

Louise Akanvou, Centre National de Recherche Agronomique

Eric Bably, BK & Associés

Binde Binde, Africa Trans-Logistics International

Bob Clark, Société TECHNOSERVE

Tata Dagnono, SCPA Bilé-Aka, Brizoua-Bi & Associés

Henri Danon, Ministère de la Poste et des Technologies de l'Information et de la Communication

Jean de Foucauld, Ceva Santé Animale

Kouadio Jean Esse, Ministère de l'Agriculture

Soumaiga Farrouna, Syndicat National des Transporteurs de Côte d'Ivoire

N'Datien Séverin Guibessongui, Cabinet ICT Consulting

Peter Harlech Jones, GALVmed

Bachir Hervé Dissou, Agro Afrique

Simplice Houphouët, BK & Associés

Kinèdèni Koukouni Kignelman Koné, SCPA KONE-N'GUESSAN-KIGNELMAN Société Civile Professionnelle d'Avocats

Edmond Koffi, Centre National de Recherche Agronomique

Nestor Kouakou Koffi

Kan Marcel Konan, Société Coopérative Anouanzè-Douekoue

Sekou Konaté, Foncier Rural, Ministère de l'Agriculture

Augustin Kone, Ministère de l'Environnement, de la Salubrité Urbaine et du Développement Durable

Michel Kouakou, Centre National de Recherche Agronomique

Sylvain Kouakou, Ministère de l'Agriculture

Bamba Moussa Mahan, Mahan Group Industries

N'Guessan M'Bahia, Africa Pure Technology

Jean Patrick N'doume, Office Ivoirien des Chargeurs (OIC)

Boni N'Zue, Centre National de Recherche Agronomique

Jean Thierry Oura, CÔTE D'IVOIRE AGRI

Philippe Sabot, Merial

Idrissa Seynou, Ministère de l'Agriculture

Didier Medard Sossah, Bureau national d'études techniques et de développement (BNETD)

Lacina Soumahoro

Assiongbon Têko-Agbo, Commission de l'Union Economique et Monétaire Ouest Africaine (UEMOA)

Jean Philippe Touré, Versus Bank

Kalifa Touré, Office Ivoirien des Chargeurs (OIC)

Jessica Nanou Waota, SCPA Bilé-Aka, Brizoua-Bi & Associés

Stanislas Zézé, Bloomfield Investment Corporation

Emmanuella Zoro, AnyRay & Partners

DENMARK

Danish Agency for Digitisation

Danish AgriFish Agency

Danish Agro

Danish Business Authority

Danish Veterinary and Food Administration

Finanstilsynet (The Danish FSA)

Nykredit Bank A/S

Yara

Hans Abildstrøm, Horten Advokatpartnerselskab

Mathias Neumann Andersen, Department of Agroecology, Climate and Water, Aarhus University

Lidde Bagge Jensen, The Danish Nature Agency

Marie Blanner, The Danish Nature Agency

Niels Borum, Lexsos Advokater

Jean de Foucauld, Ceva Santé Animale

Håkun Djurhuus, Bech-Bruun

Peter Fenger, Bryggeriforeningen (Danish Brewers Association)

Søreen Kolind Hvid, Seges P/S

Eva Juul Jensen, The Danish Nature Agency

Julie Bak, Ministry of Food, Agriculture and Fisheries of Denmark

Jakob Kamby, Kammeradvokaten

Ulf Kjellerup, COWI A/S

Louise Lundsby Wessel, Bech-Bruun

Birgitte Lund, Danish AgriFish Agency

Michael Svane, DI Transport

Jakob Møgelvang, Danish AgriFish Agency

Mark Villingshøj Nielsen, Bech-Bruun

Peter Odifier, G.O. Transport & Spedition A/S

Per Olsen, Danish Agriculture and Food Council

Henning Otte Hansen, The Royal Danish Agricultural Society

Peter Pedersen, Fasterholt Maskinfabrik

Jan Persson, Danish Transport Authority

Robin Philip, Bruun & Hjejle Law Firm

Kenny Rasmussen, Ministry of Justice

Anders Refsgaard, COWI A/S

Alexandre Latif Schleimann-Jensen, Bech-Bruun

Anders Ankær Sørensen, Danish AgriFish Agency

Jakob Sørensen, Holst

Søren Stenderup Jensen, Plesner

Andreas Tamasauskas, Ronne & Lundgren

Mette Thomsen, Danish AgriFish Agency

Lise Viftrup, Danish Environmental Protection Agency, Ministry of the Environment

ETHIOPIA

Ethiopian Agricultural Transformation Agency (ATA)

Tigray Agricultural Research Institute

Teshome Gabre-Mariam Bokan Law Office

Muradu Abdo Srur, Addis Ababa University

Tigistu Abza, Ministry of Agriculture

Achamyeleh Gashu Adam, Institute of Land Administration

Melaku Admassu, Pioneer Hi-bred Seeds Ethiopia P.L.C

Alishume Ahimed, Ethiopian Biodiversity Institute

Bassam Alayyat, Alayyat Group Ethiopia

Amsalu Alemayehu, Wasasa

Belachew Yirsaw Alemu, Institute of Land Administration

Abenezer Asfaw, Boot Coffee Consulting & Training

Fikadu Asfaw, Fikadu Asfaw and Associates Law Office

Getenesh Ashenafi, Agricultural Input Supply Enterprise

Girmaye Ayalew, Global Africa

Workneh Ayalew, Ethiopian Agricultural Transformation Agency (ATA)

Aga Amsalu Ayana, Integrated Seed Sector Development

Ashinafi Ayenew, Ethiopian Biodiversity Institute

Million Bekere, Cooperative Bank of Oromia

Diliba Beyene, Oromia International Bank

Zewdie Bishaw, International Center for Agricultural Research in the Dry Areas (ICARDA)

Andrea Bues, Leibniz Institute for Regional Development and Structural Planning (IRS)

Moti Cheru, Veterinary Drugs and Feed Administration and Control Authority (VDFACA)

Aberra Debelo, Sasakawa Global 2000

Ephrem Demeke, Ethio Telecom

Asaminew Deribew, Commercial Bank of Ethiopia

Motuma Didita, Ethiopian Biodiversity Institute

Yibeltal Dubale, Ethiopian Road Transport Authority

Fikadu Dupasa, Limu Inara Farmers Multi-purpose Cooperative Union

Tesfa-alem Embaye, Mekelle University

Dilnesa Fentahun

Adugna Fite, Oromia Agriculture Bureau, Participatory Small scale Irrigation Development Program (PASIDP)

Teshome Gabre-Mariam Bokan, Teshome Gabre-Mariam Bokan Law Office

Teklay Glibanos Gebrehiwot, Mochaland PLC

Zelalem Gebretsadik, Veterinary Drugs and Feed Administration and Control Authority (VDFACA)

Alehegn Gebru, Moenco Kalitiy Machinery Branch

Seyoum Getachew, Ethiopian Agricultural Transformation Agency (ATA)

Rajiv Ghandi, Hester Biosciences Ltd

Fikremariam Ghion, Ethiopian Biodiversity Institute

Yodit Gurji, Fikadu Asfaw and Associates Law Office

Kedir Bushira Hassan, Addis-Vet-Pty Ltd/PLC

Abdulmen Ibrahim

Haftom Kesete, Haftom Kesete Kahsay Law Office

Kibret Alemayehu, Dejen Cross Border Level 1-A Freight Transport Owners Association

Teshome Lakew, Ministry of Agriculture

Gezahegne Lemma, Alpha Truckers Association

Hailu Leta, Aggar Micro Finance S.C.

Patrick Maluku, Monsanto

Getnet Yawkal Mebratu, Mebratu

Henoki Melaku, Ethiopian Agricultural Transformation Agency (ATA)

Zelalem Mesele, ZK flowers P.L.C

Kedir Musema, Ries Engineering

Robson Mutandi, The International Fund for Agricultural Development (IFAD)

Mearaf Nur, Mearaf Bedru Law Office

Philippe Sabot, Merial

Manaye Abera Shagrdi

Eleni Shiferaw, Ethiopian Biodiversity Institute

Getachew Shimels, GAWT International Business PLC

Ermias Teshome, Ethiopian Agricultural Transformation Agency (ATA)

Misikire Tessema, Ethiopian Biodiversity Institute

Fekadu Tilahun, Ethiopian Agricultural Transformation Agency (ATA)

Daniel Weldegebriel Ambaye, Institute of Land Administration

Netsanet Woldekidan, Awash International Bank

Dagninet Yimenu, Damtit Vet Pharma Trading Co.

Teshome Yohannes, Buusaa Gonofaa Microfinance Share Company

Emiru Zewdie, ALPPIS

Tewodros Zewdie, Ethiopian Horticultures Producers and Exporters Association

GEORGIA

Colibri Law Firm

Tea Abramidze, Notary Chamber of Georgia

Tina Adamia, Caucastrans Express Ltd

Giorgi Begiashvili, Begiashvili & Co

Alexander Bolkvadze, BLC Law Office

Archil Chachkhiani, VTB Bank

Zurab Chkheidze, Begiashvili & Co

Jean de Foucauld, Ceva Santé Animale

Malkhaz Dzadzua, MFO Crystal

David Egiashvili, National Agency of Public Registry

Levan Gachechiladze, Isragreen LLC

Nata Ghudushauri, LLC MFO Credo

Archil Giorgadze, Dechert LLP

Lasha Gogiberidze, BGI Legal

Levan Gotua, Begiashvili & Co

Irakli Gvilia, BLC Law Office

Nana Janashia, Caucasus Environment NGO Network

Vakhtang Janezashvili, BGI Legal

Rusudan Kacharava, Terra DeNovo LLC

Nino Kharitonashvili, Notary Chamber of Georgia

Nino Khopheria, Notary Chamber of Georgia

David Khrikadze, BDO Legal

Avtandil Korakhashvili, National Academy of Sciences of Georgia

Ana Kostava, Dechert LLP

Tamar Mamporia, DLA Piper

Nicola Mariani, Dechert LLP

Ekaterina Meskhidze, National Agency of Public Registry

Irakli Mgaloblishvili, Mgaloblishvili, Kipiani, Dzidziguri (MKD)

Tamar Mtvarelidze, Caucasus Environment NGO Network

Kakha Nadiradze, Association for Farmers Rights Defense

Eka Naobishvili, Ministry of Agriculture

Sophio Natroshvili, BGI Legal

Nana Phirosmanashvili, Association for Farmers Rights Defense

Irakli Pipia, DLA Piper

Rusudan Gergauli, LPA Law Firm

Philippe Sabot, Merial

Nino Sesitashvili, BLC Law Office

Ilya Shapira, Isragreen LLC

Irakli Sokolovski, Dechert LLP

Nino Suknidze, DLA Piper

Rusudan Tchkuaseli, BLC Law Office

Tamar Tevdoradze, BGI Legal

Nino Tevzadze, Caucasus Environment NGO Network

Tamara Toria, Georgian Farmers' Association

Bela Tskhvediani, VTB Bank

Nino Zambakhidze, Georgian Farmers' Association

GHANA

Ministry of Food and Agriculture (MoFA)

Shawbell Consulting

OLAM

Samuel Achaw Ofosu, Veterinary Council

Adingtingah Apullah Patrick, Savanna Seed Services Company Limited

Prince Afful, EB-ACCION SLC

Maxwell Agbenorhevi, USAID Feed the Future

Anthony Akunzule, Veterinary Services Directorate, Ministry of Food and Agriculture (MoFA)

Martin Ali, Ministry of Food and Agriculture (MoFA)

Emmanuel K.M. Alognikou, International Fertilizer Development Center (IFDC)

William Amanfu

Daniel S. Amlalo, Environmental Protection Agency

David Andah

Patrice Annequin, International Fertilizer Development Center (IFDC)

Kwasi Anokurang-Budu, EB-ACCION SLC

Asamoah Owusu-Akyaw, Private Transport Association of Ghana

Issac Asare, AGRA

Emelia Desiree Atta-Fynn, EB-ACCION SLC

William Awuku Ahiadormey, Agricare Limited

Johnson Kwadzo Badzi, EB-ACCION SLC

Kwaku D. Berchie, Pan-African Savings & Loans

Charles A. Biney, The Volta Basin Authority

Isabel Boaten, AB & David

Goh Charles, Vodafone Ghana

CK Djan-Suleiman, Zaklan Consult

Raymond Codjoe, R.A.Codjoe Law Offices

Wilson Darkwah, Irrigation Development Authority, Ministry of Food and Agriculture

Siegfried Kofi Debrah, International Fertilizer Development Center (IFDC)

Bazaanah Fidelis, Ghana Cooperative Credit Unions Association (CUA)

Peace Gbeckor-Kove, Environmental Protection Agency

Sergio Godoy, Yara

Michael Gyan Nyarko, AB & David

Peter Harlech Jones, GALVmed

Abdul Razak Haruna, Alfayi Co. Ltd

Thomas Havor, Seed Producers Association of Ghana (SEEDPAG)

George K.A. Brantuo

Kwabena Kankam-Yeboa, Water Research Institute

Isaac Karikari, Karicel Foundation

Japhet Lartey, International Fertilizer Development Center (IFDC)

Francis Mensah, African Fertilizer and Agribusiness Partnership (AFAP)

Andrew Mercer, Mercer & Company

Kwabena Nimakoh, Mercer & Company

Anita Nsiah, Mercer & Company

Samuel Nuamah Dankwah, Nwabiagya Rural Bank

Ben Nyamadi, Irrigation Development Authority, Ministry of Food and Agriculture

Kwame Oppong-Anane, Opporhu Agricultural and Rural Development Consultancy Ltd.

Isaac Kofi Osei, Mechanical Lloyd Co. Ltd.

Richard Osei-Amponsah, University of Ghana

Francis Owiredu, Advans Ghana Savings and Loans

Gyasi Poku, Indchem Royal Ltd.

George Prah, Ministry of Food and Agriculture (MoFA)

Philippe Sabot, Merial

Elizabeth Rosebud Afua Alifo Tetteh, Erat Services

George Agyemang Sarpong, G.A. Sarpong & Co.

Emmanuel Kaaviele Tinsari, Lands Commission

Isaac Yaw Azadagli, Agricultural Development & Mechanization Limited (ADEMEC)

Albert Yeboah Obeng, Foresight Generation Club

GREECE

Ministry of Rural Development and Food

Mediterranean Plant Conservation Unit, Mediterranean Agronomic Institute of Chania (MAICh)

Tampakis Fresh Co

Yara

Manolis Agrimanakis, TROXOI & TIR

Nikolaos Athanassiadis, AP & GENERALIS Law Firm

Evangelia Balla

Savvas Balouktsis, Machinery Importers' - Representatives' Association (MIRA)

Evangelos Baltas, National Technical University of Athens

Sofia Chatzigiannidou, Zepos & Yannopoulos Law Firm

Jean de Foucauld, Ceva Santé Animale

Sotirios Douklias, KG Law Firm

Elisabeth Eleftheriades, KG Law Firm

Maria Giannakaki, Karageorgiou & Associates

Anthony B. Hadjioannou, Kyriakides Georgopoulos Law Firm

Stavros Karageorgiou, Karageorgiou & Associates

Ioannis Karavokyris, G. Karavokyris & Partners Consulting Engineers s.a.

Nikolaos Kondylis, N. Kondylis & Partners Law Office

Ioanna Kontopoulou, Hellenic Telecommunications and Post Commission (EETT)

Ilias Kotsopoulos, OTE S.A

Theodora Kouloura, Hellenic Fertilizers and Chemicals ELFE s.a.

Georgia Kourakli

Marinos Kritsotakis

Irene C. Kyriakides, Kyriakides Georgopoulos Law Firm

Persa Lampropoulou, Ilias G. Anagnostopoulos Law firm

Evagelia Liakopoulou, Hellenic Telecommunications and Post Commission (EETT)

Spiros Livieratos, Hellenic Telecommunications and Post Commission (EETT)

Christina Manossis, ZEUS KIWI SA

Evangelia Mantzou

Marinos Kandylis, Olympias SA International Transport

Ioanna Michalopoulou, Michalopoulou & Associates

Maria Mimikou, National Technical University of Athens

Anthony Narlis, Geodis Calberson GE

Maria Oikonomou, Ministry of Reconstruction of Production

Ioannis Panagopoulos, National Technical University of Athens

Stefanos Panayiotopoulos, Zepos & Yannopoulos Law Firm

George Parissopoulos, National Agricultural Research Center & Institute of Agricultural Machinery

Kalliroi Passiou, G. Karavokyris & Partners Consulting Engineers s.a.

Michael Paterakis, Dr. Paterakis and Partners

Alexandros Protofanousis, Protofanousi Fruits SA

Nikos Protofanousis, Protofanousi Fruits SA

Evangelia Rammou, Public Notary Greece

Kyriaki-Korina Raptopoulou, Kyriakides Georgopoulos Law Firm

Antonios Sifakis, Haidarlis - Sifakis Law Offices

Panagiotis Stamatopoulos, Agroconsults

Neoklis Stamkos, KEPA

Katerina Tassi, Karageorgiou & Associates

Kimon Tsakiris, KG Law Firm

Eleftherios Vagenas, V. ATTIS LTD

Antonios Voulgarakis, Nature sa

GUATEMALA

All Logistics S.A.

Anavi Guatemala

Superintendencia de Bancos de Guatemala

Pedro Arias, Duwest

Adolfo Brito Gómez, Marroquín Pérez & Asociados, S.C.

Abraham Buezo, Asociación de Semilleristas de Jocotán (ASEJO)

Ana Beatriz Clavería, Duwest

Alejandro Cofiño, QIL+4 ABOGADOS

Carlos Roberto Cordón Krumme, Cordón Ovalle & Asociados

Jean de Foucauld, Ceva Santé Animale

Héctor Fajardo, Camara de Transportistas Centroamericanos (CATRANSCA)

Gilvert Garcia, Aimar Group

León García, Yara

Harald Himsel

Julio Artemio Juárez Morán, Asociación de Transportistas Internactionales (ATI)

Miguel Juarez Pelaez, Dirección General de Transportes

Karen Larson, Friendship Bridge

Herver López, Tecnica Universal, S.A. (Tecun Guatemala)

Maria Lucía Soto Santos, Consejo de Usuarios del Transporte Internacional de Guatemala

Maria Mercedes Marroquín de Pemueller, Marroquín Pérez & Asociados, S.C.

Pedro Pablo Marroquín Pérez, Marroquín, Pérez & Asociados, S.C.

Vivian Lucía Morales Herrera, Arias & Muñoz

Pedro Aragón Munoz, Aragón & Aragón

Oswaldo Oliva, National Federation of Financial Cooperatives

Verónica Orantes, QIL+4 ABOGADOS

Victor Orantes, SERCA, S.A.

Guillermo Austreberto Ortiz Aldana, Ganaderia y Alimentacion Unidad de Normas y Regulaciones Coordinacion, Ministerio de Agricultura

Mélida Pineda, Carrillo y Asociados

Ana Gabriela Platero Midence, Arias & Muñoz Guatemala

Paris Rivera, INSIVUMEH

Bernhard Roehrs, AgroAmérica

Maricarmen Rosal de Donis, Integrum

Jorge Eduardo Salazar, Ministerio de Agricultura, Ganadería y Alimentación

Ligia Salazar, Arias & Muñoz Guatemala

Juan Salvador Sandoval, Ministerio de Agricultura, Ganadería y Alimentación

Edwin Sánchez, FUNDEA

Ricardo Santa Cruz Rubi, Agexport

Yashira Shutuc, Aimar Group

Aura Cristina Son Icú, Duwest

Daniel Humberto Sosa Casasola, Ministerio de Agricultura, Ganadería y Alimentación

Armando Soto, Duwest

Arturo Soto, Sosa & Soto Abogados

José Daniel Tistoj Chan, Ministerio de Agricultura, Ganadería y Alimentación

Enrique Toledo-Cotera, ARTLEX- Attorneys at Law

José Urrutia, BK Consulting

Neftali Villanueva

JORDAN

Central Bank of Jordan

Department of Lands and Survey Jordan

Monsanto

Zahra Wa Shajara For Agricultural Services

Alaa Abbassi, Abbassi Law Office

Raed Abd el Qader, The National Center for Agricultural Research and Extension (NCARE)

Jamal Abu Umaro, Nagel Company

Zeinab Ahmad Al Momany, Specific Union for Farmers Productive

Sultan Al Fayez, Ali Sharif Zu'bi Advocates and Legal Consultants

Jawad Al-Bakri, University of Jordan

Abdullmalik Al-Eassawi, Telecommunications Regulatory Commission

Ahmed Al-Fayad, Ministry of Agriculture

Nada Al-Frihat, Ministry of Agriculture

Al-Ansari Almashakbeh, Telecommunications Regulatory Commission

Monther Al-Reefai, Ministry of Agriculture

Jamal Alrusheidat, The National Center for Agricultural Research and Extension (NCARE)

Hazim Al-Smadi, Ministry of Agriculture

Ibrahim Amosh, Amosh Legal Services & Arbitration

Emad Awad, Ministry of Agriculture

Rakan Baybars, Rakan Baybars Law Office

Ahmad Ekor

Ahmad Faidi, Faidi Law Firm

Ziad A. Ghanma, Central Bank of Jordan

Baha Halasah, Information and Communications Technology Association of Jordan

Zuhair Hattar, Land Transport Regulatory Commission LTRC

Lubna Hawamdeh, Ali Sharif Zu'bi Advocates and Legal Consultants

Khaled Hudhud, Information and Communications Technology Association of Jordan

Zeyad Jadan

Afram Jamil, Information and Communications Technology Association of Jordan

Mazen Kalbouneh, Green Produce Fodder Hydroponics System

Sameh Mahariq, Alwatani (National Microfinance Bank)

Mohammad Majdalawi, University of Jordan

Luma Mdanat, Ali Sharif Zu'bi Advocates and Legal Consultants

Ghassan Obeidat, Jordan Valley Authority

Fida Rawabdeh, Ministry of Agriculture

Yahya Shakhatreh, The National Center for Agricultural Research and Extension (NCARE)

Bassam Snobar, University of Jordan

Ali Subah, Ministry of Water and Irrigation

Sami Telfah, Telfah Trading Company

John Yancura, FINCA

KENYA

Monsanto

One Acre Fund

Syngenta Foundation

Yara

Aisha Abdollah, Anjarwalla & Khanna (A&K)

Carilus Ademba, Sacco Societies Regulatory Authority

Pamella Ager, Halmiton, Harrison & Mathew

David Joseph Angwenyi, Mohammed Muigai Advocates

Francis Chabari

Grace Chilande, International Fertilizer Development Center (IFDC)

Gilly Cowan, GALVmed

Harm Duiker, SNV

Martin Fisher, KickStart International

Paul Gacheru, Igeria & Ngugi Advocates

Rajiv Ghandi, Hester Biosciences Ltd

Hugo De Groote, CIMMYT

Anthony Frederick Gross, A. F Gross Advocate

Antony Guto Mogere, Mohammed Muigai Advocates

Peter Harlech Jones, GALVmed

Richard Harney, Coulson Harney Advocates

Samir Ibrahim, SunCulture

Paul Isako, SNV

Sameer Jaywant, SunCulture

Duncan Ndiguran

Sammy Kamanth, Equity Bank Limited

Sarah Kiarie-Muia, Kaplan & Stratton Advocates

Brenda Kihara, Kenya Revenue Authority

John Kinaga, KickStart International

Evelyn Kyania, B.M Musau & Co. Advocates

Mary Njuguna, SNV

Paul Makepeace

Nathaniel Makoni, ABS TCM Ltd

Michael Mbiti, Anjarwalla & Khanna Advocates

Laura Mburu, Orange

Saidi Mkomwa, African Conservation Tillage Network (ACT)

Mona Doshi, Anjarwalla & Khanna Advocates

Gillian Kadenyi Muriithi, Deepa Industries Ltd.

Benjamin Musau, B.M Musau & Co. Advocates

John Mutunga, Kenya National Farmers' Federation

Timothy Mwangi, DAMCO

Eunice Mwongera, Hillside Green Growers and Exporters

Charles Nichols, SunCulture

Peter Njuguna, Sacco Societies Regulatory Authority

Martin Nyamweya, SNV

Gilbert Obati, Egerton University

Fred Ojiambo, Kaplan & Stratton

Bridget Okumu, International Fertilizer Development Center (IFDC)

Phillip Onyango, Kaplan & Stratton

Edwin Oseko, Ministry of Agriculture, Livestock and Fisheries

Anne Marie Ran, Deutsche Gesellschaft für Internationale Zusammenarbeit (GIZ) GmbH

Ben Roberts, Liquid Telecom Kenya

Nat Robinson, Juhudi Kilimo LLC

Philippe Sabot, Merial

Dirk Schaefer

Sonal Sejpal, Anjarwalla & Khanna Advocates

Denis Tiren, International Fertilizer Development Center (IFDC)

KYRGYZ REPUBLIC

CJSC Agrimatco Ltd

Ministry of Agriculture and Melioration

Public Association AgroLead

Vega Plus

Azizbek Abdiev, ARIS

Maksat Abdykaparov, AVEP Public Fund

Myrzagul Aidaralieva, Lorenz International Lawyers

Niyaz Aldashev, Lorenz International Lawyers

Abdybek Asanaliev, Kyrgyz National Agrarian University

Kerim Begaliev, Colibri Law Firm

Kydykbek Beishekeev, On-Farm Irrigation Project

Ruslan F. Beishenkulov, State Inspectorate for veterinary and phytosanitary safety under the Government of the Kyrgyz Republic

Abdelhak Benyagoub, IGCC Logistics Group LLC

Turkmen Bootaev, Association of the International Road Transport Operators

Daria Bulatova, Lorenz International Lawyers

Ruslan Derbishev, OJSC Commercial Bank "KYRGYZSTAN"

Samara Dumanaeva, Lorenz International Lawyers

Natalya Galivets, IGCC Logistics Group LLC

Kymbat Ibakova, Lorenz International Lawyers

Abduhakim Islamov, Seed Association of Kyrgyzstan

Daniar Jasoolov, Association of Farms (KARAGAT)

Gulchehra Kamchibekova, Aiyl Bank

Evgeny Kim, Lorenz International Lawyers

Nurlan Mamatov, Kyrgyz-Turkish Manas University

Umtul Muratkyzy, Lorenz International Lawyers

Niazbek Aldashev, Lorenz International Lawyers

Rafael Nurahunov, CronaTrans

Ulan Orozbekov, Ministry of Transport and Communications

Olesya Paukova, Companion Financial Group CJSC MFC

Tulegen Sarsembekov, Eurasian Development Bank

Temirbek M. Shabdanaliev, Association of Carriers of Kyrgyzstan

Baktybek Shamkeyev, Central Asia International Consulting

Nurlan Smanov, State Communications Agency under the Government of Kyrgyz Republic

Talant Soltobekov, LBD Consulting

Chynara Suiumbaeva, United Nations Development Program (UNDP)

Nurlan Tokonov, AVEP Public Fund

Mirlanbek Torobekov, Frontiers

Anastasiia Tsoi, Lorenz International Lawyers

Baktybek Tumonbaev, CJSC Atrium Holding

Kunduz Turgumbaeva, Frontiers

Uran Tursunaliev

Gulnara Uskenbaeva, Association of Supplier (Producers and Distributors)

Aleksei Vandaev, Kalikova & Associates

Dmitriy Vetlugin, Sky Mobile LLC Beeline

Zhigitaly Zhumaliev, Department of Crop Production Development

LAO PDR

EXIM Company Limited

Microfinance Association

PK Interfreight Co., Ltd

Agroforex Company

Department of Agriculture Extension and Cooperatives (DAEC), Ministry of Agriculture and Forestry

Agnès Couriol, DFDL

Vinay Ahuja, DFDL

Vincent Bounleua, Sengarthit Development Co., Ltd

Phachone Bounma, Department of Livestock and Fisheries, Ministry of Agriculture and Forestry

Chay Bounphanousay, National Agriculture and Forestry Research Institute (NAFRI)

Jakkrit Bunmee, Tilleke & Gibbins Lao Co., Ltd.

Somsadasak Canlayany, Lao Freight Forwarder Co., Ltd

Chanthone Chanthavong, Ministry of Posts and Telecommunications

Nawika Charoenkitchatorn, Lao Premier International Law Office

Syyang Chertoi, Ministry of Posts and Telecommunications

Phoukong Chidhouplok, Ministry of Post and Telecommunications

Malavan Chittavcong, National University of Lao

Aristotle David, VNA Legal Sole Co. Ltd.

Michael Dwyer, Center for International Forestry Research

Rupert Haw, DFDL

Konrad Hul, VNA Legal Sole Co. Ltd.

Xayluxa Insyxiengmai, Ministry of Post and Telecommunications

Alexia Jolliot, VimpelCom Lao co., Ltd

Nonxay Keosysom, M-FLAC Trading Sole Co., Ltd

Khamouane Khamphoukeo, Department of Agriculture Extension and Cooperatives (DAEC), Ministry of Agriculture and Forestry

Natchar Leedae, Lao Premier International Law Office

Khamkong Liemprachanh

Thavisak Manodham, Ministry of Post and Telecommunications

Keochai Mayyavongsink, ACLEDA Bank Lao Ltd

Sonevilay Nampanya

Somlack Nhoybouakong, Lao Freight Forwarder Co., Ltd

Somphone Phasavath, Lao Freight Forwarder Co., Ltd

Kingkeo Phengmixay, M-FLAC Trading Sole Co., Ltd

Sengchanh Phetkhounluang, Department of Agriculture Extension and Cooperatives (DAEC), Ministry of Agriculture and Forestry

Khamphaeng Phochanthilath, VNA Legal Sole Co. Ltd.

Vanthieng Phommasoulin, Ministry of Agriculture and Forestry (MAF)

Oudom Phonekhampheng, National University of Laos

Kham Phoui, Ministry of Agriculture and Forestry (MAF)

Phoumy Phoumanivong, Department of Agriculture Extension and Cooperatives (DAEC), Ministry of Agriculture and Forestry

Yatkeo Phoumidalyvanh, Ministry of Agriculture and Forestry (MAF)

Vichit Sadettan, Lao International Freight Forwarders Association (LIFFA)

Vanpheng Sayakone, Ministry of Posts and Telecommunications

Bouaphet Sayasane, Ministry of Public Works and Transport

Visone Saysongkham, Bank of the Lao PDR

Andy Schroeter, Sunlabob Rural Energy Systems Co., Ltd

Senesakoune Sihanougong, DFDL

Sinouk Sisombat, Sinouk Coffee

Viengkham Sodahak, Department of Agriculture Extension and Cooperatives (DAEC), Ministry of Agriculture and Forestry

Saiya Thammavongseng, SCU Huasae Chaleun

Sikhoun Tiamtisack, Lao Freight Forwarder Co., Ltd

Arpon Tunjumras, Lao Premier International Law Office

Sounthone Vong, Department of Livestock and Fisheries, Ministry of Agriculture and Forestry

Settha Vongpuckdy, ACLEDA Bank Lao Ltd

Manivone Vongxay, Ministry of Industry and Commerce

Soulivanh Voravong, Ministry of Agriculture and Forestry (MAF)

Huang Wei Jie, M-FLAC Trading Sole Co., Ltd

Sisomphone Yangnouvong, Department of Agriculture Extension and Cooperatives (DAEC), Ministry of Agriculture and Forestry

MALI

Autorité Malienne de Régulation des Télécommunications/TIC et des Postes (AMRTP)

Conseil Malien des Transporteurs Routiers (CMTR)

Eurolait Mali

International Fertilizer Development Center (IFDC)

Kafo Jiginew

Syngenta Foundation

Rhaly Ag Mossa

Daouda Ba, Vaughan Avocats

Abou Berthe, Sasakawa Africa Association

Cheickna Bounajim Cissé

Abdoulaye Cissé, Africa Trade & industry system

Aminata Coulibaly, MALIMARK A2F

Oumar Kalifa Coulibaly, Direction Générale des Douanes

Cyril Achcar, Groupe Achcar Mali Transit

Jean de Foucauld, Ceva Santé Animale

Elie Dembele

Fanta Dembele, MicroCred

Fanta Diallo, Office de Protection des Végétaux

Samba Diallo

Boubacar Diawara, DYNAPHARM

Messotigui Diomande, Mali Protection des Cultures (M.P.C)

Oumar Ampoural Dolo, Cabinet d'Expertise en Développement Agricole et Rural

Bakary Doumbia, Socimex SARL

Seydou Doumbia, La Ficelle - SCPA

Michel Havard, CIRAD

Abdoulaye Keita, Assemblée Permanente des Chambres d'Agriculture du Mali (APCAM)

Mama Koné, Institut d'Economie Rurale (IER), Ministère de l'Agriculture de l'Elevage et de la Pêche

Hady Ly, Carrières et Chaux

Souleymane Niaré

Amadou Ongoiba, ARC EN CIEL SARL

Philippe Sabot, Merial

Nafo Samaké, Groupe Achcar Mali Transit

Idrissa Nonmon Sanogo, Direction Régionale des Services Vétérinaires de Kayes

Amadou Sidibé, Institut d'Economie Rurale (IER), Ministère de l'Agriculture de l'Elevage et de la Pêche

Frédéric Sidibé

Assiongbon Têko-Agbo, Commission de l'Union Economique et Monétaire Ouest Africaine (UEMOA)

Abdoulaye Traoré, Etude, Formation, Evaluation et Conseils (EFEC - sarl)

Amadou Traoré, Vesta Industries

Bakary Yaffa, Etablissements Yaffa et Frères

MOROCCO

Société Nationale des Transports et de la Logistique (SNTL)

Yara

Soufiane Alami, Agridata Consulting

Saleh M. Amine, Cour Internationale de Médiation et d'Arbitrage (CIMEDA)

Chakib Ben El Khadir, Association Marocaine des Importateurs du Matériel Agricole (AMIMA)

Youssef Bencheqroun, Al Amana Microfinance

Hanane Boumehdi, Maroc Agroveto Holding

El Hassane Bourarach, Institut Agronomique et Vétérinaire Hassan II

Baptiste Dungu, MCI Santé Animale

Mustapha El Khayat, Association Marocaine de la Logistque

Talhi Faouzi, Maroc Agroveto Holding

Ali Hajji, SEWT

Peter Harlech Jones, GALVmed

Zouhir Imad, Socopim Premium Group

Amine Kandil, Charaf Corporation

Samira Khallouk, Agence Nationale de Réglementation des Télécommunications (ANRT)

Abdelatif Laamrani, Cabinet Laamrani Law

Mehdi Megzari, Sayarh & Menjra Law Firm

Ahlam Mekkaoui, Boulalf & Mekkaoui

Lamghari Omar, Africa Transcontinental Shipping Sarl

Rachid Oumlil, ANUMA

Farrouk Rajaa, Transfaro S.A.R.L

Abdelali Regag, Tamwil El Fellah

Nesrine Roudane, Nero Boutique Law Firm

Philippe Sabot, Merial

Mohamed Sabik

Omar Sayarh, Sayarh & Menjra Law Firm

Mohamed Sinan, Ecole Hassania des Travaux Publics

Khalid Tadlaoui, MCI Santé Animale

Rachid Tahri

Abdelaziz Zerouali

MOZAMBIQUE

Ajuda de Desenvolvimento de Povo para Povo

Citrum de Maputo

Couto, Graça e Associados, Sociedade de Advogados

Eduardo Mondlane University

Matanuska Moçambique Limitada

Ministry of Agriculture (MINAG)

MozFoods - Vanduzi

Otilio Assamundine

Francisco Avillez, Sociedade de Advogados (SCAN)

John Christie-Smith, Greenbelt Fertilizantes de Moçambique, Lda (GBF)

João Chunga, FRUTISUL

Alcinda Cumba, FL&A

Mario Jorge de Almeida Matos, Biochem

Fion De Vletter

Teresa Falcão, Vieira de Almeida & Associados (Atlas Lda)

Tito Fernandez, Lurio University

Alexander Fernando, International Fertilizer Development Center (IFDC)

Aase Ditlefsen Ferrão, First Natural Choice (Mocambique), Lda

Ana Isabel Fotine Mponda, Ministry of Public Works and Housing

Italino Francisco, Caixa Comunitária de Microfinanças

Tom Holloway

Luis Junaide Lalgy

Donovan Liedeman

Anselmina L. Liphola, Ministry of Land, Environment and Development

Fernanda Lopes, FL&A

Bernardo Luís Tembe, Hluvuku

Neves Macuacua

Elcidio Madeira, Astros

Natalino Magaia, Medimoc SA

Bernardo Mahoro, Sal & Caldeira, Advogados, LDA.

Paulino Munisse, Instituto de Investigação Agrária de Moçambique (IIAM)

Pedro Murreriua, Ministério dos Transportes e Comunicações (MTC)

Simon Norfolk, Terra Firma Lda

Munyaradzi Amos Nyambiya

Afonso Osorio

Marino Pascoal, Caixa Comunitária de Microfinanças

Enoque Raimundo Changamo, Caixa Comunitária de Microfinanças

Philippe Sabot, Merial

Fernando Sequeira, AgriFocus

Elsa Adélia Timana, Ministry of Agriculture (MINAG)

Adriaan van den Dries

Lourenço Veniça, Fundo Nacional de Estradas

Carlos Zandamela, Ministry of Agriculture (MINAG)

Llionel Zisengwe, iDE

MYANMAR

East-West Seed International Ltd.

Ministry of Agriculture and Irrigation

Ministry of Communications and Information Technology

Ministry of Co-operatives

Ministry of Transport

Myanmar Microfinance Bank

Myanmar Livestock Federation

SGS (Myanmar) Limited

Than Aung, E.F.R Express Services Limited

U Myint Aung, International Fertilizer Development Center (IFDC)

U Soe Htun Aung, Ministry of Agriculture and Irrigation

Myint Aye, UN Habitat

Darrel Chon, OV Logistics

Patricia Curran, Telenor

Bridget Di Certo, DFDL

Katherine East, DFDL

Ei Ei Mon, Ministry of Construction

James Finch, DFDL

Rajiv Ghandi, Hester Biosciences Ltd

William D. Greenlee, Jr, DFDL

Alvi Hakim, DFDL

Min Aung Hein, Harmony Myanmar Agro Group Co, Ltd.

Robert Htun Nwe, Harmony Myanmar Agro Group Co, Ltd.

U Hla Htun, Agricultural Mechanization Department, Ministry of Agriculture and Irrigation

Grahame Hunter, International Fertilizer Development Center (IFDC)

Thin Khaing, United Nations Development Program (UNDP)

Thin Khaing, United Nations Development Program (UNDP)

U Ko Ko, Agricultural Mechanization Department, Ministry of Agriculture and Irrigation

Dolly Kyaw, International Fertilizer Development Center (IFDC)

U Han Thein Maung, Ministry of Agriculture and Irrigation

U Win Myaing, Ministry of Agriculture and Irrigation

Aung Khin Myint, Myanmar International Freight Forwarders Association

Daw Yi Yi Myint, Ministry of Agriculture and Irrigation

Wazo Win Myint, Aquamarine Shipping

Nay Lin Zin, Myanmar Rice Millers' Association

Nichole Cross, DFDL

San Oo, Ministry of Environmental Conservation and Forestry

Michael Rodenmark, YOMA Strategic Holdings Ltd.

Daniel Susnjar, Telenor

U Htun Thein, Customs Department

Yi Mon Thu, E.F.R Express Services Limited

U Aung Kyaw Sow, Myanmar Rice Millers' Association

U Aung Thein, Myanmar Rice Millers' Association

U Thaung Win, Myanmar Rice Millers' Association

U Tint Aung, Myanmar Rice Millers' Association

Benjamin K. Wagner, BNG Legal

U Min Wai, Ministry of Agriculture and Irrigation

U Aung Win, Ministry of Agriculture and Irrigation

Kyaw Win Htun, Telenor

Ko Ko Ye'lwin, DFDL

U Zaw Win Naing, Myanmar Microfinance Bank Limited

NEPAL

Nepal Telecommunications Authority

Bipin Adhikari, Kathmandu University

Chandramani Adhikari, Allied Law Services

Durga Prasad Adhikari, Seed Entrepreneurs' Association of Nepal (SEAN)

Madan Bhatta, Nepal Agricultural Research Council (NARC)

Jibaraj Bhattaraii, Federation of Truck Transport Entrepreneurs

Shashi Bisht, Department of Irrigation (DoI)

Devendra Gauchan, Bioversity International

Pankaj Joshi, Salt Trading Corporation Limited

Khoj Raj Katwal, Nepal Drip Irrigation Pvt. Ltd

Bishal Khanal, Kathmandu University

Bharat Kharel, Bhrikuti Development Bank

K.B. Lama Syangtan, Bindhavasini Savings Co-operative Society Ltd. (BISCOL)

Sanjay Kumar Mandal, Jeevan Bikas Samaj

Yogendra Mandal, Jeevan Bikas Samaj

Atul Nagar

Mahendra P Khanal, Seed Quality Control Center

Pratima Pandey, Nepal Agricultural Research Council (NARC)

Tung Raj Pathak, Mahakali Irrigation Project

Rabindra Pradhan, Himalayan Bank Ltd.

Netra Prasad Osti, National Animal Science Research Institute

Padam Bahadur Rana

Damodar Regmi, Jeevan Bikas Samaj

Pramod Kumar Shah, Shivam Organisation

Bhola Shankar Shrestha, Nepal Agricultural Research Council (NARC)

Dipesh Shrestha, Suva Transport

Shreemat Shrestha, Nepal Agricultural Research Council (NARC)

Bhuwon Ratna Sthapit, Bioversity International

Prabin Subedi, Paramount Legal Advisory Services Pvt. Ltd.

Mahesh Kumar Thapa, Sinha-Verma Law Concern (SVLC)

Pradip Thapa, Bindhavasini Savings Co-operative Society Ltd. (BISCOL)

Satya Narayan Verma

Manoj Nidhi Wagle, Department of Customs

NICARAGUA

Agro Éxito S.A

Agroalfa

Asociación de Productores y Exportadores de Nicaragua (APEN)

ChamAgro

CISA AGRO

Instituto de Protección y Sanidad Agropecuaria (IPSA – MAGFOR)

Maquipos, S.A.

Nicaragua Machinery Company

Ramac S.A.

Marvin Altamirano, ATN Asociación de Transportistas de Nicaragua

Eddy Francisco Ampié, Instituto Nicaragüense de Telecomunicaciones y Correos (TELCOR)

Daniel Araya, Arias & Muñoz Nicaragua

Hilda Argüello, Asociación de ganaderos de Chontales (ASOGACHO)

Silvio Arguello, Consortium Taboada y Asociados

José Blandón, Comisión Nacional Ganadera de Nicaragua (CONAGAN)

Annely Bravo, Instituto Nicaragüense de Telecomunicaciones y Correos (TELCOR)

Maria Auxiliadora Briones

Bismarck Cardoza Delgadillo, GANASOL

Milton Castillo, Heifer International

Salvador Castillo, Federación de Asociaciones Ganaderas de Nicaragua (FAGANIC)

Ana Cecilia Chamorro, Arias & Muñoz Nicaragua

Luis Chamorro, MERCONCOFFEE

Sergio Antonio Chamorro Urcuyo

Mario Davila, Finca Vida Joven

Gloria Maria De Alvarado, Alvarado y Asociados

Jean de Foucauld, Ceva Santé Animale

Celina Delgado Castellón, Instituto Nicaragüense de Telecomunicaciones y Correos (TELCOR)

Michael Edwin Healy Lacayo, Federation of Agricultural Producers of Nicaragua (UPANIC)

Maricarmen Espinosa Segura, Central Law Molina & Asociados

Pablo Flores, GANASOL

Armando Gómez, Federation of Agricultural Producers of Nicaragua (UPANIC)

Solón Guerrero, Federación de Asociaciones Ganaderas de Nicaragua (FAGANIC)

Lucía Guevara, Central Law Molina & Asociados

Myriam Jarquin, Corte Suprema de Justicia, Instituto Altos Estudios Judiciales

Edmundo Lacayo, Instituto Nicaragüense de Telecomunicaciones y Correos (TELCOR)

Rodolfo Lacayo Ubau, Autoridad Nacional Del Agua

Marlón López, GANASOL

Orlando López, Aquatec S.A.

Eduardo Martinez Silva, Agricons S.A.

Fernando Medina Montiel, Oficina de Leyes Dr. Fernando Medina Montiel

Lea Montes Lagos, Abogado Nicaragua

Lesbia Moreno, Abogado Nicaragua

Julio Munguía, Instituto Inter-Americano de Cooperación para la Agricultura (IICA)

Manuel Narvaez

Claraliz Oviedo, Alvarado y Asociados

Roger Pérez Grillo, Arias & Muñoz Nicaragua

Mirian Reyes, Ministry of Transport and Infrastructure

Ana Teresa Rizo, Arias & Muñoz Nicaragua

Denis Salgado

Alfonso José Sandino Granera, Consortium Centro América Abogados

José Evenor Taboada, Consortium Taboada y Asociados

Carlos César Úbeda Torres, Consortium Centro América Abogados

Alejandro Vargas, MERCONCOFFEE

Alvaro Vargas, Federación de Asociaciones Ganaderas de Nicaragua (FAGANIC)

Roberto Villegas, PROCOCER R.L.

Eduardo Zamora

Frederik Zeuthen, Café Nor

NIGER

Abattoir Frigorifique Régional de Maradi

AFCOM

Agrimex

Centrale d'Approvisionnement en Intrants et Materiels Agricoles

Chambre de Commerce, d'Industrie et d'Artisanat du Niger (CCIAN)

Direction Générale du Génie Rural

Haut Commissariat à l'Initiative 3N

Ministère de l'Agriculture

Réseau National des Chambres d'Agriculture du Niger (RECA)

Mahatan Sani Abdou, Ministère de l'Agriculture

Salou Abdou Doro, L'Autorité de Régulation des Télécommunications et de la Poste (ARTP)

Adamou Kodo Abdourahamane, PADMIF

Buckner Akouete Koffi, International Crops Research Institute for the Semi-Arid Tropics (ICRISAT)

Abey Bazou Alhou, Secrétariat permanent du Code Rural

Idrissa Ambalam, Groupe SANECOM/GPSA

Maliki Barhouni, Chambre de Commerce, d'Industrie et d'Artisannat du Niger

Moussa Bola, Projet de développement des exportations et des marchés agro-sylvo-pastoraux (PRODEX)

Adamou Danguioua, Haut Commissariat à l'Initiative 3N

Fadjimata Gali Adam Dantia, Ministère de la Communication et des Relations avec les Institutions

Jean de Foucauld, Ceva Santé Animale

Abdoulaye Djadah, Banque Agricole du Niger

Boube Issouf, Negoce International Niger

Salifou Karimou, Airtel Niger

Aboubacar Malam Massou, Institut National de la Recherche Agronomique du Niger (INRAN)

Moudy Mamane Sani, Direction Générale de la Protection des Végétaux

Illya Miko, Food and Agriculture Organization of the United Nations (FAO)

Maman-Lawal Mossi Bagoudou, Banque Agricole du Niger

Aïchatou A. Nasser, Ferme Semencière Ainoma

Mahamane Nasser Laouali, Institut National de la Recherche Agronomique du Niger (INRAN)

Zalika Maiga, Ets Kazali & Fils

Amadou Ouattara, Food and Agriculture Organization of the United Nations (FAO)

Mamoudou Oumarou, Chambre de Commerce d'Industrie et d'Artisanat du Niger

Zakary Rhissa, Fondation Taboghor

Philippe Sabot, Merial

El-Hadj Saminou, Office National des Aménagements Hydro Agricoles (ONAHA)

Ousmane Mamane Sani, ONG Karkara

Idrissa Tchernaka, Etude d'Avocats Marc Le Bihan & Collaborateurs

Assiongbon Têko-Agbo, Commission de l'Union Economique et Monétaire Ouest Africaine (UEMOA)

Labaran Yahaya, Office National des Aménagements Hydro Agricoles (ONAHA)

Wouro Yahia, Etude d'Avocats Marc Le Bihan & Collaborateurs

Attaoulahi Zakaouanou, Ministère du Transport

PHILIPPINES

Allied Botanical Corporation

Fortuna Ranch

Oldreach Trucking Services

The Bangko Sentral ng Pilipinas

Universal Harvester, Inc.

Ruben P Acebedo II, Sycip Salazar Hernandez & Gatmaitan

Jescel Alday-Salvaleon, Bayer Animal Health

Ferdinand Castillo, AKC Trucking

Ferdinand Correa, Correa Trucking

Rubina Cresencio, Bureau of Animal Industry, Department of Agriculture

JJ Disini, Disini & Disini

Pablo M. Gancayco, Gancaycos, Balasbas & Associates

Rajiv Ghandi, Hester Biosciences Ltd

Nicolette Gica, 1st Valley Bank

Norlito Gicana, Fertilizer and Pesticide Authority

Reynaldo Gregorio, Philippine Center for Postharvest Development and Mechanization (PHILMECH)

Tanya Hotchkiss, Cantilan Bank, Inc.

Rose Marie M. King-Dominguez, Sycip Salazar Hernandez & Gatmaitan

Franco Aristotle G Larcina, Sycip Salazar Hernandez & Gatmaitan

Victor P. Lazatin, Angara Abello Concepcion Regala & Cruz Law Firm

Paul Limson, Bureau of Animal Industry, Department of Agriculture

Romualdo C. Martinez, Philippine Center for Postharvest Development and Mechanization (PHILMECH)

Edgardo V. Olego, Confederation of Truckers Association of the Philippines

Joel R. Panagsagan, Super Trade Enterprises

Felix C. Paraguya, Jr., FPJMLP Customs Brokerage

Roel R. Ravanera, Xavier Science Foundation

Lailani Rose Rico, Bureau of Animal Industry, Department of Agriculture

Philippe Sabot, Merial

Joaquin V. Sayoc, Romulo, Mabanta, Buenaventura, Sayoc & De Los Angeles

Delfin C. Suministrado, Agricultural Machinery Testing and Evaluation Center

Rodolfo H. Tamayo, Agri Component Corporation

Raul Urbiztondo, Cantilan Bank, Inc.

Rolando Victoria, ASKI (Alalay Sa Kaunlaran, Inc.)

Rey Yparraguirre, Cantilan Bank, Inc.

POLAND

Clifford Chance LLP

General Veterinary Inspectorate

International Cooperation Department, Agricultural and Food Quality Inspection (IJHARS)

Kancelaria Adwokatów i Radców Prawnych Lipiński & Walczak

National Water Management Authority

Office of Electronic Communications (UKE - Urząd Komunikacji Elektronicznej)

Polish Financial Supervision Authority (KNF)

Polish Seed Trade Association (PIN)

Ulenberg Sp. z o.o.

WBW Weremczuk Bobel & Partners, Attorneys at Law

Monika Adamin, Clifford Chance LLP

Wojciech Andrzejewski, Kancelaria Prawna Piszcz, Norek i Wspólnicy Spółka komandytowa

Aleksandra Auleytner, Domański Zakrzewski Palinka (DZP)

Igor Bąkowski, Bąkowski Kancelaria Radcowska

Agnieszka Bieda, Department of Geomatics, AGH University of Science and Technology

Marta Bryjak, White & Case LLP

Zofia Bulińska-Radomska, Plant Breeding and Acclimatization Institute (IHAR)

Jarosław Bydłosz, Department of Geomatics, AGH University of Science and Technology

Dariusz Godzisz, Ipsen Polska Sp zoo

Agnieszka Dawidowicz, University of Warmia and Mazury in Olsztyn

Jean de Foucauld, Ceva Santé Animale

Michał Fereniec, Greenberg Traurig LLP

Maciej Gorgol, Warsaw Bar of Advocates

Olaf Günther-Borstel, Yara

Kamil Jankielewicz, Allen & Overy

Wiesława Kasperska-Wołowicz, Institute of Technology and Life Sciences

Anna Klimach, University of Warmia and Mazury in Olsztyn

Anna Kluczek-Kollar, Misiewicz, Mosek & Partners Counsellors - at - Law

Anita Kwartnik-Pruc, Department of Geomatics, AGH University of Science and Technology

Leszek Łabędzki, Institute of Technology and Life Sciences

Mirosław Leszczyński, John Deere

Przemysław Musioł, Kancelaria Prawna Piszcz, Norek i Wspólnicy Spółka komandytowa

Marcin Olszak, Polish Financial Supervision Authority

Joanna Organiściak-Płachta, Salt City Pharma Center

Małgorzata Pałysa, Polish Agency for Enterprise Development

Piotr Parzych, Department of Geomatics, AGH University of Science and Technology

Agata Pawlak-Jaszczak, Kancelaria Prawna Piszcz, Norek i Wspólnicy Spółka komandytowa

Paweł Piotrowski, Clifford Chance LLP

Marcin Piszcz, Kancelaria Prawna Piszcz, Norek i Wspólnicy Spółka komandytowa

Piotr Smolarczyk, Greenberg Traurig LLP

Mikołaj Steppa, Rural Development Foundation (RDF)

Katarzyna Szczepaniak, National council of agricultural chambers

Maciej Tomaszewicz, Chamber of Merchants, Grain Processors and Foodstuff Producers (Izba Gospodarcza Handlowców)

Dominik Wałkowski, Wardyński & Partners

Witold Studziński, Studziński i Partnerzy Adwokacka Spółka Partnerska

Jolanta Wyszatkiewicz, Ministry of Agriculture and Rural Development

Marcin Zaczyński, Plant Breeding and Acclimatization Institute (IHAR)

Izabela Zielińska-Barłożek, Wardyński & Partners

Leszek Zielonka, Zielonka-Steckert-Wspólnicy

RUSSIAN FEDERATION

Avakov Tarasov & Partners

Central Bank of the Russian Federation

John Deere

Monsanto

Marc Bartholomy, Clifford Chance LLP

Aleksey Belugin, Eurasian Center for Food Security, Moscow State University

Valentin Borodin, VB & P

Olga Brovkina, Association of International Road Carriers (ASMAP)

Konstantin Chaykin, Altayskiy Fond Mikrozaymov

Ekaterina Dudina, Beiten Burkhardt

Irina Glazkova, Avakov Tarasov & Partners

Alexey Konevsky, Pepeliaev Group

Evgeniya Konovalova Dudinova, Cargill

Polina Krymskaya, Federal Service for State Registration Cadastre and Cartography in Moscow

Alexey Kuzmishin, Beiten Burkhardt

Vladislav I. Kvashnin, Digesta ILC

Anton Lachinov, VimpelCom

Maxim Levinson, Baker Botts LLP

Anastasia Likhacheva, National research university

Alexander Nadmitov, Nadmitov, Ivanov & Partners

Ella Omelchenko, Clifford Chance LLP

Maksim Prigon

Dmitry Raev, Morgan Lewis

Artem Rodin, CMS Legal

Anastasia Serebrennikova, Clifford Chance LLP

Elena V. Syrykh

Robert Woolley

Sergei Yudaev, ZAO "Ambar"

RWANDA

Nyiombo Investments

One Acre Fund

Rwanda Natural Resources Authority (RNRA)

Alexis Bizimana, KCB Bank Rwanda

Vianney Bizimana, Banque Populaire du Rwanda

Jeanne d'Arc Nyaruyonga, International Fertilizer Development Center (IFDC)

Moses Kiiza Gatama, Equity Juris Chambers

Bob Gatera, Balton Rwanda Ltd

Jonathan Gatera, National Bank of Rwanda

Henry Gitau, Balton Rwanda Ltd

Peter Harlech Jones, GALVmed

Pie Hibamana, Amicus Law Chambers

Gafigi Jean Paul, Pannar

Potel Jossam, Kayonza District

Channy Kalisa, Kigali Golden Farm

Jonas Kamili, Banque Populaire du Rwanda

Regina Kayitesi, Private Sector Federation

Brian Kirungi, Airtel Rwanda Limited

Kizito Safari, Bona Fide Law Chambers

Elonie Mukandoli, National Bank of Rwanda

Jean Baptiste Mutabazi, Rwanda Utilities Regulatory Authority (RURA)

Sylvain Muyombano, Rwanda Natural Resources Authority (RNRA)

Dominique Mvunabandi, Smartfarming Rwanda Ltd

Mwitende Ladislas, Top Services Enterprises Ltd

Susan Nambi, Equity Juris Chambers

Kannan Narayanan, Hawassa University

Jules Theoneste Ndahayo, Umutanguha Finance Company Ltd. (UFC)

Emmanuel Ngomiraronka, Ministry of Agriculture and Animal Resources

Peter Ngugi, Yara

Theogene Niyibigira, Rwanda National Genebank

Beatrice Niyokwizigirwa, Rwanda Agriculture Board (RAB)

Felicien Niyoniringiye, Rulindo District

Alfred Nkubili, ENAS

Bernard Nsengiyumva, National Bank of Rwanda

Livingstone Nshemereirwe, Access to Finance Rwanda

Jean Bosco Rusagara, Intraspeed Ltd

Philippe Sabot, Merial

Didier Sagashya, Rwanda Natural Resources Authority (RNRA)

Gerard Mutimura Sakufi, Banque Populaire du Rwanda

Mohammed Salim, Green Age International Ltd.

Jean Damascene Serugero, National Bank of Rwanda

Josephine Umurewa, Development Bank of Rwanda

Grace Umutoni, Private Sector Federation

Esperance Uwimana

Kabalisa Vincent de Paul, Rwanda Natural Resources Authority (RNRA)

SPAIN

Asociación Nacional de Obtentores Vegetales (ANOVE)

Bioibérica S.A.

Catalan Water Agency

Compagnie Fruitière España

Compañía Maquinaria 93

Grupo AN

Grupo Fertiberia

John Deere

MIGASA

Ministerio de Agricultura, Alimentación y Medio Ambiente (MAGRAMA)

Yara

Margarita Arboix Arzo, Autonomous University of Barcelona

Ignacio Cantonnet, TERGUM

Alberto Cortegoso Vaamonde, Cuatrecasas Gonçalves Pereira

David Cota Mascuñana

Rafael de Sádaba

Alfonso de San Simón, San Simón & Duch

Diego de San Simón, San Simón & Duch

Paulo Felix, CEPEX Spain

Alfredo Fernández Rancaño, J&A Garrigues, S.L.P.

Juan José Gil Panizo, Federación Nacional de Asociaciones de Empresarios de Transporte Discrecionales de Mercancías (FENADISMER)

Juan González, Garrigues

Matías González, Vodafone España, S.A.U.

Rosa Huertas González, Confederación Hidrográfica del Duero

Vicente Izquierdo Garcia, Departamento de Aduanas de la Agencia Tributaria de España

Jaime Jaume, Semilla

Carlos Jimenez

Álvaro López-Jorrín, Garrigues

José Luis Mauri Alarcón, Irritec Iberia SA

Juan Muguerza Odriozola, J&A Garrigues, S.L.P.

Luis Murillo Jasol, Cuatrecasas Gonçalves Pereira

Adrián Nogales, Colegio Oficial de Ingenieros de Telecomunicación (COIT)

José Luis Palma Fernández, Gómez-Acebo & Pombo Abogados S.L.P.

Juan Pardo, Asociación Comercial Española de Fertilizantes (ACEFER)

Nicolás Nogueroles Peiró, Colegio de Registradores de la Propiedad y Mercantiles de España

Luis Pérez de Ayala, Cuatrecasas Gonçalves Pereira

Pedro Portellano, Garrigues

Millan Requena Casanova

Lourdes Rodriguez Lopez, Plaza Forwarding SL

Elicia Rodríguez Puñal, Cuatrecasas Gonçalves Pereira

Alicia Sánchez Muñoz, Ministerio de Economía y Competitividad

Emilio Sidera Leal, Ministry of Public Works

Ignacio Solís Martel, AgroVegetal

Gonzalo Ulloa Suelves, Gómez Acebo & Pombo, Abogados, SLP

SRI LANKA

CIC Agribusinesses (Pvt) Limited

Dilmah Tea Ltd

Empire Teas Pvt Ltd

Sri Lanka Council for Agricultural Research Policy (CARP)

Ranjith Abeykoon, Tea Exporters Association (TEA)

Asanka Abeysekera, Tiruchelvam Associates

Asoka Ajantha, Janathakshan

Asela Angammana, AgStar Fertilizers PLC

A.R Ariyaratne, Sri Lanka Council for Agricultural Research Policy (CARP)

M. Ziard Caffoor, Ceylon Grain Industries

Jean de Foucauld, Ceva Santé Animale

Savantha De Saram, D.L. & F. De Saram

Anil de Silva, Dave Tractors & Combines (Pvt) Ltd

Sashanee de Silva, Gowers Law Firm

Sameera S Dissanayake, Sri Lanka Council for Agricultural Research Policy

Manjula Ellepola, F.J. & G. De Saram

Anjali Fernando, F.J. & G. De Saram

Lakshman Fernando, CIC Agribusinesses (Pvt) Limited

Mayuri Fernando, D.L. & F. De Saram

Rohan Fernando, Tea Exporters Association (TEA)

Bhavani Fonseka, Center for Policy Alternatives (CPA)

Tilani Ford, F.J. & G. De Saram

Tharindu Gallage, Empire Teas Pvt Ltd

Helani Galpaya, LIRNEasia

Dilum Gamage, Julius & Creasy

Rajiv Ghandi, Hester Biosciences Ltd

Dilini Gunaratne, Julius & Creasy

Thilanka Haputhanthrie, Julius & Creasy

Hettiarachchi Hemaratne, The Colombo Tea Traders' Association

Anura Herath, The International Fund for Agricultural Development (IFAD)

Ranila Hurulle, Julius & Creasy

Shanika Jayasekera, Sri Lanka Council for Agricultural Research Policy (CARP)

Nilusha Kapugama, LIRNEasia

Uma Kitulgoda, F.J. & G. De Saram

Navindra Liyanaarachchi, SANASA Federation Ltd.

Waruna Madawanarachchi, C.I.C. Seed & Foliage

Ameer Mahuroof, Gowers Law Firm

Ashwini Natesan, Julius & Creasy

Chaminda Nissanka, Brown & Company PLC

Simon Padmini, Sri Lanka Council for Agricultural Research Policy (CARP)

Ranga Pallawala, Janathakshan

Laknadhi Perera, Julius & Creasy

Nihara Perera, Sudath Perera Associates

Oswin Perera, University of Peradeniya

Sudath Perera, Sudath Perera Associates

Ranjith Rajapakse, Jinasena (PVT) Ltd.

Saman Rajapaksha, AgStar Fertilizers PLC

Shobitha Ranasinghe, Empire Teas Pvt Ltd

J.M. Swaminathan, Julius & Creasy

Nuwanthi Upeksha, CL Synergy Pvt Ltd

Roshana Waduge, Ceylon Fertilizer Co. Ltd.

Aruna Weerakoon, Agro Culture Trends Pvt Ltd.

Anil Wickremasinghe, Jinasena (PVT) Ltd.

Udara Widanagamage, CL Synergy Pvt Ltd

Sameera Wijerathna, Dialog Axiata PLC

SUDAN

Alpha Group

Family Bank

Kenana Sugar Company

Ministry of Water Resources, Irrigation and Electricity

Muhammed Kamal Abass, CTC Group

Hassabo Abbas, Ministre de l'Agriculture et de l'Irrigation

Ula Makkawi Abdelrahman, Ministry of Agriculture & Irrigation

Wala Hassan Aboalela, El Karib and Medani Advocates (EKM)

Ahmed Adam

Faisal Ahmed, Transnile for Trade & Agriculture

Mohamed Alhassan Ahmed, National Seed Council

Alawia Alhamadabi, National Information Center

Inaam Attiq, Aztan Law Firm

Sarah Badreldin, Raiba Land Transport, Elnefeidi Group

Sami Balla Ibrahim, Widam Food

Omer El Dirani

Mustafa Elbashier, Mustafa Elbashier Law Office

Salah Eldin Elaghbash, Brilliance for Development and Services

Afaf Elguzouli, Ministry of Agriculture and Irrigation

Shaimaa Elhassan, Raiba Land Transport, Elnefeidi Group

Yahia Awad Elkareem

Sami Freigoun, CTC Group

Rajiv Ghandi, Hester Biosciences Ltd

Amr Hamad, Haggar Holding Company

Salih Hamid, Savings & Social Development Bank

Peter Harlech Jones, GALVmed

Tayeb Hassabo, Aztan Law Firm

Hawaii Abdulwhab Almahdi, Ministry of Transport, Roads and Bridges

Mohamed Alhadi Ibrahim, Elnilein Engineering & Spare Parts Co.ltd

Nawal Ibrahim, Agricultural Mechanization Administration

Idris Idris

Mubarak Mahgoub, AL Nelein Engineering & Spare Parts

El Tahir Ibrahim Mohamed, Agricultural Research Corporation

Insaf Mohammed Musa, Agricultural Research Corporation

Mahmoud Numan

Osman Elmakki Osman Elmakki

Abdul Hamid Rhametalla, Landell Mills Ltd

Philippe Sabot, Merial

Salman Salman

Mahmoud Seddon, Harvest Hybrid Seed Co

Hassan Shakir

Vickram Swaminath, Raiba Land Transport, Elnefeidi Group

Mohamed Tangasawi

Azhari Traifi, Aztan Law Firm

TAJIKISTAN

AccessBank Tajikistan

BDO Academy Tajikistan

Legal Consulting Group

OJSC "Agroinvestbank"

Zhanyl Abdrakhmanova, Colibri Law Firm

Firdavs Abdufatoev, Ltd. "ORO Isfara"

Aiembek Akramov, National Association of Derkhan farms

Bahtier Bahriddinov, Neksigol Mushovir

Dzhamshed Buzurukov, Ltd. "ISFARAFUD"

Nargis Hamidova, International Road Transport Association (AIATT)

Zafar Hudoikulov, Yovar

Davron Isaev, USAID Farmer Advisory Services in Tajikistan (FAST)

Davlatyor Jumakhonov, First MicroFinance Bank

Matraim Jusupov, Kyrgyz Republic Research Institute of Irrigation

Alisher Khoshimov, Colibri Law Firm

Matazim Kosimov, Livestock Institute TAAS

Nurlan Kyshtobaev, Grata Law Firm

Shirinbek Milikbekov, Colibri Law Firm

Firdavs Mirzoev, Nazrisho & Mirzoev Law Firm

Azam Murtazaev, Neksigol Mushovir

Zulfiya H. Odinaeva, Ministry of Transport and Communications of the Republic of Tajikistan

Amindjon Parpiev, Bard & Co

Kurbonali Partoev, Cooperation for Development

Tulegen Sarsembekov, Eurasian Development Bank

Marina Shamilova, Legal Consulting Group

Azizbek Sharipov, National Association of Derkhan farms

Sherzod Sodatkadamov, Nazrisho & Mirzoev Law Firm

Mahinakhon Suleymanova, Neksigol Mushovir

Matluba Uljabaeva, National Association of Small and Medium Business of the Republic of Tajikistan

Nargis Usmanova, National Association of Derkhan farms

Alimardon Azimov, Center for implementation of land cadastre system

TANZANIA

Advans Bank Tanzania Ltd.

ByTrade Tanzania

Davis & Shirtliff

Engiteng Dairy

ETC Agro Tractors and Implements Ltd

Forbix Attorneys

International Fertilizer Development Center (IFDC)

LonAgro Tanzania Ltd

Metl Agro Tractors & Implements Ltd

Ministry of Agriculture, Food Security and Cooperatives

Ministry of Livestock and Fisheries Development

Ministry of Water and Irrigation

Tanzania Bureau of Standards

Tanzania Farmer Services Center Ltd (TFSC)

Tanzania Fertilizer Company Ltd.

Tanzania Meat Board

Tanzania Official Seed Certification Institute (TOSCI)

Yara

Julie Adkins, SNV

Joy Alliy, VELMA Law

Mahmoud Ahmed Ally, Allied Transport

Stephen Axwesso, Brevis attorneys

Hamisi Chimwaga, Mwanga Community Bank

Raphael L. Daluti, Ministry of Agriculture, Food Security and Cooperatives

George Fernandes, East African Law Chambers

Rajiv Ghandi, Hester Biosciences Ltd

Edward Greenwood, FINCA

Sharif A. Hamad, Breeders Tanzania

Niko Janssen, SNV

Peter Harlech Jones, GALVmed

Theresia Hubert, Tanzania Bureau of Standards

Aron Johson Kitaka, Ministry of Transport

Vian Karamaga, Allied Transport

Buberwa Kafanabo, BEST-Dialogue

Peter Kasanda, Clyde & Co

Neema Lwise Kileo, Astute Attorneys

Agapiti E. Kobello, Bank of Tanzania

Canuth Komba, Ministry of Agriculture, Food Security and Cooperatives

Gunga Kumar Gunga, DAMCO

Barney I. S. Laseko, Prime Minister's Office

Amalia Lui, Clyde & Co

Peter A. Lupatu, Ministry of Transport

Elvin Lwakabare, DAMCO

Justo N. Lyamuya, Ministry of Lands, Housing and Human Settlement Development

Mashiku Majo, National Irrigation Commission

Eli-Tunu Mallamia, Tanzania Truck Owners Association (TATOA)

Patrick Maluku, Monsanto

Victor B. Mrema, Brevis attorneys

Hassan Mruttu, Ministry of Livestock and Fisheries Development

Deonice Mshida, Agricultural Seed Agency

Benjamin Mtaki, Tea Research Institute of Tanzania

Arnold Munisi, Brevis attorneys

R.J. Mwageni, Posta na Simu SACCOS Ltd.

Paul Myovela, OLAM

Joseph Mwaipaja, Tanzania Bureau of Standards

Yaya Ndjore, TIGO

Adolf Ndunguru, Tanzania Revenue Authority

Martha Ngalowera, Vice President's Office

Leo Ngowi, Surface and Marine Transport Regulatory Authority (SUMATRA)

Patrick Ngwediagi, Ministry of Agriculture, Food Security and Cooperatives

John Nkoma, Tanzania Communications Regulatory Authority

David Nyanye, Michigan State University

Ravi Periyasamy, Balton Tanzania Ltd

Edimitha Protace, Tanzania Bureau of Standards

Hassan Tino Rajab, CBS Law Offices

Juma Reli, Bank of Tanzania

Kelvin Remen, Tanzania Horticultural Association (TAHA)

Hem Chandro Roy, BRAC Tanzania

Martin Ruheta, Veterinary Services, Ministry of Livestock and Fisheries Development

Philippe Sabot, Merial

Charity Safford, Vodacom

Ial Samakande, Irrigrow

Sebastian Sambuo, Rural Urban Development Initiatives (RUDI)

Ulhas Sardesai, OLAM

Ujwalkanta Senapati, OLAM

Amish Shah, ATZ Law Chambers

Cecilia Boniface Shiyo, CBS Law Offices

Baldwin Shuma, Tanzania Seed Trade Association (TASTA)

Nahson Sigalla, Surface and Marine Transport Regulatory Authority (SUMATRA)

Emmanuel Simbua, Tea Research Institute of Tanzania

Lait Simukanga, National Irrigation Commission

Tariro Sithole, Quton Tanzania Limited

Elia Timotheo, East Africa Fruits Farm and Company Ltd.

Sixtus Toke, Ministry of Agriculture, Food Security and Cooperatives

Raymond Wigenge, Directorate of Food Safety, Tanzania Food and Drug Authority (TFDA)

Nicholas Zervos, VELMA Law

TURKEY

Turkish Cooperative Association

Türkiye Yem Sanayicileri Birliği

Can Adamoglu

Fulya Koc Arslan, Monsanto

Sedat Bakici, General Directorate of Land Registry and Cadastre

Barlas Balcioglu, Balcıoğlu Selçuk Akman Keki

Nevzat Birisik, Ministry of Food, Agriculture and Livestock

Hamdi Çiftçiler, May-Agro Seed Co.

Jean de Foucauld, Ceva Santé Animale

Gülperi Eldeniz, GPE Law Firm

Hakkı Emrah Erdogan, Ministry of Food, Agriculture and Livestock

Bilal Erkek, General Directorate of Land Registry and Cadastre

Özgür Eryüz, John Deere

Ismail G. Esin, Baker & McKenzie

Ali Can Gören, Balcıoğlu Selçuk Akman Keki

Ceylan Kara

Ali Kasaci, Ministry of Food, Agriculture and Livestock

Yalçın Kaya, Trakya University

Aysegül Kibaroglu, MEF University

Ayhan Kullep

Ahmet Kumru, Kumrular Livestock

Orhan Yavuz Mavioğlu, ADMD Mavioglu & Alkan Law Office

Yaşar Orhan, Ministry of Food, Agriculture and Livestock

Senem Kathrin Güçlüer, Law Office Kunt & Partners

Fatih Şener, Association of International Freight Forwarders

Vakur Sümer, Selcuk University

Seyma Gozde Tokyay, Bicak Hukuk Law Firm

Sevilay Topcu, Çukurova University

Ümit Yıldız, Ministry of Environment and Urbanization

Yusuf Yormazoğlu, May-Agro Seed Co.

UGANDA

Abdunassar Olekwa, Ministry of Lands, Housing and Urban Development

Charles Abuka, Bank of Uganda

John Anglin, Paramount Dairies Ltd

John Atalyeba, ATACO Freight Services Ltd.

Robert Ayume, Brazafric Enterprises Ltd

Justine Bagyenda, Bank of Uganda

Sudhir Balsure, DSV Swift Freight International (Uganda) Ltd.

Jonathan Bukenya, Bora Agro-Technologies Ltd

Arthur Byara, Onyango Advocates

Rajiv Ghandi, Hester Biosciences Ltd

Andrew Gita, USAID Feed the Future

Peter Harlech Jones, GALVmed

Moira Imong

Brian Kaggwa, Impala Legal Advocates and Consultants

Ronald Kaggwa, National Environment Management Authority

William Kambugu, Ministry of Lands, Housing and Urban Development

Andrew Kamugisha, Bank of Uganda

Eldad Karamura, Bioversity International

Emmanuel Kasimbazi, Makerere University

Harriette Kasirye, Orange Uganda Limited

Nicholas Kauta, Ministry of Agriculture, Animal Industry and Fisheries (MAAIF)

Robert Kintu, FIT Uganda LT

Halid Kirunda, National Livestock Resources Research Institute

Allan Kobel, Magezi, Ibale & Co. Advocates

Timothy Kyepa, Development Law Associates

Sylver Kyeyune, Pride Microfinance Ltd.

Bob Paul Lusembo, Pride Microfinance Ltd.

Alex Lwakuba, Ministry of Agriculture, Animal Industry and Fisheries (MAAIF)

John Magezi, Magezi, Ibale & Co. Advocates

William Martovu, Heifer International

Richard Masagazi, Pearl Seeds Ltd

Astrid Mastenbroek, Wageningen UR Centre for Development Innovation

Jim Middleton, Engineering Solutions (U) Ltd

Asa Mugenyi, Mugenyi & Co Advocates

John Mulumba Wasswa, National Agricultural Research Organisation (NARO)

Augustine Mwendya, Uganda National Farmers Federation

Irene Nabwire Jingo, Bank of Uganda

Brenda Namulondo, National Agricultural Research Organisation (NARO)

Viola Namuyaba, Pride Microfinance Ltd.

Nicholas Ndawula

Donald Nyakairu, ENSafrica Advocates

Bosco Ochira Lawino, Tropical Trade International Co. Ltd

Patrice Ocungirwoth, Housing Finance Bank

James Olobo, Uganda Chamber of Commerce

Robert Opio, Ministry of Lands, Housing and Urban Development

Richard Oput, Ministry of Lands, Housing and Urban Development

Peter Otimodoch, Otis Garden Seeds

Samuel Powell, Northern Uganda Agricultural Centre

B.W. Rwabwogo, Mukwano Group

Richard A. Saasa, Agricultural Engineering and Appropriate Technology Research Institute (AEATRI)

Philippe Sabot, Merial

Abraham Salomon, Agriworks Uganda Ltd.

Illa Sanjeevi, Grow More Seeds and Chemicals Limited

Seruwo Solomon, Bukoola Chemical Industries Ltd

Irene Ssekyana, Greenwatch

Phinehas Tukamuhabwa, Makerere University

Stephen Tumwesigye, Onyango Advocates

Eva Zaake, National Agricultural Research Organisation (NARO)

UKRAINE

National Bank of Ukraine

State Veterinary and Phytosanitary Service of Ukraine

Anton Babak, Lavrynovych & Partners

Eugene Blinov, Astapov Lawyers International Law Group

Alexander Borodkin, Vasil Kisil & Partners

Myroslav Denis

Bohdan Dmukhovskyy, Astapov Lawyers International Law Group

Dmytro Donenko, Engarde Attorneys at Law

Vitaliy Fedchuk, Monsanto

Oleksandr Fedorov, KWS

Viacheslav Gavrylianchyk, Syngenta

Volodymyr Gopchak, KWS

Andrii Grebonkin, Clifford Chance LLP

Artem Khaliavka, Creative Group (PJSC)

Alexey Khomyakov, Asters

Peter Kovalenko, International Commission on Irrigation and Drainage (ICID)

Alexander Kravchenko, Bayer Animal Health

Lesya Kravchuk, CLAAS Ukraine

Igor Kutovoy, John Deere

Olga Kutsevych, Taras Shevchenko Kyiv National University

Tatyana Kuzmenko, AiG Law Firm

Anton Lukovkin, Misechko & Partners Law Firm

Iryna Marushko, Lavrynovych & Partners

Sergiy Oberkovych, Gvozdiy & Oberkovych Law Firm

Pavlo Odnokoz, Asters

Roman Ognevyuk, Engarde Attorneys at Law

Maxim Oleksiyuk, WTS Tax Legal Consulting, LLC

Pavlo Oliinyk, Engarde Attorneys at Law

Mark Opanasiuk, Inyurpolis Law Firm

Vitali Polishchuk, Institute of Hydraulic Engineering and Land Reclamation

Roman Puchko

Mykola Pugachev, Institute of Agrarian Economics

Alexey Pukha, Aleksey Pukha & Partners

Victor Ryabchun, Plant Production Institute nd. V. Ya. Yuryev of NAAS

Philippe Sabot, Merial

Irina Selivanova, Inyurpolis Law Firm

Viktoriya Taran, KWS

Viktor Teres, Heifer International

Roman Volkov, ICT-Zahid

Yulia Yashenkova, AiG Law Firm

Olga Zhovtonog, Institute of Hydraulic Engineering and Land Reclamation

Anton Zinchuk, Inyurpolis Law Firm

Olena Zubchenko, Lavrynovych & Partners

VIETNAM

C.P. Vietnam Corporation

Institute of Policy and Strategy for Agriculture and Rural Development (IPSARD)

Petrovietnam Fertilizer and Chemicals Corporation

State Bank of Vietnam

Tilleke & Gibbins Consultants Limited

Le Duy AnW, Yara

Tran Tu Anh, SNV

Pham Quoc Bao, SANCO Freight Ltd

Quoc Doan Bao, Syngenta

Rajarshi Chakravorty

Nguyen Ba Chat, Vietnam Institute of Agricultural Engineering and Post-Harvest Technology (VIAEP)

Nguyen Thi Quynh Chi, General Department of Vietnam Customs

Va Linh Chi, Vietnam Academy of Agricultural Sciences

Kim Van Chinh, Institute of Policy and Strategy for Agriculture and Rural Development (IPSARD)

Pham Hung Cuong, Vietnam Academy of Agricultural Sciences

Duc Dang, Indochine Counsel

Thuan Dinh Quang, Phuoc and Partners

Doan Doan Tuan, Institute for Water and Environment (IWE)

Pham Van Dong, Department of Animal Health, Ministry of Agriculture and Rural Development (MARD)

Do Huu Dung, Department of Animal Health, Ministry of Agriculture and Rural Development (MARD)

Nguyen Quy Duong, Plant Protection Department, Ministry of Agriculture and Rural Development (MARD)

Viet Thanh Duong

Nguyen Duy Dang

Andrew Fitanides, Baker & McKenzie

Rajiv Ghandi, Hester Biosciences Ltd

Huong Thanh Ha, Plant Protection Department, Ministry of Agriculture and Rural Development (MARD)

Le Son Ha, Plant Protection Department, Ministry of Agriculture and Rural Development (MARD)

Nguyen Ha, DFDL

Tran Thu Hang, Vietnam Cooperative Alliance

Nguyen Hiep, Transworld Cargo Logistics

Nguyen Hoa, DFDL

Nguyen Hong Hai, Duane Morris

Vu Thi Huong, SNV

Nguyen Huy, Rigonfruit

Tran Huy, Rigonfruit

Thang Huynh, DFDL

Tran Mai Kien, Vietnam Institute of Meteorology, Hydrology and Environment (IMHEN)

Cuong Le, DFDL

Nguyen Thi Kim Loan, HSBC Bank

Bui Van Minh SNV

Nguyen Dong Nghia, Rigonfruit

Huyen Tram Nguyen, Gide Loyrette Nouel Law Firm

Lam Nguyen, PEJA (S.E.A.)

Mau Dung Nguyen, Vietnam National University of Agriculture

Oanh H. K. Nguyen, Baker & McKenzie

Thanh Lam Nguyen, Vietnam Seed Trade Association

Thi Hong Duong Nguyen, Indochine Counsel

Thi Nguyet Nga Nguyen, Ministry of Transport

Thi Phuong Loan Nguyen

Trung Anh Nguyen, Vietnam Made Co., Ltd

Tuan Nguyen, ANT Lawyers

Nam Nguyen Hoai, Ministry of Agriculture and Rural Development (MARD)

Khanh Nguyen Hong, Directorate of Water Resources

Chung Nguyen Thi Phuong, Phuoc and Partners

Nguyen Nang Nhuong, Vietnam Institute of Agricultural Engineering and Post-Harvest Technology (VIAEP)

Ha Phuong Nguyen, SNV

Hac Thuy Nguyen, Fertilizer Association of Vietnam (FAV)

Hiep Pham, Hiep PK Cafe

Thu Thien Pham, YKVN

Tuan Pham Quoc, Phuoc and Partners

Vu Phan, Indochine Counsel

Nguyen Anh Phong, Institute of Policy and Strategy for Agriculture and Rural Development (IPSARD)

Pham Ngoc Phuoc, SANCO Freight Ltd

Marieke van der Pijl, Gide Loyrette Nouel Law Firm

Franck Renaudin, Entrepreneurs du Monde

Mehdi Saint-Andre, Yara

Yee Chung Seck, Baker & McKenzie

Vivek Sharma

Gaël Stephen, ACE (Anh Chi Em)

Nguyen Thac Tam, Co-operative Bank of Vietnam (CPCF)

Nguyen Thi Thanh Binh, SANCO Freight Ltd

Duyen Nguyen Thi, Vietnam Academy of Agricultural Sciences

Nguyen Thi Thuy, Ministry of Agriculture and Rural Development

Tran Thanh Thuy, Vietnam Institute of Meteorology, Hydrology and Environment (IMHEN)

Ha Thuy Hanh, National Agriculture Extension Centre

Nguyen Tram Anh, Transworld Cargo Logistics

Thuy Thanh Thi Tran, Tien Giang Capital Aid Fund for Women's Economic Development

Trung Kien Tran, S&B Law

Kien Tran Trung, Multico (Vietnam) Co Ltd

Tran Quang Truong, SNV

Tran Van Trang, General Department of Vietnam Customs

Vi Sieu Trinh, Bayer Crop Science

Hoang Trung, Plant Protection Department, Ministry of Agriculture and Rural Development (MARD)

Nguyen Diep Tuan, DKSH Vietnam Co., Ltd.

Tran Duc Tuan, Vietnam Institute of Agricultural Engineering and Post-Harvest Technology (VIAEP)

Torsten Velden, Bayer Crop Science

Nguyen Quoc Viet, Vietnam Institute of Agricultural Engineering and Post-Harvest Technology (VIAEP)

Dzung Vu, YKVN

Vu Ngoc Quynh, Vietnam Codex Office

Hoa Xuan Vuong, Vietnam Institute of Meteorology, Hydrology and Environment (IMHEN)

Terence Wilson

ZAMBIA

Airtel

Bank of Zambia

Community Markets For Conservation (COMACO)

Copperbelt Universty

Kasensa Collaboration

Terrafirma Engineering and Surveying Consult (TESCO)

Zenith Business Solutions

Alan McNab, Backloads Zambia Limited

Milind Amin, Saro Agro Ltd

Chris Bishop, AgDevCo

Habasonda Calvin, Bank of Zambia

Simon Cammelbeeck, World Food Programme

Phillip K. Chibundi, Chibundi & Co. Law Practice

Chris Chiinda, Hitech Logistics Limited

Prisca Chileshe, IITA

Abigail Chimuka, Africa Legal Network (ALN)

Sydney Chisenga, Corpus Legal Practioners

Arshad Dudhia, Musa Dudhia & Co

Robin Durairajah, Chibesakunda & Co

Emmanuel Manda, Musa Dudhia & Co

Reagan Blankfein Gates, The Judiciary of Zambia, High Court Ndola

Rajiv Ghandi, Hester Biosciences Ltd

Shuller Habeenzu, ITM Consult

Nsondo Hamulondo, NWK Agri-Services

Coillard Hamusimbi, Zambia National Farmers Union (ZNFU)

Wilhelm Hesse, Agland ltd

Chance Kabaghe, Indaba Agricultural Research Policy Institute

Michael Kalimamukwento, Bridgepac Investments Ltd

Lazarous Kalumba, Nishati Clearing and Forwarding

Chapwa Kasoma

Linda Kasonde, Mulenga Mundashi Kasonde Legal Practiners

Humphrey Katotoka, Zambia National Farmers Union (ZNFU)

Jones Kayawe, Zambeef Products plc

George Liacopoulos, Zdenakie Commodities Ltd

Caesar Lubaba, National Livestock Epidemiology and Information Centre

Banji Milambo, Bank of Zambia

Gerald Monga, Central Veterinary Research Institute

Christian Morris, NWK Agri-Services

Kenneth Msiska, Zambia Agricultural Research Institute (ZARI)

Robert Mtonga, Truckers Association of Zambia (TAZ)

Parick Muchimba, Amiran Ltd.

Victor Musabula, Ventus Legal Practitioners

Mioamba Musambo, Stanbic Bank Zambia

Chanda Musonda, Africa Legal Network (ALN)

Godfrey Mwila, Zambia Agricultural Research Institute (ZARI)

Patricia Nachilima, Ventus Legal Practitioners

Perry Ngoma, CropLife Zambia

Dickson Ng'uni, Zambia Agricultural Research Institute (ZARI)

Ashok Oza, Saro Agro Ltd

Sharad Oza, Saro Agro Ltd

Nathan Phiri, Official Seed Testing Station Mount Makulu, Seed Control and Certification Institute

Musenge Sakala, Africa Legal Network (ALN)

Jessica Schicks, AB Bank Zambia

Dick Siame, The International Fund for Agricultural Development (IFAD)

Peter Sievers, COWI

Mike Sikazwe

Armando M Sirolla, AB Bank Zambia

Judith Tembo

Wesley Litaba Wakun'uma, Hivos Foundation

www.ingramcontent.com/pod-product-compliance
Lightning Source LLC
Chambersburg PA
CBHW061135030426
42334CB00003B/44